MAPPING BIHAR

Written Indian history begins in sixth century BC with the history of Magadh (present day states of Jharkhand and Bihar). For almost a millennium Magadh dominated Indian history. The situation changed when Islamicized Turks entered India. The Mughals who followed the Turks ensured Bihar's economic prosperity; Patna became the most important centre of Himalayan trade. European Companies visited Patna to obtain a variety of goods, local as well as Himalayan. In the mid-eighteenth century Bihar and Bengal fell into the hands of Englishmen. A new chapter began.

At the turn of the nineteenth century, Industrial Revolution began in Britain.

The East India Company stopped trading in textiles. Instead, they promoted cotton cultivation in order that cotton was available to British textile factories. They promoted cultivation of indigo, needed by the textile manufacturing factories coming up. Land revenue source of the government's prime income, was collected even when agricultural output suffered massively. The government took deep interest in opium production but paid the cultivators less than the market price. British interference in agricultural matters caused wide spread agrarian distress.

Indian society encountered many socio-religious reform movements. Raja Rammohun Roy and Swami Dayanand were major proponents of the new order. Stress was laid on gender equality, women empowerment and the modern system of education. Institutions for training doctors, engineers and scientists were opened. As time progressed, by and large, Biharis accepted the changes. Eventually social reform movements turned into the freedom movement in which Biharis played a leading role.

This comprehensive volume is indispensable for scholars working on Bihar and modern and medieval South Asia.

Surendra Gopal served as Lecturer, Reader and Professor in History Department, Patna University between 1958 and 1996. Along with teaching he carried out significant research work. The result has been more than 100 research papers and eight books. His latest book is *Born to Trade: Indian Business Communities in Medieval and Early Modern Eurasia* (2016).

Dr. Gopal has collected data for his works from English, Hindi, Urdu, Bengali and Russian sources.

MAPPING BIHAR

From Medieval to Modern Times

SURENDRA GOPAL

Routledge
Taylor & Francis Group

LONDON AND NEW YORK

First published 2018
by Routledge
4 Park Square, Milton Park, Abingdon, Oxon OX14 4RN
605 Third Avenue, New York, NY 10017

First issued in paperback 2023

*Routledge is an imprint of the Taylor & Francis Group, an
informa business*

Publisher's Note
The publisher has gone to great lengths to ensure the quality
of this reprint but points out that some imperfections in the
original copies may be apparent.

Print edition not for sale in South Asia (India, Sri Lanka,
Nepal, Bangladesh, Afghanistan, Pakistan or Bhutan)

British Library Cataloguing in Publication Data
A catalogue record for this book is available from the British
Library

Library of Congress Cataloging in Publication Data
A catalog record for this book has been requested

ISBN-13: 978-1-138-49093-2 (hbk)
ISBN-13: 978-1-03-265325-9 (pbk)
ISBN-13: 978-1-351-03418-0 (ebk)

DOI: 10.4324/9781351034180

Typeset in Warnock Pro 11/13
by Ravi Shanker, Delhi 110 095

MANOHAR

For
Dr. Kusum (wife)
Parag & Piyush (sons)
Shalini & Soumya (daughters-in-law)
Kriti, Aslesha, Poorva & Anvesha (granddaughters)

Contents

Preface

It gives me great pleasure in presenting a collection of research papers on the history of Bihar. These papers were written over the last half-a-century and deal with a variety of subjects but the focus remains on Bihar.

The ancient history of India is of course primarily the history of Bihar, but my abiding interest has been in the late medieval and early modern period.

These papers were written for a variety of reasons. Some were part of commemoration volume to be published to show respect for historical researches done by a scholar; some to show respect for scholars who had enriched the field of history. Some papers were written to mark a particular event.

While writing the papers I came across an important revelation. The late medieval and early modern period is rich in evidence, not available unfortunately for writing the history of earlier period.

First, by and large, the textual evidence both printed and handwritten was in plenty. Thanks to the advance of printing. Also, during this period geographical discoveries made in the fifteenth century encouraged world-wide travel. The traveller considered his duty to note down carefully whatever he saw. Several of them published their impressions on return. As a matter of fact, local history has become a part of general history.

The case of Bihar is an example, where for the nineteenth century, we have historical evidence available in Hindi, Urdu, Bengali and English. They provide significant facts. An example being the case of Babu Kunwar Singh who in 1857 challanged British rule during the uprising. To this day Kunwar Singh is revered as great freedom fighter. But the fact remains that Kunwar Singh and the British were good friends before they parted. The British gave Kunwar Singh Rs. 10,000 for increasing the cultivation of cotton in area under his control. The English were keen to ensure regular supply of raw cotton needed for the newly set up textile factories.

Dayanand Saraswati the founder of Arya Samaj came to Bihar and lived as a guest of an Englishman. Second, as an Arya Samajist, he was a stauch believer in the supremacy of the Vedas. But we find him to be rational and a firm believer in science and emerging technology.

A rich Indian went to Dayanand and told him that his wife was unable to conceive. In order to have a heir he wanted to marry again. Dayanand believed in one marriage and so refused to support his proposal for another marriage while the first wife was living. Dayanand, in fact, advised him to go to an English doctor. Dayanand despite his firm faith in the Vedas refused to ignore the achievements of modern science and technology.

There was gender inequality. Women were supposed to live in the house and not show their faces in public. Traditionally they were supposed to remain illiterate. They were not supposed to go to school. Even this was challenged by some. Aghor Kamini Devi (mother of Congress leader B.C. Roy, Chief Minister of Bengal) publicly moved in the city singing religious songs. Back in Patna later on she opened a girls school.

The ruler of Dumraon, in 1881 opened a girls school too. The number of students was around 200.

Tradition, we find in Bihar, was challenged in different walks of life.

It is my pleasant duty to thank people who have helped me in differet ways in carrying out my studies. They are numerous and it is not possible to name them.

I am grateful to the Indian Council of Philosophical Research for permitting to include my article on Science College, Patna in this anthology. I cannot forget the name Sri Ramesh Jain who regularly inspired me to complete this work. Other prominent helpers include Sri Ghufran, Prof. Hetukar Jha, Prof. A.K. Gupta, etc.

I alone am responsible for all the inadequacies that readers may discover in the volume.

Patna   SURENDRA GOPAL

CHAPTER 1

Ideas in Ancient and Medieval Bihar

Recorded history of India begins in the sixth century BC. At this point Magadh emerges as a political entity. Magadh became the core of the present day state of Bihar, a bigger entity with the Ganga River running through its centre. Eventually its border touched Himalayan foothills north of the Ganga and extended up to the mountainous region of Chhotanagpur in the south. Kosi River running from the Himalayan mountains met Ganga River and formed the eastern boundary of Bihar. Smaller kingdoms, virtually city states, existed on Magadh's western boundary.

In 327 BC Alexander the Great entered India through the north-west. Local rulers resisted. Alexander the Great immediately realized India was no Iran which he had recently subjugated. He decided to return. Alexander's invasion had shown weak points in Indian political order. Some Greek soldiers settled down in conquered areas. Interaction between Greeks and Indians produced momentous cultural results. Indians interacted with Greeks and Iranians, admired their art and architecture.

Many Indian scholars from the Greek-occupied territories fled to Bihar. Patna, the capital city of Magadh, became an important centre for scholars.

Chandragupta Maurya took advantage of the political disunity. He defeated smaller states; he created the first pan-Indian empire around Magadh. For the next millennium Magadh remained in the limelight, both politically and intellectually.

More importantly, political unity helped scholarship. His mentor Kautilya wrote the *Arthashastra,* a manual for governance.

Bhadrabahu, a Jain saint was another famous intellectual.[1] The concept of 'three philosophies', 'Sankhya, Yoga and Lokayat' became popular among scholars.[2]

Magadh led the way politically as well as intellectually; the ruling elite was intellectually motivated. No wonder Ashoka the Great, the grandson of Chandragupta Maurya and successor to the throne became an admirer of Buddhism and decided to propagate it within his empire (now larger than that of his grandfather). Two major results followed. He wanted the populace to follows the teachings of Buddha. For this purpose Buddha's teaching were translated in local language Prakrit or Ardhamagadhi. They were carved on stone pillars and hills. During Ashokan era stone architecture and sculpture reached new heights of excellence. Even after two millennia the polish on Ashokan pillars is intact. The major point to note is, for the first time attempt had been made to make public language also the language of administration. Maybe it was a step to develop a common language for the people of the empire.

After the death of Ashoka, the Mauryan Empire declined, but the culture of scholarship in Bihar continued and flourished.

Patanjali wrote *Mahabhashya*, a textbook on Sanskrit grammar. Scholars still use it. In *Yogasutra*, he propounds the basic proposition of the philosophy of yoga.[3]

Some Jain saints of the period are remembered even today as important writers and mathematicians. Jain saint Bhadrabahu (313 BC) was a contemporary of Chandragupta Maurya, Uma Swati, a Jain saint and writer lived in Patna in 150 BC; the Jain work *Anuyogasutra* (100 BC) mentions numbers greater than 1029.[4] It has been remarked that Jain philosophy '. . . was born and took shape in Bihar.'[5]

Scholarship in Patna received a new boost when the Gupta Empire with capital at Patna emerged in the fourth century AD.[6]

The Gupta rulers created an empire which replicated that of the Mauryas. They were tolerant: they permitted the Ceylonese ruler Meghvarma to build a monastery at Bodh Gaya,[7] where Buddha had attained enlightenment.

They patronized litterateurs and scholars. Kalidas, the eminent Sanskrit poet and dramatist was a member of the royal court. *Amarkosh* the famous Sanskrit dictionary was compiled, during the Guptas.

The Gupta rulers were firmly committed to the promotion of scholarship and arts and crafts. Repeated invasions of Central Asia Huns did not deter them. They continued to promote scholars and helped educational institutions. Two major events deserve our notice.

First, the contribution of Aryabhatta: Born in AD 476 Aryabhatta wrote *Aryabhattiyan* in AD 499, a treatise on mathematics and mathematical astronomy. He affirmed the concept of heliocentric universe. He contemplated that the earth moved on its axis and also around the sun. He explained the scientific reasons for solar and lunar eclipses. He correctly stated that the value of π was 3.1416. Aryabhatta proposed an original solution in whole numbers to the linear equation with two unknowns that closely resembles modern solution.[8]

Even today places in the vicinity of Patna are known as Taregana (place from where stars could be observed), Khagaul (observation point for watching the movements of stars in the sky), Phulwari (garden which surrounded the observation posts). Contemporary and later scholars appreciated the seminal contribution of Aryabhatta.

Aryabhatta's fame soon spread. Several Indian scholars commented upon his treatise in centuries that followed. Among these scholars were Brahmagupta (AD 628), Bhaskar I (AD 629), etc.[9]

The second major event was the establishment of Nalanda University. Gupta ruler Narsimha Gupta Baladitya who had defeated the Hun aggressor Mihirkula in AD 520 established a monastery in Nalanda. Eventually it took the shape of a teaching institution. The Gupta rulers were past their prime. Even then they extended their support to the Nalanda University. The last ruler Vishnu Gupta ascended the throne in AD 550-1 Vasubandhu, a Brahmin from Gandhar motivated Gupta rulers to help Nalanda to develop. Two Brahmins from south India, Dignaga and Dharmakirti established their schools in the Nalanda monastery.

The institution continued to function for the next six centuries when it was destroyed by foreign invaders. 'At Nalanda there was an enormous university complex attended by over ten thousand students, . . .'[10]

The fame of Nalanda spread widely; scholars and students came from all parts of India and South-East Asia. Scholars from Nalanda went to Tibet and propagated Buddhism.

Two more important educational institutions developed in Bihar. They were in Bihar Sharif (in the vicinity of Nalanda) and Kahalgaon near the modern town of Bhagalpur.

Nalanda University was known more for Buddhist studies.[11]

The most illustrious foreign student was Hiuen Tsang from China in the reign of Harshavardhan in the seventh century AD. He studied here for more than a decade and half. He collected manuscripts relating to Buddhism and Buddha and carried them to his homeland. Some of them were translated into Chinese. Many Buddhist texts are not found in India but their Chinese versions are available.

Scholars from Nalanda were invited to Tibet. They propagated Buddhism. Acharya Shantarakshita reached Tibet in the early years of the eighth century AD. He asked seven more Buddhist saints from India to help him in this task.[12] In the eleventh century, Atisha from Vikramshila University arrived in Tibet.[13] Their preachings persuaded Tibetans to accept Buddhism. Tibetan students and scholars studied at Nalanda.

After the Guptas, Palas of Bengal ruled Bihar. Academically Bihar remained vibrant. Pala rulers supported Nalanda University; they granted a village for its upkeep. Sena dynasty rulers, who succeeded Palas continued to support Nalanda University.

Buddhism competed with Hinduism for becoming the religion of the masses.

In Mithila (north Bihar), scholarly activities had begun to be quite visible since the ancient period. A Jain text *Nyaya dhammakahao* contains the story of Malli, the daughter of a king of Mithila who became one of the *Tirthankars* before Mahavira (see Hardy, 1995, *The Religious Culture of India: Power, Love and Wisdom*, Cambridge Studies in Religious Traditions 4, pp. 456-9).

The great philosopher Yajnavalkya of *Brihadaranyaka Upanishad* fame lived in Mithila in the court of Janak (Upendra Thakur, 1988, *History Mithila: From the Earliest Times to 1556 AD*, Mithila Institute, Darbhanga, pp. 502-3). Gautam who wrote *Nyaya Sutras*, Shatananda, Rishyashring, Vibhandaka, and others were outstanding scholars in Mithila at that time (ibid., p. 507). Later, Udyotakara, Mandan Mishra, Vachaspati, Udayana, Gangeshopadhyaya and a large number of scholars produced treatises in different fields. They are considered have made a great contribution to Indian civilization.

Proponents of Hinduism were also active. Under their auspices Sanskrit studies flourished. Two streams are marked. First, scholars specially in Mithila (north-east of Patna) concentrated their attention on Hindu scriptures and six schools of philosophy that had emerged in the country.[14] The second stream sought to downplay the influence of Buddhism. They carefully studied works by Buddhist scholars, and repudiated their doctrines. They also replied to questions raised by Buddhist scholars against Hindu religion.

The scholars of Mithila and Bengal practiced the philosophy of *Navya Nyaya*, that was created in Mithila in the thirteenth century by Gangesh Upadhyaya.

At this point an important change in politics of the country had significant consequences.

II

Towards the end of the twelfth century, Muslims from Central Asia attacked north India. Muslims controlled Sindh and Punjab, the latter after the raids of Muhammad Ghazni. Towards the end of the eleventh century and beginning of the twelfth century, the nature of Muslim attacks changed.

They moved eastwards, towards the Gangetic Valley. In the

course of the century, they brought almost the whole of north India under their sway.

Both Hindus and Buddhists were killed and their property looted by aggressors. In the changed political situation, educational institutions lost patronage of the ruling elites. They disintegrated. All the three universities in Bihar ceased to exist.

Nalanda University, however, continued for around a quarter century more though in a highly depleted form.

Dharmasvami (AD 1197-1264), a Tibetan scholar came to Nalanda in AD 1234. He says that only one scholar was available. He was ninety years old. He had ninety students. Dharmasvami stayed at Nalanda for four months. Then he went back home. On his return journey he met King Ramsinha, the Kamat ruler of Tirhut.

At another place he says that there were no scholars who could read the books still left. People were afraid of death and therefore those who could, did not reveal their competence.

The political change was accompanied by major social change.

Buddhists throughout India (with minor exceptions) for fear of death, came back to Hinduism. After almost two millennia Buddhism as a religion ceased to exist in India. Aggression by Muslims was the immediate reason for the disappearance of Buddhism from the land of its birth.

Secondly, study of Buddhism as a specialized discipline was given up. In the long run, scholars forgot Pali, the language of many original Buddhist texts.

Finally, the emergence of Islam as a force compelled Indian scholars to devise ways and means to confront the Islamic challenge believing in conversion. Islamist rulers had recorded their repeated superiority in battle fields. The only way, they thought, that would save Hinduism was to study scriptures intensely and apprise common people about the finer points of their religion and philosophies. Also, a section emphasized the regular performance of rituals associated with day to day living. Mithila scholars were very active in this field. This is reflected in Sanskrit works produced by them during this period.

It is clear that from sixth century BC onwards to the end of the twelfth century AD, state and individuals sponsored and supported scholars and scholarly institutions in Bihar. Absence of state patronage meant absence of institutions imparting higher education. There were no foreign students or scholars now as Buddhist studies had been abandoned in absence of specialized institutions and scholars. However, dedicated individuals continued the study of Hindu scriptures and philosophy.

In the Mithila region of Bihar, available evidence indicates a number of individuals devoted to higher studies. Sometimes acquisition of knowledge was family-based. The focus remained on Hinduism, Hindu philosophical works and Hindu social rituals. It appears that no attempt was made to study Islam. It is difficult to explain why scholars became steeped in studying knowledge that has been discovered in the past. Scholars were no longer interested in creative research. Stress was on producing literary works and writing critiques of religious and philosophical works of the past.

There were some exceptions. The first important work in this category was Jyotirishwar's *Varna Ratnakar*. The author describes the sociopolitical and cultural conditions in Mithila. This is a very important source for studying the social life in Mithila.

Chandeshwara Thakur, a great statesman of that era, according to P.V. Kane (*Dharmashastra ka Itihas*, Hindi trans., vol. 1, p. 85), was first in India to stress that anyone having capacity to protect people (*praja*) could become a king superseding the old notion of *Shastras* that only a Kshatriya was entitled to be a king (K.P. Jayaswal, 'Introduction', *The Rajniti Ratnakara* by Chandeshwara, Bihar and Orissa Research Society, 1936, p. 24).

Mithila during this period saw the rise of its greatest writer and scholar Vidyapati.

Vidyapati wrote in three languages, Sanskrit, Avahatta and Maithili; the last was the spoken language of the people. He produced literary works in Maithili, the language of the masses. His books *Kirtilata* and *Kritipataka* are in Avahatta. He wrote

Purush-pariksha and *Vibhag-sara* in Sanskrit. Vidyapati lived during the time of eight or nine rulers.[15]

The period is also known for works on Indian philosophy, especially Nyaya. Gangesh Upadhyaya's work *Tattva Chinta-mani* is well known. Within a couple of centuries, this branch of philosophy became popular in Bengal where it was introduced by Raghunath Shiromani and Sarvabhaum.[16] It soon gained ascendancy in Bengal. In 1503 an institution to study this branch intensely was established at Navdeep in Bengal.[17] The most well-known scholar of Nyaya philosophy in Bengal was Raghunath Shiromani, who had studied in Mithila.[18] Vacaspati Misra who flourished in the ninth century is described as the greatest commentator on all the six schools of Indian philosophy. He is hailed an equal to the great commentator Adi Shankar (propagator of Hinduism). He wrote to expound the doctrine of Udyotakara and his *Bhamati* is a commentary on Shankara's *Brahmasutra*.

His other works number fifteen.[19]

Vacaspati Misra wrote a lot on social behaviour, rites and rituals to be practised by an individual. Following are his major works:

Acara-cintamani deals with daily rites of Vajaneyins, including the daily worship of deities.

The *Krtya-cintamani* describes five sacred places.

The *Nitti-cintamani* deals with kingly duties.

The *Vyavhara-cintamani* is on legal procedure and evidence.

The *Sudra-acara cintamani* touches on the daily duties of a Shudra.

The *Vivada-nirnaya* deals with points of civil and criminal law.

The *Suddhi-nirnaya* describes purification due to impurities, death, birth, etc.

The *Gaya-shraddha-paddhati* is a manual of the funeral rites to be performed at Gaya.

He claimed to have written 10 works on the Shastra (Nyaya) and thirty on Smriti.[20]

III

Muslim administration meant the presence of Muslims in cities and villages. Though numerically small, their presence could not be ignored. Public saw their religious rituals. For their prayer mosques were built; mausoleums came up. Minarets became a familiar sight.

Along with Islam, Sufi order arrived in Bihar as well. Followers of Sufi saints Abu Najib Abdul Qadir Suhrawardi (d. AD 1168) and his disciple Shaikh-us-Shaykh Suhrawardi (d. AD 1234), etc., came to Bihar[21] and resided here. They preached the message of Saints that they worshipped. The Muslim scholars collected letters and utterances of these saints, *Dabistan-i-Madhib*, the Persian text, written in the suburbs of Patna in the sixteenth century informs us about various religious practices of Bihar.[22]

The most famous Sufi saint of Bihar was Sharafuddin Yahya Maneri (d. AD 1381). His descendents stay in Maner. Devotees from all corners of India and abroad visit these places. His letters have been published in book form, *Sharafuddin Maneri: The Hundred Letters* by Paul Jackson, S.J. These letters, written throughout the year 1346-7, are addressed to his disciple and Governor of Chausa (in western Bihar) and were compiled by Zain Badr Arabi.[23]

Muslim rulers made Persian the language of administration. The study of Arabic (the language of the holy book Koran) and Persian languages was introduced in Bihar. A new system of education appeared. Its prime aim was teaching recitation of verses of the Koran in original. Knowledge of Persian helped a person to get a government job or patronage. The followers of mysticism or Sufism accepted the local language since they were expected to talk to the common man regarding their faith. This added to the popularity of local languages.

During the first three hundred years of Islamic rule in Bihar no history of the area in Persian language was written. This was strange since history writing in Persian was encouraged by rulers right from the beginning of the thirteenth century.

The Muslims also brought the Unani system of medicine. It is, of course, true that the system did not replace the Ayurvedic system with which the masses were familiar. The two systems of treatment were continued simultaneously.

Babur, the Mughal ruler, captured the throne after defeating Ibrahim Lodi in the first battle of Panipat in 1526. In consonance with the policy of previous Muslim rulers, Babur advanced eastwards. He reached the vicinity of Maner. His son Humayun after ascending the throne followed Babur's policy of eastward expansion. He established Mughal rule in Bengal. As the climate did not suit him, he decided to return. Sher Shah, the Zamindar of Sasaram intercepted him on the banks of the Ganges at Buxar. Sher Shah recorded a decisive victory. Humayun was forced to quit India. He took shelter in Iran.

Sher Shah, a soldier from Bihar became the ruler of Delhi. His brief rule of five years set a pattern of governance for the good of the people. It became a model for the subsequent rulers in Delhi. Two millennia ago Chanakya of Magadh had provided the theoretical framework for stable government. Now another Bihari had demonstrated its practicality.

After a decade and half Humayun returned to the throne of Delhi but within a year he was dead. He brought Shiism. His successor Akbar wrote a new chapter. He was keen that important Sanskrit texts should be translated into Persian so that Muslims could appreciate Hinduism and understand why Islam could not repeat its achievements of Central Asia, West Asia, etc. Political stability and royal patronage to scholars helped the revival of love for knowledge.

Contacts with Persian scholars helped Mithila scholars to write in areas which they had ignored. The way was shown by Mahesh Thakur.

Akbar gave to Mahesh Thakur the right to collect land revenue in Tirhut on his appreciation for his scholarship. His *Sarvadesha Brittant Sangrah* gives a picture, of Indian society.

After him in the reign of Shah Jahan, Hemangad Thakur a descendant of Mahesh Thakur wrote a book on astronomy and recounted the methods of predicting solar and lunar eclipses.

CONCLUSION

The study shows that Bihar has almost a continued history for promoting scholarship for almost two millennia. It remained steeped in a culture of scholarship. The result was astounding.

The first regular treatise on government was written in the fourth century BC.

It produced a great scholar like Aryabhatta, who predicted heliocentric universe and paved the way for mathematical astronomy.

To sustain this culture three universities came up at Nalanda, Bihar and Vikramsila. Students from different parts of our country and abroad studied here. These institutions survived for almost six hundred years. Changed political situation hastened their disintegration.

Within Bihar the region of Mithila emerged as true bastion of traditional Indian scholarship. Scholars of Mithila kept the torch of knowledge burning despite all obstacles.

India survives because Indian scholars never gave up studies, whatever the difficulty. Our deep regards to them.

NOTES

1. Antonova, Bongard-levin and G. Kotovsky, *A History of India I*, Progress Publishers, Moscow, 1979.
2. Dinanath Sahni, *Mahan Khagolbid-Ganitgya Aryabhatta* (in Hindi), Prabhat Prakashan, Delhi, 2012.
3. Dr. G. Roerich, *Biography of Dharmasvamin*, Kashi Prasad Jayaswal Research Institute, Patna, 1959.
4. R.R. Diwakar (ed.), *Bihar Through the Ages*, K.P. Jayaswal Research Institute, Patna, 2001.
5. Ritu Kamal and Gopal Kamal, *Prapanch Kanya Indian Philosophy in the Second Millennium*, Viva Books, New Delhi, 2008.
6. Syed Hasan Askari and Qyamuddin Ahmad, *The Com-prehensive History of Bihar*, vol. II, pt. I, K.P. Jayaswal Research Institute, Patna, 1983.
7. Rajendra Ram (ed.), *Intellectual Perspective of Rahula Sankrityayana: Essays and Reminiscences*, Janajagran Prakashana, Patna, n.d.

8. Shyam Narayan Singh, *History of Tirhut from the Earliest Times to the End of the Nineteenth Century*, Darbhanga, 2012.
9. S.H. Askari, *Islam and Muslims in Medieval Bihar*, Khuda Bakhsh Oriental Public Library, Patna, 1989.
10. Paul Jackson, S.J., *Sharfuddin Maneri: The Hundred Letters*, Khuda Bakhsh Central Library, Patna, 2002.
11. Hardy, *The Religious Culture of India, Power, Love and Wisdom*, Cambridge University Press, 1995.
12. Upendra Thakur, *History of Mithila*, Darbhanga, 1988.
13. P.V. Kane, *Dharmasastra ka Itihas*, vol. I.
14. K.P. Jayaswal, *The Rajniti Ratnakar of Chandeswara*, Patna, 1936.
15. *Bihar through the Ages*, p. 442.
16. *History of Bihar*, vol. II, pt. II, p. 318.
17. Ibid.
18. *Prapanch*, p. 87.
19. Shyam Narayan Singh, pp. 169-70.
20. Ibid., pp. 110-12.
21. Askari, p. 3.
22. Ibid., p. 5.
23. Jackson, p. i.

CHAPTER 2

Bihar Peasants in the Early Decades of the Eighteenth Century

In the second half of the seventeenth century, the Bihar peasant was exposed to the full-range of the activities of the European trading companies especially, the English, the Dutch and the French, whose agents scoured the urban and rural markets in search of cotton textiles, opium, turmeric, saltpetre, etc.[1] A pattern of agricultural production and an urban-rural economic nexus emerged to satisfy the European demands and caused a spurt in the output of raw cotton, opium, turmeric and saltpetre. While the cotton textiles were primarily meant for the European markets, opium was sent by the Dutch and the English to South-East Asia. The Dutch export of opium from Bihar had begun in 1648.[2]

The desire to secure opium was intense. In 1701, the Patna agents of several Armenian and English traders disclosed that they had orders to procure as much opium as they could, irrespective of the price they had to pay. The following year, some English traders bought a substantial amount of opium at Patna, that the Dutch had earlier rejected for being of too poor a quality. In 1706, the Hugli factors reported that, as usual, 'a number of English traders had sent to the archipelago, that year, a total of 58,000 pounds of opium procured at Patna and an unspecified amount procured at Hugli. . . .'[3]

Saltpetre and turmeric were used as ballast for Europe-going ships. Saltpetre commanded a large market in strife-torn Europe because it was an essential constituent of gunpowder. The major European exports from Bihar, towards the end of the seventeenth century, thus had a strong rural base. According to a Dutch estimate, Bihar, in 1688, produced 226,200 maunds of raw saltpetre which, when refined, came to 127,238 maunds.[4] In 1719/20, the average price of saltpetre was Rs. 5 per maund.[5] The European paid for these items in cash.[6] They brought either bullion or coins, which were re-issued as local coinage, either in the mints of Patna or Rajmahal.[7]

The import of bullion in Bengal, by the English, increased after the death of Aurangzeb in 1707, when the Mughal Court shifted to the north and the import of the Madras rupee ceased to be profitable. Hence, from 1709, the English decided to import bullion and get it minted. In order to make it profitable, they sought the permission of the Nawab for the free use of the mint. The Nawab, Murshid Quli Khan, however, wanted a fat sum, which the English were not willing to pay and the negotiations thus dragged on.[8] But the point to note is that, Eastern India was experiencing monetization of the economy at an accelerated pace.

The countryside thus received cash which was variously used. The peasant paid his land-revenue to the zamindar and the zamindar remitted his due to the provincial *Diwan*, eventually to be transferred to the centre.[9] The surplus cash, thus acquired—be it fully understood—varied considerably from individual to individual. At the one extreme, were the zamindars of Darbhanga, Dumraon, Hathwa, etc.,[10] and at the other was a *khudkasht* peasant owning a small plot of land. The former received thousands while those at the other extreme, maybe only a few rupees. The Mughal state had arranged for the availability of coins by opening two mints at Patna and Rajmahal.[11] The Bihar peasant, at the opening of the eighteenth century, was thus exposed to the forces of monetization of the economy and the commercialization of agriculture.

The last of the Great Mughals, Aurangzeb, had remained in the Deccan during the second half of his reign and gradually the central hold over the eastern provinces was weakening, though it was the treasure of the eastern provinces, which sustained the Mughal military campaigns. Therefore, the need for more and more cash from the area had become a necessity and the peasant was called upon to generate more and more surplus cash.

The process had been further stimulated because of the decision of the European trading companies to shift the focus of their activity from the western coast to the eastern coast and to concentrate upon Bihar and Bengal, rather than on Orissa, as was the case earlier. For the purchase of cotton textiles, the European no longer considered Gujarat, but eastern India, consisting of Bihar and Bengal, as their prime market. They enlisted the services of Manik Chand, a member of the House of Jagat Seth, to obtain permission for free trade in Bihar in 1706.[12] In Bihar, the Europeans primarily sought to procure opium and saltpetre. Saltpetre could be obtained cheaply and of better quality if the producers were given *dadni* (advance money) in the month of November or December.[13] The peasant was also required to supply turmeric as an alternative ballast to saltpetre for ocean-going ships. The Bihar peasant, it seems, had also become a supplier of sugar, which was exported from the ports of Bengal to Asian and European markets.

As can be seen, these developments involved increasing transactions in cash between the producer and land-controller and the traders, both indigenous and foreign. For the conduct of their business, the European traders maintained establishments in rural areas. For example, in 1716, the English were stationed at Singia, Futtua and Chowndee.[14] Later on, we learn that one Raghu Pandit was associated with the Futtua establishment and the English had dealings with Gulalchand Shah's agents at Coora, Jahanabad. At Futtua, they left five camels and at Coora one camel, which they wanted to be sold.[15]

It would seem that there was a great infusion of cash in the countryside; the different strata of society had benefited from the increased pace of the commercialization of agriculture and the monetization of the economy. Quantitative data are, however, lacking. We do not know the volume of cash generated in the economy and the share received by the different groups. However, certain impressionistic assessments can be made and the overall impact of this new feature on the peasant can be delineated. We can make a guess from the following instances and draw certain inferences.

In 1702, the Mughal governor of Bihar ordered the seizure of the goods of the English East India Company. In the Rajmahal Factory, the Company complained that its loss amounted to Rs. 70,000.[16] In October 1717, the English East India Company officials drew two Bills of Exchange, each worth Rs. 5,000, from Bolchund for payment to Saw Biparry (Byopari, businessman). The second was taken from Gowoldass Gossaulray for payment to Kissoray Gocolchund.[17]

But the process was obstructed by the short-sighted policies of the Governor, Sarbuland Khan, who levied a special tax, called *budruks* on merchants, ostensibly to provide escort to them during their journeys. He took from the Dutch Rs. 13,200 instead of the customary Rs. 10,000 to allow them to trade. Besides, he had already extorted Rs. 50,000 from them during the year.[18]

The extent of Dutch trade can be realized from the fact, that, when in 1712, Farrukhsiyar confiscated the goods of the Dutch factory at Patna, their value came to Rs. 1.5 lakh. In the same year, the Dutch paid Rs. 2 lakh to the Prince when he realized money from all traders and bankers to raise an army for the impending war against his uncle.[19] Subsequently the Dutch were allowed the use of the mint as well.[20] The French also obtained the privilege of trading in Bihar on the payment of 2.5 per cent customs duty.[21]

The European trading activities, along with that of the indigenous merchants, further increased when the English obtained from the Mughal Emperor Farrukhsiyar, the right to duty-free trade in Bihar and Bengal in 1717, after John Surman negotiated the terms in Delhi.[22] However, the Mughal bureaucrats continued to raise obstacles in the smooth conduct of the trade.[23]

The landlords and/or the land-controllers were, socially and economically, a heterogenous group. The most important Rajput, Brahman and Bhumihar zamindars were those of Dumraon,

Darbhanga and Hathwa respectively. The untouchables, the Dusadhs, the Musahars, the Mochis, etc., who supplied the bulk of labour power, hardly owned even their homestead lands. The peasant communities primarily consisted of Yadav, Koiri and Kurmi castes. Some among these peasant communities owned considerable land on which they worked themselves or cultivated it with the help of hired labour-power. These were the real producers. The large landholders, the upper caste Hindus, Brahmans, Rajputs, Kayasthas, Bhumihars, etc., were ritually barred from ploughing and therefore, preferred to get the land worked by share-croppers or through hired labourers.

The peasant communities, by themselves, were in no position to completely switch over to opium/turmeric/sugar cane as food shortages immediately sent the cereal prices soaring, beyond the reach of the common man. Hence, to keep body and soul together, the peasant had no option but to continue to cultivate cereals to meet his own needs and the needs of the hired labour-force. The cash only enabled him to pay for his land-revenue and meet other incidental expenses, in connection with life-cycle rituals, medicine, clothing for ceremonial occasions, etc. The big landholders/land-controllers were the greatest bene-ficiaries. But their pattern of expenditure and attitude was such that they hardly bothered about long-term changes in the economy, which they were in a position to bring about.

Control of land involved an increasing desire to become a zamindar; this was particularly true of the upper castes among the Hindus, since most of the zamindars came from within their ranks. They remained unconcerned about changes in agricultural techniques for enhanced production. Secondly, a zamindari meant raising a retinue of armed followers and workers for collecting and keeping accounts of the land-revenue. In case of large zamindars, the number of armed followers was large enough to be called upon to provide military contingents to the provincial/central authorities whenever they needed such support. These contingents would also be asked to provide escort to travellers and/or treasures passing through their zamindari at the behest of the provincial authorities.

Sometimes these zamindars would collect taxes or *rahdari* duty from traders transporting goods through their territories. Thus the Dutch company asked its officials to pay to Raja Dhir, in 1708, under whose territory the saltpetre station of Chuprah lay, so that he would permit them to travel unmolested.[24] Of course, it was part of their duty to maintain law and order within their jurisdiction. Thus the zamindar replicated the state apparatus and the capital at his command could only accidentally be diverted to economic channels. Furthermore, as one embodying the state power, he was psychologically inclined to go in for conspicuous consumption; he built palaces, spent lavishly on weddings and other socio-religious functions, and hardly gave a thought to economically viable and productive long-term investment.[25] Hence, the surplus cash in his hands seldom motivated him to plan for increased agricultural productivity by ensuring improvement in technology.

The medium and large-scale producers reduced the area under cereal cultivation and went in for cash crops on a part of their holdings. The primacy was accorded to cereal production as the labour force was mostly paid in grains. This mode of payment was preferred as shortages of food grains enhanced their prices so much that they remained beyond the reach of a substantial part of the population. Import of food grains from surrounding surplus areas failed to relieve the distress. The experience of famine of 1670-1 can be cited as an example.[26] Hence, the peasant's wisdom dictated that, whatever be the demand for cash crops, he should continue the cultivation of cereals, as it was his best protection against scarcities and it also insulated him against the fluctuating demand and prices of cash crops. After all, the peasant could not predict the behaviour of the market, which stretched from Southeast Asia to the Atlantic littoral of Northwest Europe.

As regards saltpetre, the situation in practice was not much different. The actual producers, the *Nonias,* belonged to the lowest rung of the social order. They seldom owned the land from which saltpetre was extracted. They sold their labour power, and even here, they could not bargain with the master, who was socially, economically and politically dominant. But the rural beneficiaries were subject to the manipulations of the big traders and the political authorities. Since saltpetre was an essential ingredient of gunpowder, the top bureaucrats had no hesitation in interfering with its sale and transportation. Thus, in 1699, Prince Azim-us-Shan asked his agent at Patna to purchase 40-50 thousand maunds of saltpetre on the plea of attacking Arakan. But his plan of earning 100 per cent profit on an investment of Rs. 1 lakh fell through.[27] Also, Haji Ahmad, the elder brother of Alivardi Khan and the Nawab of Patna, indulged in a private trade in saltpetre and was angry with the English when they refused to purchase his stock in Hughli.[28]

The mechanism of the market, that evolved, also did not permit the peasant to innovate. In actual practice, the peasant was hardly a free agent; if he produced small quantities, he was not in a position to go to the market. He had to sell it either to the local merchant or to the zamindar or to the big farmer or to the agent of the European trading companies. The price was determined, not by him, but, by and large, by purchasers. Consequently, his cash earnings remained meagre, just enough to meet his land-revenue obligations and part of expenses incurred in connection with life-cycle rituals, religious festivals and purchase of clothes, spices, medicines, ornaments, etc. The net result was that hardly any investible surplus was left with them; in fact, often they had to borrow. Such a situation did not provide them with any material incentive to improve production techniques to increase the yield. In fact, they were so vulnerable that, any setback to the harvest on account of flood or drought for a couple of years continuously, led to their pauperization and indebtedness to the village moneylender, who could be the zamindar, the big farmer, the merchant or the agent of the European companies.

The middle and big farmer had a better deal; he could pro-duce cereals, not only for his immediate consumption and the consumption of his workers, but also for the market; at the same time, he could spare enough land for cash crops such as cotton, opium, turmeric, sugar cane, etc. He was in a position to market his own produce either within the village itself or at the nearest rural or urban market place. He could claim market-price for his produce and could not always be dictated to in this regard. But here the cultural factors intervened and constrained his role as a economic being. Generally, these big landholders belonged to the upper castes and the entire agricultural operations were carried on by hired employees belonging to the cultivating communities, lower castes and untouchables. They performed only supervisory functions. Hence, their personal involvement in increased yield was peripheral, so long as their economic needs were met and their social status remained unquestioned. The land-controllers, therefore, had little interest in or knowledge of the techniques of agricultural production.

Consequently, a situation had been created that despite the increasing monetization of the economy and the commercialization of agriculture, the land-controller or producer in the country side was hardly giving any thought to the accumulation of capital and to investing in economic enterprises. He was more prone to spend it on non-economic and non-productive matters. The Bihar peasant and landholder/controller remained unconcerned with the larger economic implications of the commercialization of agrarian output. It did not automatically galvanize him to switch over to cash crops and benefit from the new economic opportunities. His conservative stance continued; the countryside remained steeped in poverty and the economy stagnated. Saltpetre, opium, turmeric and sugar cane failed to bring about significant improvements in the life of the peasantry.

The political environment further inhibited the peasant. Safety, during journeys, was a perpetual problem; this may have been due to a general law and order problem but it must have acted as a dampner to economic prosperity. Even the Mughal Emperor was not sure that, presents for him carried from Patna to Delhi by the English East India Company, would reach him safely. Hence, in 1714, he not only sanctioned a large sum but also provided an armed escort under a Mansabdar of 1,000 men, to conduct these safely to him.[29] The English were still not sure and hence they entered into a private arrangement with the Ujjainiya chief of Bhojpur, Sudhist Narain, not to molest them in transit through his territories.[30] Also, for their own safety, they decided to appoint 400 peons and buxeries, and 50 horsemen.[31] Even the Nabob was apprehensive of the designs of the Ujjainiyas and felt that 500 horses and 500 buxeries were needed to protect them.[32] Eventually, the Ujjainiyas assured them safe conduct.[33]

The powerful zamindars often found themselves in a state of confrontation with their political masters. This did not mean only absence of peace but also their economic deprivation. This is illustrated by the events which followed the accession of Shuja-ud-daulah to the governorship of Bengal. Shuja-ud-daulah obtained the Nizamat of Bihar and appointed Muhammad Ali Vardi Khan to be his Deputy Governor in Bihar. After assuming charge, Ali Vardi associated with himself, Abdul Karim, the Chief of the Afghans of Darbhanga, and sent him to subdue the Banjarah tribe, who were a class of marauders and murderers, and who in the guise of traders and travellers used to plunder the imperial domains and treasures. He gained a large booty. Ali Vardi then advanced against the Rajas of Bettiah and Bhawarah, who were refractory and turbulent. Their regions had never previously been trod upon by the feet of the armies of former Nizams, nor had their proud heads ever bended before to any of the former Subadars. Indeed they had never paid the imperial revenues and taxes. Ali Vardi Khan carried off a large booty amounting to several lakhs. And settling with the Rajas the amounts of tribute, presents and the imperial revenue, he raised an immense sum. Ali Vardi also subdued the Chakwars, and invaded the domains of the turbulent Zamindar of Bhojpur and of Raja Sunder Singh, Zamindar of Tikari, and of Chieftain Namdar Khan Muin. Ali Vardi levied revenues on them and reduced them to subjection.[34]

If such was the situation with some of the zamindars of Bihar at that time, one can only deduce the miserable condition of the Bihar peasants in that uncertain political environment.

Thus it becomes clear that, despite the monetization of the

economy and the commercialization of agriculture in the early decades of the eighteenth century, the Bihar peasants could not make much progress. They found themselves subject to the tyranny of the zamindars, the machinations of the bureaucrats and the manipulations of the traders and their agents. Consequently, the inflow of money into the Bihar countryside at that time merely enabled the peasants to pay off their dues and to fulfil their obligations but it did not contribute towards the betterment of either their economic or social status.

NOTES

1. Surendra Gopal, 'Coins and Trade: A Study of Bihar Economy in the Seventeenth Century', in Amal Kumar Jha (ed.), *Coinage, Trade and Economy*, Anjaneri, Nashik, 1991, pp. 210-13.
2. Om Prakash, *The Dutch East India Company and the Economy of Bengal, 1630-1720*, Princeton, 1985, p. 169.
3. Ibid., pp. 154-5.
4. Susil Chaudhuri, *Trade and Organization in Bengal, 1650-1720*, Calcutta, 1975, p. 161.
5. Ibid., p. 168.
6. Gopal, op. cit., p. 211. It is stated that between 1663 and 1700 the Dutch imported bullion worth 47 million florins.
7. Ibid.
8. Abdul Karim, *Murshid Quli Khan and His Times*, Dhaka, 1974, pp.154-5.
9. Ghulam Hussain Salim, Text and English translation by Abdus Salam, *Riyazu-s-Salatin*, Calcutta, 1902, p. 289. Shuja-ud-din Muhammad Khan, when he became the Nawab of Bengal, Bihar and Orissa, immediately raised Rs. 1 crore and 50 lakh, which he remitted to the Imperial Treasury through the banking agency of Jagat Seth Fatah Chand. He sent Rs. 40 lakh more to Emperor Muhammad Shah after selling the household effects of the late Nawab. Only after this, 'and after the Abstract Balance-sheet of the Annual Accounts was prepared, he remitted to the Imperial Capital the stipulated annual tribute of the Nizamat, besides the Imperial Revenue, according to the established usage'.
10. A.R. Khan, 'Chieftains in Bihar during the Mughal Period', *Proceedings, Indian History Congress*, Goa, 1987, pp. 197-205.
11. Jagdish Narayan Sarkar, *Glimpses of Medieval Bihar Economy*, Calcutta, 1978, pp. 104-5.

12. Karim, op. cit., p. 118.
13. C.R. Wilson, *The Early Annals of the English in Bengal*, III, Calcutta, 1917, p. 46; Sushil Chaudhuri, 'Saltpetre Trade and Industry in Bengal Subah', *Proceedings, Indian History Congress*, Chandigarh, 1973, pp. 263-4.
14. Wilson, op. cit., II/1, p. 243, doc. no. 972.
15. Ibid., II/2, p. 238.
16. Karim, op. cit., II/2, p. 236.
17. Wilson, op. cit., II/2, p. 236.
18. Ibid., p. 236.
19. Ibid., p. 197.
20. Ibid., p. 199.
21. Ibid., p. 201.
22. Karim, op. cit., Section III.
23. Ibid., Section IV, 'The Working of Farrukh Siyar's Farman, 1717-27'.
24. Om Prakash, 'The Dutch East India Company in Bengal', *Indian Economic and Social History Review*, September 1972, p. 278.
25. Syed Najmul Raja Rizvi, 'The Life Style of the Zamindars of Eastern Uttar Pradesh in the Eighteenth Century', *Proceedings, Indian History Cngress*, Burdwan, 1983, p. 280.
26. Sarkar, op. cit., pp. 111-14. Marshall, an eye-witness to the tragedy, wrote that over 10,000 people died of starvation.
27. Jagdish Narayan Sarkar, *Private Traders in Medieval India: British and Indian*, Calcutta, 1990, p. 126.
28. Ibid., p. 120.
29. Wilson, op. cit., II/1, p. 1995, doc. no. 874, 8 November 1714.
30. Ibid., II/2, p. 12.
31. Ibid., p. 15.
32. Ibid., p. 20.
33. Ibid., p. 26.
34. Salim, op. cit., pp. 295-7.

CHAPTER 3

Changing Bases of Peasant Movement in Bihar, 1917-1975

THE SETTING

A century after Vasco da Gama discovered the sea-route from Europe to India in 1498, European merchant capital began to penetrate the landlocked region of Bihar where they secured cotton textiles and what was probably even more important, saltpetre, an ingredient for making gunpowder. European merchants were joined by their Asian as well as Indian counterparts and therefore, several areas of rural Bihar experienced acceleration of the process of monetization of economy, commercialization of agriculture and intensification of rural-urban economic nexus.[1] These processes received impetus after trade in the region prospered on account of the arrival of more and more traders such as, Indians, Asians and Europeans who were finding it difficult to ply trade in western and southern India on account of the prevailing political situation.[2] Rural Bihar continued to be the happy hunting ground of merchant capital in the first half of the eighteenth century as it supplied mostly saltpetre and cotton textiles to Europeans, and items such as, indigo, silk, sugar, etc., were exported also by other traders.[3] The presence of a large number of traders of diverse ethnic background ensured good income to farmers and we do not hear of any major peasant unrest during this period.

The picture began to change sharply in the second half of the eighteenth century when indigenous political authority became subservient and subsequently was replaced by the English East India Company. First, the East India Company used its political might to eliminate European competitors and later on reduced other Asian and Indian merchants to insignificance.[4] The Company, thereafter, sought to use the instrument of land revenue to enrich itself and in the process rural Bihar was impoverished. It was ravaged by the terrible famine of 1770 when 1/3 of its population perished.[5] However, the Company encouraged the cultivation of opium which it exported to China[6] and opium replaced saltpetre as the main export commodity of rural Bihar. Meanwhile, in 1793 they introduced Permanent Settlement, i.e. the amount of land-revenue to be collected was fixed and a class of hereditary intermediaries for its collection was brought into existence. The induction of this class of rentiers added a set of exploiters whose elimination became a major demand of the peasantry.[7]

The Permanent Settlement remained the determining in-fluence on the agrarian structure in the province during the next century and a half. The peasant movements in the State have to be studied and evaluated against this background during the colonial era and in the years after India became Independent.

During the next half of the nineteenth century, the rural society did see a number of new elements: the English search for textiles disappeared as England witnessed the Industrial Revolution; instead, the English began to bring the factory-made textiles.[8] Secondly, the position of the zamindars was consolidated; the zamindars by and large became the bulwark of English rule and the government spokesmen in the rural areas.[9] Thirdly, in this period the English popularized the cultivation of potatoes, which in a way seems to have warded off hunger, a striking feature during the first four decades of the English rule.[10] Finally, the English and other Europeans began to settle down in villages first as sugar manufacturers and then as indigo planters.[11]

No major food shortages are recorded; however, it is not clear as to why rural poverty had increased. A British visitor reported that the people of Bihar could not afford even salt and hence, sprinkled ashes to make the food tasty.[12]

Possibly, emigration to the tea plantations, then being set up,

to metropolitan and mining areas and to outside India helped to
minimize rural distress.[13]

The backdrop to the rural scene in the second half of the
nineteenth century was provided by the events of 1857, when
the English rule was challenged over a vast stretch of north
India, including parts of Bihar in which both the zamindars
and peasants were active participants. As a result, the British
Government became aware of the problems facing the rural
society and the first tenancy legislation—Bengal Tenancy Act
of 1859 was passed.[14] It sought to defuse tension between the
tenant and the zamindar— an issue which the government was
repeatedly called upon to resolve, since neglect might have
resulted in rural upheaval and threatened the continuance of
the *Raj*.

The introduction of railways added a new dimension to the
society and economy by making long distance travel quicker,
safer and cheaper; it enabled the rural population to migrate to
various parts of this country where work was available and this
to some extent mitigated rural poverty.

During this period, a number of Europeans settled down in
rural areas as indigo planters; their numbers increased after the
indigo revolt of 1859-60 and Pabna revolt of 1871 in adjoining
Bengal.[15] They were like the local zamindars a new source of
oppression to the peasantry; they also leaned heavily on the
government for a variety of privileges and remained loyal. The
peasantry resented their oppression as it was resenting the
oppression of Indian zamindars.

During the second half of the nineteenth century, rural Bihar
was repeatedly devastated by famines;[16] the government was
forced to adopt measures to alleviate the sufferings of the people;
a famine code was evolved; new rail lines and link roads were
built so that people working at these places might get the much
needed purchasing power; irrigation facilities were created by
repairing old or constructing new canals, ponds, wells, etc.[17] It
was hoped that besides acquiring the much needed purchasing
power, these irrigation and transport facilities would promote
agricultural productivity. However, they failed to generate the

required economic well-being, and only migration of Bihari labourers to other parts of India and abroad such as, West Indies, Mauritius, Fiji, etc., alleviated rural sufferings. But the government was conscious of the simmering rural discontent.

Several other forces of social change such as, spread of education, growth of printing-press and journalism, consciousness about colonial exploitation, began to seep in the rural areas. To forestall the outbreak of any trouble, the government passed a new tenacy legislation, The Bengal Tenancy Act of 1885.[18]

In the second half of the nineteenth century the State sought to contain peasants' discontent by mediating between them and the zamindars. However, the governmental measures met with limited success and the peasant question remained alive.

In 1885 the Indian National Congress was formed and gradually the peasantry of Bihar began to entertain the hope that the foremost national political organization would look into its grievances.

PEASANT QUESTION BECOMES A NATIONAL QUESTION: CHAMPARAN SATYAGRAHA

Raj Kumar Sukul, a peasant from Champaran district, bordering on the kingdom of Nepal and a place where indigo planters had become prominent, went to the annual session of the Indian National Congress in 1916 at Lucknow and narrated the tale of the peasantry and its oppression by the indigo planters. Braj Kishore Prasad, a respected leader of the party from Bihar, raised the question in the highest party forum and a resolution was adopted.[19] At the same time, Raj Kumar Sukul was persuading national leaders to take a personal interest in the question. He persuaded Mahatma Gandhi to visit Champaran who arrived here in April 1917. His arrival signified a new stage in the peasant question.

Hitherto the peasant question had been apolitical; now it had been politicized and became a national concern. Local peasant struggles came to be viewed as an integral part of the anti-colonial movement. Rectification of local grievances was sought in the resolution of general problems such as, reform of the agrarian structure, promotion of socio-economic and cultural well-being of the rural folk. These new dimensions from now onwards shaped and affected the course of the peasant movement.

In the colonial set up, the peasant question sooner or later becomes a part of the freedom movement; otherwise its viability and effectiveness diminish; it cannot achieve even its limited objective, i.e. the redressal of small grievances. The Champaran movement set in motion a new trend in the peasant movement.

Furthermore, the movement brought to surface the future political leadership of the state, especially of the Congress party to which Mahatma Gandhi belonged. Mention may be made of men like Rajendra Prasad who rose to be the first President of the Republic of India, Anugraha Narayan Sinha who became an important provinical level leader, Braj Kishore Prasad, Dharnidhar Sinha, etc.[20] All of them became full-time Congress activists and the Congress party secured a cadre of dedicated leaders who made pursuit of India's Independence the sole aim of their lives and gave mass base to the anti-colonial struggle in the province. The peasant question had transformed the freedom movement into a mass movement; the urban based educated professionals had thrown in their lot with the rural folk.

As a result of Gandhi's intervention, the government set up an inquiry committee and passed legislation to concede some of the demands of the peasantry.[21] Emboldened local leadership brought forth peasants' grievances and fought for their redressal. As a result, in coming years, peasant agitations under the aegis of local leaders became a matter of national concern and continued to appear in one part or the other.

One of the important movements started at this point of time was led by Swami Vidyanand in 1919 in the Darbhanga district of north Bihar dominated by the biggest landlord of India, Maharaja of Darbhanga. Peasant attention had shifted to the tyranny of landlords and their servants. The movement soon spread to the adjoining districts of Muzaffarpur, Bhagalpur and

Munger. He was supported by affluent as well as middle and poor peasants of both high and low castes. But he failed to gather enough political support and despite personal popularity, he had to remain content with only partial success.[22] The colonial administration, of course, sided with the landlords.

The point of note was that during this phase the movement was all inclusive, i.e. peasants of all categories and all castes participated in it. It created an atmosphere of fearlessness to such an extent that when Mahatma Gandhi unleashed his Non-Cooperation movement in September 1920, masses thronged to it. Simultaneously, contradictions in the peasant movement appeared. Different categories of peasants became conscious of their identity and the homogeneity of the movement gradually ended; sectional peasant interests came to the fore and hereafter the peasant movement became fragmented.

A section of the peasantry, especially belonging to the upper castes who were landholders and/or tenants and/or petty zamindars, became vocal. Some of them had received new education and so they concluded that only through group action could they secure their demands. They were more concerned with their economic grievances than with the restructuring of the political machinery. Political action was to be only one of the means of redressal of economic grievances. Nationalist leaders quickly realized this character and direction of the peasant movement but consented to support it in the hope of broadening the Congress-led anti-colonial front.

Nevertheless, a section of the Congress leadership was sceptical of the usefulness of such a movement since the peasant mobilization was partially along caste-lines. Thus the Bihar Provincial Kisan Sabha, formed on 18 November 1929, did have among its office-bearers committed Congressmen such as, Shrikrishna Sinha[23] who headed the first Congress government in the province both in the pre- and post-Independence periods, but Braj Kishore Prasad, another Congress stalwart did not permit his name to be associated with it.[24] This incident showed that the nationalist movement was not yet strong enough to subsume all sub-movements. Henceforth, it had to contend with a movement which would turn against it, whenever it felt, its immediate economic interests were threatened. At this point of time, the nature of the peasant movement, instead of strengthening the freedom struggle, could even weaken it.

The Kisan Sabha, instead of reflecting the aspirations of the broad spectrum of the peasantry, was wooing only a section, mostly upper caste occupancy tenants. However, it adopted an anti-zamindar stance and this struck a sympathetic chord amongst those Congressmen who were ardent supporters of agrarian reforms in which abolition of landlordism had top priority. Henceforth, the peasant movement under the auspices of the Kisan Sabha generally ran an independent course. Peasant movement was assuming an autonomous character.[25]

FRAGMENTATION: THE PEASANT MOVEMENT

The 1930s opened with a worldwide depression which caused a steep fall in agricultural prices. The distress of petty, landholders and sharecroppers was more pronounced. Hence, the Congress set up an Agrarian Enquiry Committee so that it could formulate its politics towards the peasantry. At the same time, the Kisan Sabha gained in support among a section of the peasantry whose economic demands it was primarily championing.

THE DECADE OF THE KISAN SABHA

The Kisan Sabha, true to its composition, promoted the interest of small and intermediate peasantry and tenantry. It opposed the commutation of produce rent into cash rent since the fall in agricultural prices had adversely affected its followers. This brought them in conflict with the zamindars. Furthermore, it pleaded occupancy rights on land for tenants who had been arming it continuously for a certain number of years. Under the leadership of Swmai Sahajanand, it launched several local struggles.

When the All India Kisan Sabha was formed in 1936, Swami

Sahajanand became its top ranking leader and was either its President or General Secretary continuously for a decade.

The Kisan Sabha could not have an easy relationship with the Indian National Congress for a variety of reasons.[26] First, the Congress professed belief in non-violence as a means to achieve its ends, but for the Kisan Sabha violence was not undesirable. Secondly, for the Congress the attainment of freedom was the primary goal, whereas the Kisan Sabha was keen to promote economic interest of its membership. Thirdly, the Congress had formulated its non-agrarian policy at the national level, and therefore, in Bihar it was bound to act within its parameters. Finally, when the Congress took up the reins of the government, it was constrained to coordinate all its policies and hence, agrarian reforms could be implemented only as a part of the overall administrative policy.

Before the 1930s ended, the Congress members had severed relationships with the Kisan Sabha and the Congress members were explicitly banned from establishing any contact with the Kisan Sabha.

The Kisan Sabha, though professing to be a non-political organization, began to lean for support on other political parties. Swamiji first became an admirer of Forward Bloc, a break away group from the Congress under the leadership of Subhas Chandra Bose and later showed strong affinity with the Communist Party of India (CPI) which came into being in Bihar in 1939.[27] The Kisan Sabha, while professing an anti-British stance, mostly emphasized economic demands of a distinct section of the middle peasantry. It explicitly excluded the landless labourers from its purview. Hence, though it waged several local struggles, it could never arouse the enthusiasm of masses. Instead, the Indian National Congress which professed to be fighting for India's freedom and was only, in general terms, espousing the cause of peasantry drew greater support as was evidenced during the Quit India movement, started by the party in 1942.

However, by the end of the 1930s, the influence of three political parties on the peasant movement was becoming clear;

that of the Indian National Congress, the Congress Socialist Party and the Communist Party of India. The latter particularly benefited from its association as it drew a substantial section of its cadre from those who worked among the peasants as members of the Kisan Sabha.

Those sections of the peasantry in the State whose interests were not being served by the Kisan Sabha also tried to organize themselves. The peasant communities, especially the Yadavas, the Kurmis and the Koeris, i.e. those who personally carried on operation connected with farming formed in 1934 the Triveni Sangh.[28] The organization was promoted by pro-British Indians in the hope that it would further split up the peasants and prevent them from supporting the Indian National Congress and thus weaken the freedom movement. The aim was not realized, but the organization helped establish caste identities among these castes. Though for the moment this new organization did not have any significant political repercussions, it prepared the ground for a new politico-economic group in the post-Independence period, i.e. the organization of the so-called backward castes, which is politically a force to reckon with.

The landless agricultural labourers whose interests had been ignored by all and who were mostly Harijans or untouchables also formed in 1937 an organization of their own, Khet Mazdoor Sabha led by Jagjivan Ram who had already joined the Indian National Congress. However, this organization failed to make any mark in favour of those whose interests it was supposed to represent.[29]

During the War, the peasant movement, on the whole, entered a quiet phase. The British Government followed a policy of severe repression: most of the political and Kisan Sabha activists were put behind the bars.

WAR YEARS: COLLABORATION

The CPI whose members were taking a leading part in the peasant movement was banned, but when the Soviet Union entered the War on the side of Allied Powers, a compromise was reached between it and the British Government. The CPI activists were released; Sahajanand agreed to collaborate with them and he was also set free. Now collaboration became the key note.[30] No struggle was waged by the Kisan Sabha. Since the beginning of the War depression had ended; agricultural prices were rising, more employment was generated and, on the whole, economic hardship of the period of Economic Depression was a thing of the past. The Congress was engaged in a movement to overthrow the British rule. The Socialists sided with the Congress.[31] Hence, the peasant movement was passing through a quiet phase.

The period following the end of the Second World War witnessed hectic political activities; the British Government realized that it could no longer hold on to Indian empire; the Congress and the Muslim League felt that they were nearing their cherished goal of achieving a free India and Pakistan. The agrarian question remained in the background; the Government and the political parties negotiated a settlement, while the people anxiously waited for die outcome.

The Kisan Sabha leadership now realized the futility of its past policies: Swamiji dissolved the organization, severed his connection with the CPI, and the Kisan Sabha after about two decades became defunct.[32]

It must be pointed out that several of the Communist activists in the post-Independence Bihar such as Indradeep Sinha, (former Member of Parliament), late Karyanand Sharma, etc., acquired their political and organizational skill as workers of the Kisan Sabha. They took over the Kisan Sabha organization and reorganized it as a full-fledged wing of their party.

FREEDOM COMES: AGRARIAN CHANGE THROUGH LEGISLATION

Within two years after the end of the Second World War the British Government and the major Indian political parties had come to an understanding. The Congress had won the elections to the Provincial Assembly of Bihar and formed the

Ministry. During the poll campaign it had reiterated its promise to end zamindari or landlordism. It was now in a position to implement its agrarian policies and fulfil its pledges to the peasantry. The peasantry too did not force governmental hands in the early years of Independence in spite of high prices of food grains and shortages, since it realized that the government was pre-occupied with the problem of refugees from Pakistan. Of course, debates and discussions concerning the peasant question did not cease, and so Bihar, in the late 1940s, did not witness any major peasant unrest or upsurge.

In the Congress which had pledged to eliminate the landed intermediaries, i.e. the zamindars, the debate ranged round how soon and in what manner zamindari could be ended. The radicals opposed the payment of any compensation, but the Congress refused to toe their line. In spite of strong opposition from the zamindars, who took the matter to the law court, the Zamindari Abolition Bill became a law and a major change in the agrarian structure was achieved.[33] Of course, it was the result of sustained political activity, but there was no immediate peasant movement to bring it about.

The quiescent phase in the movement did not last long. The political leadership, having achieved freedom from foreign yoke, devoted itself to the task of socio-economic regeneration of the country. An immediate task was to bring about all round changes in the agrarian economy and structure. First, agricultural productivity had to be enhanced to feed the growing population and to reduce dependence on foreign food imports. Secondly, in order to avoid rural unrest or outbreak of violence, land reforms in the shape of promulgating land-ceiling, redistribution of surplus land amongst the landless, consolidation of land-holdings, etc., had to be carried out. But the Congress sought to achieve all this without violently provoking one section of the rural society against the other. Hence, in the changes that followed there were no sharp breaks. The government's policy was to contain rural discontent through development and thus it began to engineer changes in agrarian structure.

The government passed legislation concerning *bakasht* land, i.e. land cultivated by sharecroppers but deliberately left it so vague that many ex-zamindars were able to hold on to the lands which should have gone to tenants.[34] Of course, there were clashes between the ex-landlords and sharecroppers, but these did not amount to more than local and sporadic incidents.

While peasant movement was passing through a quiescent phase, important politico-economic changes were taking place which profoundly affected the direction and character of the peasant question.

First, the government had accepted the principle of adult franchise and elected bodies were established from village level upwards. Secondly, the government had made up its mind to transform the villages and the main agency to bring it about was the Community Development Programme which envisaged transformation of Indian agriculture through increased productivity. As a matter of fact, the food shortage prevailing in the country immediately after India gained Independence had forced the government to accord priority to the problem of raising agricultural productivity and the First Five Year Plan aimed at this by popularizing the use of chemical fertilizers and high yielding varieties of seeds. The government also provided increased irrigation facilities by constructing dams, canals, etc. Of course, these concerted efforts bore fruit and agricultural production began picking up.[35] Hence, the peasant communities, i.e. those who had been traditionally regarded as fanners and who in social hierarchy came below the upper castes gained in economic strength. The process was helped by the fact that after the zamindari system was abolished, a substantial number of upper caste zamindars left villages and settled down in towns and their land became available to farmer communities under a variety of arrangements. The exodus of zamindars thus provided more opportunity to farmer communities to improve their economic situation and at the same time a vacuum in the local power structure was created which these peasant communities began to fill up. As the time progressed, these peasant communities realized that since they outnumbered the upper castes, they could dominate elective offices from the village up to the state and national legislatures. Hence, along with the accretion of economic strength, the peasant communities were gaining political clout. In the 1950s, there was tension but no worthwhile peasant movement.

Of course, the policies of the Congress government also helped in ensuring rural peace. It followed a conscious policy of accommodating the educated or influential members of the so-called backward castes (i.e. farmer communities, now called intermediate castes) in the political power structure. The two ministries formed in 1952 and 1957 showed increase in the representation of peasant communities.

Processes were initiated to appease the land hunger of the landless. The most important voluntary experiment was initiated by the disciple of Mahatma Gandhi, Vinoba Bhave who started the *Bhoodan* movement which sought to persuade landholders to gift away their surplus land, which was to be subsequently distributed amongst the have-nots. Vinoba Bhave succeeded in converting to his views, Jayaprakash Narayan—a Left revolutionary of the 1940s and a widely respected leader.[36] Some hopes were entertained that the land question might be solved. However, it was obvious that *Bhoodan* had failed, but it had temporarily helped to contain rural turbulence and prevented the peasant communities from organizing any planned and violent movement for the redressal of their grievances.

But the peasantry had become conscious of its strength and its first manifestation was seen in the canal agitation launched in the Sone Canal area in the Shahabad district in 1952 which continued upto 1962-3 and united all political parties against the ruling Congress party. The movement was directed against the government's decision to enhance irrigation rates.[37] All the peasant communities actively participated in it and got embedded in their consciousness.

The various political parties were becoming aware of the potentiality of the peasant support in their electoral battles and hence, were keen to mobilize them under their banner. Ram Manohar Lohia who started his political career as a member of the Indian National Congress and then became a top leader of the Congress Socialist Party took the lead in this and under the aegis of the Socialist Party (the name kept on changing) organized the peasant community against the Congress party.

The 1950s and the 1960s saw the emergence of peasant communities as a political force and that they had stabilized themselves became evident after the State Assembly elections in 1967. The Congress for the first time lost its majority and a combination of opposition parties ranging from the extreme Right such as, Jan Sangh to the CPI on the Left formed a coalition government. The peasant communities had shown their political might and though the combination could not work, it was clear that peasant communities could no longer be ignored as a political force. True, the peasant communities too did not share the same perception of interests and were divided along caste-lines and hence, were given to factionalism. Besides, they lacked the cementing force of a coherent ideology and this enabled the Congress to topple the ministry after one year. However, from now onwards it was clear to the peasantry that it was a powerful political force and hence, to achieve its ends, it need not launch concerted mass movements; only political planning and electoral effort would secure for it the desired results. The direction of change precluded the farmer communities from resorting to mass movement and they were keen to exploit the opportunities afforded by improved technology and means of transportation to enrich themselves. They now competed with upper caste peasants and so economically, socially and politically contradictions between the two appeared. When the peasant community became rich and politically powerful, it was also riven by dissensions.

While the peasant communities had been consolidating their power and rising in political hierarchy, another sector, the landless labourers, whose services were vital for production purposes and who mostly belonged to the untouchable castes, were languishing.

The untouchables, however, were also growing conscious of the significance of their numbers and realized that enbloc voting by them could make substantial difference to results in election contests. In several village level elections, they were assiduously wooed by rival parties in order to win their support; some of their members had been offered offices in the village panchayats.[38] But nothing substantial had been done to improve their economic lot. In fact, when they looked at other peasant communities, they found that the latter's lot had considerably improved as compared to their status in the pre-Independence days. Hence, they felt jealous of peasant communities who had grown affluent, risen in social hierarchy and acquired political power in the decades following the Independence. At the same time, the electoral process had generated new consciousness about their political rights and were not prepared to put up with humiliations heaped on them by the intermediate castes, whom they found to be no less tyrannical than the upper caste peasants and zamindars in pre-Independence days. The new section tried to exploit them economically as well as socially. As a result, for the first time the landless labourers were at logger heads with the peasantry and they did not try to hide their resentment and anger.

The Indian National Congress had realized the importance of Harijan votes and therefore, it presented itself as the champion of the cause of the Harijans. The Congress could legitimately do so since Mahatma Gandhi in pre-Independence days had worked hard to remove untouchability and bring about trans-formation in the socio-economic status of the community. He had given them a new name *Harijans*, meaning 'the men of God' and had lived amidst them. So when the Congress party staked its claim for the leadership of the Harijans, the latter believed in them. When the Congress came to power, it did try to help them through a number of legislative enactments. This certainly gave more confidence to the Harijans and made them resentful of the atrocities committed on them by the peasant communities. But at the same time, it was clear that the Congress support to Harijans in no way resolved the Harijan versus peasant communities contradiction. It seemed to them that the legislative enactments could not help them much in their struggle against the peasant communities. To counter them, they should take to arms in the same way the peasant communities, a little while ago, had done against the upper caste landlords.[39] The cult of armed resistance thus was accepted by the Harijan community as a means of asserting their rights, and its ideological justification was discovered in certain interpretations of Marxist-Leninist-Maoist doctrines. In the initial stages of their armed struggle, they were helped by outsiders, usually city-bred and well-educated political activists who had been attracted towards Marxism-Leninism as an instrument of political transformation. But as the movement grew, the Harijans began to throw up their own leadership. Thus for the first time, Harijans belonging to different parts of the State began to be influenced by an ideology which rose above local issues and could genuinely compete with the ideologies of the national political parties. Furthermore, Naxalites who came to be widely known as the followers of this ideology began to draw the attention of various other sections of the society and other political parties. It was feared that if the Naxalite ideology took roots amongst the landless peasantry, countryside might be rocked with violnce; the green revolution may be red.

All parties wanted to win over Harijan votes and hence, when the United Front ministry fell down and was followed by ministries of other parties, they vied with each other in passing a series of Land Ceiling Laws which, however, remained merely on paper. The Harijans decided that the governmental machinery was slack; and hence, they began to occupy fields, harvest the standing crops and a Land Grab movement started (1971-2).[40] The initial momentum of this movement stunned the onlookers; they had never expected the have-nots to be so militant. Now that the die was cast, no political party in the State wanted to remain unassociated with the movement. The fact that political parties plunged into it resulted in pulls and counter-pulls and the movement did not survive for long.

But the new militancy among the landless did not die out. In different pockets of the State news of physical retaliation began to trickle in. The immediate cause was not always economic;

the landless would not consent to be treated as sub-human beings in day-to-day intercourse. Their ire was raised not only against the upper caste farmers, but even against the peasant communities who treated them equally badly. Thus the new phenomenon showed the landless labourers fighting two enemies simultaneously: the upper caste as well as the intermediate caste peasantry. The militancy of the landless is now known by the common name of *Naxalism* or extremism. There are several pockets where such elements became prominent. Mention may be made of Ekwari, Musahari, Chauradano, etc.

Thus the peasant movement by 1975 had taken a new shape: the landless labourers had been drawn into its vortex and the state apparatus was forced to use its repressive might in order to quell them. The Twenty-Point Programme enunciated by Mrs. Gandhi in 1975 sought to focus attention on this problem.

It was discovered that within the category of landless labourers, there was another category, the bonded-labourer whose fate was hardly better man that of the slave. The government through legislation put an end to the system; it has succeeded to some extent, but the overall problem of the landless labourers has remained. A decade has passed; the problem has defied solution; tensions in rural areas have increased and the State is now engaged in seeking its solution.

NOTES

1. Surendra Gopal, 'Jains in Eastern India in the Seventeenth Century', in D. Tripathi, ed., *Business Communities in India*, Delhi, 1984.
2. See Surendra Gopal, *Commerce and Crafts in Gujarat, XVI-XVII Centuries*, Delhi, 1975. In western India the Marathas grew powerful under the leadership of Shivaji (1627-80) and challenged the Mughal rule. They repeatedly sacked the port of Surat in Gujarat, then the most prosperous port in India. Aurangzeb followed an expansionist policy with regard to the Deccan Sultanates, resulting in prolonged war-fare which undermined the local economy.
3. K.K. Datta, ed., *The Comprehensive History of Bihar*, vol. III, pt. I, Patna, 1976, Chap. XII.
4. Ibid., Chap. II.

5. Ibid., p. 139.
6. Till 1816, the manufacture of opium was confined to the area of Bihar and the adjoining tract of Benares, see H.R. Ghoshal, *Economic Transition in the Bengal Presidency (1793-1833)*, Patna, 1960, p .119.
7. Sunil Sen, *Agrarian Relations in India*, Calcutta, 1979, Chap. I; A.C. Guha, *A Brief Sketch of the Land Systems of Bengal and Bihar*, Calcutta, 1915, Chap. III.
8. Ghosal, op. cit., p. 257.
9. Guha, op. cit., pp. 11-12.
10. Datta, op. cit, p. 458.
11. Ghosal, op. cit., pp. 306-7; Datta, op. cit., pp. 461-2.
12. Surendra Gopal, 'The Roots of Rural Poverty in Bihar', *Current Studies*, Patna, 1984.
13. Ibid.
14. Guha, op. cit., p. 135.
15. Sunil Sen, *Peasant Movements in India*, Calcutta, 1982, pp. 11-18.
16. Datta, op. cit., p. 495. Between 1860 and 1880, Bihar experienced five major famines and three local scarcities. See C.E. Buckland, *Bihar Under the Lieutenant Governors*, Delhi, 1976, vol. I, pp. 393-555; vol. II, pp. 556-93, 872.
17. Buckland, op. cit., vol. II, p. 732: 'The opening of the Sone Canals had given a great impetus to the extension of sugarcane cultivation and had caused a considerable increase in the agricultural wealth of the tracts supplied.'
18. Ibid., p. 811.
19. Datta, op. cit., vol. III, pt. I, pp. 263-4.
20. Ibid., p. 266.
21. Stephen Henningham, *Peasant Movements in Colonial India: North Bihar, 1917 to 1947*, Australian National University South Asia Monograph Series, Canberra, 1982, p. 49. The Champaran Agrarian Act quietened unrest by substantial concessions.
22. Ibid., Chap. 3.
23. N.M.P. Srivastava, 'Peasant Movement in Bihar', *The Journal of the Bihar Puravid Parisad*, 1980-1, pt. II, p. 210: 'Within these nine years the raiyat grew from infancy to adulthood'; Arvind N. Das, *Agrarian Unrest and Socio-Economic Change 1900-1980*, Delhi, 1983, p. 88.
24. Ibid.
25. Swami Sahajanand Saraswati, *Kisan Sabha ke Sansmaran* (in Hindi), Allahabad, 1947.
26. For details, see Das, op. cit., pp. 130-6; Swami Sahajanand Saraswati, *Mera Jeewan Sangharsh* (in Hindi), Patna, 1952.

27. Indradeep Sinha, *Bihar Mein Communist Party ka Vikas* (in Hindi), Patna, n.d.
28. Hetukar Jha et al., *Social Structures and Alignments*, Delhi, 1985, p. 21.
29. Das, op. cit., p. 139.
30. Ibid., pp. 168-70.
31. Srivastava, op. cit., p. 222. The Congress Socialists parted company with the Kisan Sabha in February 1941.
32. Ibid., pp. 223-4.
33. Das, op. cit., Chap 8. The final legislation was named Bihar Land Reforms Act, 1950 and it became a law in 1952.
34. Ibid., p. 187. *The Bakasht Disputes Settlement Act, 1947* may be construed as a continuation of the Congress policy of pre-World War II days.
35. Datta, op. cit., vol. III, pt. II, pp. 555-8.
36. Jayaprakash Narayan became so enthusiastic that he gave up active politics and devoted himself to *Bhoodan*. In 1974, Jayaprakash Narayan (J.P.), as he was popularly called, gave the call for total revolution which eventually led to the imposition of Emergency in the country by Mrs. Gandhi in June 1975; Das, op. cit., pp. 202-3.
37. Jha et al., op. cit., p. 23.
38. Ibid., Chap. II.
39. Sen, op. cit., pp. 225-8.
40. Das, op. cit., p. 231.

CHAPTER 4

Peasant Movement in Bihar during the Second World War
(Some Newspaper Sources)

The movement launched by Gandhiji against the indigo-planters in the district of Champaran was the first peasant movement of the state in the twentieth century. Although the momentum was soon lost, yet peasants had entered into the calculation of political workers. By the end of the 1920s, Bihar Kisan Sabha (Peasant Conference) had been organized by Swami Sahajanand and his fellow-workers. The peasant movement received further impetus in the province when the Congress Socialist Party, a leftist group in the Indian National Congress, came into existence in 1934 at Patna. But the movement was subjected to a number of pulls.

The Indian National Congress had been concerned with the fate of the peasants.[1] Several members of the Congress Socialist Party accorded priority to work among the ruralities. When the Communist Party was formed in Bihar on 20 October 1939, it tried to strengthen its position by attracting the peasantry to its banner.[2] The Kisan Sabha was active in the field. Therefore in spite of divergent pulls, the movement continued to expand. It remained a part of the national freedom movement, directed against alien rule.

The outbreak of the Second World War was a signal for the nationalist forces to intensify their activities. A section of left-oriented workers assumed radical postures. They denounced the Congress leadership which had failed to remove the grievances of the peasantry during its ministry. The movement was now led by moderate as well as extremist factions. The picture changed after Hitler attacked the Soviet Union on 21 June 1941.

The new turn in international politics stunned the Communists. They feared that the defeat of the Soviet Union would ensure the victory of Fascism, a possibility, which they viewed with grave concern. Hence, they decided to work wholeheartedly for the defeat of the fascist powers. The war was now a people's war. Nothing had to be done, which would hinder the outcome of the war in favour of the Allied powers, who now became the ally of the Soviet Union, 'the only state of the peasants and workers on the earth'.

The changed attitude of the Communist Party towards British imperialism owing to the exigencies of war affected the course of the peasant movement.

The Communists did not give up their work among the peasants but instead of exhorting them against the British rule, they sought to mobilize them to render help to the Britishers.[3] Their attitude was by and large shared by the leaders of Kisan Sabha, particularly Swami Sahajanand and his chief lieutenants Yadunandan Sharma and Yamuna Karji.

This considerably strengthened the position of the Communists in the peasant movement in the State because Swami Sahajanand, as one of the founders of Kisan Sabha in Bihar and also as one of the prominent activists of the all India body commanded considerable respect among a section of the peasantry.

But the Indian National Congress and the Congress Socialist Party thought that the nation ought to combine to drive out the British. Hence, they wanted to use the peasantry against the British. They refused to accept the plea that any weakening of the British would facilitate the victory of the Fascists. The peasant movement was being pulled in opposing directions.

A year of debate and discussion showed the irreconcilable position of the two sides. The CPI brought out in July 1942 an English weekly from Bombay, the *People's War* and its Hindi counterpart, *Lok Yuddha*. They wanted to educate the masses regarding the policies of the party. The two journals devoted considerable attention to peasant movement and regularly printed news and reports about its progress from all parts of the country. Most of the news and reports were based upon information supplied by party activists or those having ideological affinity.[4]

The data thus collected from news and reports regarding Bihar, reveal two things. It sheds light on the activities of the Kisan Sabha because most of the Communists involved in peasant movement, worked on behalf of the Kisan Sabha. Secondly, we get a glimpse into the nature of the leadership of the movement.

It appears that many of the local secretaries or organizers were either Communists or sympathizers of the CPI. Eventually some of them rose to high positions in the party hierarchy. The top leadership in Bihar Communist Party consisted of several persons who started their career as workers and organizers of peasant movement during the war. In fact, this also explains why certain areas, became traditional pockets of Communist influence. The study of the files of the *People's War* gives an insight into not only the peasant movement in the province against an all India perspective but also helps us to trace the growth of the Communist Party.

The *Lok Yuddha* serves an identical purpose but in one respect is more informative. Many of the activists in interior villages sent their reports in Hindi and were published in the *Lok Yuddha* straightaway. They were far more comprehensive and accurate than those which had been translated or summarized into English for being used in the columns of the *People's War*.[5]

These weeklies give us the broad outlines of the course of the peasant movement. A more comprehensive and authentic picture is obtained by supplementing the above facts by those secured from another Hindi weekly, the *Hunkar*, started at Patna in mid-1942.

The chief promoters of the paper were Swami Sahajanand and Pandit Yamuna Karji, who were in the Kisan movement of the province since the late 1920s. The former was the secretary of the All India Kisan Sabha in 1943 and its president in 1944.[6] They made the *Hunkar*, the chief organ of the Kisan Sabha, on which now fell the mantle of the leadership of the peasant movement because after the Quit India movement of 9 August 1942, the Indian National Congress and the Congress Socialist Party had been severely repressed. The files of the *Hunkar* during this period, therefore, give *us* detailed information about different facets of the movement. The journal was not disturbed by the British government like other newspapers of the period because of its policy of cooperation with the ruling authorities. Here we have almost a day-to-day record of the activities of the Kisan Sabha.

The *Hunkar* regularly carried articles by Swami Sahajanand which expounded the policies and attitudes of the organization.[7] We learn of the arguments defending the policy of collaboration and opposing the policy of confrontation pursued by the National Congress. There are reports on tours and meetings addressed by Swami Sahajanand.[8] The areas and extent of the influence of the Kisan Sabha can be inferred. Further, we learn of the organizational structure.[9] We discern that many of the office-holders occupied and occupy eminent position in the CPI. Mention may be made of late Shri Karyanand Sharma ex-MLA who was the secretary of State Council,[10] Shri Bhola Prasad MP was a full time worker of the Kisan Sabha. Yogendra Sharma MP also took prominent part in Kisan Sabha work. Uma Shankar Shukla ex-MLA was active in the district of Champaran. Rahul Sankrityayan worked in the Saran district. Indradeep Sinha, MLC started his career as an activist in the peasant movement. The Kisan Sabha work proved to be an ideal training for the emergent leadership of the Communist Party in the province.

As a part of its policy of collaboration with the British authorities, the Kisan Sabha, on the political front advised its members and sympathizers to refrain from supporting the 1942 movement. They were not to participate in violent activities.

As the war proceeded, prices rose and scarcity conditions prevailed. The Kisan Sabha lent full support to the Government in their efforts to hold prices and prevent shortages of essential commodities. It became an ardent supporter of the Grow More Food campaign initiated by the rulers.

The Kisan Sabha workers asked peasants to cultivate fallow land so that production would increase.[11] Through collective efforts, the peasants constructed bunds and irrigational channels, which would help them to raise better crops.[12] The journal published information about the type of fertilizers to be used by the peasants for different crops.[13] The peasants were told about the crops they should plant and the return they could expect. However, technically these suggestions were elementary. They failed to rouse the enthusiasm of the peasantry and hardly made any difference to the quantum of the produce.

The peasants were exhorted to sell grains to the government, to report against profiteers and hoarders.[14] The pages of the journal indicate the extent of the collaborationist policy followed by the leadership of the Kisan Sabha and the peasant movement in Bihar.

But no movement, claiming to be a popular one, can survive by adopting conciliatory tones with an alien regime. This is all the more true for a period of national soul-searching which India was undergoing following the August movement. The leaders of the Kisan Sabha appeared to have realized this shortcoming. They tried to remedy the situation by putting forth their own rationale as distinct from the line of the Communist Party.

Swami Sahajanand claimed that the Kisan Sabha had nothing to do with politics or political parties. It was concerned purely with the redressal of economic grievances.[15] In effect, he sought to delink economics from politics. This attitude created rift in the movement. The Communist Party refused to accept the distinction made between politics and economics by Swami Sahajanand. The Communists and the followers of Swami Sahajanand began to drift apart. The debate and discussion that ensued is preserved in the pages of the *Hunkar* and the *People's War.*

Other type of information can also be secured. The leaders of Kisan Sabha continued to agitate on local issues in order to maintain their image as fighters for the cause of the impoverished peasantry. Thus they pressed for the abolition of the *Bhavli* system of land tenure, widely prevalent in the districts of Gaya, Patna and Monghyr. They protested against the tyrannical conduct of specific landlords. They opposed the attempt on the part of the zamindar to evict the actual tiller or his efforts to harass him by forcibly harvesting his standing crops or by demanding exorbitant rent from him. But these were isolated attempts. Their success did not add to the strength of the movement. The leadership tried to win over a section of the peasantry by demanding increase in the purchase price of sugar cane by the sugar mills. Some of the Kisan Sabha activists became members of Joint Sugar Control Board formed by the Government.[17] As a part of this policy they vehemently opposed restrictions imposed on the manufacture of *gur* or *jaggery*,[18] and asked the peasants to prepare it. The policies of Kisan Sabha did not cut ice with the peasantry.[19] The leadership began to feel their isolation from the main stream of national life. Therefore by 1944, the leaders of the Kisan Sabha adopted a more conciliatory tone towards the Indian National Congress and its leaders. The futility of conducting a purely economic movement became obvious. The non-Communist leadership of the Kisan Sabha went out of limelight.

NOTES

1. K.K. Datta, *History of Freedom Movement in Bihar,* vol. II, Patna, 1957, pp. 233, 235.
2. Indradeep Sinha, *Bihar Mein Communist Party ka Vikas,* Patna, p. 1.
3. They took up the work of Grow More Food Campaign, *People's War,* 19 September, 1943.
4. *People's War,* vol. II, no. 2, 11 July 1943, carries a report on the 10th Provincial Kisan Conference held at Sonepur on 12 and 13 June 1943 under the presidentship of Swami Sahajanand.
6. *People's War,* 7 November 1943 and 26 March 1944.
7. *Hunkar,* 6 December 1942. The editorial supported the policy of helping British war efforts; *Hunkar,* 27 December 1942 and 3 January 1943.
8. Ibid. Report on Swamiji's tour in the district of Monghyr; *Hunkar,* 31 January 1943. Report on his tour of Gaya district.
9. *Hunkar,* 28 February 1943. On p. 10 we have a list of district officials

in eleven districts. The issue of 28 March tells us of training camps for workers.

10. *Hunkar,* 14 February 1943.
11. *People' War,* 22 August 1943. Comrade Bindeshwar Singh helped to secure 1,500 *bighas* of waste land for the Grow More Food campaign.
12. *People's War,* 19 September 1943; *Lok Yuddha,* 17 October 1943, and 14 November 1943.
13. *Hunkar,* 27 December 1942.
14. *Lok Yuddha,* 13 February 1943. Sunil Mukherjee became a member of the Legislative Assembly issued a statement to this effect.
15. Swami Sahajanand, 'Samrajyavadi Yuddha aur Jan Yuddha', *Hunkar,* 3 January 1943, p. 9; idem, 'Kisan Sabha aur Rajniti'. *Hunkar,* 10 and 17 January 1943; see also the issue of 2 July 1944.
16. *People's War,* 26 March 1944. P.C. Joshi wrote in this issue about Sahajanand, 'He was a victim to (such) depressing sentiments . . .'.
17. *Lok Yuddha,* 31 October 1943. The Kisan Sabha celebrated a sugar cane week from 10 October 1943. Ibid., 16 January 1944; *Hunkar,* 20 December 1942; *Hunkar,* 20 August 1944.
18. *People's War,* 26 September 1943; *Hunkar,* 20 December 1942, 7 February 1943.
19. *People's War,* 26 March 1944; it was admitted, 'The Kisan Sabha finds itself at the lowest ebb'.

CHAPTER 5

Opium Raiyats in Bihar in the First Half of the Nineteenth Century

Along with indigo, opium was another widely cultivated and important cash crop in the plains of Bihar in the eighteenth and nineteenth centuries. As, a cash crop Bihar farmers had cultivated opium at least since the seventeenth century. The Europeans, the Dutch and the English were the exporters.[1] The English East India Company, having seized power after the battles of Plassey and Buxar, systematically ousted all the other European rivals from the purchase of opium: by the end of the eighteenth century it emerged as the sole exporter and it was keenly interested in promoting the cultivation of opium since 'Bengal opium' as the Bihar opium was euphemistically called, was the most sought after commodity in China and was the chief 'economic foundation of the triangular commerce between England, India and China'.[2] Opium was also 'The third principal Branch of the East India Company's territorial revenue in India'.[3] The English East India Company took measures to regulate its cultivation and sale.

Like indigo, opium was cultivated in all the districts in the plains of Bihar but with a crucial difference. The Europeans did not take up its cultivation; the cultivation of opium remained outside the ambit of European planters. It was carried out exclusively by indigenous farmers. Secondly, in 1790s the Company procured its requirement of opium through contractors, both Indian and British. Opium contracts were exposed to public competition

Among European contractors, in the 1790s David Colvin was the most important person. The Company advanced to him in 1794-5 a sum of 50,000 *sicca* rupees, in 1796-7 a sum of 1,34,800 *sicca* rupees, for the supply of opium.[5] Another European contractor Playdell received in 1797-8 a sum of 84,000 *sicca* rupees for the same purpose.[6] This gives us an idea of the economic importance of poppy cultivation and the quantum of cash it injected in rural economy.

In view of the great economic importance of the opium crop, the government monopolized its production. No one could cultivate it without its sanction. For the strict enforcement of its monopoly the Collectors were asked to secure written assurances from the landholders 'that they will not knowingly permit the cultivation of the poppy on their estates except on account of Government and they will report the District Judge of any illicit cultivation'.[7]

In 1820 the Collector of Shahabad was informed that opium cultivation was prevalent in the district since the turn of the century. 'Hundreds of Koeris can now produce it'.[8] This is in contrast to the situation described by Buchanan during his tour of the countryside of the district in 1812-13. About one stretch he says 'some poppy' and about the other he remarks 'a good deal of poppy.'

The keen interest displayed by the government in promoting poppy cultivation can be seen from the letter written by the Collector of Shahabad to Secretary, Board of Revenue, Central Province in 1823. He noted he had visited 'villages in the eleven of the thirteen pergannah of the District' and 'enquired into the state of poppy cultivators'.[10]

He found that the cultivators were primarily Koiris. The Koiris complained of two difficulties coming in the way of poppy cultivation. First, they regretted that neither the zamindars nor the farmers did not care about the maintenance of irrigation facilities such as wells or water courses. Secondly the rent on land which they cultivated was arbitrarily enhanced frequently either by the zamindar or the person who had farmed the land from him. The Collector was constrained to observe that whenever 'an estate is let in farm' the poppy lands are the first to be overburdened with taxation which left the farmer with 'a bare subsistence' .[11]

The Collector noted that the cultivation of poppy was decaying since in one village he saw only ten wells operative out of the existing sixty.

Furthermore, the Koiris did not always cultivate poppy on the best land, i.e. the high lands or Dhee or Komar lands near the villages because of their high rents. Instead they cultivated it on 'inferior lands' where the rent was low. As a result the output of poppy was reduced and its quality was inferior.[11]

The state of poppy cultivation in the Patna district was much better. Buchanan in 1811-12 noted 'The poppy is always cultivated near village in garden land, which is carefully watered, and gives at least one other crop, while some things are almost always sown along with it especially onions, garlic and coriander, while a hedge of carthamus is usually raised round the plot'.[13]

He noted modes of oppressing the opium cultivator. First, at the time of appraisement, the *Parkhya* or the appraiser extracted illegal gratification from the seller and if he offered any complaint, the *Parkhya* threatened to dub it as 'adulterated'. While weighing, the *Dundydar* or the weigher extracted some money or some gift. Finally the Brahmin at the Factory also took a share from the sale-proceeds.[14] Consequently according to the Collector, 'Thus the Koiri is not paid for much more than half the quantity delivered by him'.[15]

In order to better the condition of the opium cultivators, the Collector made certain suggestions. He stated. 'My own observation enables me to state the deficiency of water is great and unless the evil can be remedied, no large increase of the poppy cultivation can be relied on'.[16]

It was in pursuit of this recommendation that he suggested to the Board of Revenue that a sum of Rs. 10,000 be advanced for the repair and construction of wells. Out of this sum Kunwar Singh, the zamindar of Jagdishpur wanted Rs. 3,000 and the rest Rs. 7,000 was to be distributed among smaller zamindars.[17]

The government was keen to involve the zamindars in the expansion of poppy cultivation since their intransigence could create a log of hurdles. The zamindars by and large cooperated as poppy would bring cash to the raiyats and strengthen their capacity to pay their zamindari dues. Moreover, the zamindar could always charge higher rent for lands on which poppy was cultivated.

The government's interest in ensuring availability of irrigational facilities to the opium cultivator persisted throughout the century. Rivett-Carnac noted in 1894 that the Opium Agency continued to make advances . . . to the cultivators for the construction of permanent masonry wells and for digging small temporary wells unprotected by masonry, for the purpose of irrigating their fields. The advances made for wells are repayable by installments.[18]

Opium cultivation brought the Koiris in close contact with the zamindars or the leaseholders, who tried to impose greater financial burden on them as compared to the cultivator of cereal crops. An element of exploitation marked the relationship between the opium cultivator and the zamindar or the leaseholder. Since the ritual status of the Koiri in the social hierarchy was low, the local Brahmin used his superior status to extract some part of his hard-earned income. This was a continuous reminder to him to continue to defer to the Brahmin even in spheres where he had no social or ritual standing.

It should be noted that poppy cultivation was not the exclusive prerogative of the Koiris. Other castes, engaged in farming also raised this crop since the monetary returns were tempting.

Finally, the government was concerned with the fate of poppy cultivators since it was keenly interested in ensuring a stable output of opium. As distinguished from indigo, the opium cultivators did not have to launch any agitation to make the government aware of their problems. One could trace government's desire to keep the poppy cultivator satisfied right from the early days of the nineteenth century.

The government on its own initiative tried to solve the problems of the opium cultivators and ensure their minimal . . . well-being so that the required quantum of . . . would be available.

In a letter written in 1827 to the Board of Revenue, the

Collector hoped that the interest on the amount disbursed for the purpose of constructing wells would be waived for 'the sum advanced . . .'. The principal would be realized in installments.[19]

The keen governmental interest was probably due to increase sale of opium in China from 1824-5 onwards as revealed from the figures given in the endnote.[20] In 1822 one chest of Patna opium fetched the highest price in China. It was worth Spanish Dollars 2,500 per chest.[21]

The government's initiative was well received. The Collector reported that he had received applications for such (financial) assistance from different parts of the district and many peasants were even prepared to pay enhanced rent if improvements were made.[22]

The opium cultivators appreciated the steps of the government and were willing to join hands with it in order to enhance its productivity since it was economically a viable proposition. In spite of the element of coercion exercised by the zamindars, the leaseholders, the employees of the Opium Agency and the Brahmins, they fell the need to offer their cooperation to safeguard their economic interests. An idea of popularity of opium cultivation can be had from the fact that in 1832-3, it was cultivated on 1,72,489 *bighas* in Benares and Bihar while in 1797 it was cultivated only on 46,000 *bighas*.[23]

The popularity of opium cultivation in the district of Saran was primarily due to the fact that on the same soil three crops could be grown, 'the first is Muchye or Jonera, and what is sown after the poppy is cut is China, Metrtice and Sang. Where the land is near any large town and are cultivated by people of low caste. . . . With ready means of disposing of the produce they are made to yield many crops of vegetables, the profits are consequently much greater and the rent is high.[24] Of course it was realized that it was a labour intensive crop, 'labour is required in watering, weeding and constant attention during cultivation'.

The Collector further reported,

those ryots who have only a beegah of land seldom cultivate the whole with poppy probably only half and the remainder of the ground with potatoes, brinjals and other vegetables. And ground of the same description culti-vated with other produce whenever allowed to lay idle yields greater produce and profit.[25]

Convergence of economic interests of the peasant, the zamin-dar and the government on the question of opium cultivation brought them together; cooperation and not confrontation shaped their relationship.

It may be noted that in several of these letters the opium cultivators are referred to as Koiris which suggests that the Koiris were basically engaged in its cultivation in the Shahabad district.

A letter of Collector in 1812 noted. 'The opium cultivators or Koirees are the most industrious if not the only laborious cultivators we have in this district. . . .'[26] Subsequently, he sup-plied the Koiris of all the thirteen parganas in the district with New Orleans cotton seed although they were reluctant to experiment with it.[27]

This is a tribute to the industriousness of the Koiri peasants that they were trusted with the experiment of cultivating cotton from New Orleans cotton seed in spite of their reluctance. The cultivation of cotton did not bring in greater economic gains and therefore, could never replace opium cultivation.

Other sections of the peasantry also took to opium cultivation because of its profitability. By 1850s opium cultivation had considerably expanded. In this district of Patna, opium was cultivated in four out of twelve parganas.[28] In the district of Saran opium was an important crop in sixteen out of seventeen parganas.[39] In the Sarkar Champaran which then formed a part of the Saran district, poppy was a popular crop as it was produced in all the four parganas.[30] A Sub-Deputy Opium Agent was stationed in Bettiah.[31] In the district of Monghyr, poppy was grown in twelve out of twenty-two parganas.[32] In 1847-8, the area under poppy cultivation was about 20,315 *bigha* and the output was about 4,040 maunds.[33] The poppy cultivators worked for both the Tirhoot and Bhagalpur Sub-Deputy Opium Agencies.[34]

In the district of Tirhoot, opium cultivation was fairly wide-

spread. Wyatt refers to the existence of three opium factories
in the district; viz., at Muzaffarpur, Lalganj and Russolganj-corf
Koilee.[35] Buchanan had already spoken of the industrious Koiris
of Bhagalpur, who were well-known opium producers.

In short, in Bihar plains opium was an extensively cultivated
crop. Despite its contribution to the economy, the opium cultivator could not escape oppression by the concerned government
employees as well as the intermediaries and the zamindars.
Even low-ranked employees of the Opium Department used
their powers to oppress and harass him and indulged in corrupt
practices.

HARASSMENT OF POPPY CULTIVATORS

Even in the first quarter of the nineteenth century opium cultivators attached to the Lalgunge factory were complaining of
malpractices. The Collector of Tirhoot admitted that while
the receipts (*chittahas*) with the cultivators showed that they
had delivered '11 maunds and three seers of opium', the factory
records show the delivery of only thirty seers and 12 chataks.[36]

In 1830, the Collector of Saran reported that the opium
cultivators of the estate of Raja 'Tejpertaub Tejna' complained
to him in 'Rammnuggur'. Their main complaint was directed
against two of the *ticcadars* or agents of the Raja, 'Omur Doss'
and 'Leela Mahtoo'.

Hitcha Bhuggut of the village Dubouba complained that
Ticcadar Cheelya Pandu was demanding more than the rent
specified in the 'pottah' for poppy fields. The stated rate was
Rs. 1 annas 8 per *bigha*. His request was that the *ticcadar* be
restrained from collecting this excess amount.

Other cultivators Buloth, Sheodeen, Sheonath, and Shaikh
Mushid also complained against the *ticcadars* and *putwaree*
who were asking an amount more than that specified in the
agreement. They complained that if they refused payment they
would not be permitted to cultivate their lands.

Heera Mahto in his application also made similar allegations
against the *ticcadar* and stated that because of his tyranny
'inhabitants of ten houses' had run away from their village.

The petition of Rummun and Ruttun on village Quela Kunnya again accused the *ticcadar* of raising the rent from Rs. 3 per *bigha* as noted in *pattah* to Rs. 7 per *bigha*.[37]

The Collector found out that the cultivators could not expect any justice from the Raja since the Raja got from *ticcadar* a share in the collected amount known as *Russom* 'as expence for the village'. The Raja also levied a tax at the time of marriage which the *ticcadar* collected from the village. The Collector concluded that the cultivator could hope for no respite from the zamindar's tyranny.[38] The oppression of opium cultivators in the above-mentioned manner is further proved by the complaints of Sodhee, Lokharee, Dinded and Tukkar of Majhowah pargana under the zamindari of Raja Anand Kishore of the Bettiah Raj.

The villagers complained that 'Bussunt Raout', the *ticcadar* was asking for double the amount they had paid according to the *patta* between the fasli years 1231 and 1235 from the fasli year 1236.

On inquiry the Collector found that Jukkharee tilled 6 *bighas* of land and paid Rs. 14 and 4 annas. Besides, he also paid Rs. 1 5 annas and 10 pies as other taxes such as *missabanah, putwaree* and a second *batta*.

Sodhee cultivated 3 *bighas* and paid Rs. 10 and also an extra 15 annas.

He found out from the receipt of the *ticcadar* that Rs. 19 had been actually realized.[39]

When he made further enquiries from the *ticcadar* and the *putwaree,* the entire pattern of tax collection became obvious.

He found, '. . . the *ticcadar* collects on the pattah to pay for the expenses of the rajah darbar one anna and a half on each rupee from every Assamee of the village'. The *ticcadar* further collected, '. . . one anna and a half as *rajank* (the rights of the raja). . .'.[40]

He noted that in the village twenty-one cultivators cultivated 65 *bighas* and 19 *biswas* of land. Besides they had some *bhowlee* land as well. For this they paid Rs. 18 anna 1 and pies 10. They paid Rs. 16 and pies 6 as *hissabanah* and Rs. 54 annas 2 and pies 3 as rajah darbar and other prohibited cesses such as *chumawan*.

The Collector issued an order to the Raja and prohibited the levying of these 'exactions'.[41]

Other evidence indicated that the *ticcadar* collected from the cultivators cesses such as *batta*, *russoom*, *putwaree* and expenses of *shadee*.

When the cultivators went to complain, the Raja refused to meet them and when they met him, the Raja refused to listen to them.

The oppression of the peasant was obvious. There was absolutely no justification for exacting these cesses.[42]

In a letter to the Acting Collector of Bhagalpur in 1836, the local government official reported that two cultivators had complained against the opium Mohurir and the peons at Rajmahal. In case prompt action was not taken against the culprits, the opium cultivators threatened to abandon cultivation. He, therefore, recommended that swift action against the employees of opium department should be taken.[43]

DIFFUSION OF POPPY CULTIVATION

The opium cultivator despite all his desire to be cooperative did resent iniquitous behaviour. He made his discontent known in clear terms to governmental authorities. Commonality of interest goaded him to join mass action programmes to secure his legitimate demands.

The willingness of the opium cultivator to persist with opium cultivation despite the tyrannical behaviour of the zamindar, *ticcadar* and the employees of the Opium Department may be explained by the fact that it brought government investment in cash to the countryside and helped him partially to meet his cash obligations and thus escape from the clutches of the moneylender and other harassments from the zamindar consequent upon non-payment of his dues.

The sale of opium to the government was important to the cultivators since it brought them cash. Thus in 1842 we hear of an employee of the Opium Department going to Sultanganj to disburse Rs. 5,000. He proposed to take along with himself a Havildar and five sepoys to guard the money.[44]

Since the promotion of opium cultivation was a considered government policy, the concerned government servants were also vigilant that its productivity did not suffer on account of factors under their control. They carefully monitored events which might have a negative effect on opium cultivation. The Sub Opium Agent, Bhagalpur wrote to his Acting Deputy Opium Agent. 'I regret the necessity I am under of bringing to your notice the conduct of Juggomohun Tagore in having taken forcible possession and cultivated for indigo, sundry poppy fields the property of government on which I had unexpired lease.'[45]

The government employees were also expected to give positive assistance to the agents of the Patna Opium Office when he went to the villages to collect opium from the cultivators. D. Campbell of Patna Opium Office requested the local Magistrate to instruct police officials to render every aid to his gomashtas in securing the delivery of the drug.[46]

The keen government interest as well as the possibility of good economic returns, besides, the expectation that being an opium cultivator might bring in governmental protection against the tyranny of the zamindar and other elements in the rural society, impelled the peasantry to adopt opium cultivation as an integral part of their economic activity.

Despite government's keen desire to promote opium cultivation, it was not prepared to allow all the sundry take to it. It wanted to keep tight control over its production. In fact anyone going for it without prior governmental permission was subject to penalty incurred under the provision of Regulation XIII of 1816.[47]

The intense involvement of the government with opium cultivation made its presence highly visible in the countryside. The government servants were able to observe at first hand, the state of agriculture, were able to devise remedial measures for the welfare of the cultivator such as protection of the cultivators from the oppression of local zamindars or officials and provide for irrigational facilities, etc. Consequently on the whole, the peasant found opium cultivation not an irritating experience as was the case with indigo-cultivation. As a result, we mark a widespread diffusion of opium cultivation; even in area where proper irrigational facilities were not available.

By 1818 opium cultivation had become popular in Saran. The rent of the opium fields ranged from Rs. 4 for *bigha* to Rs. 16 and 18 depending on the 'soil and situation'.[48]

Opium cultivation became so widespread in the Saran district by the 1850s, that besides the traditionally cultivating castes others including untouchables took to it. A report from the Collector of Saran stated. 'The opium cultivation is not now entirely in the hands of better class of cultivators-Dhosadho, Dovies and even Chumars now cultivate the drug and lodging a false report at the Thanahs are enabled to offer their opium for sale illegally'.[49]

By 1818 opium cultivation had taken roots in Bhagalpur and it was reported to have been cultivated in an area extending up to 14,500 *bighas*.[50] The *raiyats* wanted seeds to be given around the month of May and from each *bigha*, the government should not collect more than 4 seers of opium. They also wanted Rs. 4 as cash advance per *bigha*. They set the quality of opium to be delivered. It was to be 'pure opium or of the description called Sochah of Bhagalpore of 101 as they delivered when formerly the opium was cultivated in this district by contract.[51]

In Zillah Monghyr in the season 1847-8, it was estimated that poppy was cultivated on approximately 20,000 *bighas* of land and the yield amounted to more than 4,040 maunds of standard consistency of 70.[52] By 1874, the area under opium cultivation had increased to 39,960 *bighas*. In 1873, 4,775 maunds of opium were produced on 33,854 *bighas* and it was worth £95,513,14s. 0d.[53] The Monghyr Opium Sub-Agency had five collection centres.[54]

In 1867 the Deputy Collector of Jamui Sub Division reported, 'The poppy is extensively cultivated. The means of irrigation are scanty, there being no reservoirs of water during the dry season except wells to draw water from which is a very labourious process.'[55]

But the process of diffusion was not always smooth. Often unexpected problems arose and the governmental machinery had to sort these out. An instance from the Bhagalpur district may be cited.

By 1825 the government measures to popularise-opium culti-vation in the Bhagalpur district were yielding contradictory results. The zamindar of Gidhaur was unable to fulfil his obligation and so were the cultivators within his jurisdiction. Hence, both of them were intending to give it up. But the Opium Agent in pursuance of the government policy persisted. He requested the local Raja Neerbhye Singh and Raja Nawab Singh to continue to promote the cultivation of poppy.[56]

The government measures eventually yielded results. A report to the Commissioner of Revenue for the Division of Monghyr in 1829 states 'that a considerable improvement has been made in the opium provided for abkary purposes, this refinement has not been effected in the quantity of the drug but in its consistency. . .'.[57]

One reason why opium cultivation retained its popularity was the case with which it could be sold in the home market if the government did not purchase it. In spite of government's prohibition the peasant did indulge in its clandestine sale and earned some extra cash.

The price of opium in the domestic market was fairly high. The sale-price of opium to the public in Purnea and Bhagalpur was pegged at Rs. 25 per seer. The local officials insisted that price should in no case be increased since it would put 'opium beyond the reach of the common man.'[58]

The government felt no moral inhibition in promoting its use among the common men. It was concerned with its revenue: It did not bother to consider the evil social and moral consequences that might result from its increased consumption. Its apathy to the social and moral aspect of opium only helped to increase its use. We are, at the moment, not in a position to delineate its impact on the society because of absence of data.

The government patronage is obvious from the fact that the Collector was deeply involved in its retail sale for local consumption. The Saran Collector in 1847 sold it to local retailers at the cost of Rs. 10 per seer. His office could also sell it to individual users.

In February 1866 a great storm blowing from northwest towards Sonpur over a tract 35 miles long and roughly 5 to 8 miles broad, totally destroyed the poppy fields. In the past similar devastation had also taken place.[60]

Opium, however, in 1870s was described as the 'by far the most valuable crop grown in Saran district'.[61]

An idea of the local consumption of opium could be had from the requisition sent by the Collector of Purnea who put it at 25 maunds 9 seers and $^3/_{12}$ chatak in 1829.[62] The population of Purnea town could consume only a very limited amount and the major part was used by the rural population. The government remained totally unconcerned with the fact that a sizeable section of population was getting hooked to it.

The wide-spread use of opium encouraged people to its smuggling and clandestine trade. The government's effort to regulate its trade did not always succeed. Since the profits were handsome, smuggling was frequent.

The government rewarded those informants whose information resulted in the seizure of opium in unauthorized possession.[63]

We learn from the report of the Collector of Saran that he was keeping in gaol 12 prisoners forwarded to him by the Deputy Opium Agent, accused of smuggling 'small parcels of opium'. They were Bacchow Chye, Nundoo Gooerrej, Soomerun Mullah and Sembhoo Gooerrej.[64]

In 1823 opium was seized at the 'Hureehur Chutler' fair on an information given by 'Chedu Singh informer'. The opium ('11 ch. of good quality and six ch. of marketable quality') was confiscated and the accused was sent to gaol for three months in the 'Dewanny gaol' and was fined Rs. 8 annas (half a rupee). In case he failed to pay the fine, his prison term was to be extended by three months.[65]

The opium smuggling prevalent in the 1820s continued. In the 1880s, the Deputy Commissioners of Hazaribagh and Lohardagga districts reported that if the far flung areas where opium was cultivated, the cultivators kept a part of the produce for personal use and also for clandestine sale. This contraband opium was probably more than what was kept in the district of Bihar. The Opium Agent, however, disagreed with the view that such activities could be curbed by searches by excise officials or 'paid spies'. Instead he suggested 'better supervision on the part of opium subordinates'.[66] For this reason he agreed to consider 'the advisability of dispatching an assistant to reside at Daudnagar, where there is a small bungalow in order to supervise more closely the working of the Department of Palamow'.[67]

Despite harassment and oppression by the zamindars, contractors and the government employees, opium cultivation continued to expand. In Saran district in 1873-4, it constituted 2.4 per cent of the gross cropped area. In 1893-1901 the gross cropped area under opium slightly lessened and come down to 2.3 per cent but it remained a strong competitor of the indigo crop. In 1873-4 the gross cropped area under indigo was only 2.2 per cent which rose slightly to 2.6 per cent in 1893-1901. By the 1870s the area under indigo cultivation was 50,000 acres.[68]

It is significant, that in Champaran after the raiyats started actively opposing the European indigo planter in 1867, they started increasing the area of land under poppy cultivation. It was one of their ways to show their displeasure and also to compensate for the loss of cash income which they suffered after withdrawing from indigo cultivation.

NOTES

1. Surendra Gopal, 'Coins and Trade: A Study of Bihar Economy in the Seventeenth Century', in A.K. Jha (ed.), *Coinage, Trade and Economy*, Nasik, 1991, pp. 210-13.
2. J. Kumar, *Indo-Chinese Trade*, New Delhi, 1974, pp. 44-5. An idea of the increased supply of Bihar and Benares opium to China can be had from the following figures:
1802-3: 3,292 chests supplied to China.

1805-6: 1,538 chests supplied to China
1810-11: 4,968 chests supplied to China.
It was sold at nearlv Rs. 2,000 per chest. Ibid., p. 48.

3. W.R. Ferminger (ed.), *The Fifth Report from the House of Commons on the Affairs of the East India Company*, Calcutta, 1917, p. 39. No doubt, the Dutch traveller Stavorius had reported in the eighteenth century, 'Bihar opium was conveyed by inland route from India to every part of Asia'. Stavorius 1, p. 296.

4. K.K. Datta (ed.), *Selection from the Judicial Records of the Bhagalpur District Office (1792-1805)*, Patna, 1968, p. 42. 'Saoroop Chund a Native Banker and Merchant' is described as an opium contractor. He belonged to Purnea. Ibid., p. 42; James Hay was a European contractor in Bhagalpur. Ibid., pp. 43, 66, 118.

5. Firminger, ed., op. cit., p. 40.

6. P.C. Roy Chaudhury, *Muzaffarpur Old Records*, Patna, p. 126.

7. Ibid., p. 192.

8. From Colltr. of Shahabad, vol. 120, 1820.

9. *Journal of Francis Buchanan Kept During the Survey of the District of Shahabad in 1812-1813*, Patna, n.d., pp. 170-1.

10. From Colltr. of Shahabad, 1823, vol. 135.

11. Ibid.

12. Ibid.

13. Francis Buchanan, *An Account of the Districts of Bihar and Patna in 1811-12*, Patna, vol. II, p. 522.

14. Ibid.

15. From Colltr. of Shahabad, 1823, vol. 135.

16. Ibid.

17. Ibid.

18. Quoted in William Pinch, 'Poppy and the Peasants: A Look at the Structure of Agrarian Society in Twentieth Century Bihar', *Explorations*, no. 2, p. 31.

19. From Colltr. of Shahbad, 1827, to Secy. BOR, Central Provinces.

20. 1824-5: 5,960 chests of opium (Bengal, Bihar, Benares sold in China).
1825-6: 3,810 chests of opium (ibid.).
1826-7: 6,560 chests of opium (ibid.).
1827-8: 6,650 chests of opium (ibid.).
1828-9: 4,903 chests of opium (ibid.).
1829-30: 7,443 chests of opium (ibid.).
1830-1: 5,672 chests of opium (ibid.).
1831-2: 6,815 chests of opium (ibid.).
1832-3: 7,598 chests of opium (ibid.).
1833-4: 7,808 chests of opium (ibid.).

21. Ibid., p. 11.
22. From Colltr. of Shahabad, 1827, to Secy. BOR, Central Provinces.
23. Kumar, op. cit., p. 165.
24. From Colltr. of Saran, to Members of the BOR in Bihar and Benares vol. 77, 1818.
25. Ibid.
26. From Colltr. of Shahabad, 1842, to Sub-Deputy Opium Agent. vol. 155, L. no. 107. In view of this the Collector entrusted with the task of promoting the cultivation of American cotton sought to select 'two of the most intelligent cultivators in each Ph. from amongst the opium ryots to whom I will distribute the seeds in equal proportions, reserving a little for myself which I will cultivate in my own compound'. Ibid., L. no. 22.
27. To Colltr. of Shahabad from Sub-Agent Opium; from Colltr. of Shahabad, 1842, L. no. 36.
28. *Notes on the District of Patna*, n.d., probably published in 1850s, pp. 1-6.
29. A. Wyatt, *Statistics of the Districts of Saran and Sircar Saran*, n.d., but probably published in 1850s, pp. 1-12.
30. A. Wyatt. *Statistics of Sircar Champa: In the District of Saran*, n.d., but probably published in 1850s, pp. 1-10.
31. Ibid., p. 3.
32. Captain W.S. Sherwill, *General Remarks on the District of Monghyr*, 1853, pp. 3-17
33. Ibid., p. 18
34. Ibid.
35. Wyatt, *Tirhoot . . .*, pp. 58-9.
36. From Colltr. of Tirhoot, 1825, vol. 595.
37. From Colltr. of Saran, 1830, vol. 91, no. 6,
38. Ibid.
39. From Colltr. of Saran, 1830, vol. 91.
40. Ibid.
41. Ibid.
42. Ibid.
43. Bhagalpur Collectorate Khas Mahal, 1836, vol. 291. To Actg. Colltr. of Zillah Bhagalpur.
44. Bhagalpur Collectorate. Miscellaneous, 1842, vol. 396 to Actg. Deputy Opium Agent, Bhagalpur.
45. Bhagalpur Collectorate. Miscellaneous, vol. 396, 1842 to Actg. Deputy Opium Agent Bhagalpur from Sub-Deputy Opium Agent.
46. J.S. Jha, *Records of the Judge and Magistrate of Patna for the Years 1820-25*, Patna, 1966, p. 11, serial no. 109.

47. Bhagalpur Collectorate, vol. 271, 1825-8.
48. From Collectorate of Saran to Members of the Board of Commerce in Bihar and Benares, vol. 77, 1818.
49. Saran Collectorate, 18 June 1846 to 6 September 1855, vol. 30, L. no. 96 to Commr Rev. Pat Dn. from Offtg. Secy. Board of Custom, Salt and Opium, 27 May 1847.
50. Bhagalpur Collectorate, vol. 279, Letters sent, 1818.
51. Ibid.
52. Sherwall, *Monghyr. . .* , p. 18.
53. W.W. Hunter, *A Statistical Account of Bengal*, London, vol. XV, Monghyr, 1871, p. 98.
54. Ibid., p. 97.
55. *Basta*, Bhagalpur, 1860-70, L. no. 5. From Deputy Collector of Jumuice Sub Dn to the Colltr. of Monghyr, 6 April 1867.
56. Bhagalpur Collectorate, 1825-33. To the Colltr. of Bhagalpur
57. Ibid., 1829-33, to Commr. of Rev. for the Dn. of Monghyr.
58. Ibid.
59. Saran Collectorate, 18 June 1846 to 6 September 1855, vol. 30. L. no. 96 to Commr. R. Pal. Dn. from Offg. Secy. Board of Custom, Salt and Opium, 27 May 1847
60. Idem., vol. XI, Saran, p. 306.
61. Ibid., p. 287.
62. Bhagalpur Collectorate, Records, Letters Recd. from Colltr. of Purnea 1829-30, vol. 173, p. 4.
63. *Muzaffarpur Old*, p. 327.
64. From Colltr. of Saran, 1822, vol. 80. To BR. Central Provinces, Patna.
65. Ibid., 1823, vol. 83.
66. Basta Bhagalpur Commr 1890-1, no. 403B. 30 May 1890 from K.G Gupta Esq. Secy. L. P. to Secy GOB Rev. Department.
67. Ibid.
68. A. Yang, *Limited Raj: Agrarian Relations in Colonial India Saran District, 1793-1920*, Delhi, 1989, pp. 37-8.

CHAPTER 6

Revenue Roll Registers: An Aid for Quantitative Study of Agrarian History of Bihar in the Nineteenth Century

Some recent studies on the nineteenth century history of rural Bihar have concentrated on movement of land prices, sale of land holdings and the role of zamindaris. They have been based on archival materials drawn from India and Great Britain.[1] However, the Board of Revenue Library, Government of Bihar, Patna appears to have been ignored. The library contains primary sources which have authentic quantitative data and which can deepen and broaden our understanding of the forces at work in the rural society of the state. At one session of the Commission I drew attention to mouzah-war records. In this paper I would refer to Revenue Roll Registers, compiled in the 1890s and preserved in the Board of Revenue Library.

The Revenue Roll registers are devoted to each district. The undermentioned remarks are based upon a perusal of vol. XI relating to Gaya district. The data have been collected under the following columns, i.e. (a) Name of the pargana, (b) Name of the estate (c) Revenue divided into installments and finally (d) Remarks.

The first useful information to be derived is regarding the number of Zamindaris. If all the estates are added up, we can get a near accurate total of Zamindaris existing in the district. A study of Revenue rolls of each district would indicate the number of Zamindaris in the respective districts. If all of them are added up, we know[1] the number of the Zamindaris in the province. Of course, the real total can never be determined since the process of fragmentation as well as amalgamation of

the Zamindaris never ceased. From the vantage point of later
day experience, it may not be wrong to assert that in areas,
where there were large number of Zamindaris, the sufferings
of the actual tillers of the soil were greater and along with them
the state of agricultural labourers was appalling. Consequently,
when political consciousness grew in course of the progress
of freedom movement, such areas became centres of peasant
agitation and movement. This would explain, why the peasant
movement in the state which first started in the district of
Champaran under the leadership of Mahatma Gandhi did not
prosper there, while it became more intense in Gaya district,
which had many times more Zamindars than Champaran.[2]

If we add up the amount of revenue which was to be collected
we would know the exact amount of land revenue, levied in a
district. A simple arithmetical exercise would enable us to find
out the total land revenue that was to be collected. For the first
time, we can have an exact idea of the total amount of land
revenue of the province and also its break up down to district
level and even below.

The data can be used in various ways. For example, if we
relate it to the total area under cultivation, we can find the
incidence of taxation per unit area in each district. Similarly,
if put it against the value of agricultural produce, we could
learn which districts were over assessed or under assessed. In
fact, the data would enable us make a comparative study of the
burden of the land revenue in different districts. Maybe this
would permit us in conjunction with other factors to make
generalizations about the regional economic imbalances that
subsequently developed in the province. Of course, the data
regarding land under cultivation and the value of crops, have
to be culled from sources such as mouzah-war records, Census
reports or District Gazetteers, etc.

From the information contained in the Revenue Rolls, we
can also infer the size of the village. Thus the register devotes
thirteen pages, i.e. from pp. 58 to 70 to describe the amount
of revenue due from Gopalpur.[3] Obviously, the fragmentation
here was much greater. But at the same time the total amount

due was meagre. This would suggest that area concerned was poorly cultivated probably because of soil-conditions and lack of irrigational facility. Of course, for the confirmation of the latter two hypotheses we have to turn to other sources. In addition to this information, we can have revenue as an index for categorizing the villages. The new category would reflect their relative economic prosperity or backwardness. Thus within the district itself we can identify pockets of poverty. It may serve us as a starting point of investigation for the stress and strain to which the district might have been subjected thereafter. Another interesting piece of information to be gleaned from the Revenue Rolls concerns the timing of the payment of the revenue. The months when the land revenue is expected to be paid, are all given according to the Hindu calendar, i.e. Chait, Baisakh, Sawan, Bhadon, Asadh, etc. The Government was undoubtedly aware of the fact that the masses better understood the indigenous calendar than the Gregorian and hence preferred to follow the local one for the purpose in place of the official one. Furthermore, the period of payment probably followed the cropping pattern of the area and the selected months showed the time when the peasant's capacity to pay the revenue was the best.

From a perusal of the Rolls, we also find that the payment was generally made in installments. Usually the installments were quarterly but in certain cases they were also biannual. In rare instances they were monthly as well. Maybe, the break-up was necessitated by the inability of the people to pay in one lump sum. Hence, it would not be far-fetched to surmise that the government took into account the varying local conditions, such as the crops produced, their value, and the harvesting cycle and finally the capacity of the people to pay before fixing up the time for the realization of the land revenue. Another bit of information also deserves notice.

In a number of cases, the Rolls show that the amount of revenue due is crossed in red ink and a new amount has been substituted. The sum is less than the original. For example, in Barabar Khurd Paperahi of pargana Goh the revenue amount

was decreased from Rs. 300 to 202 in 1892.[4] In another village
the amount was reduced from Rs. 196 *annas* 11 only to Rs. 71.[5]
The steepest decrease is in case of Jaitipur Baranwan where
the revenue demand was brought down from Rs. 1,116 to 55.[6]
The remarks column mentions the reason also. The reduction
was done in pursuance of a letter of the Commissioner dated
17 October 1882. The remark is written in Devanagari script but
no summary of the letter of the Commissioner is given. These
reductions in revenue demand probably followed appeals put
in after the assessment was felt to be oppressive or beyond the
capacity of the peasant to pay. Was it in some way connected
with slump in agricultural prices? In certain cases, the British
government thought it wise to climb down in order to contain
the accumulating discontent. It is not to suggest that the British
government was always responsive to the demands of the
people and revised its policies 'to serve or protect the interest
of the peasants. The exploitative character of the British rule
remained unabated. The point would be worth investigating
why the British made these concessions.

NOTES

1. The author expresses his gratitude to Shri Hetukar Jha of the
   Sociology Department for the help in the preparation of this paper.
2. Binay Bhushan Chaudhuri, 'The Land Marked in Eastern India,
   1793-1940', *IESHR*, vol. XII, nos. 1 and 2; ibid. 'The Process of
   Depeasantisation in Bengal and Bihar, 1885-1947', *IHR*, vol. II, no. 1.
3. Swami Sahajanand Saraswati, *Kisan Sabha ka Sansmaran*, Allahabad
   n.d.; idem, *Mera Jiwan Sangharsha*, Bihta, 1952. *Revenue Roll*, vol. XI
   (Gaya District), 1892, pp. 58-70.
4. Ibid., p. 37.
5. Ibid., p. 34.
6. Ibid., p. 87.

CHAPTER 7

Beginnings of Peasant Protest against European Indigo Planters in Bihar

G. Francois Grand, the first Collector of the district of Tirhoot (Tirhut) was also the first European to take up indigo plantation in north Bihar in 1785.[1] Subsequently, European interests in indigo developed; by the 1850s, European indigo planters could be found not only in all the districts north of the Ganges but also in several districts of south Bihar.[2]

According to *Geographical and Statistical Report of the District of Tirhut* published in 1854 there were sixty-four indigo factories.[3] Some of these were combined with sugar factories as well and all of them were located in rural areas.[4]

It seems that this expansion has been achieved without any major confrontation between the local peasantry or the zamindar and the European planters. Of course, there were occasional conflicts. In 1840s, one such encounter took place near Sucree (Sakri) village when the local zamindar after having promised renewal of lease to an indigo factory reneged and signed an agreement with the local banker. The indigo factory sent one thousand men to prevent the banker from taking possession of the fields. The banker was also fully prepared for the occasion. An affray took place; nine persons were injured.[5] An European indigo planter reminiscing about the incident noted, 'This was my first experience of a fauzdery and, though I had to act in similar ways on one or two occasions. I am glad to say that rows of this kind are now seldom heard of Planters and zamindars fight their battles in civil courts.'[6]

This was in contrast to the situation in Bengal where the European indigo planters and the peasantry in the late 1850s were locked in a bitter tussle. Though Bihar produced around 30 per cent of exportable indigo from India,[7] the relations between the planters and peasants were harmonious. The officiating Collector of Tirhoot wrote, '. . . prior to the cold season of 1866-7, disturbances in connection with indigo cultivation were unknown in Tirhoot. The planter and the ryot were on good term.'[8] But by mid-1860s, the situation in Bihar had dramatically changed; conflicts between the European indigo planters and local cultivators broke out. For the next half a century, these turmoils became a major source of tension in rural Bihar. Only after Mahatma Gandhi's intervention in Champaran in 1917 on behalf of the Indian peasantry these disturbances ceased.

II

The conflict between the Pandoul Indigo Factory and the peasantry started in the winter of 1866-7. Pandoul is presently a small town in Madhubani district of north Bihar; it was then a part of the zamindari of Darbhanga Raj, the biggest in Bihar and one of the biggest in the whole of India. The 'Pundowl' indigo factory also had a sister concern, 'Pundowl Steam Engine Sugar Factory'.[9] The manager of the Pandoul Indigo Factory was Mr. John Gale.[10]

The problems were sorted out within a few months, but its reverberations were heard for long; officials referred to the incident and commented upon it. The Officiating Collector of Tirhoot analysed the situation when the dust had settled down and passions somewhat cooled. In his letter to the Commissioner of Revenue, Patna, dated 9 April 1868 he traced the genesis of the conflict.

According to him, the disputes commenced toward the close of 1866 when the ryots refused to sow indigo as desired by the Manager of the Pandoul Factory, who construed it as a breach of contract on the part of ryots. In many instances he found that the lands that had been prepared for indigo were sown with Cheena and other crops.[11]

The disputes had arisen in villages leased to the Pandoul concern from the Darbhanga estate. The Officiating Magistrate explained this unwillingness and defiance to a pernicious system of sublease to factory *amlahs* (servants) which had been allowed to grow up in the concern, 'under which whilst the planter demanded his full share of indigo from the ryot, he sublet his villages to his factory servants who on their side endeavoured to exact the highest rent they could obtain.'[12] 'He went on to add that such leases described as 'Khushkma' 'were in direct contradiction of the terms of the planter's own lease from the Court of Wards.' He concluded,

To me it is a matter of surprise not that contracts were repudiated and disturbances took place but that under such a system they had not taken place long before. It is right, I should mention, that from all enquiries I have made, I believe this system to have been confined to Pandowl and to have been attempted in no other concern.[13]

The Collector's analysis was partially true but did not explain why the disputes broke out at this particular juncture.

III

The Pandaul concern, as stated earlier, situated in the village of Pandoul fell under the Darbhanga estate, the biggest in Bihar.[14] After the death of Maheshwar Singh, the zamindar of Darbhanga in 1860, his successor was his two-year old son Lakshmishwar Singh. Under Maheshwar Singh, there had been gross mismanagement and the zamindari was burdened with a huge debt. The government thereafter stepped in and took the zamindari under the Court of Wards and appointed Mr. Forlong an Englishman and a former indigo planter as the manager.[15]

The new Manager tried to introduce some semblance of order into collection of land revenue. For the purpose he decided that the *thicadari* system was best suited for its collection. Individuals were empowered to collect land revenue after they had agreed to pay a lump sum to the coffers of the estate. It was in pursuit of this objective that the European—managed indigo concerns were granted leases to the villages by the Darbhanga estate. The lessee thought that they had virtually inherited the rights of a zamindar.

The Manager of the Pandoul concern, Mr. John Gale, an Englishman, in violation of the terms of the lease, appointed as sub-lessees Indian employees of the concern. Gale hoped that new manager of the estate, an Englishman as well as a former indigo planter would overlook this violation. The Indian sublessees, too, felt confident about the support of the two Englishmen and went about behaving in an arbitrary manner unconcerned either with the interest or the sentiments of the peasantry. But in Mr. Borbour, the Subdivisional Magistrate, Gale found an officer, who felt genuinely concerned about the right of the Indian peasantry. He refused to lend his weight, even indirectly to Mr. Gale. His view was that Mr. Gale could not coerce the peasantry to sow indigo. Mr. Gale was dissatisfied with the stand taken by Mr. Borbour. This emboldened the peasantry to defy the dictates of the European indigo planter and his employees. The rigid stand taken by the two sides appeared to be irreconcilable. The situation was ripe for the outbreak of violence. The Commissioner, Patna Division Mr. Mangles intervened.

Mr. A.C. Mangles, in his report mentioned this view of Mr. Borbour, the Subdivisional Magistrate. He noted,

Mr. Borbour . . . gives it in his opinion that the present trouble has been in a great measure caused by the practice which exists in the Pondoul concern of sub letting the villages taken in lease by it to the Factory servants and Omlahs; by which means he says that the sublessee stands between the Ryot and the Factory and intercepts what the latter allow the former. He adds also that the Ryots had been complaining of this practice for some years back . . . the Sublessee who had the proper deductions allowed him in his rent from the Factory, not allowed them to the Ryots.

Mr. Borbour's perception was shared by other European indigo planters in the area. This was conveyed to the Government of Bengal by the Patna Commissioner. He noted[16] '. . . the general opinion among planters to be that the present dispute had arisen from special cause of complaint owing to the system of subletting to rapacious Factory Servants. . . .[17]

One cannot possibly disagree with the cause of grave dissatisfaction among the Indian peasantry as described by the Subdivisional Magistrate and the neighbouring European indigo planters. But they do not answer the question as to why at this juncture the discontent turned into defiance.

IV

While the peasant had a cause to be extremely unhappy as a result of the system of subletting and arbitrary behaviour by the planters and his employees, he was compelled to seek a solution because of the continuing drought during the preceeding two years which had depleted his stock of cereals and wiped out his purchasing power. A severe drought in 1865 had created famine conditions in the Nepal Tarai, the districts of Champaran, Tirhut and Bhagalpur. Things then did not go out of hand as conditions were not so bad in the Saran district and also in districts south of the river Ganga, viz., Patna, Munger, Shahabad and Gaya.[18] Prompt relief measures in 1865 minimized distress which became acute from April 1866 when price began to soar as crops failed again. Further relief measures had to be adopted. Timely rains revived cultivation and by December when the rice crop was harvested, life became normal.[19] Experience of two consecutive seasons when crops had failed convinced the peasant that only availability of food grains could bail him out of a situation of scarcity like that of 1865 and 1866. But has concern was not shared either by the government or the indigo planters. On the top of it the Government took no steps to prevent export of food grains when people were facing starvation. The peasant's sense of alienation was heightened.

Mr. Borbour had pointed towards this factor when he wrote that 'owing to large exports of grain from the subdivision, the distress and scarcity may exist towards the close of the year in which case . . . it would no doubt embitter the indigo dispute.'[20]

The experience had taught the peasants a bitter lesson. They felt that the cultivation of cereals would at least stave off starvation and death. Besides, when there was a shortage of food grains, cereals would fetch better and higher prices than indigo and therefore, the cultivation of the dye did not make any economic sense; in the circumstances it was suicidal.

Mr. Maclean in his official letter of the Commissioner accep-

ted this assessment of the situation by the peasantry. He stated
'Prices are very high and lands occupied by indigo would [fetch
more] in other crops.' 'The ryots are in consequence dissatisfied
and have combined to make a stand against the factories.'[21] Mr.
Maclean's opinion on the economics of indigo cultivation by the
peasantry was accepted by his superior who also noted, '. . . I
question whether the ryots will assume cultivation unless some
concessions are made to them.'[22] The opinion of another official
confirmed Maclean's view. He pointed out that the indigo
cultivators were paid 'Rs. 7 and 8 annas per beegha, which does
not remunarate the ryot.'[23] He was also convinced that soon an
increase in the amount to be paid to the indigo cultivators was
inevitable.[24]

The peasant found indigo cultivation economically inadvis-
able; he also found it repugnant on other scores as well. They
were coerced to grow it on their best 'Bheet' land, which they
loathed. They strongly resented the conduct of the sublessees,
the factory employees, who arbitrarily enhanced the rents to
be paid by them. As if this was not enough, the peasantry was
harassed and humiliated in many other ways.

An example of the harassment of cultivators by the indigo
planter and his employees was given by Mr. Mangles on the
basis of Police reports. The adjoining

Doulatpur Factory had instituted a charge of loot of indigo seed against
some of the inhabitants of Renerah village. The villagers instituted a
counter charge against the Factory to the effect that some of the Factory
servants had themselves thrown the seed into the tank in the village for
the purpose of getting up a false complaint against them. On investigation
the police have sent B form with regard to the Loot, on the ground that
the factory servants themselves had thrown the seed into the tank.[25]

The false police cases caused a lot of inconvenience, unnecessary expense and undeserved humiliation to the peasants.

The Factory commandeered the bullocks of peasants for
ploughing their own field; its employees carried away their
ploughs and requisitioned their carts to transport the produce
of the Factory during the 'manufacturing season.'[26] Their fruit
trees and bamboos were seized.[27] For all these services rendered

by the peasant, he was paid virtually next to nothing. In fact, the European indigo planter and his subordinates had perfected a system in which the peasant had been reduced to an object of exploitation and rapacity.

The peasantry could not narrate their tale of woe to anyone or seek redress. Formerly, the zamindar would listen from a sense of community solidarity. Now their zamindar was a minor, a child; the zamindari was administered by an Englishman, an ex-indigo planter. The governmental machinery was geared to the maintenance of law and order. It was unconcerned with their economic problems and would stir only when peace was threatened and violence errupted. This can be seen subsequently; when clash between the peasantry and the employees of the factory became imminent, the government took notice and intervened.

The peasant's sense of grievance was heightened by the cultural tradition in which he was born and brought up. The area, situated in the heart of Mithila, was from ancient days a seat of learning. Both the Brahmins and the Kayasthas, the two literate communities were also the principal landowners. They had been fairly mobile, especially the former, whose members had been invited to the courts of other indigenous rulers and feted and honoured for their scholarship.[28] They had been given land grants either revenue free or at concessional rate by the chief of the Raj as a recognition of their scholarship. Now they had to submit to the atrocities of the indigo planter and his staff. The Maharaja of Darbhanga, a Srotriya Brahman, who had bestowed these gifts of land, had levied rents at reduced rates. He also shielded them on account of caste affiliation from other vexatious imposts. At the moment the Maharaja was powerless to do anything in their favour. The fusion of indignation and grievances directed against the European indigo planter produced a rare unity among the peasantry belonging to all castes and communities.

Though at the moment direct evidence suggesting Brahmin and Kayastha leadership in this confrontation is lacking but a subsequest incident is revealing. In 1867-8, when a similar situation developed in Champaran, one of the reasons ascribed for it by the Europeans was the influx of discontented elements from Tirhoot and their exhortation to the local peasantry to keep up the fight against their exploitation.[29]

It is known that Maithils have been coming to the Bettiah Raj at least since the eighteenth century; the local zamindar lavishly gifted land to them. Pandit Ghanashyam Jha was made the Raj Purohit.[30] Hence, it is just possible that the relations of Maithils settled in the Bettiah Raj may have been coming and encouraging and inciting the local peasantry to fight against the oppressors.

The sense of injustice on the part of the upper caste Maithil landholders and a strong feeling of economic hurt among all sections of the peasantry forced them to decide that the cultivation of cereals in spite of objections by the Factory was the surest method for escaping starvation. This led to the emergence of the first organized peasant protest movement against European indigo planters in Bihar in the nineteenth century.

The outbreak of the movement was reported in a letter of 25 January 1867. It describes it as 'serious disputes with ryots which have arisen in the Pandoul indigo concern in Tirhoot and which threaten to expand to other factories.'[31] It went on to add that on 15 January 1867, Mr. Borbour, officer-in-charge of the Madhubani subdivision informed the Officiating Magistrate Mr. Maclean that the ryots of number of villages in lease to the Pandoul concern who had been in the habit of cultivating indigo for the concern under the conditions current in Tirhoot and who had this year up to that engaged in preparing the indigo lands had now united in refusing either to finish the preparation of the lands or to allow the Factory to do so. . . .'[32] Borbour wanted instructions whether 'he should allow the Factory to prepare the lands [against] the wishes of the ryots'.[33] Mr. Maclean told him that if the ryots refused to honour their contractual obligations, the Factory should seek a remedy in the court of law.[34] He could not support the Factory in its attempt to cultivate the land of ryot.[35] He was asked to preserve peace and punish trespass.[36] Borbour was asked to advise the Factory manager from desisting from any attempt 'that might provoke resistance.[37] In short, the concern of the government was to prevent armed clashes between the contending parties.'

Mr. Borbour acting on the instruction received, 'issued a notice to Mr. Gale, the Manager of the Pandoul concern' and directed him to abstain from ploughing the 'assamewar lands' of a certain village that has encouraged the ryots to plough the lands for themselves.'[38] Mr. Borbour was apprehensive that if Mr. Gale persisted in his conduct, the peasantry, connected with indigo might become equally defiant.

Mr. Gale objected to this by saying that 'Mr. Borbour's order was passed *ex parte* and that the lands of which he had been deprived by it were in fact "Zeerat lands" belonging to the Factory but made over to the ryots to cultivate indigo and other crops for the Factory.'[39] But Mr. Gale's contention was rejected.

Mr. Borbour's rejection of Mr. Gale's plan was construed by die peasants as support extended to their cause by the government. The peasantry felt that they had on their side right as well as government's might; Mr. Borbour's order encouraged them to persist with their defiance of the Pandoul concern and its employees.

Mr. Gale realized that he had bitten more than he could chew and beat a hasty retreat. In March 1867 it was reported, 'Mr. Gale is getting rid of the obnoxious subleases as fast as he can, and is making many important concessions to his ryots and that they are gradually withdrawing their opposition to the Factory.'[40] One section of the government was also convinced that things would be fine throughout the district if the European indigo planters 'put their houses in order' and '. . . there will be a very improved state of feeling on the part of the ryots regarding Indigo.'[41]

V

Though the peasant resistance continued only for a few months, the nature of their defiance caused deep concern among the

European indigo planters as well as the bureaucracy. The European indigo planters feared that if they went on making concessions their profits would plummet. They wished that the experience of Pandoul should not be repeated.

The bureaucracy was conscious of the feelings of the European indigo planters. It wanted the European indigo planters to flourish despite occassional bureaucratic dislike of their lifestyles[42] and their overbearing behaviour. But more than that it did not want disputes and dissent to lead to violent clashes. The memories of 1857 were still fresh in their minds. Hence, the bureaucracy devised a plan of crisis management aiming to localize the dispute, prevent it from becoming an inspiration for other indigo peasants of the area and finally, to reassure the European indigo planters that their interests would be safeguarded.

Mr. Borbour was advised to exercise restraint in passing orders in favour of the peasantry. At the same time it was recommended that Mr. Borbour should be given full magisterial powers so that he could 'settle these disputes'.[43] Mr. Borbour took the hint and promised a spot inquiry before sending a detailed report.[44]

The official position was that even though the ryots were justified in refusing the cultivation of indigo since it was not profitable to them but this is a matter with which Government officers cannot interfere. They can only keep the peace and settle questions of disputes possession and punish trespass and mischief.[45]

The same letter also showed where the government sympathy lay. Although it affirmed that 'peace has been preserved' yet it did not approve Mr. Borbour's action in stopping the Indigo Factory from coercing the ryots to cultivate indigo. In fact, he was asked to desist from it.[46] 'I do not consider that Borbour's explanation of his order under Sec. 2 is satisfactory' but 'the harm which it was calculated to do has since been arrested.'[47] It further asserted 'Mr. Borbour willfully though by mistake misled Mr. Maclean as to the real nature of the dispute between the Factory and the Ryots. . . .' It however, added that 'in the event the facts represented by Mr. Borbour were correct, then Mr. Maclean's order were 'quite proper.'[48] At the same time Mr. Maclean's conduct was also censured for not joining Mr. Borbour's camp in spite of clear instructions and rejected his excuses justifying his absence.

The incident continued to haunt both the planters and the government as it was for the first time that the peasantry had successfully defied the planters and had forced the government to concede the justice of the cause.

A letter dated 22 February 1867 conveyed the substance of an interview which took place between the Commissioner and Mr. Gale, who was accompanied by Mr. Becher, the Manager of the adjoining Jayanagar Factory at Muzaffarpur. Earlier he had also met the General Manager of the Darbhanga estate. Both the Indigo planters assured that the dispute would 'settle down' as Mr. Hinky whom the ryots treated as zamindar and to whom they had been talking had 'disabused them [the ryots] of the idea that the Government was opposed to indigo planting.'[49] The indigo planters also promised 'to enquire into and redress the ryots' complaints.'[50]

The indigo planters, however, at that point refused to increase the emoluments of the indigo cultivators 'in the face of a strike' but agreed to consider 'if its necessity was established.'[51] On behalf of the government it was simply stated that 'Indigo cultivation should be carried on terms which were satisfactory both to the planter and the ryot.'[52] The opinion of the government was conveyed to them that enhancement of the rates paid to the peasantry was necessary but 'whether this should be given now or at a future time was a matter of which they [the planters] ought to be the best judge.'[53] The government wanted that the dispute should be localized.[54] As can be seen, the government had no intention to formulate a pro-ryot policy though they could not close their eyes to the iniquitous conduct of the planters. At the same time they tried their best to prevent the impression going round that they were in any way anti-Planters.

As a fall out of the movement a number of criminal cases were registered by the Factory and its servants for 'criminal trespass' and counter-cases were instituted by the indigo cultivators. In some cases, the Factory's contention was upheld and the ryots appealed to the superior court. But the government directive to the officers was,

they were to leave all questions of right to land and of the legal obligation of the raiyats to cultivate indigo for the factories to the decision of the Courts, and to impress on the planters the wisdom of viewing the subject in a broad and conciliatory spirit, especially with reference to the statement that the cultivation of cereals and other crops offered longer inducements to the cultivators than indigo at the rates paid for it.[55]

The judiciary helped to absorb the immediate shock resulting from a clash of interests. A time span would elapse before a judgement would be pronounced one way or the other. Meanwhile economic necessity would force the parties to find a *modus vivendi*.[56] In Bihar in the nineteenth century, this pattern to resolve conflict between the peasantry and the planters became widely prevalent.

The official perception was on similar lines; it was reported,

Some of these (cases) have been decided in favour of the Factory, these are now pending in appeal before the judge and as the same question is involved in all the cases the deciding of those pending one way or the other would no doubt go a great way to bring the parties to an understanding especially if Mr. Borbour's orders are upheld.[57]

The judicial process was invoked to maintain the *status quo.*

NOTES

1. Askari and Ahmed (eds), *Comprehensive History of Bihari*, vol. II, pt. II, Patna, 1987, p. 414.
2. See the map no. 2: Country South of Ganges, compiled in the office of the Surveyor General of India and published at Calcutta in June 1860, lithographed by H.M. Smith.
3. A. Wyatt, Esq. (Revenue Surveyor), *Geographical and Statistical Report of the District of Tirhoot*, Thos. Jones, 'Calcutta Gazette' Office, Calcutta, 1854, pp. 58-9.
4. Ibid.
5. An Old Planter, *Reminiscences of Behar*, Thacker Spink & Co., Calcutta, 1857, pp. 55-8.

6. Ibid., p. 58.
7. C.E. Buckland, *Bengal under the Lieutenant Governors,* vol. I, Deep Publications, Delhi, 1976, pp. 243-57.
8. Letter no. 2. Confidential from Officiating Collector of Tirhoot to Commissioner, Revenue, Patna, 9 April 1968. Patna Commissioner's Record Series (PCRS), vol. 1, Basta VI.
9. Wyatt, op. cit., p. 59.
10. *Reminiscences of Bihar,* p. 13. 'Mr. G. was devoted to gardening and showed great taste in the way he laid out the grounds. It was said that his pineapples were so plentiful that he fed his pigs on them, and that every fruit and flower that India could produce might be found in his garden.'
11. Letter no. 2. Confidential. From Officiating Collector to Commissioner, Revenue, Patna, 9 April 1868. PCRS, vol. I, Basta VI.
12. Ibid.
13. Ibid.
14. Jata Shankar Jha, *Biography of an Indian Patriot Maharaja Lakshmeshwar Singh of Darbhanga,* Patna, 1972, p. 6.
15. Stephen Henningham, *A Great Estate and its Landlords in Colonial India,* Oxford University Press, Delhi, 1990, p. 31.
16. Letter no. 25, 5 March 1867, from Commissioner Patna to Secretary, Government of Bengal, PCRS, vol. I, Basta V.
17. Letter no. 60, 15 March 1867, From Commissioner Patna to Secretary, Government of Bengal, PCRS, vol. I, Basta V.
18. Buckland I, p. 393.
19. Ibid., p. 394
20. Letter no. 25, 5 March 1867, from the Commissioner Patna to Secretary Government of Bengal, PCRS, vol. I, Basta V.
21. Letter no. 40, 7 February 1867, from Commissioner, Patna to Secretary, Government of Bengal, PCRS, vol. I.
22. Ibid.
23. Letter no. 60, 15 March 1867, from Commissioner Patna to Secretary, Government of Bengal, PCRS, vol. I.
24. Ibid.
25. Letter no. 25, 5 March 1867, from Commissioner Patna to Secretary, Government of Bengal, PCRS, vol. I, Basta V.
26. Buckland I, p. 329.
27. Henningham, op. cit., p. 42.
28. J.C. Jha, *The Migration of Matthil Pandits,* Patna, 1991, p. 234.
29. S.K. Mittal, *Peasant Uprisings & Mahatma Gandhi in North Bihar,* Anu Prakashan, Meerut, 1978, p. 67.
30. Jha, op. cit., p. 244.

31. Letter no. 27, 25 January 1867, from Commissioner Patna to Secretary, Government of Bengal, PCRS, vol. I, Basta V.
32. Ibid.
33. Ibid.
34. Ibid.
35. Ibid.
36. Ibid.
37. Ibid.
38. Ibid.
39. Ibid.
40. Letter no. 25, 5 March 1867, from Commissioner Patna to Secretary, Government of Bengal, PCRS, vol. I, Basta V.
41. Ibid.
42. John Beames, *Memoirs of a Bengal Civilian*, London, 1961, pp. 172-3, 174.
43. Letter no. 27, 25 January 1867, Commissioner Patna to Secretary, Government of Bengal, PCRS, vol. I, Basta V.
44. Ibid.
45. Letter no. 48, 7 February 1867, Commissioner Patna to the Secretary to Government of Bengal, PCRS, vol. I, Basta V.
46. Buckland I, p. 328; The Governor Cecil Beadon forced the Assistant Magistrate to withdraw his proclamation.
47. Letter no. 48, Commissioner Patna to the Secretary, Government of Bengal, PCRS, vol. I, Basta V.
48. Ibid.
49. Letter no. 130, 22 February 1867, Commissioner Patna to Secretary, Government of Bengal, PCRS, vol. I, Basta V.
50. Ibid.
51. Ibid.
52. Ibid.
53. Ibid.
54. Ibid.
55. Buckland I, p. 328.
56. Ibid., p. 329. 'The necessity of increasing the rates paid for indigo was recognised by several of the Tirhut planters, and the Pandoul raiyats came to terms with the factory'.
57. Letter no. 25, 5 March 1867, Patna Commissioner to Secretary, Government of Bengal, PCRS, vol. I, Basta V.

CHAPTER 8

Small Towns in Bihar in the First Half of the Nineteenth Century
(A Study in the Character of Urban Growth)

In the first half of the nineteenth century under the impact of a new polity and the economic, political and administrative measures adopted by the English East India Company after their victories in the battles of Plassey (1757) and Buxar (1764), a new trend was visible in the process of urbanization in Bihar.

The paramount interest of the Company was to collect land revenue regularly. After a series of experiments, a major step was taken in 1786 when the Acting Governor-General McPherson created thirty-five revenue districts in the Bengal Presidency, each under a European Collector to supplement the existing districts. By 1793, Bihar comprised the districts of Tirhut, Saran, Purnea, Behar, Bhagalpur, Shahabad with headquarters at Arrah (1787),[1] Ramgarh and a portion of the Jungle-Mahals.[2]

The chief administrative seat of these districts soon developed into urban centres, since they became the focal point of revenue, civil and judicial administration of the respective areas. They became adjunct to the capital city of the erstwhile *suba* of Bihar, Patna, which for historical and commercial reasons, retained its dominant position.

With the passage of time the bureaucracy went on expanding and its powers went on increasing. The Collector in 1787 was vested with powers of Judge and Magistrate. Though Regulation II of 1798 divested the Collector of judicial powers, another European covenanted servant was empowered to exercise it. He was to preside over the Criminal Courts of Circuits stationed at the same place. Each district had a Collector as well as a Judge-Magistrate.[3] As the number of subjects to be dealt by the administration increased, more offices were created and new officers were appointed to man them. Regulation 1 of 1829 created twenty divisional commissionerships in the Bengal Presidency and out of these three were located in Bihar, viz., at Patna, Saran and Bhagalpur. The commissionership of Saran was abolished in 1834.[4]

In 1837 separate District Magistrates were appointed and the posts of the Collector and Magistrate were separated. Each district had an Englishman as a Civil and Session's Judge, a Collector and Magistrate.[5]

These officers had a number of subordinates. The Collector, the Judge and the Magistrate had Europeans as their Secretaries. Other European officers included a Deputy Collector, Surgeon, sometimes a Deputy Opium Agent, an Engineer and a sprinkling of indigo-planters.[6] Some retired European servants who preferred to spend their last days on the Indian soil, had also settled in these urban centres.

The district headquarters thus acquired a physical character and a demographic composition, distinct from traditional urban centres.[7]

The new urban centres, undoubtedly the product of colonial rule, had a ruling elite which differed from the old. The Europeans held all the top offices. With very few exceptions, none ever thought of settling down in this country. They made no pretence of acquiring urban immovable property except in the early years when the Company did not provide them with residential accommodation. Even then, as soon as they were transferred to another place, they sold it off. This arrangement was unsatisfactory and soon the Company built suitable and big houses for its top officers such as the Collector, the Judge and Magistrate, Surgeon, etc., along with offices for them. Circuit houses meant for providing accommodation to officials on tours came up in all district towns.[8] The colonial administration became one of the biggest real estate owners in these urban centres. It determined the physical shape of the town as well as the style of architecture . . . the Raj or colonial, basically functional but with European trappings.

The houses meant for European officers and offices were situated at one end of the town; they had very high ceilings to protect the occupants against the awful summer heat. As a further safeguard, the spacious rooms were surrounded on all sides by wide verandas. The compound was large with provision for stables for horses, rooms for carriages and housing for the army of domestic servants such as *ayahs*, cooks, coachmen, syces, sweepers, washermen, water-earners, guards, etc. The area had good roads lined with shady trees and was generally kept clean. In many instances a park was laid out, known as Company Bagh. A large flat ground was also provided where parades could be held; horse-races could take place or games like polo could be played.

Since the Britishers professed Christianity, a church was built sooner or later to serve their spiritual and ritual needs.[9] Often a clergyman also resided. Besides, a Christian graveyard was also provided since mortality was then fairly high.[10]

Generally, this quarter came up at a distance from the localities inhabited by locals because these European bureaucrats out of a sense of racial superiority did not want to mix up socially with the indigenous people. Further, they were keen to live in a world which, they thought, was a replica of 'their homeland thousands of kilometres away'. Hence, after sometime, a club was also established where they could meet in the afternoons and evenings, socialize, chat, play games and drink. This was the focal point of their collective social life and leisure-time activities. They celebrated Christmas and New Year, organized balls and dramatic performances, etc.

The colonial urban centre became a twin city — the new area had government offices and officer's quarters; in the other part lived the native population. While the first was open and was generally known as Civil Lines, the second remained congested with mud and brick houses standing cheek by jowl and was reputed to be the old town. While the first was basically residential, the second was the centre of trade and crafts and supplied the material needs of everyday life. The main bazaar was located in the old town. The tailor, the barber, the washerman as well as the army of domestic servants, the palanquin-bearers, the carriage-driver, etc., all lived there. Hence, it was thickly populated, dirty and with only pockets of affluence. The official quarter had a sparse population, was clean and prosperous.

The nature of the new colonial urban centre Arrah, in 1812, has been described by Buchanan in the following words,

> . . . but towards the west and on its (road) north side is an open lawn in which are placed the court houses, the accommodations for the judge of circuit and the houses of the judge and surgeon,[11] all buildings sufficiently commodious but no sort of ornament to the place. . . . This is the handsomest part of the town. At the west endure the collector's office, his and his assistant's houses and those of other Europeans not in the service; none of the buildings in any degrees ornamental.[12]

Subsequently European engineers also became a part of district administration.[13]

The European population though very small in numbers, hardly ever running into three figures, was administratively and politically dominant and had a social life of their own. The Indians whether in the service of the Company or belonging to the zamindar or mercantile or professional classes kow-towed to them.[14]

The population of the urban centre grew since people were drawn to it for several reasons. Property disputes were to be decided in the law-courts located here; government revenue matters concerning either the zamindars or the ryots were to be sorted out here; directions for dealing with law and order problems were to emanate from here; those who had been sentenced to imprisonment by the courts were to be lodged here in the gaols.

To meet the day to day material requirements of such a varied population, traders and artisans came as possibilities of earning a livelihood emerged. There was an influx of grocers, vegetable-vendors, traders in household utilities, artisanal groups such as masons, carpenters, blacksmiths, potters, braziers, goldsmiths, etc., and members of service sector such as washermen, barbers, tailors, etc. The professionals, the lawyers, the physicians, the teachers, etc., also arrived here. To serve the spiritual and ritual needs, there was an immigration of Hindu priests, Muslim Maulvis and Christian clergy. In short, the population of the new urban centre was mixed, the members professed different religious beliefs and pursued a variety of occupations.

This character of the colonial urban centre is apparent from Buchanan's description of Arrah. He estimated the number of houses to be 2,775. 'The buildings are in general mean and close huddled together, but some decent roads have been made through it, forming tolerable streets.'[15] But of course affluent Indians such as zamindars, lawyers, merchants, etc., lived well. He remarked, '. . . several of the natives seem fond of gardens, in which are a great variety of trees and a good many flower.'[16]

Of course, in order to cater to the religious needs, places of collective worship such as temples, mosques and subsequently churches were also erected. The new urban centres opened market in small plots of land, basically to be used for housing and/or trading purposes.

An example of the growth of colonial urban administrative centre was that of Chhapra, a village in the seventeenth century, where the English and the Dutch flocked to collect saltpetre. By the mid-eighteenth century, it had become a *qasba* or semi-urbanized or a big village as it had to cater to a large number of Europeans as well as indigenous traders. After the area was annexed following the defeat of Mir Kasim, the Nawab of Oudh and Mughal emperor Shah Alam II in the battle of Buxar, the British felt the need to have an administrative point from where they could follow the goings on in the territory of Gorakhpur across the border as well as to keep an eye on the turbulent chiefs of Bettiah and Hussenpur. In this case, strategic need and administrative requirements helped in the rise of a new urban centre.[17]

As these districts were extremely large, the need was felt to create subsidiary administrative centres so that the distant parts of the district could be effectively administered.

The district of Saran also included the Mughal Sarkar of Champaran and therefore, 'to look after the territory of Champaran a Magistrate was stationed at Motihari in 1837.[18] Of course, this decision was prompted by other factors as well.

Champaran bordered on Nepal and commanded the land-routes to the valley of Kathmandu. Furthermore, several indigo-planters had from 1813[19] started operating in the area and in a short-while had spread in the countryside. The Europeans also began to take interest in the setting up of steam sugar factories but when profits from indigo became substantial after 1850s, they gave it up.[20]

At Motihari, European indigo-planters of the surrounding area socialized, planned hunting expeditions,[21] relaxed and discussed matters of mutual interest. Moran, an indigo-planter built his house in Motihari. He and Henry Mill had purchased the Turkulia indigo factory from William Wood on 12 July 1816. The Hull family retained the possession of the factory till 1927-8 when it sold it to the Bettiah Raj.[22]

The British decision to have an administrative infrastructure at Motihari adjoining the Nepal border was correct since in 1840, the Nepalese forces taking advantage of British reverses in the first Afghan war took control over a strip of territory 25 miles long and 8 miles wide. Colonel Oliver was asked to lead British forces against Nepal and the Nepalese reluctantly evacuated the ninety-one villages they had occupied.[23]

The perception of defence requirements persuaded the government to declare the neighbouring town of Bettiah as the headquarters of a subdivision in 1852, which further reinforced Motihari's character as an urban centre.[24]

The European indigo-planters who had spread all over north Bihar felt the need of a common meeting place, to interact socially and to talk over their mutual problems. Muzaffarpur, the district headquarters of Tirhut was chosen for the purpose since it was centrally located and almost equidistant from north-west, north-east and south. It assumed, a pronounced European character with the erection of a race-course, formation of an exclusively European Club and a polo ground.[25]

In the Tirhut district, Darbhanga, the seat of the largest zamindari in Bihar also developed as another urban centre.

In some cases old urban centres within the district remained active even though they could have withered away after the withdrawal of administrative officers. Munger in the newly created Bhagalpur district was one such centre. A number of factors ensured their survival. Some of them were located on the convergence of various routes; some were centres of specialized crafts; some were pilgrim centres; in some cases a combination of two or more factors operated. Occasionally the presence of monuments from antiquity also helped them to survive.

The case of Munger, the capital of the Bengal *suba* for some time under Mir Kasim is important. When the English emerged victorious, they did not accord it the status of an administrative centre although Monghyr (Munger) had been the headquarters of a sarkar of the same name under the Mughals. Despite deliberate neglect Munger was saved from extinction because of its strategic location on the banks of the Ganga. Its fort commanded the river route between Bihar and Bengal. Besides, its climate was wholesome. The Europeans treated it as a health resort. Governor-General Warren Hastings on way to Benares in 1781 had left his wife there to recoup her health. Hence, in the early nineteenth century it was converted into a depot for army clothing, an invalid station for British soldiers. The English established a lunatic asylum for treating the British soldiers.[26] All the British ships going up and down the river Ganga halted here, and we have numerous descriptions of the place by European visitors, whose love for its products helped to sustain traditional crafts, such as arms, cutlery, art objects of horn, etc.

Eventually the British realized that the administrative status of Munger ought to be raised. Hence, in 1812, Mr. Ewing was appointed to assume charge of Monghyr criminal court, called 'the court of the joint magistrate of Monghyr.' He was to act as a subordinate to the Magistrate of Bhagalpur.[27] In 1832, the jurisdiction of the Munger court was further raised; 'it became the revenue receiving centre under the name of the

Deputy Collectorship.' This office was conferred upon the Joint Magistrate.[28]

The growing administrative importance of Munger sup-plemented by its location as a halting place for steam-ships and boats plying up and down the Ganga, helped it to survive as a significant urban centre and a centre for the production of a variety of artisanal goods. An official British surveyor in 1850s noted,

Monghyr, the principal town, with a probable population of 40,000 souls, is well built, substantial and flourishing place, with about, 300 brick houses and numerous markets, carrying on a brisk trade in brass-ware cutlery of an inferior kind, guns, rifles, pistols and iron-ware in general, but of a very doubtful and dangerous nature as regards the fire-arms; furniture of every description, leather work, consisting of boots, shoes and rough saddlery, gunpowder, fancy and elegant mat-work of every description, besides various kinds of birds and chameleons, brought from the Southern hills, which are sold to travellers at the ghat, who may be passing either in the steamers or in boats; printed cloths and native dhoties, which are woven in adjoining villages, many hundred families being in the occupation. . . .

During the cold and hot weather, from November to June, a large temporary bazar, giving cover to about 500 natives, is built upon the sand-bank immediately to the north of the fort; and being on the edge of the harbour, from hence is shipped the exports of the town, and imports are received, besides giving cover to numerous tribes of mat and basket-makers, grain sellers, sweet-meat shops, artificers, grass and bamboo-cutters, the whole of which disappear upon the commencement of the rains.[29]

Bhagalpur became the district headquarters in the early days of the rule of the English East India Company, it was chosen because of its location on the banks of the Ganga near Munger and for easy accessibility.

The traditional silk industry of the place remained buoyant. Miss Fane noted, '. . . Bhagalpur is famous for its manufacture of silk, of a very ugly texture but useful here and very serviceable in England, where it washes well and lasts for ever.'[30] According to one estimate Bhagalpur annually exported silk textiles worth Rs. 90,000 to Calcutta alone.[31]

Sasaram, an urban centre dating back to the sixteenth century and containing a number of Sur monuments retained its character because it lay along the 'great military road' which ran from Calcutta in the east to the banks of the Indus river in the west. Its importance increased when the stretch of the road lying between Calcutta and Kanpur was metalled in 1840s.[32] We have a description of the town from Buchanan.

Sasaram is a large country town, not much short of a mile each way and closely built. Many of the houses, partly of brick and partly of stone, have tiled roofs. Some of the streets are tolerably wide and exceedingly rudely paved with stone. Some people keep their houses and streets opposite tolerably clean, but this is of little avail as seldom more than 2 or 3 such persons live adjacent to each other and their neighbours are involved in every species of Hastiness. Most of the streets are as usual narrow crooked lanes.[33]

These urban centres lacked cleanliness and except for the central street, other roads were extremely narrow. There was no planning behind their growth.

These points are brought into sharper focus when we examine the physical lay out of another traditional urban centre Gaya, an important pilgrim centre of the Hindus.

Gaya was made the headquarters of the district of Rohtas carved out in 1784.[34] The first Collector Thomas Law tried to make the city a little more functional in view of the new role it had to play. He built a market-place. But when Buchanan visited it in 1813, he did not find it much different from the other urban centres in Bihar. He noted,

. . . This town is large and built mostly of brick and stone, but the stones are not squared except such as have been taken from ruins, and the whole building whether brick or stone is often covered with plaster. . . as many of the houses are large they look tolerably well at a distance, but a near approach fills with disgust. . . . The streets are narrow (6 to 10 feet) dirty and crooked. The galleries which serve for shops are mostly very slovenly, and even of those which are neat and gaily painted some corner or other is usually defiled by smoke or dust, and cobwebs. The very best houses are rendered slovenly by cakes of cow dung for fuel patched of their walls, and the jealousy of men prevents any reasonable number or size for the apertures intended to intermit air or light, while the small ones that are tolerated are secured by rude wooden shutters without paints or polish.

In walking through the town, precautions are necessary as formerly in Edinburgh. The passenger must call out to prevent inundation from above.[35]

The pilgrim centre, by acquiring an administrative status was transformed simultaneously into a colonial urban centre. The zamindars of the district began to acquire land and build their houses.

Bihar or Behar, another traditional urban centre survived for two principal reasons. The government had not totally withdrawn its patronage. A government appointed *amil* with subordinate officers resided there. The town still had a flourishing paper-making industry. The area where paper-makers lived was described as, the neatest that I have seen. 'The houses though small are built of brick or mud, plastered, and are covered with sheets of paper stuck on to dry. This gives them a clean look.'[36]

The place had an important sufi *khanqah*, that of the fourteenth century Firdausiya saint Sharafuddin Yahya Maneri.[37] Devotees from outside regularly visited the shrine. The place was also located on the route to Rajgir and Pawapuri, sacred to Hindus, Buddhists and Jains. From Behar also radiated routes to Patna in the north, Nawada and Gaya in the south; hence, Bihar also acted as a distributing and collecting centre for merchandise both imported and exported.

Indigo-planters contributed to the continuation of one urban centre, Purnea. An official estimate in 1832 shows that indigo was cultivated on an area of 1,31,487 *bighas*, the biggest area in any district in Bihar. Eight European indigo-planters managed sixty-five factories.[38] To meet their credit needs, seven banking houses including that of Jagat Seth functioned.[39] Another class of dealers in money lived in the town, known as *poddars* who generally exchanged silver and cowries and advanced loans to wage-earners.[40]

These newly established colonial urban centres, however, could not meet the economic needs of their entire hinterland. Economic efficiency required that big villages should grow up all around so that producers and traders did not have to cover long distances for transacting business. That such villages had emerged as adjunct to urban centres, is apparent from Buchanan's account. While describing Sheikhpura, he wrote,

Sheikhpura is a very large village or a small town extending more than one mile from east to west. It was with great difficulty that I could squeeze an elephant through the street. . . Sheikhpura contains, some tolerable houses of brick cemented with mud. One entirely of mud, belonging to a Bangalee merchant, is a very comfortable place, being kept smooth and clean and in some places painted. . . .[41]

A unique urban centre which came into being as a result of British rule was the cantonment town. From the very beginning the British tried to develop Danapur about 18 km west of Patna as one such town. Geographically, it was so located that troops could easily be transported on the river Ganga eastwards or westwards. By crossing the Ganga they could reach many points in north Bihar. Hence Danapur was developed as a military station. To supply provisions and other necessities for the large body of troops, bazars[42] and colonies of artisans and service-personnels such as washermen, barbers, etc., sprang up. Since the officer class was manned exclusively by Englishmen, their quarters were 'very extensive and also handsome.'[43] Shops selling European provisions existed. Some European merchants had also settled down and made a considerable fortune. Thomas Mundy during his visit in 1803 found one who had made $50,000 and then lost it in England and had returned to retrieve his fortunes once again.[44]

Churches were built and some private houses with typically European architecture came up.[45] An attempt was made to create an ambience of life-style in England. Miss Fane and her family were given a fete by the local Brigadier.[46] But this type of urban centre could not develop beyond a point. It remained under the shadow of its neighbour, Patna, the main urban centre of Bihar.

The military factor helped another urban centre Buxar, located on the Ganga, to survive. It was midway between Patna and Benares. It had a shed; containing 7,000 horses for supplying, the Bengal army. Captain Mundy had noted its existence in 1853.[47] The place had three Englishmen, the M.D. of the station,

Manager of the Shed Farm and a Veterinary Surgeon.[48] It also had a coal dump to supply the steam-ships plying between Calcutta and Allahabad. Heber called it, 'a large and respectable Mussulman town, with several handsome mosques—one of the largest and neatest bazars which I have seen, and some good-looking European bungalows. He was told there were 'no less than one hundred and fifty Europeans in garrison . . .'.[49]

The introduction of the Permanent Settlement in 1793 resulted in the emergence of the institution of the zamindaris. Some of the hereditary chieftains with large holdings became zamindars. Among these mention may be made of Dumraon and Jagdishpur in the Shahabad district, Tekari in the Gaya district, Darbhanga in the Muzaffarpur district, Hathwa and Bettiah in Saran district, etc. The owners of these big zamindaris soon realized that in order to meet the new administrative requirements, they had to remodel its management. They had to induct officials with a knowledge of English to keep in touch with governmental laws. The recruitment of such gentlemen, who had received education in urban centres; began to change the nature of the seat of the zamindaris. Houses were built for the new office-staff. Kunwar Singh, the hero of the revolt of 1857, was a big zamindar with his seat in Jagdishpur. In order to collect the land revenue, he had divided the area into a number of units and had employed an hierarchy of officials.[50]

Sometimes when these big zamindaris were placed under the Court of Wards, the government sent its own officials to manage its affairs. They worked for the moral and material well-being of the local people by inducting the zamindar to establish schools[51] imparting English education and to establish allopathic dispensaries.

The zamindars still patronized traditional culture, donated to and set up religious institutions, schools imparting education in classical languages, etc. The zamindar and his seat became the cultural and administrative focal point for the surrounding areas. Hence, many of these places became semi-urbanized.

The residence of the zamindar of Tekari, Mitrajit Singh was described thus. 'It is abundant size for the residence of a man of rank, and has at a distance a picturesque castle like appearance, being built very irregularly with many projections and elevated towers.' Further, 'at a little distance is a garden surrounded by a brick wall with turrets at the corners, and containing some small buildings of bricks. Also a tank were a sannyasi resides in a good brick house, and entertains mendicants at the Rajah's expense' . . . . 'On each side of the fort is a large bazar, and in some places the streets have been made wide and straight like those of Sahebganj. The houses are mostly of mud, tiled but in general poor and slovenly.'[52]

In view of this fact, it is hardly surprising that when the local self Government Act was passed in the 1860s and Municipalities were established many of these seats of big zamindaris were automatic choices for these institutions. The district headquarters emerged as educational centres for modern education when in 1833 the government began to follow the policy of opening zillah schools, which imparted English education up to the Matriculation level. Since local teachers were not available, generally teachers from the neighbouring province of Bengal were employed. Students from the surrounding countryside came to study in these institutions. The district headquarters now had the largest number of literate persons as compared to other places. It, therefore, emerged as the torchbearer of new ideas and new culture.

The zamindars also felt the need of having a residential quarter in the district towns since they were always saddled with numerous law-suits which involved frequent visits there. Also for purposes of education and treatment, visits to the district headquarter were necessary. Hence, a residence was considered a necessity for the zamindars in the district headquarters.

The zamindars began to invest in urban property, not as a commercial proposition but as a symbol of status. This step strengthened rural-urban nexus and urban influences could be transmitted more easily and more quickly. However, this nexus ensured that rural features would appear in urban areas. This became gradually pronounced when many small zamindars took to newly emerging professions and jobs in the government to supplement their income and to acquire power and position. Thus urban centres could in some senses be described as 'overgrown villages.' Nevertheless, urban values began to seep in the countryside which presaged the beginnings of Westernization and modernization.

It is interesting to note that during this period no significant commercial centre development which could stimulate urbanization. Of course, there can be no talk of the emergence of any industrial centre as industrial revolution had not come down to Bihar.

The processing of indigo dye was carried out in villages where the crop was grown. Opium was carried to Patna where it was processed in a government-owned factory. The Europeans did try to develop the manufacture of sugar by using new machineries and steam boilers. In this case again the concerns were situated in the countryside where sugar cane was cultivated. Hence manufacturing activities largely remained confined to the rural areas. During the period under review economic factors did not contribute to the emergence of any urban centre.[53]

In these urban centres, the artisans and the members of service groups were liberated from the bonds of the Jajmani system, which still prevailed in the villages. Hence, they had greater freedom to practice their occupation. Secondly, some of them could give up caste-occupation and move over to new ones because several constraints had disappeared. They had now access to new education, the key to a new career and a fresh opportunity to earn livelihood by adopting new crafts or by opting for new occupations for which they had acquired qualifications.

But these centres did not make the expected impact on the society or economy. For example, the district of Patna had 11,74,740 acres of land.[54] The area of Shahabad district was 4,403.64 sq. miles and its population 16,02,274 souls.[55] The district of Saran had an area of 6,394 sq. miles.[56] The district of Tirhoot had an area of 614.40 sq. miles.[57] Thus the district headquarters catering to the needs of extensive areas with hardly a couple of subsidiary towns could not have much impact, especially when railways had not appeared. True, an attempt was made to connect the urban centres through roads with Patna and also to join these urban centres with each other with 'Cusbah Towns' through newly built roads.[58] But in the absence of rapid means of transport, the interaction with the rural areas remained perfunctory. The village located around the urban centre could experience certain impulse when the population was drawn into establishing some sort of economic nexus either through exchange of goods or services, but those located at a greater distance retained their old ways. Only later the coming of the railways and development of better surface transport facilities made them conscious of the newly emerging socio-economic, cultural, administrative and political forces.

It should be recorded that the British administrative policy contributed to the decay of several urban centres which had now lost their administrative position. The most important among them was Rajmahal, the Mughal capital of Bihar and Bengal in the seventeenth century. Its palaces and buildings had decayed. In 1809 Valentia had noted, 'no vestiges even of its ancient munificence remain.'[59] When Miss Fane visited it in 1836, she found marble-tiled halls being used as coal depots for supplying coal to the steam-vessels playing up and down the Ganga.[60]

The first three-quarters of the British colonial rule may be described as a period fostering a new type of urban centre in limited numbers. But soon this infrastructure provided the bedrock for the development of another type of urbanization which imbibed the fruits of Western technology and industrial revolution, such as the printing press, the telegraph, the railways, etc. This stage begins after the middle of the nineteenth century.

The new urban centres may be described as beacons of modernization since they embodied the principle of rule of law, administered through the law-courts; they were the seats of secular and scientific education, which was accessible to all irrespective of caste, race, religion or language. These urban centres by providing modern medical help showed the efficacy of Western scientific achievements. They became the symbols of Western technology. These urban centres had mixed habitation which had replaced the dominant pattern of lay out in the village where the population occupied localities on the basis of caste, occupation or religion. This fostered a new sense of community living where inter-personal relationship had objective basis. The intermingling of the various strands of Indian, and non-Indian population widened the mental horizons of the local citizenry.

NOTES

1. J.A. Hubback, I.C.S., *Final Report on the Survey and Settlement Operations in the District of Shahabad 1907-1916*, Patna, 1928, p. 11. Brooke took over charge as the first Collector of Shahabad with headquarters at Arrah on 21 September 1787.

   It should be noted that by and large the boundaries of the earlier districts coincided with the eight sarkars into which the *suba* of Bihar was divided in the Mughal times, viz., Saran, Champaran, Hajipur, Tirhut, Shahabad, Rohtas, Bihar, Monghyr. Rowland N.L. Chandra, *Village in the Province of Bengal*, Calcutta, 1909, p. 18.

2. K.K. Datta (ed.), *Catalogue of Patna Commissioner's Records (1813-53)*, Patna, 1963, p. XVIII.

3. Ibid., p. XVI.

4. Ibid., p. XVIII.

5. Ibid., p. XVII; In 1831 Civil Judges were given session's work and their magisterial work was transferred to the Collectors (ibid., pp. XVI-XVII). The different geographical and statistical reports published in 1850s recount the same hierarchy of officials. 'The capital of Tirhoot, is Muzafferpur, where a Judge, Collector, Magistrate, Civil Surgeon, Sub-Deputy Opium Agent, and other Subordinate Judicial and Revenue and Police Officers are located'. Wyatt, *Geographical and Statistical Report of the District of Tirhoo*t, Calcutta, 1854, p. 5.

6. In early 1850s, William Tayler who assumed the Judgeship of Shahabad with headquarters at Arrah reported: 'The residents then at Arrah were: Travers the Collector; A. Swinton, Magistrate with his sister-in-law, Miss Norman; G. Field, Sub-Deputy Opium Agent; and Dr. Hutchinson, Civil Surgeon'. William Tayler, Esq., *Thirty-Eight Years in India*, vol. II, London, 1882, pp. 132, 217, 221.

7. Heber in mid 1820s, while talking of Munger/Monghyr said: 'There are besides his/Mr. Templer, the Judge and Magistrate/own family,

five or six others here of the upper and middling classes, and above thirty old English pensioners, many of them married and with families, . . .' In 1837 Emily Eden wrote from Munger, 'All the English residents, six in number (and that is what they call a large station), came on board immediately', Emily Eden, *Up the Country* (rpt., Curzon Press, Dublin, n.d.), p. 3.

8. Reginald Heber, *Narrative of a Journey Through the Upper Provinces of India, from Calcutta to Bombay 1824-1825*, vol. I, London, 1849, p. 124. 'I arrived at Boglipoor, or Bhaugulpoor . . . my friends the Corries still there, established very comfortably in the circuit-house (a bungalow provided in each of the minor stations for the district judges when on their circuit), and which had been lent to them by the Judge and Magistrate, Mr. Chalmers.'

9. The construction of a church was commenced in Danapore in 1827 and completed in 1830. Kumod Verma, 'Khagaul', *Times of India* (Patna), 2 November 1992.

10. Heber, op. cit., pp. 124, 132. He speaks of meeting Christian clergies in Bhagalpur and Munger. Chhapra had a Christian cemetery.

11. Buchanan, *Journal of Francis Buchanan Kept during the Survey of the Districts of Patna and Gaya in 1811-12*, Patna, 1925, p. 60. Mr. Jameson was the Surgeon at Gaya.

12. *Journal of Buchanan Kept during the Survey of the District of Shahabad in 1812-13*, Patna, 1925, pp. 8-9. It may be pointed out that the house of the Judge covered an area of 42 *bighas* or about 30 acres of land.

13. *Reminiscences of Behar*, Calcutta, 1887, p. 62.

14. Prof. K.K. Basu compiled a list of 414 Europeans both officials and non-officials who lived in Bhagalpur, Munger and the surrounding countryside between the last quarter of the eighteenth and the end of the first half of the nineteenth centuries. K.K. Basu, 'The Early Europeans in Bhagalpur', *Proceedings, Indian Historical Records Commission, 15th Session*, Poona, December 1938, pp. 90-106.

15. *Shahabad . . .*, p. 7.

16. Ibid., p. 8.

17. Heber wrote about Chhapra, 'It is now the chief town of the district of Sarun, and the residence of the Judge and Collector and contains also, a good many large, handsome native houses . . .', Heber, op. cit., p. 145.

18. *District Gazetteer, Champaran*, Patna, 1938, p. 36.

19. Ibid., p. 74.

20. Ibid.

21. *Reminiscences of Bihar*, Chaps. II and X.

22. *District Gazetteer, Champaran*, p. 168.
23. Ibid., p. 34.
24. Ibid., p. 36.
25. The Muzaffarpur races were revived in January 1854 after they had stopped for sometime owing to differences within the European community. *Reminiscences of Behar*, p. 118.
26. *District Gazetteers, Monghyr*, p. 50.
27. Ibid., p. 51. Its jurisdiction extended to five police stations, viz., Monghyr, Tarapur, Surajgarha, Mallipur and Gogri.
28. Ibid. From that time the officer, although he did not obtain the title, exercised most of the powers of a full Magistrate Collector and from the first corresponded directly with the chief executive and revenue authorities and not through the Bhagalpur Collector, whose deputy he nominally was. The new revenue district comprised of Collectors of *parganas* from the neighbouring districts of Bihar, Bhagalpur and Tirhut. Ibid., pp. 51-2.
29. Captain W.S. Sherwill, *General Remarks on the District of Monghyr* (n.d., probably 1850s, place of publication probably Calcutta), pp. 11, 12; In 1824 Heber had also referred to Munger in glowing terms. 'The town is larger than I expected, and in better condition than most native towns. Though all houses are small, there are many of them with an upper storey, and the roofs, instead of the flat terrace or thatch, which are the only alterations in Bengal, are generally sloping, with red tiles, of the same shape and appearance with those which we see in Italian pictures; '. . . I was surprised at the neatness of the kettles, tea-trays, guns, pistols, toasting-forks, cutlery, and other things of the sort, which may be procured in this tiny Birmingham', ibid., p. 132; Emily Eden in 1837 had noted '. . . the inlaid tables and boxes were tempting, and there was the prettiest dolls' furniture possible, tables and cane-chairs, and sofas, arid foot-stools, of such curious workmanship'. Emily Eden, op. cit., p. 10. Almost a similar picture was painted by William Tayler in 1848. 'A confused and clamourous host of Hawkers invaded the steamer directly she anchored. Punkhas, mats, baskets, straw bonnets, avadavats, chameleons, toasting forks, gun-screws, sticks, tables, with diverse other miscellaneous manufactures were pressed upon us by rabid dealers, with a zeal and pertinacity which was striking but unpleasant', Tayler, vol. I, p. 48.
30. John Pemble (ed.), *Miss Fane in India*, London, 1885, p. 123.
31. H.R. Ghosal, *Economic Transition in the Bengal Presidency*, Patna, 1950, p. 157.
32. *Miss Fane in India*, p. 25.

33. *District Gazetteer, Shahabad*, p. 105.

34. *Catalogue . . .* , p. 288.

35. V.H. Jackson (ed.), *Journal of Francis Buchanan kept during the Survey of the Districts of Gaya and Patna in 1811-12*, Patna, 1925, pp. 40-1.

36. Ibid., p. 91.

37. Paul Jackson (trans.), *Sharfuddin Maneri: The Hundred Letters*, New York, 1980, p. 1.

38. Ghoshal, op. cit., p. 306.

39. Ibid., p, 286.

40. Ibid.

41. *Patna and Gaya*, p. 87.

42. Ibid., p. 168. The bazars are extensive. We have a beautiful description by Heber also. 'As we approached Dinapoor, symptoms began to appear of a great English military station, and it was whimsical to see peeping out from beneath the palms and plantains large blue boards with gilt letters, "Digha Rarm Havell victualler," & c.; "Morris, Tailor"; "Davis, Europe Warehouse", & c. The cantonment itself is the largest and hansomest which I have seen, . . . there are, likewise, several indigo-planters in the neighbourhood, many of them with families, . . . 'There had been a school for the European children and those recruits who could not read, but this had fallen to decay. . .'

43. ' . . . I found that to avoid the fury of the stream they had moored her [pinnance] in a narrow nullah, which constitutes of vessels, while one of the banks was covered with all kinds of vessels, while one of the banks was covered with warehouses, and the other occupied by a great cattle-fair.' Heber, op. cit., pp. 143, 144, The place continued to flourish. William Tayler in 1848 wrote, 'The moment the steamer anchored, a stream of table-cloth and towel vendors, wax candle makers, and Patna toymen, flowed in upon the deck, in a repetition of the commercial transactions which had been carried on at Monghyr' William Tayler I, p. 489.

44. Ibid. The garden of the General was described in these words, 'The General has a very good garden, in which he has English apples and Bukhara plums both of which he says produce excellent fruit. . . . He has also peaches with a depressed fruit, which I have seen nowhere else. Having a taste of cultivation as a florist, he has procured some plants from Nepal especially the fine Porana.' *Miss Fane in India.*

45. Captain Mundy, *The Journal of a Tour in India*, vol. I, London, 1803, p. 172.

46. *Miss Fane in India*, pp. 127-8.

47. Ibid., p. 128.

48. Captain Mundy, op. cit., Dee, 'Just opposite, there is a grand establishment of the Company's shed, the Superintendent, Major Hunter, having a pretty house at the latter place.'

49. *Miss Fane in India*, pp. 128-9. Emily Eden, op. cit., p. 18. She along with her brother Lord Aucland halted here and visited the stud; William Tayler, also visited it in 1848. William Tayler, p. 469.

50. Heber, op. cit., pp. 146, 147.

51. *Aj* (Patna), 23 April 1992, p. 7.

52. Ibid.

53. *Patna and Gaya*, pp. 156-7.

54. A. Wyatt, Esq., *Geographical and Statistical Report of the District of Tirhoot*, Calcutta, 1854, pp. 58-9. In all sixty-four sugar factories run by steam engines are mentioned, all located in rural areas and some of them as parts of indigo and Steam Engine Sugar Factory, Dynee Steam Engine Sugar Factory, Husna Steam Engine Sugar and Indigo Factory, etc.

55. *Statistics of the District of Patna, n.d.* but published from Calcutta in 1850s. The area has been calculated on the basis of data furnished by the Officiating Deputy Surveyor General, Calcutta on 22 September 1847.

56. Travers. *Statistics of Zillah Shahabad*, Calcutta, n.d. but 1850s.

57. A. Wyatt. Esq., *Statistics of the District of Sarun and Sircar Sarun*, Calcutta, n.d. but 1850s.

58. Wyatt, *Geographical and Statistical Report of the District of Tirhoot*, p. 57.

59. Ibid., pp. 11, 28.

60. Valentia, *Voyages and Travels to India, Ceylon, The Red Sea*, vol. I, London, 1809, pp. 79-80; Ann Deane who passed through the place after Valentia wrote about the place, 'Here the ruin of a magnificent palace, formerly belonging to the Rajah, may be seen; and here, every day about noon, the postman from East to West meet, and exchange their dispatches, either way, Ann Deane, 'A Guide Up The River Ganges, from Calcutta to Cawnpore', *Bengal Past and Present*, vol. XXXI.

CHAPTER 9

A New Pattern of Urban Growth: Emergence of Zamindari Towns in Bihar

(A Case Study of Dumraon in the Second Half of the Nineteenth Century)

The colonial period in eastern India began with the take over of the administration of Bihar and Bengal after the battles of Plassey and Buxar and the grant of the Dewani of Bengal and Bihar by the Mughal Emperor Shah Alam to the English East India Company. The Company's rule ushered in important changes in society, economy and polity.

A new pattern of urban growth emerged out of the colonial policies; the Company promoted new urban settlements because of their administrative needs.

II

In early modern times, an urban centre, by its very nature is a concentration of multi-ethnic, multi-lingual, multi-religious populace who gather at a particular place to earn their living by non-agricultural pursuits. These urban centres have a significant presence of traders (wholesalers and retailers), artisans, serving bureaucrats, professionals such as lawyers, doctors, teachers and journalists, etc. The density of population is much higher than a rural settlement.

The needs of sanitation, education, are looked after by a definite body of citizens created by the law of the State.

The intellectual environment of this urban area is definitely superior to a rural settlement since here the proportion of literates in the population is much higher. They are forward looking and are capable of appreciating and accepting the advantages that changes in science and technology bring about. They become the propagators of scientific ideas in the surrounding countryside.

The last characteristic was the logical outcome of the Industrial Revolution of the late eighteenth century which had begun to affect many nations and societies across the globe by the mid-nineteenth century.

The advent of new science and technology, as in the other parts of the world, was accompanied by the rise of a new middle-class in India which included a category aware of the advantages of the new science; it was keen to imitate the life-style of their European counterparts in dress, food and even in forms of entertainment. The Indian rural society was slowly imbibing the ethos of the culture that was emerging in Presidency towns, provincial capitals and district headquarters. Improvements in communication (the new postal system, the telegraph), in transportation (first the steam-ships and then the railways) facilitated this strengthening of linkages between the towns and the countryside. The needs of colonial administration and economy which required opening up of the rural markets for the goods manufactured in the industries of Manchester and Liverpool and other industrial centres in England also gave a fillip to this.

The zamindari urban centres, mostly situated amidst rural areas helped to achieve this colonial objective.

In Bihar these zamindari towns emerged in a number places, such as Darbhanga, Bettiah, Hathwa (in north Bihar) and Dum-raon, Surajpura, Tekarai (south of the Ganga River).

Undoubtedly, the preconditions for the emergence of such zamindari towns were created by the introduction of the Permanent Settlement in 1793, envisaging the collection of land revenue through the agency of zamindars (recognized and set up by the Government) and not directly by the State. The land revenue to be paid by the zamindars from their respective areas was fixed in perpetuity and any amount collected over and above it was the remuneration of the zamindar. The zamindari rights were made hereditary; the owner could sell or mortgage it in full or in part. Zamindari was private property.

Zamindars assured of the continuation of their Estate as family property accepted the norms fixed by the colonial administration because the uncertainty prevailing in the Mughal and Nawabi times had ended. But they also realized that any transgression or violation of norms set up by rulers would invite dispossession and penalty and punishment. So they decided to adopt the colonial administrative practices. In this transformation the model was the structure of the district headquarters, set up by the colonial rulers. However a significant role was played by the nature and inclination of the zamindar as well.

In this paper we discuss the emergence of Dumraon, the headquarters of the Dumraon Estate, one of the oldest zamindaris in Bihar, situated south of the river Ganga in the old Shahabad district as a prominent urban centre under the stewardship of Maharaja Radha Prasad Singh between the late 1860s and 1894 when he passed away.

III

For Maharaja Radha Prasad Singh the model was the township of Arrah, the headquarters of the district of Shahabad and the seat of its Collector.

The British Collector who was responsible for land-revenue collection and the maintenance of law and order and also for the enforcement of governmental laws within his jurisdiction called district (roughly equivalent to sarkar of the Mughal and Nawabi times). He had a large civil and police staff to assist him. Invariably the employees belonged to different castes, religions, provinces and countries. Arrah attracted a floating population because people came from villages to sort out their problems with the government and also to avail of the latest educational and medical facilities that had developed there. The permanent population had a significant segment of artisans, barbers, tailors, washermen, cobblers, carpenters, iron-smiths, jewellers and professionals.

Dumraon moulded itself into a replica of Arrah. Dumraon was the largest zamindari in the Shahabad district. Its importance had increased when the English East India Company confiscated the zamindari of Jagdishpur after its proprietor Kunwar Singh raised the flag of opposition against the British rule in 1857.

The British success opened the eyes of the zamindars and the Indian intelligentsia. The zamindars knew that armed opposition to the British rule in order to force them to accept their demands was futile. Armed coercion had been successfully practised during the Mughal and the Nawabi rule. Now they had to seek legal remedies for their grievances against the various measures of the colonial rulers. They had to carefully confirm to the laws and norms laid down by the British authorities so as not to irk them and to invite their wrath. For this they knew they had to give up their traditional methods of working and imitate the British pattern of administration.

Dumraon was no exception to this changed thinking. Maheshwar Baksh Singh who was at the helm of affairs during the stormy days of 1857 had already initiated this process. His successor Radha Prasad Singh intelligently carried it forward.

This is clear from the Census Report of 1891. It shows the population of Dumraon in that year at 18,384 including 3,384 Muslims. It mentions the presence of Christians as well.

The layout of the town shows its urban character. The center of the town was called the 'chowk'. From here roads radiated to all the four directions (IV.33). The city administration attached much importance to these roads; water was sprinkled on them every day. In the evenings lights were put on the light-posts, erected at regular intervals. Several streets branched out from these roads. The Municipality counted 119 streets but they admitted there were many more which had not been numbered.

Earlier there were sixteen mohallas or quarters in the town. Their number was now forty-nine because of continuous increase in population (IV.30). The names of the new mohallas suggest that the population growth was possible because of the arrival of professional and service classes; new groups of Muslims also arrived.

The names of some of the new mohallas are: Mir Shikar Toli, Shah Sahab ka Takia, Nathu Khan ka Hatha, Manihar Toli, etc. (IV.31). Obviously the majority residing in these *mohallas* were Muslims.

New *mohallas* where professional and service groups resided were: Manihar Toli (sellers of bangles), Lohar Toli (iron-smiths), Julaha Toli (weavers), Darji Toli (tailors), Hajjam Mohalla (barbers), Kewat Toli (fisher-folk), Sonar Toli (goldsmiths), Mochi Toli (cobblers), etc.

Some of the *mohallas* were also named after caste groups: Ahir Toli (milk-men), Tiwari Mohalla (Brahmins), Kahar Toli (potters), etc. (IV.32).

The civic authorities ensured that pukka roads connected the centre with the periphery as well as the railway station (IV.33).

Markets were built to cater to the needs of the towns people as well as the neighbouring population. This was necessary because traders of Dumraon imported goods from Bombay (now Mumbai) as well as Calcutta (now Kolkata) and re-exported a part to the hinterland. Businessmen from the adjoining district of Palamau made their purchases in Dumraon. The major exports from Dumraon consisted of cotton, wheat, barley, peas, sugar, sweet potato, mustard, etc. (IV.34).

According to one estimate there were 45 shops selling clothes (IV.34).

The town had several ponds. Out of which four were famous. Maharaja Jai Prakash Singh had built a pond, known as Naya Talab or New Pond (IV.34).

The town was beautified by several gardens and orchards laid out by the Dumraon ruler and his family members.

The estate had constructed a number of buildings to house public offices such as the Survey Office, the Printing Press, Tahwil Office, Sarista Office, Revenue Department, Agriculture Office, Law Department, Dewan's Office, English Office, Farsi Office, Treasury, a Hall for meeting, etc. (IV.42).

There was a separate store where food grains, provisions

and eatables were kept. Whenever estate guests arrived, this organization supplied food of their choice (IV.41).

Most of the rulers built temples and places of worship. The estate financially helped individuals who wanted to construct a place of worship irrespective of their faith. The estate provided hospitality to all holy men visiting the town without any discrimination.

The town catered to the material and moral needs of its inhabitants.

IV

After Maharaja Radha Prasad Singh assumed the reins of power, he tried hard to bring modernization to his subjects. He knew that in this new education as introduced by the colonial administration would play a vital role because it was secular, scientific and accessible to all irrespective of race, religion or creed. Furthermore, administrative needs dictated that the Estate should have its own cadre of English-knowing experts as English was the language of colonial administration. The Colonial Laws were in English, the administrative decisions were conveyed in English and English was the medium of official communication and personal conversation with bureaucrats. He therefore decided to promote new education and extended all support to Raj High School established in 1856.

The Maharaja had become aware of the need for gaining expertise in English because he had been frequently meeting the Governor-General and other high officers whenever they passed through Sasaram on way to Calcutta or from Calcutta to north India since 1859 (IV.2). He had himself studied English with tutors, Pandit Dwarka Nath Kashmiri, Sri Kali Kant Bhattacharya and Sri Jai Prakash Lal.

As soon as he assumed charge of the estate after Maheshwar Baksh Singh abdicated the throne in 1869, he decided to put his ideas into practice. He elevated the Raj High School to Intermediate standard (then known as F.A. or Fellow of Arts). He offered a prize of Rs. 50 to students who passed the I.A.

examination (IV.50). He sent them to Patna or Benares to write their examinations.

He encouraged students to study engineering and medicine at Calcutta and in 1890 offered two scholarships worth Rs. 10 each to them (IV.22).

While promoting English education, he patronized traditional Sanskrit and Perso-Arabic learning in the town by giving books to students studying these subjects. The estate also met their boarding expenses (IV.49).

V

Radha Prasad Singh ensured that like all urban centres Dumraon also became the torch-bearer of social reform. It shows that he was aware of the wave of social reform then blowing in the country.

Both the Government and social organizations were promoting it.

A major dimension of this social reform movement was the uplift of the status of women. Raja Rammohun Roy through Brahmo Samaj had started propagating it. The Governor-General William Bentinck had abolished the Sati system; Vidya Sagar had agitated and the Government had passed the Hindu Widows Remarriage Act. Social reformers thought that spread of education was a powerful force for emancipating women from the chains of tradition and conservatism. In this respect some effort had been made in Bihar. Mokshda Girls School was opened in Bhagalpur. Radha Prasad Singh's mind was working in that direction.

Probably impelled by this desire he invited Sivanath Sastri, the famous Brahmo leader to Dumraon since Brahmo Samaj was in the fore-front of women emancipation movement in eastern India. He stayed there for quite sometime. We do not know what transpired between the two but in 1882 the Maharaja established a girls' school (IV.13). This was a very bold initiative. The school had on its rolls, Hindu and Muslim girls. Hindu girl students belonged to several castes. The wife of the Lt. Governor of Bengal on visit to Dumraon inspected the school in 1887.

The estate extended financial support to widows who had no relatives to look after them. They received food sufficient to support them each month. They were also given some money (IV.49).

If parents did not have money to marry their daughters, they got financial support from the estate without any distinction of religion or caste (IV.49).

The estate budget had provision for such expenses.

Quietly but efficiently the estate was trying to send the message of social transformation to its residents.

VI

Modern urban centers showcase latest achievements of technology directly impinging upon the life of common man. Maharaja Radha Prasad Singh was keen that advances made by science and technology should be known to the residents of Dumraon.

Geography also helped the estate in this. Dumraon was situated near the railway line connecting Calcutta, the then capital of India, with north India. Hence, people knew how steam engine could change the life style of an ordinary person by revolutionizing the production and transportation systems.

The estate established a printing press for printing forms, receipts and other papers required for administering the estate (IV.36). People realized that the printing press was a powerful instrument in promoting literacy and bringing knowledge to the door-steps of the common man.

People became more convinced of the benefits which science conferred upon them when the estate opened a modern hospital in 1871 for treating the sick. He appointed properly qualified doctors who had studied in medical colleges. The estate also appointed the necessary supporting medical staff to assist the doctors. Its infrastructure was in no way inferior to any hospital established by the government. The estate incurred an expenditure of Rs. 4,000 (IV. 3).

A little later the estate also set up a veterinary hospital, which further showed the keenness of the Estate to demonstrate that the achievements of science were beneficial to the common man.

VII

The above measures helped to prepare the mind of the common man to accept the results of scientific researches and to use them in different walks of life.

Radha Prasad Singh knew that Dumraon's economy rested on agriculture. Economic prosperity would follow if agricultural production increased. For this it was essential that the peasantry should be familiar with the use of the latest tools and also the latest agricultural practices.

For bringing this knowledge to the peasants, the estate from 1885 onwards regularly organized annual agricultural exhibitions either in Dumraon or in the nearby Brahmapur. The estate spent Rs. 20,000 on holding the first Agricultural Exhibition (IV.14). The exhibits included various forms of ploughs and other agricultural implements. Seeds of improved variety were also on display. The queries of visitors were answered by qualified persons manning the stalls (IV.14).

Improved breed of livestocks were also on show because they were an integral part of agricultural production.

A juice extractor from sugar cane was shown because the peasants manufactured sugar and Dumraon exported it.

In short, these agricultural exhibitions were used as an instrument for modernizing agriculture, the basis of economy, in the estate.

The mind of the Maharaja was scientific is also clear from the fact that he had electrified his palace. He had done this at a time when electricity had just arrived.

He also had a telephone installed.

In other words, residents of Dumraon could legitimately claim that they were familiar with most of the amenities provided by scientific and technological advances to any urban centre of the times.

VIII

The Maharaja was keen to ensure that residents of Dumraon should be provided with the necessary civic amenities and they should have a say in deciding what was best for them.

The Estate gave land to the Government of India free for establishing post offices. When the Government of Bengal started establishing police stations, the estate handed over to them land without charging a single paisa for it (IV.5).

These measures meant that the quality life in Dumraon was in no way inferior to any other small urban centre in India.

The Maharaja's efforts to formally give a legal cover as an urban centre to Dumraon bore fruit in 1877 when under a notification of the Bengal Government a municipality was constituted to govern, control and regulate its civic affairs (IV.33). The Municipality became intimately associated with providing civic amenities to the residents and was in the forefront in arranging receptions to distinguished visitors to the town. It was also an assertion of the urban identity of the town.

When Sir Ashley Eden, the Lt. Governor of Bengal visited Dumraon in 1882, the Municipality accorded him a civic reception. Sri Prayag Singh, B.A., the Headmaster of the Raj High School read the welcome address on behalf of the municipality (IV.2).

The Maharaja consciously followed a policy of inviting distinguished visitors from different walks of life to the town so that the locals would have a feeling that they were not living in isolation and were part of a larger community. He ensured that the distinguished guests did not lack any comfort to which they were used. For this he built a European Guest House and whenever the estate hosted a special function on the occasion of the visit of the Governor-General or the Lt. Governor or a marriage ceremony, etc., the catering arrangements were entrusted to the Great Eastern Hotel of Calcutta (IV.24). For the entertainment of guests arrangements were made for European games. In 1893, tennis tournaments were held (IV.35, 36).

The Maharaja established the Dumraon Polo Club where competition in horse-racing was organized (6, 12).

Military bands from Dinapur Cantt provided European music and Ball Dances were held.

The idea was that the residents of Dumraon should become familiar with the lifestyle of their colonial masters and the Westernized Indians and should not entertain any preconceived ideas about them.

This was a deliberate policy. It becomes evident when we see the list of visitors to Dumraon during the time of the Maharaja.

In 1875, Sir Richard Temple, the Lt. Governor of Bengal stayed for two days in Dumraon (IV.4)

In February 1882, the Lt. Governor of Bengal personally came to Dumraon to confer upon Radha Prasad Singh the title of Maharaja Bahadur and the title of Rai Bahadur on Dewan Jai Prakash Lal (IV.6).

A festival-like atmosphere prevailed in Dumraon. The guests present constituted a cross-section of the bureaucracy as well as the zamindars in the Presidency of Bengal. The high officials present were: Mr. Hadley (the Commissioner of Patna Division), Mr. Nolan (the Collector of Patna), Chandra Madhav Ghosh (Judge, Calcutta High Court), Durga Giti (Assistant Commissioner, Patna), Collectors and Magistrates posted in the districts of Patna, Saran, Champaran, Balia, Benares, Ghazipur, etc., and Opium Agents posted in Patna, Ghazipur, Jehanabad and several military officers stationed in the Dinapur Cantt.

Among the non-official guests mention may be made of Jagtanand (Vakil, Calcutta), Bhartendu Harish Chandra (eminent Hindi litterateur from Benares), Raja Shiva Prasad (a distinguished educationist and a noted author), Munshi Newal Kishore (publisher of medieval Persian historical texts written in India, Lucknow), Munshi Diwan Chand (editor, *Rifai-i Am*), Munshi Sirajuddin Ahmed Khan (editor, *Waka-i Alam*,

Ghazipur), Pandit Chintaman Rai (editor, *Kavivachan Sudha*, Benares), editors of *The Pioneer* and *Amrit Bazar Patrika*, etc. (IV.6, 8, 9)

In 1883 when the plan for writing the history of the Ujjainiya community was taking shape, the Maharaja invited a number of distinguished scholars to Dumraon and asked them to prepare an outline to be followed by the writer.

In February 1887, the Lt. Governor of Bengal, Thomson inaugurated the third Annual Agricultural Exhibition in Dumraon (IV.15). On this occasion 150 distinguished guests were invited. The local municipality held a civic reception for the Lt. Governor who praised the efforts of the estate in promoting female literacy (IV.15).

In August 1887 the Lt. Governor of Bengal, Bailey came to Dumraon with Lady Bailey. She laid the foundation stone of the Girls' School, established in 1882 (IV.19). She expressed her happiness that 200 girls were receiving education and among them were both Hindus and Muslims.

In other words, while Maharaja Bahadur was at the helm of affairs, he ensured that the town remained the torch-bearer of modern education; the residents had the opportunity to get to know elites of the society and also had a glimpse into the new life-style that was emerging among the new middle-class. Dumraon was, as expected of an urban centre, playing its role as a modernizer and a trend-setter.

NOTE

Tawarikh Ujjainia (in Urdu) in four volumes has provided the data used in this essay.

CHAPTER 10

Endeavour and Persistence:
Brahmo Samaj in Bihar in the
Second Half of the Nineteenth Century

The Brahmo Samaj was the first movement for socio-religious
reforms initiated in India in the nineteenth century under the
impact of Western ideas, culture and technology. Its place of
origin, appropriately enough, was Bengal, the first Indian state
to come in intimate contact with the Western way of life, administration and education. The interaction with European ideas
and technology resulted in the establishment of educational
institutions with new subjects of study, and printing presses
which produced the Young Bengal Renaissance. A critical
examination of traditional beliefs and practices in different
walks of life began. It was during a ferment like this that the
Brahmo Samaj was formed in 1828 in an attempt to satisfy the
strivings of some of these questioning minds. Within a short
period, the Samaj had a well-defined organization with a clear-
cut set of ideals, and was able to make a mark on the socio-
religious scene.

The present paper is an attempt to study the results which
followed when an attempt was made by the followers of the
Samaj to propagate its ideals in adjoining Bihar, where the Western system of education spread very slowly, resulting in a near
absence of an indigenous class of English-educated professionals, such as middle and high-level government functionaries,
doctors, engineers, lawyers, etc. The study will reveal why only
certain aspects of the movement received emphasis, and why
only certain types of individuals accepted it. Furthermore, by
identifying the long-term and short-term legacies of the movement, one can appreciate their role with greater exactitude in

the general evolution of society in Bihar. We have to remember that because of geographical contiguity, there was a continuous interaction between the Brahmos of Bengal and the Biharis.

The founder of the Brahmo Samaj, Raja Rammohun Roy, and an influential body of his followers were always in close touch with the Bihar province. The Raja had intimate contacts with it even before he established Brahmo Samaj. He had come to Patna to learn Persian and Arabic in order to be able to study Muslim scriptures in the original.[1] He started his career as a *Sheristadar* in the office of the District Commissioner at Ramgarh in Hazaribagh district.[2]

A number of Bengali Brahmos resided in Bihar, because the Bengalis having received an English education manned the British bureaucracy at the officer's as well as clerical levels. Doctors, lawyers, teachers and other professionals were mostly Bengalis.[3] The English had brought them into the province to serve the administration and civic services. The influx of Brahmos and their families was a continuous process. They could be found in practically all the important urban centres. In course of their administrative and professional duties they came in contact with different strata and classes in society. It is possible that with the exception of Orissa and Assam one cannot say the same regarding the nature and level of Brahmo interaction with other parts of India. In view of these specific features, the study of the spread of Brahmos and of the Brahmo Samaj in Bihar promises to unfold the dynamics of the movement in its missionary phase and additionally it may throw light on the process of modernization going on in the province during this period.

Since the immigration of Bengalis into Bihar has a long and continuous history, it is difficult to state precisely when the first of the Brahmos arrived, but by the time of the second half of the nineteenth century, they were to be found in the chief urban centres of the province where government officials and professionals were concentrated. Their activities in Bihar increased after 1866 when Keshub Chandra Sen, in the month of November, broke away from the parent Samaj led by

Debendra Nath Tagore, formed the Brahmo Samaj of India[4] and embarked upon a conscious policy of preaching the new doctrine to win adherents. As the name implies, Keshub desired propagation of the creed all over the country and did not want to confine it to Bengal and Bengalis alone. The missionary phase of the movement thus began. This was a landmark in the organizational structure of the Samaj for a propaganda department was created to disseminate his message.

Keshub decided that social reforms were to be an integral part of the Brahmo faith.[5] He was, of course, echoing the ideas of the founder. Keshub decided to travel to different parts of the country to spread the message, and his disciples followed him. The coming of the railways had facilitated mobility. Before proceeding on a tour to preach Brahmoism in Bombay, Keshub left his family at Monghyr in Bihar which had a sizeable Bengali population and a reputation for healthy climate.[6] On his return from Bombay he again stayed in the town with his family.[7] The presence of a large Bengali population was because of the existence of a gun factory and a railway workshop in the neighbouring suburb of Jamalpur. In both places, services of English educated and technically skilled Indians were required. For historical and geographical reasons such manpower resources could be then drawn only from Bengal.

Keshub's biographer noted that during his stay Keshub held prayer sessions almost every day and several young Bengalis became his devotees. Keshub introduced the practice of collective singing of devotional hymns (*kirtan*) on roads, which proved to be an effective method of mass contact. He had incorporated the Vaishnav tradition which attached greater importance to the ritual of *kirtan,* public as well as private, as an important means for attaining God and salvation of the soul. This was the beginning of the Bhakti movement within the fold of the Brahmo Samaj.

Keshub's innovation made a deep impact. One of his early associates Bijoy Krishna Goswami reported, 'Even the utterly worldly-minded came and joined the Brahmo Samaj. The humility, the love, the mutual attachment among the Brahmos made us feel that it was something heavenly. Even the hardest heart would melt in the fire of *upasana* (worship) in Monghyre. Many sinners received spiritual life through this *bhakti*.' The *sankirtan*, the *khole, kartal,* the *ektara* (single-strin instrument) were introduced, and these evoked unexpected response and enthusiasm especially with the orthodox Hindu Community.[8] Many Brahmos came to regard the town as a place of pilgrimage. It was here that Keshub got his well known follower, Bhai Dinanath Mazumdar.[9] Keshub also visited the neighbouring town of Bhagalpur.[10]

The Brahmo Samaj movement seemed to have received great impetus after another visit of Keshub Chandra Sen to Monghyr in 1868.[11] As in the past he left his family behind while proceeding on a tour of the North-Western Province (now Uttar Pradesh). On his return he again stayed at Monghyr. His host was Prosonna Kumar Sen, an employee in the Audit Department of the Eastern Railway.[12] In this year a branch of the Samaj was established at Jamalpur.[13]

Keshub's preaching in Monghyr caused a furore as some of the Brahmo Samajists accused him of posing 'as a savior of men, commissioned by God' and encouraging 'Brahmos to pray to him for salvation.'[14] Keshub was criticized for promoting 'man-worship' repugnant to the Brahmo ideas of one God and to its anti-idol worship stance. The threatened split did not materialize. Keshub's following in Monghyr increased. This is evident from the fact that in 1870 on the request of the Brahmos of the town, led by Dinanath Mazumdar, the government granted them a piece of land measuring 1 *bigha* (approximately 75 acres) for the construction of a place of wor-ship.[15] The temple was constructed in 1872.[16]

Bhai Dinanath Mazoomdar, a railway employee of Monghyr, resigned his job in 1873 and became a full-time preacher.[17] After 1880 he was given Bihar as his special field of service, and was recognized as its local minister.[18] At Bhagalpur he started a 'Prachar Ashram' and successfully brought a number of families within its fold.[19] Later he shifted his centre of activity to Patna.

When his health failed him, he moved on to Laheria Sarai near Darbhanga.

Another indication of the spread of the Brahmos in Bihar was the establishment of the Samaj in Hazaribagh in 1867.[20] A branch was established at nearby Pachmba in 1874. However, the total population of the Brahmos in the district in the 1870s was only twenty. Keshub Chandra Sen entered into correspondence with the government for providing facilities for registration of marriage of Brahmos in 1872.[21] The government agreed. On 4 June 1872 they issued a notification laying down detailed rules for the registration of Brahmo marriages.[22] This was evidently necessary because Brahmo followers in Bihar and elsewhere in the country were encountering difficulties in following their customs. Keshub's success provided legitimacy and governmental recognition for the faith. Henceforth, some of the waverers firmly accepted this faith.

It is evident that in Keshub's success in winning adherents to his faith two factors, besides his own personality, were crucial. First, his compromise with the Vaisnava tradition made his faith acceptable to even moderately literate Bengalis, since they felt more at home with this version. Secondly, governmental recognition had removed the legal obstacles in personal law faced by earlier Brahmos – a fact that might have deterred new enthusiasts. In a conservative society a new faith can give wider acceptance only if a certain amount of compromise with behaviour patterns which have become a part of the life-style of the people is incorporated. Furthermore, the faith must secure, at some level, explicit support of the ruling authority as well. However, at this point of time the movement itself suffered another split, a section of Brahmos revolted against Keshub's leadership in 1878 accusing him of following idolatrous practices in the marriage of his daughter.

Led by Sivanath Sastri, the group announced on 15 May 1878 the establishment of the Sadharan Brahmo Samaj. But the split did not affect the progress of the movement, because, like Keshub, the votaries of the new group also believed in missionary activity. Hence, soon after the formation of Sadharan Brahmo

Samaj, Sivanath Sastri set out on a tour of the northern India to preach his views. He first visited Monghyr, a stronghold of Keshub's followers, and then went to Muzaffarpur.[23] From here he proceeded on an *ekka* (horse-drawn carriage) to the town of Motihari, situated at a distance of 50 miles.[24] It was quite an arduous journey. In the 1870's the district had 'but few followers' of the Brahmo faith.[25] On way back he halted at Patna before travelling to Lucknow.[26] While returning to Calcutta he picked up his family from Monghyr.[27]

Next year Sivanath Sastri again decided to go on a tour of north India. He was short of money. Therefore he decided to get down at Patna and request monetary help from P.C. Roy, an ardent Brahmo and a government official.[28] He stayed at his house for a week and finished a novel *Mego Ban*.[29] He learnt that a Brahmo, Brajendra Kumar Basu, resided in the nearby town of Dumraon.[30] He was financially helped by another Brahmo of Patna. Another distinguished Bengali citizen of the town, T.K. Ghose, though not a Brahmo himself, donated some money to him.[31] Sivanath Sastri visited Bihar repeatedly to propagate his faith. In July 1830 he went to Motihari to attend the celebrations of the local Samaj. He was challenged by an Arya Samajist editor of a local journal to debate the merits and demerits of their respective faiths. A public disputation was held. The debate ended amidst an uproar.[32]

The point is that even in an outlying town of the province an awareness of the broad philosophy of Brahmo Samaj had already reached and was facing opposition from the traditionalists as well as other emerging doctrines of religious change amongst the Hindus. The incident illustrates an important of facet of the process of Westernization. The impact of Western education in its early stages in societies with memories of a fairly long history produces mutually conflicting and competing ideologies. Some of these seek to preserve the old order, some stand for evolutionary change, while others opt for a radical departure. Of course, in certain cases elements from two or even all the three are intermixed at some phase of the movement.

Hereafter, Bihar was subjected to intense Brahmo missionary

activity, more than any other province of nineteenth-century India. The two stalwarts of the movement, Keshub Chandra Sen and Sivanath Sastri, gave to the province their personal attention. A host of preachers from Calcutta belonging to both the factions frequently visited the various Brahmo organizations all over Bihar in order to promote the cause. Undoubtedly, the rivalry between the two factions sometimes created jealousies and unpleasantness but the activities of the Samaj did not slacken.

After the death of Keshub Chandra Sen in 1884, the rivalry between the different groups in the Samaj considerably lessened. They began to cooperate with each other. Besides Dinanath Mazoomdar, whose activities we have already noted, Bhakt Hari Sundar Bose and his nephew Bhai Braj Gopal Niyogi, ordained in 1897, took up missionary work on behalf of the Samaj.[33]

An important development in the history of the Brahmo Samaj in Bihar was the establishment of Sadhanashram. Originally the institution was started by Sivanath Sastri in 1891 as a Brahmo worker's shelter in Calcutta, but soon it was renamed Sadhanashram. Dr. Hem Chandra Sarkar and Babu Gurudas Chakravarty were two other early members.[34] Its branches were established in Arrah in Bihar in 1894 and in Dacca in East Bengal. From Arrah, Sadhanashram was shifted to Patna in 1896[35] Babu Gurudas Chakravarty was put in the charge.

Rajni Kant Guha entered the Ashram on 10 October 1896 and became the Headmaster of Rammohun Roy Seminary which was founded in November 1896 and began functioning in 1897.[36] With his friend Gurudas Babu he went to Bhagalpur where he contacted other Brahmos. Bhagalpur was another important point of Brahmo concentration in the province. From here they moved on to Monghyr. They discussed problems facing the Samaj with local Brahmos. They participated in collective prayers.[37]

The fact that Brahmo families could be found in all important places in Bihar can be inferred from the appointment of Registrars for solemnizing Brahmo marriages subsequently. In

1886 the Sub-Registrar of Motihari Sadar was appointed as an ex-officio Registrar for the Champaran district.[38] Mr. C. Shanne, Bar-at-Law, became a Marriage Registrar in Moghyr after the death of Babu Mohendra Nath Roy in 1900.[39] Babu Jay Kali Datta was appointed as the Registrar for Ranchi by a notification of 1901.[40] Babu Kshetra Nath Ghosh of Deoghar became the Registrar for the district of Santhal Parganas in 1904.[41] Babu Tin Couree Bose, the Secretary of the Brahmo Samaj, Giridih, a sub-divisional town (now a district town) in Hazaribagh district, requested the Inspector-General of Registration of Bengal in 1906 to appoint a permanent Marriage Registrar, as the earlier appointee, Babu Umesh Chandra Dutt, had been unable to carry on his duty on account of ill-health.[42] The government acceded to his request and allowed the rural Sub-Registrar of the sub-division to function in that capacity.[43] In 1907, two Brahmos from Deoghar, Babu Sukumar Ghosh and Babu Satish Chundra Ghosh, requested the Deputy Commissioner of Santhal Parganas to appoint Dr. Fakir Chandra Sadhudhan, L.M.S., as Marriage Registrar in place of Khetra Mohan Ghosh, who had been transferred from the place.[44] Babu Nalin Bihari Gupta, the Vice-Chairman of Dumraon Municipality, was appointed as Marriage Registrar for the purpose of registering a marriage in the family of Babu Brajendra Kumar Basu in 1908.[45]

The Census Report of 1881 noted the presence of Brahmos in Patna.[46] The Census Report of 1901 mentions their existence in almost all the districts of Bihar.[47] In short, by the end of the nineteenth century, Brahmos could be found in all the important urban centres of Bihar though numerically they were small.

In spite of assiduous propagation for three decades, the tenets of the Brahmo Samaj failed to influence even educated Hindu Biharis significantly. Even Sivanath Sastri lamented, 'yet it is a sad reflection that the mission of the Brahmo Samaj has not touched even the crust of the indigenous population of these provinces.'[48] Very few Bihari Hindus accepted the Brahmo faith, though, as W.W. Hunter noted, many Bihari Hindus were in secret sympathy with it.[49] Bhai Baldeo Narain, who was born near Gaya, and who was serving in the Gaya Collectorate, fell under the spell of Bhakt Hari Sunder Bose while he was preaching at Gaya.[50] The orthodox Bihari Hindu opinion did not view with favour the propagation of Brahmo ideas.

The Brahmos continued to encounter hostility, this is well illustrated by the case of Brahmdeo Narain. When his wife died, he called Bhai Hari Sunder Bose from Bhagalpur and Bhai Dinanath Mazumdar from Patna to perform *shradh*. But both of them along with other Brahmos were forcibly turned out of the house by Bishnudeo Narain, the younger brother of Brahmdeo Narain.[51] At Gaya there was another Bihari Brahmo, Hazariklal. He was employed in the Collectorate and was attracted towards the Brahmo Samaj through the example of Brahmadeo Narain. Later on he was transferred to Bhagalpur, and on the death of his first wife he married a Bengali lady, a daughter of Nav Vidhan missionary Bhai Durga Nath Rai.[52] He later on became Assistant Manager of Bettiah Raj.

Other Biharis who became Brahmos under the influence of Bhakt Hari Sunder were Munshi Rewalal, Babu Bhikharilal, Babu Bajrang Bihari Lal and Babu Bhusan Singh.[53] Bhakt Hari Sunder had written books in Hindi and translated into Hindi some works on the Brahmo Samaj.[54] Munshi Rewalal helped Bhakt Hari Sunder in securing a place for worship when he was refused permission by a Jain gentleman to continue collective worship in his premises,[55] as the house-owner became angry at his disparaging references to idolatry.

Bhai Braj Gopal Niyogi came to Gaya in 1880 and was initiated into Nav Vidhan by Bhakt Hari Sunder in 1884.[56] He initiated Bhai Baldeo Narain and Bhai Ganesh Prasad, two Biharis into the faith.[57] Both of them helped him to run smoothly 'Bidhan Ashram', a hostel for students.[58] Bhai Baldeo Narain was ordained in 1887. He began preaching in Muzaffarpur, but the local Hindus did not view with favour his activities and once garlanded him with shoes.[59] Bhai Baldeo Narain travelled all over India to preach Brahmo ideals.[60] A Bihari Brahmo, Srirang Bihari, was sent by Sivanath Shastri to Presidency College, Calcutta to study for the M.A. in English.[61]

However, some of the Hindus, who never became Brahmos,

sympathized with the new faith. They used to attend its meetings. This was specially true when in 1871 Keshub Chandra Sen toured Patna, Gaya, Bhagalpur and Monghyr. In fact, some of the important preachers of the faith preferred to speak in Hindi in order to communicate effectively with the local population.

An interesting instance of a convert Brahmo is that is that of a Muslim, Azimuddin, who later became an engineer.[62] He stayed with Hari Sunder Bose for two years at Bhagalpur. Unfortunately he died young. Obviously Hari Sunder's knowledge of Persian[63] and his contact with the keeper of the mausoleum of Makhdum Saheb, a Muslim saint of Bihar Sharif,[64] had enabled him to strike a responsive chord in the heart of Azimuddin. He had read the Koran with a Maulvi[65] and was in close contact with Girish Chandra Sen, a Nav Vidhan missionary who made a close and intensive study of Islam and its scriptures.[66]

In fact, both in Gaya and Bhagalpur, Bhakt Hari Sunder had succeeded in creating a compact group of Brahmos who zealously upheld the principles and ideals of the new faith. In Gaya his companions included Bijaya Krishna Goswami,[67] Kishorilal Mitra, Ram Kumar Vidyaratna,[68] Ram Charan Sen, Umesh Chandra Sarkar, Gobind Chandra Rakshit, Chandranath Ghosh, Chandra Nath Chaterjee and Ishan Chandra Sen.[69] Bijaya Krishna Goswami was a close friend of Keshub Chandra Sen, and was primarily responsible for introducing Vaishnava rituals into the Brahmo Samaj. He established an Ashram near the hills in Gaya.[70] Incidentally, all the Brahmos were either government servants or professionals such as lawyers or doctors. In order to keep up the morale of the Brahmos, celebrities of the faith such as Acharyas Trailokya Nath Sanyal,[71] Sadhu Aghore Nath,[72] Girish Chandra Sen,[73] etc., from Calcutta were regularly invited.

After Hari Sunder Basu left for Bhagalpur, Braj Gopal Niyogi, who had been initiated into Nav Vidhan in 1884, became the most active Brahmo in Gaya.[74] He organized the weekly service and collective worship for the local Brahmos.[75] He purchased the bungalow where Bhakt Hari Sunder had established the Nav Vidhan temple.[76] But Braj Gopal Niyogi left for Patna in 1892 when Prakash Chandra Roy invited him to become the headmaster of the newly established girls' school.[77] However, Bhakt Hari Sunder continued to visit Gaya at least twice a year on the occasions of Kristotsav and Chaitanyaotsav and stayed with Braj Gopal Niyogi.[78] The father of Yamini Kant, another distinguished Brahmo who later made the province of Sindh his field of activity, also lived in Gaya.[79] By 1899 the Brahmos of the place had a new place of worship.[80]

Bhagalpur was another important centre for the Brahmos in the province. The Brahmo Samaj was established here on 22 February 1864 by the joint efforts of Braj Kishor Basu, Naba Kumar Roy and Madhusudan Sarkar.[81] Soon this band of Brahmos was joined by Dr. K.D. Ghosh, the father of Aurobindo Ghosh, and his brother Bamacharan Ghosh. On his way to a tour of the N.W. Province towards the end of 1886, Keshub Chandra Sen visited Bhagalpur.[82] The Brahmo activities received impetus with the arrival of Nibaran Chandra Mukherjee in 1868 as the headmaster of the local Zilla School.[83] Of course, Brahmo leaders from Calcutta such as Keshub Chandra Sen,[84] Sivanath Sastri and others had been regularly visiting this place.

Nibaran Chandra Mukherjee managed to create a compact group of Brahmos which included Nakur Chandra Banerjee, Sri Krishna Chatterjee gave up his job and joined the Bhagalpur Bar in 1874 and subsequently became the Law Agent of Banaili Raj, then the biggest zamindari in the district.[85] He called Bhakt Hari Sunder to Bhagalpur in 1887. Hari Sunder took up a new job and settled down there.[86] Of course, Hari Sunder Basu had regularly come to Bhagalpur from Gaya to Participate in festivals celebrated annually in honour of Chaitanya and Christ.[87] Bhagalpur was fortunate that it had intimate relations with another great Brahmo leader, Ram Tanu Lahiri, who visited the city several times in the 1870s and the 1880s and stayed there for long periods.[88] He was able to wean away a local vakil, Atul Chandra Mallik from his addiction to tobacco. In 1879 Rev. Dinanath Mazumdar, a Brahmo preacher, settled down in the town. These persons contributed to the growth of Brahmo activities. Shibchandra Bandopadhyaya, who had been ostracized by orthodox Hindus for visiting England, attached himself to the Brahmos.[89] He donated a piece of land on which the Brahmo Mandir or prayer-hall was constructed in 1880.[90] The temple was inaugurated in 1881 on 11 Phalgun, the anniversary day of the Samaj by Keshub Chandra Sen, who came down for the purpose from Calcutta.[91]

As pointed out earlier, Bhagalpur had a Muslim Brahmo. Another Muslim Brahmo, Qazi Abdul Gafoor, set up medical practice in the city.[92] The vigour of the movement is also attested to by the fact a Bihari Brahmo, Bhai Baldeo Narain preached here in Hindi.[93]

The Brahmos of Bhagalpur kept close contact with those of Patna. In 1884 Mrs. Aghore Kamini attended the Maghotsav at Bhagalpur as a representative of her husband.[94] Rajni Babu along with Gurudas Chakravarti went to Mokameh, Bhagalpur and Monghyr. At Bhagalpur they were received by the Bihari Brahmo, Brahmadeo Narayan, who among other things pleaded for the separation of Bihar from Bengal.[95]

Patna, the chief administrative centre and the most important town, was a prominent centre of Brahmo activities in Bihar. The Samaj was established here in 1866. As it was on the main line of communication, the Brahmo preachers from Calcutta frequently visited the place. When Keshub Chandra Sen left for the Punjab towards the end of December 1866, he stopped at Patna. In 1868 Keshub again visited Patna to meet the Governor-General of India, Lord Lawrence, in order to discuss with him the question of legalizing Brahmo marriages. During one of his visits Keshub Chandra Sen stayed in a villa named 'Rosy Bower', near the Brahmo temple.[96] The Brahmo girls presented before him dances and drama. From 1877 onwards, the Brahmo Samaj organization in Patna was dominated by Prakash Chandra Roy and his wife Mrs. Aghore Kamini Devi. Sivanath Sastri rightly calls him 'the soul of Bankipur Samaj'.[97]

P.C. Roy came to Bihar in 1874 in the service of the government as Relief Superintendent of Famine and was posted to Motihari.[98] He had been already initiated into the Samaj before his arrival in Patna and had stayed with Sivanath Sastri, who eventually became the founder-leader of Sadharan Brahmo

Samaj. At Motihari, P.C. Roy was the only Brahmo, but soon a group of five Brahmos was formed. When a Hindu gave up wearing the sacred thread and became a Brahmo, the orthodox Hindus launched an agitation. After some time Sadhu Aghore Nath, a Brahmo, came to the place and preached. Soon P.C. Roy was transferred to Patna. The couple became the centre of Brahmo activities in the town. They were attached to Keshub Chandra Sen, but their relations with the followers of Sadharan Brahmo Samaj were cordial. From Bankipore, P.C. Roy continued to take interest in the affairs of the Brahmos of Motihari. It was at his instance that the Brahmo missionary Amritlal Basu went to Motihari along with his family.[99]

P.C. Roy, regularly invited reputed Brahmo leaders from Calcutta to preside over functions connected with the life and death cycle rituals such as birth, naming ceremony, marriage, death, etc.[100] Pratap Chandra Mazumdar came to Patna from Calcutta around Christmas every year. He performed *upasna* and preached Brahmo ideals.[101] When he was returning from America after attending the world religious conference, he was accorded a warm welcome at Danapur Railway Station, 14 km from Patna. Amritlal Basu was another frequent visitor from Calcutta. In this manner, these occasions were availed of for the propagation of the Brahmo creed. Dinanath Mazumdar in 1892 made Patna his base for the propagation of Brahmo ideals. Around this time, Kamakhya Nath Banerji came down from Calcutta as a student in the Patna Medical School and actively associated himself with the religious work of P.C. Roy. Among other distinguished Brahmo visitors from Calcutta to Patna in the 1890s was Benoyendra Nath Sen, Professor of History at the Presidency College. Dr. Bimal Chandra Ghosh, a distinguished physician, spoke before a group of young men when he came to meet P.C. Roy. These young men assembled every week to discuss different topics. Dr. Ghosh had earlier visited the city in 1896 to meet the local Brahmos before proceeding to England for higher studies on a state scholarship.[102]

From 1889 onwards P.C. Roy and his wife Aghore Kamini initiated the practice of going to Rajgir after the Maghotsav in the company of other Brahmos.[103] This was extremely daring because a journey of around 40 miles had to be performed by bullock-carts and carts drawn by camels. They continued this practice in 1890, 1891, 1892, 1893, 1894, 1895, etc. Sometimes distinguished Brahmos from Calcutta participated in these trips. These groups consisted of men, women and children.

As was the custom of the supporters of Nav Vidhan, P.C. Roy and Aghore Kamini organized public *kirtans* in the city. The participation of Aghore Kamini in the *kirtans* on the streets of Patna was severely criticized by the Brahmos as well as other Hindus.[104] The orthodox opinion was shocked at the sight of a woman from a respectable family moving in public without covering her face. Mrs. Roy spoke in broken Hindi and Bhai Baldeo Narain also made a speech on the occasion.[105]

In Patna some non-Brahmos were sympathetic to the new faith. The most important among them was Guru Prasad Sen. When Prakash Chandra Roy was discriminated in a public dinner in the house of an orthodox Hindu, by being compelled to eat alone, Guru Prasad Sen immediately raised objections. The orthodox Hindus considered a Brahmo, however, well-educated and well-placed professionally, a social outcaste. One can only imagine the courage and faith displayed by the Brahmos in face of such humiliations and hostility. Sen offered to meet the expenses of the girls' school opened by Mrs. Roy. She did not feel the need to accept Sen's proposal, but Sen along with Amrit Babu and Brajgopal Niyogi rendered a lot of assistance which ensured the smooth functioning of this pioneering institution. As a result, deep intimacy developed between the two families and they exchanged visits. Guru Prasad Sen's daughter-in-law also became a keen supporter of the social welfare activities of Mrs. Roy.

Along with Mr. and Mrs. Roy, the members of the Sadharan Brahmo Samaj actively propagated Brahmoism in Patna. Sivanath Sastri had become well acquainted with Bihar and Brahmos in the province before he broke away from Keshub Chandra Sen. Hence, even after the schism, he made intensive efforts to propagate his faith by undertaking personal trips and sending other prominent missionaries. By 1892 Sadhanashram was established in Calcutta.[106] Soon a branch of the Ashram came into being at Arrah, where a missionary from the Punjab, Bhai Prakash Dev, came and stayed.[107] It is not clear why Arrah was selected for the purpose. Probably its climate was healthy, and there was no competition or hostility from other sections of the Brahmos. But soon the Ashram was shifted to Patna.

The Ashram was put in charge of Gurudas Chakravarti when Prakash Dev became ill. The other members were Satish-chandra Chakravarti, Rajni Kant Guha and Hem Chandra Sarkar.[108] Satishchandra Chakravarti joined in 1896. These Brahmos did not believe in mere preaching. They gave primacy to social welfare activities and regarded these as the principal instrument for taking the message of their faith to the masses. The workers of Sadhanashram dedicated themselves to social and educational work. These young enthusiastic and energetic people helped Sivanath Sastri to run the Rammohun Roy Seminary, which was opened in 1897. During the first year of the existence of the school, Sivanath Sastri visited Patna almost every month to look after the functioning of the school. Patna thus had powerful followers of the Nav Vidhan as well as the Sadhasan Brahmo Samaj, whose dedication helped the faith to leave its mark on the socio-religious and cultural life of the city. From 1897 onwards both the groups came together and began to organize Maghotsav jointly.

Monghyr had been an important centre of Brahmo activities since the town had acquired the reputation of a holy place for the Brahmos because of its intimate association with Keshub Chandra Sen.[109] On his trips to Bihar or north or west India, Keshub frequently visited this place. In 1875 he visited this place with Hari Sundar Bose. After his death, a part of the ashes was brought and buried in the precinct of the Brahmo *mandir.* His memory was perpetuated in the neighbouring township of Jamalpur by naming a street 'Keshubpur' after him.[110] Ram Tanu Lahiri also came to Monghyr along with his family members. Sadhu Aghore Nath too maintained close links with this township.

Hazaribagh was another centre where Brahmo activities started at an early date. The Samaj was established here in 1866. It attracted preachers from Calcutta. From the 1890, when Braja Kumar Niyogi, a nephew of Braj Gopal, settled down in the place where his wife Srimati Chanchala Devi was running a girls' school, the Brahmos became more active. The couple along with Kshitish Chandra Ghosh and a college lecturer of philosophy, Kharag Singh Ghosh, organized important Brahmo functions. They invited people from Calcutta to give discourses and grace the various celebrations. Pramathalal, who had studied theology in Manchester College, regularly came to Hazaribagh from Calcutta to participate in the socio-religious functions. He helped in the establishment of the Nav Vidhan Mandir in Hazaribagh. At Hazaribagh a Bihari, Lal Bajrang Bihari, left a government job to take up missionary work on behalf of the Brahmo Samaj. His son Sri Rang Bihari was also a staunch Brahmo. He later became the headmaster of the Ram-mohun Roy Seminary in Patna.

Originally a branch of the Samaj was established in 1874 at Panchamba, the then headquarters of the Giridih subdivision. But in 1881, Giridih became the subdivisional headquarters. Giridih had a number of Brahmo families. The place was considered to be a health resort by the Bengalis, and some Bengali Brahmo families had constructed houses there. M.M. Bose, the first president of Sadharan Brahmo Samaj, wanted a colony of Brahmos to be established in that place.[111] Dr. N.R. Sarkar, a Brahmo of Calcutta and an eminent physician of the day, decided to build a Brahmo colony. He purchased a large tract of land which had been advertised for sale in 1900 for the purpose. The idea was taken up by other Brahmos and soon in Giridih a colony of the Brahmos developed.[112] However, this colony did not have much impact on the course of the movement in the province, as the local Brahmo population was primarily seasonal.

Several other places in the state also had Brahmo families. We have references to the presence of Brahmos in Dumraon,[113]

Muzaffarpur, Mokameh, Arrah, Sonepore,[114] Aurangabad, Motihari, Deoghar, Madhepura, Ranchi.[115] Sen visited Arrah on 2 December 1879 and addressed a public meeting in the Arrah Zila School, presided over by the District Magistrate. He was followed by several Brahmo preachers. Sivanath Sastri came to the town in 1878, 1894, 1895 and 1896 and established the Brahmo Samaj Ashram which was in 1896 removed to Patna as there were very few adherents in Arrah. In fact, throughout the period, the Brahmo influence had remained confined to certain Bengali Brahmo families, who came to the town in course of the official duties and left it as soon as they were transferred. P.C. Roy, while posted in Arrah, held prayer-meetings in his house, which were attended by a cross-section of the English educated society, both orthodox Hindus and Muslims. After him Dr. Mitra, the Civil Surgeon, remained the most important Brahmo. Raj Narain Bose, the famous Brahmo leader, had settled down in Deoghar in 1879. He lived there till his death in 1899. After his death the work was taken up by Fakirchand Sadhu Khan.

Hence, by the end of the nineteenth century Bihar had become an important centre for the activities of Brahmo missionaries. In 1889 Brahmo missionaries visited twenty-four places in the plains and three in the Chotanagpur region of Bihar. In 1894 missionaries again toured the province. Having outlined the spread of Brahmos in Bihar, it would be interesting to discuss their long and short term impact on the local society.

As the above account shows, very few Biharis, whether Hindus or Muslims, were won over to the faith. Apparently, this was not so because of lack of effort on the part of the Brahmos or Brahmo missionaries; they did their very best to carry the message of their faith to their Bihari brethren. Bhakta Hari Sundar wrote books on the Brahmo mode of worship in Hindi. P.C. Mazoomdar, who had joined the Samaj in 1859 and regularly visited Bihar thereafter, preached in Bengali and Hindi.[116] Bhakta Hari Sundar had learnt Persian in order to be able to talk to the Bihari Kayasthas who were usually well-versed in it. But their success remained insignificant. One cause was that Bihari Hindus were still educationally backward as compared to Bengalis. Although a string of high schools covered some district headquarters, yet by 1880 there was only one college in Bihar. In the 1880s the T.N.J. College (Bhagalpur) and B.N. College (Patna) were established. In the 1890s G.B.B. College (Muzaffarpur), R.D. & D.J. College (Monghyr) and St. Columbas College (Hazaribagh) were started. If we take a look at the list of successful candidates in the B.A. examination between 1864 and 1886 from the Patna College, the first college of the province, it includes 57 Bengali Hindus and 44 non-Bengali Hindus and Mohammedans.[117] The majority of graduates were Bengalis. The Muslims of the province had taken to Western education in larger numbers than Bihari Hindus. In the Survey School of Patna, in 1875, there were 21 Muslims among 37 pupils. In the Temple Medical School, out of 165 students 75 per cent were Muslims.[118] The Brahmo Samaj, whose followers were mainly Western-educated persons in Bengal, did not thus have an adequate recruiting base among Bihari Hindus, who were unable to appreciate and were not enamored of the highly philosophical doctrines of the Brahmo Samaj. To them, Brahmo doctrines appeared to be a pale imitation of Christianity, the religion of the conquerors, and hence anathema. In reaction, Biharis sometimes tended to be extreme conservatives, however, under the impact of Western education, occasionally they tried to strike a compromise. They were attracted by the Arya Samaj with its easily intelligible doctrines, viz., back to the Vedas, attack on the caste system and anti-idolatry and anti-Christian stance. In this phase, when the educated urban Hindu still had deep rural roots, not religious radicalism but reformism was more popular with him.

The failure of the Brahmo Samaj to win a large number of followers to its fold in Bihar in the second half of the nineteenth century should not lead us to conclude that it was totally ineffective. Socially, the Brahmo Samaj exercised a beneficial influence. From 1860s the Brahmo Samaj had deliberately made social reforms an integral part of its creed, it advocated social practices such as intercaste and widow marriages, interdining and equality of sexes, and it championed the spread of Western education. The Brahmos did not merely preach but actively pursued these ideals. In 1862 the first intercaste marriage among the Brahmos had taken place.[119] In August 1864, another intercaste marriage was performed in which the bride was a widow.[120] In 1865 Keshuv Chandra Sen insisted that three reforms – of idolatry, caste and marriage customs – were vital for the regeneration of Hindu society.[121] In effect, the Brahmo Samaj now stood forth as a champion of all-round social change rather than a propagator of merely reformed religious ideas. Social change rather then religious reform became the principal Brahmo creed. Henceforth the Brahmos initiated, both by their preaching and example, significant changes in society. The spread of Brahmoism was accompanied by a number of initiatives in the field of social reforms by the Brahmos.

The most important Brahmo initiative was in the sphere of Western education. Wherever they were, they opened schools, teaching English and imparting knowledge of Western sciences along with other subjects. In many instances they met the expenses of these institutions from their own pockets, besides working there as teachers. Rammohun Roy Seminary, a high school, was started in November 1897 by a band of Brahmo Samajists at Patna. In Gaya, Bhakta Hari Sundar established a school called the Cheap School. The poor students paid a monthly fee of only 1 *anna* (6 paise in terms of the present day currency) and those who were affluent were charged only 4 *annas* per month. Another famous Brahmo, Bhai Braja Gopal Niyogi was also employed in this school.[122] Many of the teachers in high schools and colleges were Brahmos from Bengal. Besides the government, the Brahmos were the most effective agency for propagating Western education. The Brahmos not only attacked the caste system in theory but consciously tried to improve the social and cultural status of the untouchables and other depressed castes. Sivanath Sastri, who established the Sadharan Brahmo Samaj, worked among the Namasudras of Dacca.[123] Braja Gopal Niyogi opened a school in the bustee of scavengers situated on the Murli hills in Gaya in order to educate them.

When Braja Gopal Niyogi moved to Patna, to help Mrs. P.C. Roy run the Bankipur girls' school, he started Sunday School where English and Sanskrit were taught. His principal companion in this task was Kamakhya Nath Banerji. Similarly, members of Sadhanashram at Patna established a night-school for workers in 1899, and tried to organize welfare services for students.[124] The Brahmos in Monghyr organized a night school. They also ran a well-equipped library for the use of students. The Brahmos strove to spread Western education among the various sections of society. The importance of this service can hardly be over-estimated.

The Brahmo Samajists stood for the emancipation of women folk from traditional handicaps. When Keshub started the Female Improvement section, the Bengalis of Bihar including Brahmos became its members and regularly contributed money for its various activities. A look at the list shows that the contributors came from several towns of Bihar such as Monghyr, Bhagalpur, Jamalpur, Bankipur (Patna), Dinapur, Gaya, Nawada, Hazaribagh, Sherghati, Mokamah.[125] In one instance, the students of Patna College collected money and donated it to the charity section.

For improving the status and the condition of the women, the Brahmos took a number of steps. One of their songs said 'without the awakening of Indian women, India would not progress'. Braja Gopal insisted that for a bright future of the country 'disciplined and educated girls' were necessary. In pursuit of this objective, some Brahmo young men of Bhagalpur started in 1863 the Bhagalpur Mahila Samiti, the first organization exclusively concerned with the uplift of women in the province. When K.D. Ghosh, came to Bhagalpur in 1866, the movement for propagating education among women received further impetus.

Keshub had already made female emancipation an integral part of the Brahmo movement. They attached the greatest importance to education as an instrument of social change and transformation. Hence the Brahmos made determined efforts to educate the women-folk, Harisundar Bose opened a school for girls in Gaya with which Braja Gopal Niyogi was actively associated. By 1881 Mrs. P.C. Roy in Patna had been convinced that a change in the status of women was urgently called for and for this they should be educated.[126] She decided to open a school for girls in Patna. She realized that she was not adequately equipped to run an educational institution, because of lack of proper training. It speaks volumes for the courage, determination and dedication of Mrs. P.C. Roy that in spite of being the mother of five children she joined I.T. College, Lucknow, run by Christian missionaries in 1891. She stayed in the hostel for one complete session, lived the life of an ordinary hosteller submitted to the discipline, rules and regulations of the place, studied Hindi and English, and acquired the necessary training for establishing a girls' educational institution. She came back after a stay of nine months on 15 December 1891 and opened the Bankipore Girls' School.

The initial local response was of complete indifference. People would not send their daughters or sisters, as they were unwilling to expose their faces to public gaze. But Mrs. Roy never lost heart. Ten small girls took admission at the outset! Even these girls had to be brought from their homes. Soon the number rose to twenty-nine, and some non-Bengali girls also joined. She had to move from house to house to persuade parents to send their daughters to the institution. She called Braja Gopal Niyogi to help her in running the school, and he remained associated with it for five years. Among the non-Brahmos, Guru Prasad Sen took keen interest in the functioning of the school. When parents showed unwillingness to send their daughters to the school because it would violate the *purdah* system, Mrs. Roy opened a hostel inside her own house – Chhatri Niwas[127] – so that the girls would not give up their education. It became a viable institution and the torch-bearer of women's education in the state. It might also be noted that the Roy couple was often financially quite hard up. In one instance they sold a shawl for 4 *annas* and in another the chain of a pocket watch.[128]

The Interest shown by non-Bengali girls in education, though still lukewarm, should nevertheless be regarded as a major break

through, because in 1881 at a prize-distribution ceremony the
Report read by Mr. Eubank stated that '*only one Bihari girl
had entered in the last fourteen years* (i.e. since 1867) *but she
too had left*' (emphasis added).[129] In Bhagalpur the picture of
female education was similarly dismal. In 1874 there was only
one unaided girls school. Out of fourteen students only one was
Bihari. The rest were Bengali girls.[130]

Gurudas Chakravarty, who headed the Sadhanashram
of Sadharan Brahmo Samaj at Patna, took keen interest in
the promotion of female education. Another Brahmo lady,
Shrimati Chanchala Devi, a relation of Braja Gopal Niyogi, ran
a girls' school in Hazaribagh. The Brahmo example of allowing
womenfolk to receive education on par with men set the
Biharis thinking. The Brahmos preached widow-remarriage.
P.C. Roy conducted the rites when a widow remarriage took
place at Patna.[131] The orthodox Hindu opinion reacted sharply
and *Bihar-Bandhu* a Hindi journal in 1894 sharply criticized
them.[132]

At least indirectly the social reform movements amongst
the Kayastha and Bhumihar Brahmans, who were the first to
take to Western education in Bihar, might be traced back to
the influence of the Brahmo Samaj.[133] The Brahmos were in the
forefront in other spheres of social reform as well. Gurudas
Chakravarti took keen interest in the working of the Patna
Total Abstinence Society, formed to discourage the drinking
habit.[134] He gave wholehearted cooperation to the effort to shift
brothels from the vicinity of Patna College and Rammohun Roy
Seminary. In fact, Brahmos combined deep humanism with the
task of social reform. They were moved by human suffering and
tried to do their bit in alleviating it in their own way.

Service to man and welfare of humanity was their creed. The
nursing of the sick was considered a part of their duty. One can
visualize the great sacrifice of the Brahmos when we remember
that in those days epidemics like cholera and plague were
frequent, and one had practically no immunization against
infectious diseases. But these Brahmos, both men and women,
considered it their duty to look after the diseased without any

discrimination of sex, religion or economic status.[135] Members of Sadhanashram gave relief to plague-stricken people of Patna by visiting the houses of the sick and removing them to hospital. They disinfected the houses and gave medicines to the needy.[136]

Even when sickness befell an individual who had no one to look after him, the Brahmos considered it their duty to nurse him. In one case Mrs. P.C. Roy took home a member of a circus party, who had fallen ill from typhoid and had been completely abandoned by his colleagues. She nursed him back to health. In another case, she went to attend a sick person at 2 a.m. in the night. We came across many instances when Mrs. Roy served the sick without any distinction of caste or religion.[137]

When famine broke out in the years 1897 and 1900 in Madhya Pradesh, Braja Gopal Niyogi went there for relief work. He took some Brahmos and stayed there for two months.[138] Two years later, the same place was again visited by a famine and Braja Gopal Niyogi again undertook relief operations. In 1897 members of Sadhanashram opened relief operations for the famine stricken people of Jagdishpur and Dumri in the Santhal Parganas.[139] For the poor, the Brahmos showed deep concern. Mrs. Roy collected clothes for the needy: when she found people in distress otherwise also, she tried to be helpful.[140]

The Brahmos stood for religious toleration. Keshub had stated, 'No sect shall be vilified, ridiculed or hated. No prayer, hymn, sermon, or discourse to be delivered or used here shall countenance or encourage any manner of idolatry, sectarianism or sin.... '[141] Harisundar Basu, while working for a lady zamindar in Bihar Sharif, met the head of the Khanquah of Makhdum Saheb in company of another Brahmo, Girish Chandra Sen, and obtained some of his letters. Girish Chandra Sen translated them into Bengali, and Hari Sunder Basu printed and published them in Gaya.[142] He studied the Koran with the help of a Maulvi.

The Brahmo Samaj also provided a forum for the local intelligentsia to meet on a common platform. Thus the Brahmo Samaj in Hazaribagh was established in 1867 as a result of the effort of Sri J.N. Mukherjee, himself a non-Brahmo. While he lived, he took keen interest in its functioning.[143] It was a Brahmo sympathizer, Guru Prasad Sen, who laid the foundations of English journalism in Bihar by bringing out a newspaper, the *Behar Herald* in 1875 from Patna. Happily the paper is still being published. Even non-Bengali Hindus associated themselves with some of the Brahmo festivals. Babu Bisheshwar Singh, another Bihari Hindu, invited Brahmos to hold their festivals at his residences.[144] Rajni Babu acted as tutor to the wards of several distinguished Biharis.[145]

Mrs. P.C. Roy decided to discard *purdah* and sought to sit with the men-folk during their prayers.[146] From Patna she went to Hilsa in an open carriage without covering her face.[147] Of course, she was ridiculed, but she did not budge from her mission. Thus not only the *purdah* system was given up among the Brahmos, but the women-folk earned the right to associate themselves publicity with men-folk on social and religious occasions. She thereafter regularly led groups of Brahmos, both male and female, to Rajgir and other places.[148] In Rajgir the Brahmo girls sang *kirtan* in the market place. She repeated this a number of times. She even put girls on the stage when a dramatic performance was organized to celebrate Maghotsav. Maybe it was the time that women appeared on the stage at Patna. For the courage in defying *purdah*, Mrs. Roy was vehemently criticized by her contemporaries. At one point some detractors even compared her conduct with that of 'women of the street'.[149]

On the question of caste, the Brahmos took an openly defiant stand. Mrs. P.C. Roy married her daughter in 1884 to a boy belonging to a lower caste, despite opposition from family members and friends. In fact the event provoked some Brahmos to renounce Brahmoism, but Mrs. Roy remained firm.[150] A sympathizer even threatened to 'horse-whip' P.C. Roy for having dared to marry his daughter to a man of a different caste. Even his mother left his house out of anger.

In short, the Brahmo Samaj as a religious movement did not substantially affect the Bihari Hindu community. A facile explanation would be that Bihar still lacked the milieu in which teachings of Brahmoism could be acceptable to a wide segment of society. It had a very thin layer of English-educated persons, and consequently of professionals such as engineers, doctors, lawyers, bureaucrats, clerks, etc., and teachers (both belonging to school and college) who constituted the main bulk of the adherents of the Samaj in Bengal, where it had the largest following. Therefore the faith failed to make headway. Furthermore, the Biharis did not feel very happy about the Brahmo mode of worship, which resembled that of service of the Christians. It remained them of Christianity, the religion of alien rulers, and they feared that it was nothing but the thin wedge of Christianity to undermine their religion. They felt repelled at the personal conduct of some of the Brahmos, who had taken to drinking and flaunting their disregard of all caste taboos, by interdining, intercaste marriages, taking out their women-folk in the open, etc. Even some of the contemporary Europeans with all their desire for modernization of the Indians disliked the conduct of these Brahmos.[151]

Furthermore, when Brahmoism was propagated in Bihar, it had to compete with emerging movements such as the Arya Samaj, the Theosophical Society, the Ram Krishna Mission – all of which tried to combine modernity with tradition, and as such attracted the attention of English-educated Biharis. Hence, the Brahmo Samaj did not have the entire field left to itself as a modernizing movement, as was the case in Bengal when it began its career.

Finally, bereft of the support of the newly educated elite, the movement failed to draw within its fold even a single big zamindar in the province, and thus could not even make a dent in the bastion of traditional leadership. A movement like the Brahmo Samaj, with its high intellectual overtones for its wider propagation, needed an environment in which intellectual skepticism had emerged, and the new elite was prepared to show its solidarity with the new ideology.

Nevertheless the social content of the movement had a demonstrative effect and it gave new orientation to the emerging Hindu intelligentsia in the province by putting up a model which could be imitated in its course of modernization. As Gordon points out, 'Work in the Brahmo Samaj prepared men for public life, imbued them with the idea of selfless labour, and suggested to them that reformed Indian traditions might have some special role to play in meeting the needs of modern man.'[152]

Acceptance of change and denial of *status quo* were two ideals imbibed from the Brahmos. The need of the hour was to induce an attitude which would discard immobilism and accept dynamism. Thus the Brahmo Samaj did succeed in introducing these values though to a limited extent only.

NOTES

1. Sivanath Sastri, 'Rammohun Roy: The Story of his Life', in *The Father of Modern India: Commemoration Volume of the Rammohun Roy Centenary Celebrations*, Calcutta, 1933. Rammohun Roy and Kissory Chand Mitter, *Rammohun Roy and Tuhfatul Meshwahhiddin*, Calcutta, 1975, 6-7; M.C. Kotnala, *Rammohun Roy and Indian Awakening*, Delhi, 1975, 15. The Raja came to Patna around 1780.

2. R.R. Diwakar, ed., *Bihar through the Ages*, Patna, 1958, 677. Rammohun Roy was in Ramgarh from 1805 to 1807, and in Bhagalpur from 1808 to 1809.

3. This is illustrated by the professions of some of the prominent Brahmos of Bihar, as follows: P.C. Roy, Deputy Magistrate, Patna; Hari Sundar Bose, Postmaster, Gaya; Krishna Gopal Ghose, Assistant Surgeon, Bhagalpur; Prosonno Kumar Sen, E.I. Railway, Monghyr.

4. John Campbell Oman, *The Brahmans, Theists and Muslims of India* Delhi, 1973, 113-14.

5. David Kopf, 'The Universal Man and the Yellow Dog: The Orientalist Legacy and the Problem of Brahmo Identity in the Bengal Renaissance', in Rachel van M. Baumer ed., *Aspects of Bengali History and Society*, Delhi, 1976, 53.

6. Anon, *Keshub Charit* (n.p., n.d.), 135.

7. Ibid., 136

8. Sushma Sen, *Memoires of an Octogenarian*, Delhi, 1971, 3.

9. *Keshub Charit*, 136-7.

10. Ibid., 387.

11. M.C. Parekh, *The Brahma Samaj*, Kathiawad, 1929.

12. N. Niyogi, *The Apostles and Missionaries of the Navavidhan*, Calcutta, n.d., 533.

13. W.W. Hunter, *A Statistical Account of Bengal*, XV, London, 1877, 59,

14. Oman, 122.
15. *Land Revenue Proceedings,* no. 48, May 1870; no. 49, May 1870; no. 59, August 1870, no. 63, April 1871 and no. 64, April 1871.
16. Niyogi, 31.
17. Ibid., 37.
18. Ibid., 38.
19. Ibid.,
20. Punyamoy Sen, 'Hundred Years of Hazaribagh Brahmo Samaj', *The Searchlight,* 30 April 1967. W.W. Hunter, however, gives the year of establishment as 1866, cf. Hunter, XVI, 85.
21. Ecclesiastical Proceedings, 1-8, June 1872 (hereafter referred to as Eccl. Progs.). Oman, 120.
22. Eccl. Progs, A, 1-8, June 1872.
23. Sivanath Sastri, *Atma Charita* (in Bengali), Culcutta, 1359 BS, 157.
24. Ibid., 158. It appears that the town had a good Bengali population.
25. Hunter, XIII, 249.
26. *Atma Charita,* 157.
27. Ibid.
28. Ibid., 166.
29. Ibid., 167.
30. We have no details about Brajendra Kumar Basu. He might have been in the service of the local zamindar, who was amongst the biggest zamindars of the province.
31. *Atma Charita,* 167. A high school named after T.K. Ghosh still functions in Patna, and includes among its alumni Sachchidanand Sinha, first president of the Indian Constituent Assembly.
32. Ibid., 180-1. The Arya Samaj was established in 1875 in Bombay.
33. *The Apostles and Missionaries of the Navavidhan,* 67.
34. V.S. Sohoni and B.B. Keskar, eds., *Spiritual Powerhouse,* Bombay, 1940, 280.
35. *Comprehensive History of Bihar,* III/3, 9.
36. Rajni Kant Guha, *Atma Charita* (in Bengali), 303-4.
37. Ibid., 304-5.
38. Eccl. File, 3, Progs. B, nos. 1-3, June 1886.
39. Eccl. File, 3A-2, Progs. B, nos. 3-5, July 1900.
40. Eccl. File, 3A-1, Progs. B, nos. 10-12, April 1901.
41. Eccl. File, 3A-1, Progs. B, nos. 6-8, October 1904.
42. Eccl. Progs. B, nos. 1-3, 10 November 1906.
43. Ibid., Notification no. 2573, 10 November 1906.
44. Eccl. Progs. B, nos. 75-8, May 1907.
45. Eccl. File, 3A-1, Progs. B, nos. 7-9, May 1908.
46. *Report of the Census of Bengal,* II (1881), 22-3.

47. *Census of India 1901*, VII, Bengal, pt. II, 26.
48. *History of Brahmo Samaj*, 524.
49. Hunter, XII, 41.
50. Satya Sundar Basu, *Bhakta Hari Sundar Basu Mahasaya Charit-Katha*, Calcutta, 1350 BS, 30.
51. Basu, 30-1.
52. Ibid., 31.
53. Ibid., 38. Babu Bajrang Bihari offered to work as a missionary in 1887; unfortunately he died in 1888.
54. Ibid.
55. Ibid., 12.
56. Niranjan Niyogi, *Brajgopal Tamshatvarshiki Shradeya Bhai Brijgopal Niyogi*, Calcutta, 1957, 3.
57. Ibid., 5.
58. Ibid., 6.
59. *The Apostles and Missionaries*, 63.
60. *History of Brahmo Samaj*, 529.
61. Satish Chandra Chakravarti, Sivanath Sastri, Calcutta, 1375 BS, 86.
62. Bax, 30.
63. Ibid., 15.
64. Ibid., 17.
65. Ibid., 18.
66. Ibid.
67. Ibid., 27.
68. Ibid., 29.
69. Ibid., 11.
70. Ibid., 27.
71. Ibid., 10.
72. Ibid., 32.
73. Ibid., 16.
74. Niyogi, 3.
75. Ibid.
76. Basu, 13.
77. Niyogi, 4.
78. Niranjan Niyogi, *Smritir-Gawrab-Smritir Saurabh*, Calcutta, 1969, 169.
79. Ibid., 254-6.
80. Guha, 330-1.
81. Nibran Chandra Mukherjee, *Brahmattatva*, Calcutta, 1931, 25; however, Sivanath Sastri gives the date as 1863, *History of Brahmo Samaj*, 524, 535.

82. Sastri, ibid., 135.
83. Mukherjee, 25.
84. *History of Brahmo Samaj*, 142.
85. Ibid., 30.
86. Basu, 37. Mukherjee (30) gives the date of arrival of Harisundar Basu as 1887.
87. *Smritir Gaurab-Smritir Saurabh*, 285.
88. Ram Tanu Lahiri, *Tatkalin Banj Samaj*, 320, 326, 333. Another important Brahmo visitor to Bhagalpur was Raj Narain Bose, a close collaborator of Maharshi Devendra Nath Tagore.
89. Basu, 32.
90. Mukherjee, 25.
91. Ibid., P.C. Ray Chaudury, ed., *District Gazetteer, Bhagalpur*, Patna, 1962, 119-20.
92. Mukherjee, 35.
93. Ibid.
94. P.C. Roy, *Aghor Prakash*, Calcutta, 1922, 50.
95. Guha, 303-4.
96. *Smritir Gaurab-Smritir Saurabh*, 293.
97. *History of Brahmo Samaj*, 527.
98. Roy, 22.
99. Ibid., 57.
100. Ibid., 40, 41, 44.
101. *Smritir Gaurab-Smritir Saurabh*, 93.
102. Prabhat Basu, *Doctor Bimalchandra Ghoser Jivan Kotha* (in Bengali) 16-17.
103. Roy, 70.
104. *Smritir Gaurab-Smritir Saurabh*, 141, 142.
105. Ibid., 142. Other Brahmo preachers were using Hindi and Urdu to put across their message to the non-Bengali population. Mention may be made of Hari Sundar Bose and P.C. Mazumdar. They published journals in these languages. For details see below, and S. Gopal, 'The Roots of Casteism and Conservatism: A Study of Social Change in Bihar in the Second Half of the Nineteenth Century', *Journal of the Bihar Puravid Parishad*, vols. IV-V, 152-67.
106. *History of Brahmo Samaj*, 327.
107. Ibid., 334; Sohoni and Keskar, p. 494.
108. Sudharkana Chakravarty comp., *Srishchandra Chakravarty Sradharghya*, Calcutta, 1361 BS, 8.
109. P.K. Sen, *Keshub Chandra Sen*, Calcutta, 1938, 68.
110. P.C. Roy Chaudhary, ed., *District Gazetteer, Monghyr*, Patna, 1960, 376.

111. Ranjita Kundu, *Shishu Sahitya Bhagirath Yogindra Nath Sarkar*, Calcutta, n.d., pt. II, 14.
112. Ibid., 21; *History of Brahmo Samaj*, 523.
113. Roy, 41; Keshub Chandra Sen had visited the place in 1879, and meditated there. He was received by the Raja of Dumraon, a big landlord, who made large monetary donations to him, but he failed to make many converts. P.C. Roy Chaudhary, ed., *District Gazetteers of Bihar, Shahabad*, Patna, 1966, 166.
114. *History of Brahmo Samaj*, 222. Lahiri, 287.
115. *History of Brahmo Samaj*, 222. Satyendra Nath Tagore, ICS, a Brahmo after his retirement, constructed a house at Ranchi. He was the son of the great Brahmo leader Devendra Nath Tagore, and elder brother of the poet Rabindra Nath Tagore. P.N. Bose, another Brahmo and an eminent geologist and indologist, also constructed his house and spent his remaining life there. Sushma Sen, p. iii.
116. P.C. Mazumdar, *Heart Beats*, Calcutta, 1935, xxxi.
117. *Patna University Golden Jubilee Souvenir*, Patna, 1970, 5, 355-6.
118. *Bihar Herald (Centenary Number)*, 69.
119. Prem Sundar Basu, *Brahmananda Keshav*, pt. I, Bhagalpur, n.d., 107.
120. Ibid., 144.
121. Ibid., 122.
122. Niranjan Niyogi, *Brajgopal Janmshatvarshiki* (in Bengali), Calcutta, 1957, 17.
123. Manmathnath Gupt, *Acharya Sivanath* (in Bengali), Calcutta, n.d., 36.
124. *History of Brahmo Samaj*, 343.
125. P.K. Sen, *Biography of a New Faith*, II, Calcutta, 1954, 330-41 *passim*.
126. Roy, 41.
127. *Smritir Gaurab-Smritir Saurabh*, 135; Roy, 143.
128. *Nivedan-Svargiya Prakashchandra Roy Mahasayer Updesh O Prarthna*, Calcutta, n.d., 12, 13; Roy, 146.
129. *Bihar Bandhu*, 18 August 1881.
130. Jharkhandi Jha, *Bhagalpur Darpan* (in Hindi) I, pt. I, Vaijani/ Bhagalpur, 1933, 128.
131. Roy, 68.
132. *Bihar Bandhu*, 7 August 1894.
133. The social reform movement among the Kayasthas began in 1889 when the first Kayastha conference took place at Patna. From 1898 caste conferences of Bhumihar Brahmans also started taking place. In 1900 a Bhumihar Brahman from Muzaffarpur married according to Brahmo Samaj custom (Letter to the Editor, *The Bihar Times*, 4 March 1900).

134. *History of Brahmo Samaj*, 343.

135. *Smritir Gaurab-Smritir Saurabh*, 159.

136. *History of Brahmo Samaj*, 369; Guha, 354-5.

137. Roy, 171-3.

138. *Brajgopal Janmashatvarshiki*, 16.

139. *History of Brahmo Samaj*, 336.

140. Roy 184, 186.

141. Cited in Kopf, 59.

142. Satyasundar Basu, 17.

143. Sen, 'Hundred years of Hazaribagh Brahmo Samaj', *The Searchlight*, 30 April 1967.

144. Guha, 331.

145. Ibid., 326, 331.

146. Roy, 41.

147. Ibid., 79.

148. Ibid., 70, 76.

149. Ibid., 183.

150. Ibid., 53.

151. 'It is true that some few members of the Brahmo Samaj – that is, the new Deist religion – have thrown off the trammels of caste openly, and are glad to frequent the European society; and many of them, unfortunately, in consequence of the removal of caste restraint, have become dissolute and drunken, and their society is not desirable'. An Ex-Civilian, *Life in the Mofussil or the Civilian in Lower Bengal*, London, n.d., 147.

152. Leonard A. Gordon, *Bengal: The Nationalist Movement 1876-1940*, Delhi, 1974, 23.

CHAPTER 11

Swami Dayanand, Bihar and Arya Samaj

An intellectual awakening in India in the second half of the nineteenth century consequent upon the spread of new education, awareness of natural sciences, machine dominated technology, and a sense of combativeness against the Western civilization resulted in intense questioning and/or affirmation, modification of tradition as reflected in religions, beliefs, customs, manners and style of everyday living. The position taken up by the newly emerging leadership varied from total rejection of the tradition to compromise and integration with the new forces as well as reaffirmation of the old order. The intellectual ferment touched in varying degrees almost all parts of India and all the major religious communities. One message which evoked significant response in the Hindi heartland was that of Swami Dayanand, the founder of Arya Samaj in 1875.

It is interesting to note that Swamiji establishing his organization had taken care to prepare the ground for this momentous step by extensively visiting the different parts of the country and by evaluating the response and reaction to his ideas which he placed before his audiences. Keeping this in view, it is not surprising that Swami Dayanand paid first visit to Bihar, the eastern fringe of the Hindi heartland, and a very populous area several years before he established the organization Arya Samaj.

Swamiji entered Bihar in 1872 from Varanasi and halted in Dumraon, then the seat of an old and important zamindari in Bihar. He stayed with the Udasi saint Naga Baba.[1] It seems to me that his visit to Dumraon was well thought out; Dumraon was one of the biggest zamindaris in Bihar and the support of its chief would have certainly helped in garnering further local support. Secondly, the two zamindars of Dumraon, Maheshwar

Singh and Raja Radhapraksh who were at the helm of affairs between 1843 and 1894 were fairly liberal in outlook. Raja Radhaprakash described as 'nature's gentleman'[2] took into his service followers of Brahmo Samaj and from time to time he welcomed Brahmo preachers at his court.[3] He was therefore familiar with attitudes opposed to traditional religious beliefs and practices. Furthermore, the need for efficiently managing the zamindari had compelled him to employ Bihari officials who had received the new education to superior positions. They included liberals, such as Harbans Rai, Jai Prakash Lal,[4] etc. Hence, Swamiji was assured of a cordial welcome and a patient hearing of his views.

Swamiji was asked to expound his religious tenets by entering into a religious disputation with Khaki Baba,[5] a venerable saint of the area and a known supporter of Hindu orthodoxy. It is said that the logic of Dayanand's arguments was unassailable and victory remained with Dayanand. We have no details of the discussion but Dayanand's forceful exposition must have impressed and caused consternation among the orthodox section since sometime later, Khaki Baba published and circulated a pamphlet entitled *'Swami Dayanand Ki Parajay'* (Defeats of Swami Dayanand).[6] However, at the same time, Swamiji must have won for himself love and respect of the Bihari intelligentsia for he was invited to the nearby town of Arrah, the district headquarter, where there was a concentration of educated Hindus: administrative functionaries, lawyers, doctors, teachers, etc.

At Arrah, Swami Dayanand stayed with Sri Harbans Rai at the garden house of Dumraon Raj.[7] He gave two public lectures in which he denounced idol-worship, *shradh* (funerary rites) performed after the death of Hindu, child-marriages and a local orthodox Saint Kanphukwa Guru.[8] He also spoke at a public meeting held in the local school.[9]

The orthodox section was appalled; the local traditional Brahmin priests Pandit Rudradutta and Pandit Chandradatta took up cudgels on behalf of the conservative Hindus and challenged Swamiji to a religious disputation. Once again,

Swamiji's knowledge of Hindu scriptures and eloquence overwhelmed his opponents. His two successive successes must have won him public esteem and Swamiji decided to set up an organization in the town to propagate his view on social and religious ills afflicting the Hindu society.[10] The organization did not last; we do not know what led to its failure, its significance lie in the fact *that it was the first public organization set up by Swami Dayanand in Bihar.*

The immediate and positive public response the message of Swamiji was primarily due to the presence of a small group of intellectuals among the Hindus, already exposed to the new education and the new socio-religious forces sweeping across the nineteenth and the early twentieth centuries. Mention may be made of Bisheshwar Singh, Saligram Singh, Raja Rajeshwari Prasad Sinha, Sir Jwala Prasad, Sachchidanand Sinha,[11] etc. Some of them actively associated themselves with the Indian National Congress in the nineteenth century. Thus when Swami Dayanand visited Arrah, the mind of the educated section of the local residents was prepared to listen to views and ideas, critical of several prevailing socio-religious practices.

From Arrah, Swami Dayanand arrived in Patna, the largest town and the chief educational, administrative and economic centre in Bihar. Here his host was Sawanmal, Deputy Magistrate and a well educated individual.[12] It may be noted that his primary supporters at this stage were those who had received the new education and were conscious of the winds of change blowing over the country.

Swamiji stayed in a garden called Bhup Singh's Bagh, situated near the ruins of the historic Pataliputra and Agam Kuan.

At Patna, Swami Dayanand delivered talks and lectures on the Vedas and their salient features. Here again, he was queried, questioned, assailed and hailed by the audience. An orthodox group led by the local Pandit Ramjivan Bhatt challenged him.[13] It is reported that Dayanand's arguments could not be countered and the Pandit and his followers left in a huff.[14] Among those who came to listen to the lectures of Swamiji were Sri Guru Prasad Sen,[15] a distinguished lawyer and a well-known citizen,

Pandit Ramavatar Tiwary, and Pandit Chhotelal Sarawat, etc. Ramnath Tiwary,[16] a student of Patna Normal School, who attended these discourses, was so much impressed that he decided to leave everything and stay with Swamiji and help him in the propagation of his ideals. Swamiji also spoke at a meeting held in the Patna Normal School.[17]

The point to note is that the educated section of the population was taking notice of the activities of Swamiji and hence the leaders of Hindu orthodoxy could not also ignore him.

Another incident during his stay in Patna is worth recalling. A group of Maithil Pandits, known for their mastery over Sanskrit language, grammer, literature philosophy, etc., took objection to his criticism of the *Bhagvat*. They contended that presently none could write eighteen thousand couplets contained in the work. Swamiji retorted by saying that he could compose thirty-eight thousand such couplets. The Pandits asked him to compose some on the theme 'Juta-Kharaon Ka Samvad' (dialogue between shoes and wooden slippers), Swamiji instantly composed and he recited some couplets and Pandits left being deeply impressed by his command over the Sanskrit language and grammar.[18]

In short throughout his stay, he drew the local intelligentsia to himself and impressed them through his scholarship.

While in Patna he also met with a local Hindu scholars of Arabic, Munshi Manohar Lal (resident of Gurhatta mohalla in Patna City) who translated for him the Koran into Hindi. Swamiji acknowledged this help in his preface to the first edition of his *magnum opus, Satya Prakash,* published from Moradabad. He wrote that 'the fourteenth chapter of the work was composed after consulting the translation of the Koran prepared by Munshi Manohar Lal of Patna City'.[19]

It could be safely said that Swamiji's stay in Bihar did help him sharpen his outlook on socio-religious questions and at the same time won for him a name among the local intelligentsia.

Swamiji left Patna City on 30 November 1872 and arrived in Munger, another town situated on the banks of the river Ganges. He stayed in a Kabir Math and during his stay of four days, he delivered four lectures on different topics. Mauni Sadhu, leader of the orthodox Hindus, entered into a religious disputation with him, but ultimately he had no answer to the arguments advanced by Swamiji.[20]

A subsequent local follower of Arya Samaj, Dr. Kartiki Prasad Deo purchased the piece of land where Swamiji had delivered his lectures and constructed a palatial building for the local office of the Arya Samaj.[21]

From Munger, Swamiji arrived in Bhagalpur, another town of Bihar on the banks of the river Ganges. He stayed in the temple of Yudhistharnath near the Chhapatia pond, situated in the Mirjan Hat mohalla.

Bhagalpur had a fair number of educated Indians including some Bengalis, who were keenly interested in socio-religious reforms. Some of them had become ardent followers of Brahmoism, another protestant faith of Hinduism, which had originated in the neighbouring province of Bengal only about four decades back. Hence, the local audience, already familiar with protestant views of reformers, listened to Swamiji's discourses and lectures with rapt attention. No one came forward to challenge Swamiji for holding a religious disputation. Nibaran Chandra Mukhopadhyay,[22] an eminent Bengali resident of the town and an ardent Brahmo, invited Swamiji to deliver a lecture on 'Duties of Man'.[23] In course of the lecture, Swamiji touched upon the futility of rituals such as *shradh* and *tarpan* performed after the death of a Hindu by his relations. The local Bengali residents were highly impressed by Swamiji's speeches in simple Sanskrit. A deeply-impressed Bengali Brahman, who had turned Christian, confessed to Swamiji that had he listened to his discourses earlier, he would not have given up his original religion.[24]

Swamiji was also invited by the zamindar of Banaili, an orthodox Brahmin and the largest zamindar in the district. Swamiji spoke to him about the harmful effects of polygamy. The zamindar, Nitya Nand Singh, was advised to use medicines if he desired to sire children.[25]

Swamiji once again showed how far he had moved away from

orthodoxy when he invited a Muslim Maulvi to sit near him even when eatables were kept there.[26]

Swamiji's simplicity and catholicity of outlook was noted by members of other faith as well.

Swamiji used to get his food from a businessman. He, however, discovered that the businessman was really interested in being blessed with a son through his blessings. Hence, he stopped taking the food sent by him.[27]

Swamiji's anguish was great when he witnessed Hindu orthodox practices performed on the banks of the Ganges for the dead. It is said that he refused to take food on that day during the night.[28]

At Bhagalpur the father of Ramnath Tiwary, who had attached himself to Swamiji at Patna, requested him to free his son. Swamiji willingly acceded to his request.

Swamiji left Bhagalpur for Calcutta on 12 December 1872,[29] and completed his first visit to Bihar.

It can safely be said that during his sojourn of nearly three months, Swamiji had an opportunity of meeting a cross section of the Hindu intelligentsia as well as the chief upholders of orthodoxy in all the important towns of Bihar, south of the river Ganges. He was able to put across his view point and win several adherents to the message he propounded.

Swamiji spent nearly four months in Bengal, meeting and forming deep bonds of friendship with the local intelligentsia and Brahmo leader such as Maharsi Debendranath Thakur and Keshub Chandra Sen, etc. There was no sense of competitiveness or hostility. Keshub advised Swamiji to deliver his lectures in Hindi to the masses and also to wear clothes, suited to different occasions.[30]

Obviously the Calcutta visit gave him newer insights into the problems facing the country. While returning from Calcutta, he broke his journey at Patna in April 1873.[31] He spoke at public meetings, answered questions, conversed with visitors and appeared before the masses.[32] People flocked in large numbers to see him. He invited the orthodox Hindus to enter into a religious disputation so that he could clarify his position, remove their doubts, but none came forward. He decided to visit other areas of Bihar where he had not gone earlier.

Swamiji then crossed the Ganges and went to Chhapra where his host was a distinguished local businessman, Rai Bahadur Shiv Ghulam Sahu.[33] A week long programme of discourses by Swamiji caused consternation among the orthodox section; it now decided to strike back. They selected the Sanskrit teacher of the local Zila School, Pandit Jagannath Mishra, to confront Swamiji on religious matters in a public debate.

Even before the public debate could take place, Pandit Mishra tried to back out; he declared that he considered it a sin to see even a face of Swamiji. Swamiji remained undaunted; he opined that Pandit Mishra could sit behind a curtain while the debate continued. The latter could not wriggle out of the commitment.

The English Teacher of the Zila School presided over the meeting. After some questions had been answered, Pandit Mishra conceded victory to Swamiji.[34]

This programme ended his second but short visit to Bihar. He proceeded thereafter to the neighbouring province of Uttar Pradesh to disseminate his message.[35]

As a result of these two visits, some of the Bihari admirers of Swamiji continued their contact with him. Among them was Madhav Lal, a resident of Dinapore Cantonment, 16 km away from Patna. Madhav Lal had established an organization 'Hindu Satsabha' in 1866 with a view to eradicating the socio-religious evils that afflicted the Hindus.[36] He was a regular visitor to the religious discourses, delivered by Swamiji, during his first visit to Patna. He and his companions Master Janakdhari Lal, Gulab Chand and his elder brother Karman Shah were convinced that they had found the right leader for the cause of socio-religious reforms among the Hindus.[37] He had entered into correspondence with Swamiji.

It is therefore not surprising that when Swamiji established Arya Samaj in Bombay, Madhav Lal, Janakdhari Lal and Thakur Prasad were present on the occasion.[38] Two years later from Gujarat in the Panjab (now in west Pakistan), Swamiji wrote a letter of appreciation for the work Madhav Lal was doing.[39]

In his letter dated 1 April 1878, Swamiji advised Madhav Lal to change the nomenclature if his organization from Hindu Satsabha to Arya Samaj since the word 'Arya' meant 'great and knowledgeable'[40] and the word 'Hindu' could alienate the feelings of the Muslims and Christians.

When Madhav Lal informed him that on 28 March 1878 he had formally named Hindu Satsabha as Arya Samaj, Swamiji expressed his great pleasure in his letter of 12 April 1878.[41] The Dinapore Arya Samaj was the first Arya Samaj on the soil of Bihar and Bengal. Its first President was Janakdhari Lal and first Secretary was Madhav Lal.[42]

The establishment of the organization strengthened the bonds between Swamiji and his followers in Bihar. His admirers in Dinapore were now particularly keen that Swamiji should visit them, inspire them and show them the correct path. Hence, they planned to bring Swamiji to Dinapore.

In 1879 Madhav Lal sent Makhan Lal to fetch Swamiji from Muzaffarpur in Uttar Pradesh. Earlier Bholo Nath and Makhan Lal had gone to Delhi to meet Swamiji and had extracted a promise that he would soon came to Dinapore.[43] Swamiji arrived at the Dinapore Railway Station in the evening of 30 October 1879.[44] This was Swamiji's third and last visit to Bihar. He stayed for twenty days and left for Benares on 19 November 1879.[45]

Swamiji stayed at the Digha Lodge, a Bungalow owned by Mr. Jones, a British Businessman,[46] though for the first couple of days, his host was Madhav Lal. This again shows that Swamiji harboured no prejudice against any race or religion.

Dinapore was an important military cantonment and prior government permission had to be taken before any public function. The local government functionaries while permitting him to deliver public lectures or discourse expressly forbade him to say anything which might hurt the religious sentiments of others.[47] The anti-Arya Samaj forces this time became very active and mibilized their forces to obstruct the progress of Swamiji's mission. Swamiji was not cowed by the virulence of their opposition; he continued to preach his message without any fear. On this occasion, members of other religions also joined hands with the orthodox sections of his co-religionists.

Swamiji gave twenty-four lectures between 2 November 1879 and 16 November 1879 at Babu Mahabir Prasad's Katghara. In course of these lectures, he touched upon topics such as idolatory, performance of last funerary rites (*shradh*) by the Hindus, social-reform, national progress and salient features of the Vedic religion. He also criticized some of the features of other religions in course of these talks.[48]

The lectures of Swamiji created a strong sense of despair amongst the conservative Hindus. They invited Pandit Chaturbhuj from Aligarh to enter into a disputation or to refute the position adopted by the Swamiji. After his arrival, he was the guest of Sri Nandlal and Ramlal. He boasted that he had defeated Panditji in debates at thirty-two places. When this was conveyed to Swamiji, he denied 'even seeing his face'. He challenged him to enter into a discussion.

When Nandlal and Ramlal learnt that Pandit Chaturbhuj was merely boasting, they asked him to leave their house. He was, however, entertained by conservative Hindus and Muslims, who were bent upon to humiliate Swamiji.[49]

They fixed the house of Kunjabehari Shah as the venue of disputation. When Swamiji arrived, Pandit Chaturbhuj hid himself in a room and his colleague Gobind Sharan, who was also the secretary of the local branch of Dharmsabha, told Swamiji to hold the discussion with him. When Swamiji asked for the reason, he advanced the lame excuse that the eyesight of Pandit Chaturbhuj was weak and hence, he would substitute for him. Swamiji countered it by saying that he could sit behind a screen.[50] However, the opponents were not keen on a through going discussion. All they wanted was to publicly humiliate Swamiji. Hence, they put off the lamp and started making loud noises. Madhav Lal and Subedar Singh chided the rowdy elements and came out the house with Swamiji.[51] Outside, the mob hurled stones on Swamiji, who kept his peace and remained smiling.[52] The cool shown by Swamiji impressed

Subedar Singh so much that he became an ardent follower of Swamiji thereafter.

The opposition to Swamiji did not die out. Once while he was delivering a speech, a Muslim Maulvi was instigated to hurl unmerited accusations against him. Janakdhari Lal called for police protection and an English Police Inspector, Gilbert, arrived. He was so impressed by the oration of Swamiji that he became a regular visitor to his meetings along with his other English friends.[53]

The intensity of opposition to Swamiji can be gauged from the fact that one of his followers Gulabchand Lal advised him not to criticize the Muslims since they quickly became violent and took to arms. Swamiji point-blank refused to heed him and insisted that he would speak the truth, come what may. He pointed out that he had criticized Bible in front of the Commander-in-Chief of India, Lord Roberts and there was nothing illegal about criticizing any religion. Therefore, there was no point in refraining from indicating certain unpalatable features in other religions.[54]

Once, Mr. Jones, his host, visited Swamiji along with his English friends, Swamiji seated them by side, an act of courtesy which considerably impressed the visitors.[55] They requested him to speak something to them. Swamiji then narrated the features of the Vedic religion. He pointed to them that the religion enunciated in the Vedas was for the well-being of the entire mankind and should therefore be accepted.[56] It stressed truth, kindness, altruism, non-possession, right thought, etc., which found place in all subsequent religions. Finally, the Vedic religion, unlike Christianity and Islam, was not entered round any individual. The Vedic religion promised deliverance as a result of right conduct, and doing good to others.[57]

When Mr. Jones queried that if the religion described by Swamiji was so liberal he should have no objection in partaking food with him. Swamiji replied that partaking of food with this or that individual did not effect the religion of any individual. Food habits depended upon local conditions.[58]

On onother occasion, Mr. Jones asked Swamiji to expound

his views on 'punya' or right action. Swamiji promptly replied that whatever was good for the society was the right action. He also dwelt upon the usefulness of banning cow slaughter. It is said that Mr. Jones was so impressed that he gave up beef-eating.[59]

Mr. Jones looked after Swamiji with great care throughout his stay.

Thus Swamiji, despite all obstacles put in his way, left and indelible impression on all those who came in contact with him. The Dinapore Arya Samaj became the torch-bearer of the new faith in the eastern region of India and played a vital role in establishing its branches subsequently.[60]

During this visit Swamiji also performed the 'sacred thread ceremony' of Madhav Lal an act which considerably roused the ire of the orthodox Hindus, who believed that only the upper castes were entitled to put on the sacred thread.[61] While his first two visits had enabled him to develop local contacts in Bihar and were prior to the establishment of the Arya Samaj, his third and last visit was after he had established his organization. Hence, this time, if the support he received was widespread, the opposition was equally well-planned, well-organized and sufficiently violent. However, the new organization had become a centre of attention as well as criticism. During the next two decades Arya Samaj expanded its support base while facing attacks of conservative Hindus as well as non-Hindus.

A letter writer in *Bihar Bandhu*[62] on 24 March 1881 called upon the readers to extend greater support to Arya Samaj, which has been established to lift Bihar from the mire of backwardness. But its support-base remained narrow. Only some of the educated Biharis became convinced followers; the rest continued to retain their faith in the old religion which enabled the conservative leaders to mount ever-increasing attack on the new sect. Thus we find that Pandit Ambika Dutta Vyas published *Dayanand-matmulocheda* (refutation of Dayanand's views) in 1885[63] from the Khadgavilas Press, the most important publishing house of Hindi books in Bihar during the last two decades of the nineteenth century.

In order to lessen the charm of the new faith, the conservatives made several features of Arya Samaj, an integral part of their programme. For example, its call for cow protection was adopted by orthodox Hindus and the Khadgavilas Press published in 1880, a book *Go Mahima* (The Glory of Cow).

Maharaj Lakshmeshwar Singh of Darbhanga, the leader of Srotriya Brahmanas and Hindu conservatives, became actively associated with the Cow-Protection Association established by Swami Dayanand in 1882. In 1888 he resolved to donate Rs. 2 per thousand of the income of his estate to the funds of the Cow-Protection Association. He became a patron of the Cow Memorial Movement and 'contributed a lakh of rupees in furtherance of the object.'[64]

The conservatives, no longer, opposed the new education since it qualified men for administrative jobs and enable them to enter into professions of law, medicine, etc.

Another section of the educated Hindus in Bihar, the Bengalis were already familiar with a protestant faith of Hinduism – Brahmo Samaj. Hence, if they felt any attraction for the new faith, they turned to Brahmo Samaj.[65] The Brahmo Samaj failed to make any significant impact on the Hindus of Bihar, Arya Samaj became a part of the socio-religious scene in Bihar without being able to disturb the general picture. However, the handful of ardent followers kept aloft its banner.

By 1901, there were sixteen branches of Arya Samaj in Bihar and it was felt that an apex body should be formed to coordinate their activities as had already been done in the Punjab and Uttar Pradesh. The idea, born during the XXIV annual meeting of Dinapore Arya Samaj fructified in 1904. On 5 October 1904, Bihar-Bengal Arya Pratinidhi Sabha was formed at Dinapore with Bal Krishna Sahay, Pleader, Ranchi as the first president and Mithila Sharan Singh, Pleader, Patna as the first secretary.[66]

The emergence of this apex organization in the State enabled the local activists of the Arya Samaj to interact more effectively and meaningfully with other Arya Samajists in the country. Hence, when on 25 September 1908 a meeting was convened in Agra for establishing a pan-Indian body, two representatives from Bihar, Mithila Sharan Singh and Shiva Gobind Singh participated. They were among twelve members present. The former was the secretary Bihar-Bengal Arya Pratinidhi Sabha and latter hailed from Gaya.[67]

Preachers from other parts of India began to arrive in Bihar and local Arya Samajists also moved to other parts of the country to preach the message of Arya Samaj. In Bihar itself, new branches were springing up and in no distant future the organization diversified its activities: it opened institutions imparting modern education[68] and preached eradication of social evils. It attacked the caste-system, supported inter-caste marriage, upheld widow-remarriage. It stood for the abolition of the *purdah* system, and pleaded for the right of women to education and equal social status with men. It asserted the Hindu identity and was prepared to resist attack on it from whatever quarters they might come. The organization actively fostered humanitarian acts for relieving the miseries of children and women; it opened orphanages and houses for homeless women. All these activities were, of course, taken up in course of time, but some immediate results were evident.

Members of the peasant and trading communities felt en-couraged to go in for modern education and subsequently, many among them took up non-caste occupations. They joined administrative positions, became lawyers, doctors, engineers, literateurs, etc. Mention may be made of eminent physicians Dr. D. Ram and Dr. M. Das. The three sons of Madhav Lal became qualified physicians and the youngest, Lakshmipati was sent to Scotland for his medical studies. This was done at a time, when sea-voyage was considered taboo by caste Hindus.[69]

Arya Samaj, dubbed as somewhat traditionalist and funda-mentalist, became a catalyst for modernization and Western-ization among the Hindus.

NOTES

1. Swami Abhedanand et al. (eds.), *Bihar Arya Prtinidhi Sabha ka Itihas* (History of Bihar Arya Pratinidhi Sabha), hereafter cited as *Bihar*

Arya Pratinidhi . . . , Bihar Arya Pratinidhi Sabha, Patna, 1985, p. 1.

2. Bimanbehari Majumdar and Devendra Kumar (eds.), *Great Men of Shahabad*, Prasad Publishing House, Patna, 1946, p. 102.

3. Surendra Gopal, 'Endeavour and Persistence: Brahmo Samaj in Bihar in the Second Half of the Nineteenth Century', *Indica,* nos. 45 and 47, pp. 33-45 and 35-49.

4. He was the Manager of Dumraon Raj and he attended the 1886 session of the Indian National Congress as a delegate. B.B. Majumdar and B.P. Mazumdar, *Congress and Congressmen in the Pre-Gandhian Era, 1885-1917,* Firma K.L. Mukhopadhyay, Calcutta, 1967, p. 324.

5. His monastery still functions and is located at Buxar.

6. Sarvendra Shastri, *Bihar Mein Swami Dayanand,* Swami Dayanand in Bihar—hereafter cited as *Bihar Mein* . . . , Sastri Sadan, Pahleja Barka, Dist. Saran, 1984, p. 6.

7. Nagendra Nath Gupta, *Reflections and Reminiscences*, Bombay, 1947, p. 15.

8. Shastri, op. cit., p. 7.

9. Gupta, op., cit., p. 15.

10. Shastri, op. cit., p. 7.

11. Sachchidanand Sinha, *Some Eminent Behar Contemporaries*, Himalaya Publications, Patna, 1944, pp. 18-24, 159-66; and B.B. Majumdar and B.P. Mazumdar, op. cit., pp. 376-7.

12. K.K. Datta and J.S. Jha (eds.), *The Comprehensive History of Bihar,* vol. III, pt. II, K.P. Jayaswal Research Institute, Patna, 1976, p. 21.

13. Shastri, op. cit., p. 7.

14. Ibid.

15. Mazumdar, op. cit., p. 372; Guruprasad attended annual sessions of the Indian National Congress in 1886, 1887, 1891 and 1892 and was an eloquent speaker.

16. Shastri, op. cit., pp. 7-8.

17. Ibid., p. 7.

18. Ibid., p. 8.

19. Ibid.

20. Ibid., p. 9.

21. Ibid., p. 9. He served the Nepal Government as a Medical Officer. Inscription on a photograph published in *Bihar Arya Pratinidhi.*

22. Surendra Gopal, 'Endeavour and Persistence . . .', *Indica*, 45, p. 44. He was the headmaster of the local Zila School and an ardent follower of Brahmo Samaj.

23. Shastri, op. cit., p. 9.

24. Ibid.

25. Ibid.

26. Ibid., p. 9.
27. Ibid., p. 10.
28. Ibid.
29. Ibid.
30. Ibid., p. 10; Keshub Chandra Sen was a frequent visitor to Bihar and hence, he had realized that only through the use of Hindi could he put across his message to the masses. Surendra Gopal, 'Endeavour and Persistance . . . , *Indica,* 45 and 47. A year later Keshub further stated that for the unity of country, it was essential to use one language and that language could only be Hindi since it was spoke almost everywhere. *Sulabh Samachar,* 5 Chaitra 1280 Bengali year (AD 1874) quoted in Dhirendra Nath Singh, *Adhunik Hindi ke Vikas mein Khadgavilas Press ki Bhumika,* Bihar Rashtra Bhasha Parishad, Patna, 1986, pp. 252-3.
31. Ibid., p. 10.
32. Ibid.
33. *Comprehensive History of Bihar,* vol. III, pt. II, p. 21.
34. Shastri, op. cit., p. 11.
35. Ibid., p. 12.
36. Sarvendra Shastri, 'Bihar Rajya Ke Pratham Asthawan Aryasamaji Svargiya Babu Madhav Lalji', *Aryasankala,* vol. X, no. 9, April 1988, p. 6; He was born in 1844 and had studied Sanskrit in Kashi. He belonged to a family of businessmen. He died in 1904.
37. Shastri, op. cit., p. 13.
38. *Bihar Arya Pratinidhi . . . ,* p. 2.
39. Ibid.
40. Shastri, op. cit., p. 14.
41. Ibid., p. 14.
42. Ibid., p. 15.
43. *Comprehensive History of Bihar,* vol. III, pt. II, p. 21.
44. Shastri, op. cit., p. 15.
45. Ibid., p. 22.
46. *Comprehensive History of Bihar,* vol. III, pt. II, p. 22, 'Bihar Rajya Ke Pratham . . .', p. 7.
47. Shastri, op. cit., p. 15.
48. Ibid., pp. 15-16.
49. Ibid., p. 17.
50. Ibid.
51. Ibid.
52. Ibid., p. 17; 'Bihar Rajya Ke Pratham . . .', p. 7.
53. Ibid., p. 18.
54. Ibid..

55. Ibid., p. 19.
56. Ibid., p. 20.
57. Ibid., p. 20.
58. Ibid.
59. Ibid., p. 21.
60. Ibid., p. 22; 'Bihar Rajya Ke Pratham . . .', p. 7.
61. 'Bihar Rajya Ke Pratham . . .', p. 8.
62. *Bihar Bandhu* was the first Hindi newspaper to be published from Patna in the nineteenth century. Surendra Gopal, *Patna in the Nineteenth Century: A Socio-Cultural Profile*, Naya Prakash, Calcutta, 1982, p. 67.
63. Dhirendranath Singh, op. cit., p. 275.
64. Jata Shankar Jha, *Biography of an Indian Patriot Maharaja Lakshmishwar Singh of Darbhanga*, Patna, 1972, pp. 70-2.
65. Surendra Gopal, 'Endeavour and Persistence . . .', *Indica*, 47, pp. 47-8.
66. *Arya Pratinidhi Sabha . . .*, p. 5.
67. *Sarvadeshik Arya Pratinidhi Sabha Ka 27 Varshiya Itihas* (Karya Vivaran: Twenty-seven Year History of All Arya Pratinidhi Organisations), Report on activities, Delhi, 1939, pp. 7-8.
68. Madhav Lal opened a school 'Arya Sanskrit Pathshala', in 1875 in Dinapore. Subsequently in 1924 the name of the school was changed to DAV High School. 'Bihar Rajya Ke Pratham . . .', p. 7.
69. Ibid.

CHAPTER 12

Dalits in Bihar:
A Historical Study

We do not exactly know the point of time when the caste cluster of Dalits or Harijans or Pancham or Antyaja or Achchhut or Untouchables came into existence. Somewhere during the last centuries before the dawn of the Christian era, untouchability became a part of the Hindu society. The protest stream against the Vedic society such as Jainism, and Buddhism, etc., failed to eliminate it. With a distinct identity it became a hallmark of the caste system of the Hindu society.

It reflects the basic philosophy of the Hindu caste system, i.e. profession determines caste. The different sections among the Dalits followed different professions and became a subcaste and occupied a distinct position in the caste hierarchy of the Dalits.

It would seem that Dalits did enjoy some social prestige around sixth century of the Christian era when Tantra emerged. The list of Siddhas include members of the Dalit community.

Their position deteriorated, in the centuries that followed. Alberuni, the Central Asian author who spent several years in India following Mahmud Gazni's invasion in the eleventh century AD puts the Dalits at the bottom of the Hindu society. In the thirteenth century we have a conclusive proof of this phenomenon.

When the invading Turks sacked the monastery of Nalanda in the first decade of the thirteenth century a Tibetan monk Dharmasvamin escaped. On the banks of a river near Gaya he sought help from a person, who declined, on the ground that he was a member of a low-caste and therefore he could not touch him.

In the following centuries though untouchability did not

disappear; evidence shows that its members continued to live as in the preceding century.

Jyotirishwar Thakur, the author of *Varna Ratnakar* in the fourteenth century compiled a list of castes in Bihar. He uses the word Manda caste to describe the various untouchable castes. As Hetukar Jha points out Tantrism still had a large following. The Tantrics were found frequenting cremation grounds and therefore the status of untouchables might not have been very depressed.[1]

Hetukar Jha further points out that *Varna Ratnakar* mentions Siddhas. Hazari Prasad Dwivedi describes them as members of the Nath cult who combined both Tantra (Buddhist) and Yoga. Dwivedi unravelled their economic background: a vaishya, a weaver (*tanti*), a washer man (*dhobi*), a wood cutter, a painter, and two *shudras*. Tantra had become popular among *doms* as one *dom* has been referred to as a great tantric.[2]

Tantra was also a feature of Lokayat philosophy, running parallel to the Hindu, Buddhist, Jain philosophical traditions. Chattopadhaya writes,

we find supreme importance being attached in tantras to . . . Chandalis, Dombi, Rajaki, Savari and others. These are all female names and they represent some of the lowest castes . . . the tantra of the Kubjika school is said to have originated among the potters . . . in another cult the queen was initiated by a Hadi, a member of a very despised caste . . . in many . . . cases of tantra practices the priestly function is known to rest upon . . . very low caste . . . tantra was no respecter of caste distinctions and caste superiority.[3]

Jha concludes, '. . . in the region of Bihar tantric cult have significant influence and due to this the life of SCs might have not been so depressed as one imagines on the basis of precepts of Brahmanic shastras until the early mediaeval period.'[4]

A new factor had compelled the people at large to continue social practices as they were, ignoring what was written in Hindu religious law books. This was the conquest of north India by Islamicized Turks in the beginning of the thirteenth century.

Islam, the religion adopted by the Turks, theoretically professes equality among its followers. It appears that upper caste

Hindus took note of this contesting ideology and persisted with a diluted caste system. This is clear in the writings of Vidyapati, who flourished in Mithila in the late fourteenth and the early fifteenth centuries. According to him marital relations were established between the families of upper castes and lower (adham) castes. In Jaunpur he found the Brahman and Chandalas moving so closely in the market place that the sacred threads of the former were seem hanging over the bodies later.[5]

The Hindus stayed in close proximity to the Muslims. Rigours of the caste system were loosened.

Another proof of this is to be found in the new paradigms of Hinduism that were being put forward.

Vidyapati in his work *Purush-pariksha* stated that Hinduism consisted of *sadharan dharma* and *kulachar*: the former late down that one should shun violence to others, not covet other man's property or women. *Kulachar* implied that one should follow the religious practices observed by one's families. In other words, Jati/Varna the core of Hindu religion was not mentioned.

In fact in centuries preceding and following Vidyapati, a numbers of social reformers such as Kabir, Nanak, Raidas, etc., were openly denouncing caste system. They spoke in local languages and idioms easily understood by the common man. Their teachings influenced a cross section of the society across the whole of north India between the thirteenth and the seventeenth centuries. Kabir was quoted widely in the eastern Uttar Pradesh and Bihar. Nanak made the greatest impact in the Punjab; Raidas belonging to the caste of the cobblers lived in Benares, the holiest city of the Hindus. Both Kabir and Raidas were popular in Uttar Pradesh and Bihar; Chaitanaya was worshipped in Bengal; Shankardev found followers in Assam; Narsih Mehta's humanism was widely appreciated in Gujarat.

However, these movements denouncing the caste system and the practice of untouchability emerged in different times; there was no coordination among them. Hence they failed to end either the caste system or the practice of untouchability. The caste system survived and the practice of untouchability survived. The Dalits occupied at the bottom of the society. The Brahmins remained at the apex.

Reform forces, though weak, continued to challenge the caste system and improve the status of the Dalits.

This is clear from the emergence of the Sheo Narayani sect in the seventeench century in Bihar: it was popular among Dushadhs and Chamars. It survives to this day. It adopted certain practices not popular among the Hindus, such as the burial of the dead body in place of cremation.

Daryapanth was another sect, started by a Muslim tailor in the eighteenth century, which aimed at improving the status of the untouchables. Buchanan during his survey of Sahabad in the opening decade of the nineteenth century was told that among its priests were seventy Hindus belonging to the upper and the non-upper castes. They had plenty of followers among Chamars and Dushadhs.

The Dushadhs were normally employed as village watch-guards. Hence, their economic position was far better than other sections of the Dalits. Hamilton Buchanan informs us that the Dushadhs were employed by Sahebzada Singh, the Zamindar of Jagdishpur and the father of Babu Kunwar Singh, the hero of 1857. He says, 'the agents (officers) he (Sahebzada Singh) employees are . . . Dushadh and the low people . . . at Jagdishpur (the administrative centre of the zamindari . . . everything is at the disposal of the Dushadhs.' Besides, the Dushadhs virtually monopolized the priesthood of village gods.

We need not be surprised that the Dalits in the opening decades of the nineteenth century were not totally devoid of literacy. William Adams who conducted a survey of village schools in Bihar and Bengal in 1830s, found children of Dushadhs, Pasis, Dhobis and Musahars reading Hindi books and learning agricultural and commercial accounts along with children of upper and intermediate castes in north and south Bihar.

The British rule which took roots in Bihar in the second half of the eighteenth century turned out to be a defining moment in the history of Dalits in Bihar, both economically and socially.

Economically, the establishment of the British rule in India almost coincided with the emergence of industrial revolution in their century. As a result, Indian crafts, both urban and rural, steeply declined. In the countryside more and more people turned to land to earn their livelihood. Craftsmen associated with weaving were either without any work or it was unremunerative. Agriculture was their sole source of income. The Dalits were the first to be deprived of their landholdings.

The story of those associated with the trade of saltpetre was similar. Saltpetre traditionally an important ingredient of gunpowder was exported from Bihar to Europe in the seventeenth and the eighteenth centuries by the English, the Dutch and the French. A large number of rural folks had jobs and income to support their families. During Napoleonic wars in the late eighteenth and early nineteenth centuries, saltpetre was replaced by an artificially manufactured chemical compound. The manufacturers of saltpetre, its traders and transporters, all were compelled to seek a living in agriculture. The ultimate losers were the Dalits who had to surrender their small patches of land. The economic condition of the Dalits went on declining.

The Dushadhs suffered after the establishment of the Permanent Settlement. Earlier, Bihar zamindars enjoyed policing rights. The zamindars employed Dushadhs for policing. The government gradually took over policing functions from the zamindars. The Dushadhs lost a regular source of their livelihood. The governments appointed its own chowkidars.

During the first half of the nineteenth century the Dalits in Bihar suffered great economic deprivation. They could not recover from this.

In the Magadh area the economic deprivation of the Dalits was far greater. Available data show there was a great fragmentation of zamindaris. These small zamindars could hardly survive from the incomes of their small zamindaris. Their dependence on land consequently had increased. Hence, they oppressed the agricultural labourers (the bulk of whom came from the cluster of the Dalits). These agricultural labourers had no other alternative, but to continue to work for their masters at subsistence wages.

However, during this period, the consciousness in the society that untouchability was a slur did not die. It ought to be removed.

Many factors promoted this feeling. The newest was the activities of Christian missionaries, who after the establishment of the British rule had begun to bring them into the fold of the Christian religion. The second factor was the spread and growth of the new education which emphasized liberal and scientific values, such as individual liberty, freedom of expression, etc. The newly-educated intellectuals seriously thought of social reforms and transformation in the society. For the first time the intellectual segment was directly involved in the social reform process.

Two important reform movements began; they emerged in two states, in Bengal and Gujarat, Brahmo Samaj and Arya Samaj. Both were explicitly against untouchability and stood for complete abolition of socio-economic and religious disabilities of the Dalits and their complete integration in the Hindu society.

It is true that nothing much was achieved but the problem had been raised and brought to the forefront.

Another factor which brought the problem in focus was increasing urbanization during British rule.

In urban areas many member of the community lived in mixed localities; they were neither excluded nor isolated. The doors of educational institutions were theoretically not closed to them. Some of them reaped the benefits of new education, profited by the mobility induced by steam ships and railways to look for more remunerative jobs and escape from the depressing atmosphere of their villages. This explains the new stirrings of change witnessed with the Dalit society. From now onwards both external and internal factors were at work for bringing about changes in the Dalit society. This was an important development which wrote much of the history of the Dalits in the twentieth century.

The Dushadh community in Bihar seems to have been the

first to grasp the importance of a collective and sustained effort to improve their lot. They in 1911 formed the Dushadh Sabha on the pattern of Kayastha Mahasabha (1887), Pradhan Bhumihar Brahman Sabha (1905), Rajput Sabha (1906), Ravani Kahar Sabha (1906), etc.

Undoubtedly a small group of Dalits had felt the direction in which the new social mores were evolving. They did not want to be left behind.

Professor Hetukar Jha refers to a poem, published in the Hindi monthly *Saraswati* in 1914, published from Allahabad. The author was Hira Dom of Patna.

The editor Mahabir Prasad Dwivedi was a Brahman; *Saraswati* was a literary magazine. The publication of a poem by an unknown untouchable poet was a bold step. The poem expressed the aspirations of the community to become an organic part of the Hindu society. It also graphically described their problems.

The turning point came around come in 1917 when Mahatma Gandhi visited Champaran on the persuasion of a simple peasant Raj Kumar Shukla.

Mahatma Gandhi had arrived to free the peasants from the atrocities of European indigo planters. Soon many important citizens of Bihar such as Braj Kishore Prasad, Anugraha Narayan Sinha, etc., also joined him.

Each of these had brought his own cook as common eating was supposed to be against caste rules. Mahatma Gandhi told them this simply was a wastage of precious time; and a common kitchen was established. Mahatma Gandhi had achieved a breakthrough in breaching the barriers erected by the caste system.

Mahatma Gandhi and his colleagues in the Ahmedabad Ashram had taken a vow to fight against the evil of untouchability. He in Champaran unhesitatingly met locals irrespective of their caste or religion and listened to their woes. His message to masses was clear reform the society, on march to economic and political independence.

When Gandhi started the Non-Cooperation movement in 1920, the common man joined him because the political movement for the independences of the country was a part of efforts for the upliftment of the county as a whole. He had declared in 1920: 'Untouchability cannot be given a secondary place in the programme: without the removal of that taint, Swaraj is a meaningless term.'[6] It was no wonder he made it a part of his Constructive Programme.

Gandhi's message had reached even the Dalits.

His call for a temperance movement was heeded even by the Dalit Pasi community, the toddy-tappers in Bihar. Dr Datta notes, 'In Gaya the Pasis themselves held meetings at which resolutions were passed that they could no longer take the settlement of toddy trees.'[7] The Dalit response emboldened the leaders of the Non-Cooperation movement to call upon the Dhobis (washer-men), another Dalit community to refrain from 'washing European clothes' and to exhort ekka drivers 'to decline to carry persons wearing foreign materials. . .'.[8]

Patna City Municipal Committee's welcome address to Gandhiji during his visit to Patna on 23 September 1925 clearly stated, '. . . we deeply regret we have not as yet made special efforts for ending untouchability and improving the lots of the Dalits, a problem very dear to your heart. But we are running two schools for the Dalits and there is no restrictions on the entry of Dalits in our schools. . . .'[9]

The people in Bihar were concerned with the question of ending untouchability.

A peasant leader Swami Vidyanand painted untouchability as a grave social evil. In his speeches before the masses in Darbhanga district, Swami Vidyanand advocated 'the unity of Hindus and Muslims but even appealed to the peasants to look upon Untouchables as brothers in conflict with the British planters and Indian landlords, the zamindars.'[10] He had already declared in 1920: 'Untouchability cannot be given a secondary place in the programme: without the removal of that taint, Swaraj is a meaningless term.'[11] It was no wonder he made it a part of his constructive programme.

After Mahatma Gandhi had withdrawn the movement; he called upon the masses to follow a constructive programme in

1922. People were asked to spin yarn and use hand-made clothes (*khadi*), so that the poorest of the poor could earn something in addition to meagre income. The social causes taken up were (1) prohibition and (2) abolition of untouchability and integration of the Dalits in the society.[12] Both the issues provoked national debates and national concern.

The stress on ending untouchability signified that it occupied a special place in the march towards social transformation. This was now a component of national ideology.

This was the greatest service Mahatma Gandhi rendered to the cause of the Dalits; he had made abolition of untouchability a part of the national agenda; it became a part of our struggle for emancipation from foreign yoke. From 1922 onwards it was a live national political issue. In Bihar freedom fighters took up the issue in right earnest.

Shri Krishna Singh, who subsequently became the first Congress Prime Minister (now redesignated as chief minister), pleaded for removal of untouchability, promotion of education, their economic development and entry in to Hindu places of worship,[13]

Around this period Dr. Rajendra Prasad became the Chairman of Patna Municipality. He found that most of the sweepers within a few days spent their salaries on drinks; thereafter they borrowed money at exorbitant rate of interests to feed their families. The lenders waited at the gates of the office on the day the sweepers received their salaries to collect their capital and interest. The result was more economic hardship for the families.

Rajendra Prasad was also appalled by the unhygienic conditions in which the Dalits lived simply because they did not realize the value of sanitation and education.

Dr. Prasad took remedial measures. He visited their places regularly and convened meetings where religious songs were sung and at the conclusion of the function, sweets were distributed as *prasad*.

At his initiative salary was distributed fortnightly. The money-lenders were forbidden to come to the gates of the office on the day of payment of salary. There was some resistant but eventually the Dalits accepted the new measures. This change solved the problem to some extent.[14]

The top Congress leaders no longer observed this social custom. Anugraha Narayan Sinha, was once sent to Champaran during the Salt Satyagraha of 1930s. At Bettiah he states that the communal kitchen was managed by a Dalit. A Brahmin visitor refused to eat there but later on relented and shared the food.[15] There were people who were concerned with improvements in the lot of the Dalits but Gandhi's intervention had made it a national issue. He had set in motion a debate over the issue. The famous Hindi monthly *Chand*, published from Allahabad, brought out an issue devoted to the problems of Dalits in 1927. Some scholars of Hindu Dharmashastras in Varanasi also analysed the issue.[16]

Jagjivan Ram, a Dalit from Bihar, who was studying in Calcutta, formed the Ravidas Sabha in 1928. He later on turned to be a very important Dalit leader in the country.

National consciousness on this question was revealed in different ways. Maharaja of Baroda extended support to B.R. Ambedkar; he helped a brilliant student of Mahar caste to pursue higher studies abroad. On return from his foreign trip Ambedkar took up the cause of the community and soon emerged as a powerful leader.

In Bihar freedom fighters took up the issue in right earnest.

When Vidyapeeths or educational institutions were established by the Congress party during the days of the Non-Cooperation movement, some Dalits studied here. One of them was Bhola Paswan Shastri of Bihar, who in post-Independent India became a Chief Minister of Bihar and also a Cabinet Minister in the Central Government.

In 1930 Mahatma Gandhi started the Civil Disobedience movement. The government was forced to negotiate with political leaders of diverse hues in India; Ambedkar was party to these negotiations. Ramsay Macdonald, the British Prime Minister put forward his Communal Award in August 1932; he suggested that Harijans should be, like the Muslims, treated as a separate electorate and granted them 71 seats.[17] Mahatma Gandhi was thoroughly opposed to this plan because it would further fragment the society instead of uniting it. B.R. Ambedkar favoured the plan. Mahatma Gandhi went on a fast. Eventually Ambedkar agreed to give up his demand of separate electorate. In return Mahatma Gandhi agreed that 151 seats of the Hindus would be reserved for the Harijans.[18] Certain seats for the Dalits were also reserved in the Central Legislative Council. Candidates for this seat would be elected by Hindu and Dalit voters jointly. This was the famous Poona Pact of 1932.

The Poona Pact marks a dividing line in the history of Dalits in our country. Hereafter Mahatma Gandhi launched a nation-wide campaign to banish this evil practice. He personally visited different parts of India and sought donations for Harijan Fund. He asked the masses to eschew this practice. He renamed the journal *Navjivan* published from Sewagram as *Harijan*. The *Harijan* was published in English and Gujarati; it virtually became the mouthpiece of Gandhiji. The Anti-Untouchability Association was also rechristened as Harijan Sevak Sangh.

Gandhiji's campaign for the emancipation of the Dalits was as vigorous as his movement for the freedom of the country.

Gandhi's efforts for eradication of untouchability found its echo in Bihar as well.

Jagjivan Ram organized a joint meeting of Dalits and caste Hindus at Arrah following Gandhi's ending of the fast.

Soon an anti-untouchability all Bihar meeting was called at the Anjuman Islamia Hall at Patna under the Presidentship of Raja Radhika Raman Prasad Singh of Surajpura. Jagjivan Ram also attended it along with Hindu Mahasabha and Arya Samaj leaders and Congressmen such as Rajendra Prasad and Vindyeshwari Prasad Verma. His speech condemning untouchability was listened with rapt attention. Rajendra Prasad was deeply impressed and sometime later he was called to Patna and made him the Secretary of Harijan Sevak Sangh.[19]

In August 1933 Gandhiji was released from his gaol. Now he decided to devote himself to the emancipation of the Dalits. He wrote in *Harijan* that service to Harijans was as dear to him as his own breath. It was more precious to him than his daily food.

Gandhi's commitment gave a further impetus to this movement.

In 1933, Har Singh Das at a meeting of caste Hindus in Sitamarhi asked the audience to improve the condition of Harijans. In the same year the second Harijan Conference was organized at Bhagalpur.[20]

In fact the political atmosphere was suffused with the desire to improve the condition of Harijans. The Patna University Syndicate in 1933 passed a resolution whereby it undertook to reimburse a part of the examination fee levied on Harijan students.[21]

The Dalit question agitated the academics as well.

Mahatma Gandhi's deep concern for the Dalits is shown in the following examples.

In 1934 a severe earthquake jolted Bihar. Mahatma Gandhi was in south propagating the cause of Harijans. He was pained at the suffering of the common man. He came out with the statement, 'God was punishing Biharies for their sin of untouchability.' Speaking at a mass meeting at Tinnevelly on 24 January 1934 he said,

You may call me superstitious if you like, but a man like me cannot but believe that this earthquake is a divine chastisement sent by God for our sins.

... For me there is a vital connection with between the Bihar calamity and the untouchability campaign. . . . It is a curse brought upon ourselves by our own neglect of a portion of Hindu humanity which this calamity in Bihar damages the body, the calamity brought about by untouctability corrodes the very soul.[22]

He repeated the above view the same day while speaking at Tuticorin. 'I want you to be superstitious enough with me to believe that the earthquake is a divine chastisement for the great sin we have committed and still committing against those whom we describe as untouchables.'[23]

Gandhi now formally declared the end of Civil Disobedience movement, started in 1930 because it was languishing; he decided to concentrate fully upon the elimination of the evil of untouchability, a problem at the centre of his attention. He exhorted Congressmen to follow in his footsteps.

Gandhiji visited Bihar to see the damage and to collect money for providing relief to the sufferers. He was accompanied by Dr Rajendra Prasad and Jagjivan Ram, a Dalit himself.

Mahatma Gandhi also made it a point to call upon the masses to give up the practice of untouchability, wherever he addressed a meeting in Bihar. His speeches against untouchability were resented by orthodox Hindus. In Buxar and Deoghar (a place of pilgrimage for Hindus) his car was attacked. It was extensively damaged at Deoghar though he escaped physical harm.[24]

Nevertheless, Mahatma Gandhi kept on speaking about the evils of untouchability. At Motihari he said, 'Today, more than ever our hearts need a thorough cleansing and I would go so far as to say that even the earthquake would not be too great a price to pay, if it, enabled India to cast out the canker of untouchability.'[25]

Speaking at another meeting Mahatma Gandhi said,

But so long as untouchability exists we are reminded about our miseries. Some people consider untouchability as their religion, and if it disappears, it would be a some sort of calamity to them. . . . Those also who call themselves *Sanatanists* understand that untouchability is indefensible, . . . In the light of this divinal lesson we ought to become more humble and do away with the sins of untouchability. . . .[26]

During his visit to Arrah on 25 April 1934, he addressed a mass public meeting at the Ramana Maidan. The welcome song was sung by 'some Harijan boys, who also garlanded him.' The welcome addressed read by Chaudhury Sarafat Hussain, M.L.C., informed him:

You will be pleased to learn that the members of the Chamar community of this town are more enlightened and educated than their fellow brethren elsewhere.

Of the Harijan Pathshalas in this town, we give grants-in-aid to two institutions.[27]

The Sanatanists here and at his next meeting at Buxar showed Black Flags but they hardly mattered. At Arrah Raja Radhika

Raman Prasad Sinha (the proprietor of the estate of Surajpura and chairman of the Shahabad District Anti-Untouchability League) presented a purse of Rs. 500 to Mahatmaji.[28]

On 25 April 1934 Mahatma Gandhi arrived at the railway station of Jasidih enroute Baidyanath-Deoghar, an important pilgrim centre of the Hindus. The local Pandas or priests demonstrated against Mahatma Gandhi; the rear windows of the car in which he was travelling was broken. He came out of the car, walked for about a mile amongst the hostile demonstrators and tried to reason with them. Mahatma Gandhi's move to lead a group of Harijans into the temple at Baidyanath Deoghar was also opposed by a section of Pandas; Mahatma Gandhi failed in his attempt to arrange temple entry for the Harijans. Gandhiji left the place a disappointed person.[29]

But his attempt certainly gave rise to a debate among scholars of Hindu theology. The pro-entry section was led by Pandit Lokshmashastri and no-entry section was represented by Pandit Akhilanand.

The debate was held at the Rajendra Bose Library. Both the rivals spoke in Sanskrit.

Henceforth, the Sanatanists stopped holding meetings against Harijan entry on the campus of the temple. Dr. Jha rightly observes, 'the Deoghar event thus proved to be crucial in the history of Harijan movement in Bihar in the modern period.'[30]

The year 1934 may be said to be a landmark in the history of fight for removal of untouchability in Bihar.

Mahatma Gandhi was deeply impressed by the organizing ability of Jagjivan Ram, who hailed from a village near Arrah. He was made Secretary of the Congress party of Bihar. This marked the beginning of the illustrious political career of Jagjivan Ram, who within a decade emerged as one of the most important leaders of Dalits not only in Bihar but also in the whole of the country.

Jagjivan Ram established the League of Depressed Classes in 1934 during the first annual general meeting of Ravidas Mahasabha held at Calcutta.[31] It was officially formed at Kanpur

in 1935 with Rasiklal Biswas as President and Jagjivan Ram
and P.N. Rajbhoj as secretaries (Sumitra Devi, p. 120). Jagjivan
Ram established its Bihar branch in August 1935 (ibid.). He
became its president in 1936.[32] The League was not a rival but
an associate of the Indian National Congress.

He participated in 1935 in a meeting presided over by Pandit
Madan Mohan Malaviya at Poona and moved a resolution
demanding that the Scheduled Castes should have access to
temples, wells, schools, etc.[33]

Thakkar Bappa, the Secretary of Harijan Sevak Sangh was
not in favour of Jagjivan Ram taking part in political activities.
He wanted him to confine to the work of Harijan Sevak Sangh.
Jagjivan Ram refused and resigned from Harijan Sevak Sangh
and devoted himself to political activities.[34] Jagjivan Ram's argument was that change in administrative set up was vital for
accelerating improvement in the conditions of the Dalits.[35]

He helped to keep the Dalits close to the Congress. He expressed his faith in Congress, he opposed separate electorates for
the untouchables of India.

His associaton with the Congress prevented the Dalits from
supporting Dr. Ambedkar *en masse.*

These efforts yielded results. Consciousness among Harijans
was growing about the importance of higher education although
it was still sporadic. In 1934-5 session, a Dusadh of Monghyr
and one Dhobi from Patna took admission in Patna College.

In 1934 Palamau Harijan Sangh was organized. It emphasized
the need for promoting education among Harijans.

The Congress efforts were now directed at integrating Harijans in the Hindu society both socially and politically. It was
argued that both the efforts should go together in tandem: they
would strengthen each other. The Congress kept its promise in
the elections held for provincial Legislatives Assemblies under
the Government of India Act of 1935.

In Bihar Jaglal Chaudhury, a Harijan (Pasi by caste), and
Jagjivan Ram won on Congress tickets. When the Congress
formed its ministry, Jaglal Chaudhury was made a Cabinet
Minister. Jagjivan Ram another Harijan was appointed Parlia-

mentary Secretary, although at one stage Jagjivan Ram was a strong candidate for the post of Cabinet Minister. Eventually Jaglal Chaudhury got the party's nod as he was senior and was associated actively with the Congress since the days of Non-Cooperation movement when he quit his medical studies to become a Satyagrahi. Both played important role in Indian polity in the post-Independence period. The new Congress government actively pursued the cause of upliftment of the Dalits. It should be noted that Mr. Yunus who formed the first ministry under the Government of India Act of 1935 tried hard to win Jagjivan Ram by offering to induct him as a minister, but he refused to betray Congress.[36] Jagjivan Ram was appointed Parliamentary Secretary.

Dr. Syed Mahmud, the Education Minister enthusiastically promoted education among them. He noted, 'Caste Hindus as well as Harijans sat side by side to acquire knowledge.'[37]

Jaglal Chaudhury in 1938 pleaded for reservations of jobs in government services for members of the Dalit cluster on the ground, 'the less advanced communities should be allowed a certain amount of weightage and this weightage should vary inversely with the degree of advancement of various communities.' It should be noted that Jaglal Choudhury did not plead for blanket reservations probably because he felt this would create vested interest in the community.

In Bihar this was the first important voice for reservation of government jobs for the Dalits.

An Association named as 'Servants of the Untouchable Society' also came into existence.[38]

Dalits' cause undoubtedly progressed within the short span the Congress Ministry remained in power. They now had a political voice; it continued to gather strength. Their socio-economic progress was now linked to their political clout and success of the freedom movement of the country. Hereafter no ministry was formed either by a party or a coalition of parties without adequate representations to the Dalits.

The Congress Ministry resigned at the outbreak of the Second World War because of policy differences with the colonial power. The Congress party continued to fight for independence.

Jagjivan Ram became a Secretary of Bihar Congress Committee in 1940.[39] The Congress called for individual Satyagrah; Jagjivan Ram was arrested in this connection.

During the Quit India movement of 1942 many members of this cluster took part. The young son of Jaglal Chaudhury lost his life while participating in a public demonstration against British Rule. Jaglal Chaudhury was arrested and sentenced to prison for ten years. Jagjivan Ram was also put in jail.

After the war ended, the British government released Congress leaders from jail and started negotiations with them on the issue of Indian Independence.

As a sign of their good faith, the government simultaneously announced elections to Provincial Legislatures under the Government of India Act of 1935. Once again the Congress fielded Dalit candidates for the reserved seats and won all of them. The Congress also won majority of seats and was called to from this ministry. Dr. Shri Krishna Singh became the Prime Minister for the second time. He formed a Cabinet of four members including himself. He released Jaglal Chaudhury and made him a minister along with Anugraha Narayan Sinha and Dr. Syed Mahmud.

The Congress had reaffirmed its commitment to the cause of the Dalits. In fact, henceforth, the Dalits became a permanent fixture on the political agenda of all Indian political parties. They found representation in all popular governments, formed any political party or coalition of political parties.

India was inching towards independence; the British announced the formation of the Interim government in September 1946 and made Pandit Jawaharlal, the Prime Minister of India. Pandit Nehru inducted Jagjivan Ram as the Labour Minister. It was the beginning of a long political innings for Jagjivan Ram in India's national governance and politics.

India attained Independence on 15 August 1947. The ministry continued; at the same time India decided to prepare a new Constitution for governance. True to their promises to the Dalits and other disadvantaged sections, the new Constitution included adequate safeguards for their interests and for improvement of their socio-economic and political status. This brought about many meaningful and desired changes in their condition.

From now onwards, the Dalits progressed in all walks of life, thanks to the policies of the Government of India and the commitment of political parties in this regard.

The new Constitution was promulgated on 26 January 1950. India became a republic. The Constitution incorporated provisions for promoting and protecting the rights of the Scheduled Castes and the Scheduled Tribes. From now onwards the Constitution set the pace for uplifting the status of the Dalits and the Scheduled Tribes all over the country.

The Constitution reserved seats in the Lower House of the Parliament and the Legislative Assemblies for the Dalits and the Scheduled Tribes in proportion to their population. It meant that politically the Dalits were empowered at a fast pace.

Under the new Constitution the first elections to the Lower House of the Parliament and State legislations were held in 1952. It had been decided that all the seats would by turn be declared reserved seats for the Harijans. During this time some seats for the State legislature had two candidates, a Harijan and a general candidate. The same voters cast votes for both the seats.

In this election the Congress fielded candidates for all the Dalit seats. Sometimes they had to make effort to find a suitable Dalit candidate.

Henceforth, the Dalits become an important factor in Indian electoral battle. In the initial decades the electoral success of the Congress party was the whole-hearted support of the Dalits.

The Congress party took many other steps to empower the Dalits. In compliance with the constitutional provision, the Bihar Harijans (Removal of Civil Disability) Act was passed although Article 17 of our Constitution had already abolished untouchability. A Welfare Department came into existence. In every district a Welfare Officer along with an Assistant Welfare Officer and Welfare Inspectors was posted. They were to work for the all round development of the Dalits.

A section of orthodox Hindus was still not prepared to

accept the Dalits as full members of the Hindu society. Acharya Vinoba Bhave's attempt to enter Baidyanath Dham temple along with Dalits was stoutly opposed by some Pandas. Hence, legal safeguards were needed by the Dalits so that they could enjoy rights at par with other citizens of India.

They were to promote education among Scheduled Castes and Scheduled Tribes by opening schools, offering stipends, medicines and loans, etc. They also built hostels for Harijan students. The scheme was successful in the sense that those Harijans who were keen to shift from traditional to an alternative occupation, it provided a wonderful opportunity. By getting new education they could acquire new skills and could become eligible for new jobs—a passport for economic well-being social mobility not only within the Hindu society but also within the Indian society as a whole.

The Harijans enthusiastically joined educational institutions, opened for the purpose. According to Rai Chaudhary in Saran district six Harijan Kalyan Hostels were opened and twenty-six Harijan Lower Primary School were established.[40] The story was more or less the same in other districts.

For improving their economic life, sixteen grain *golas* were set up in Darbhanga. They disbursed seeds on credit. In years of food scarcity, these *golas* helped the Dalits by giving them food grains.

To improve their living conditions, new residential colonies were set up. In 1953 the government took up a ten-year scheme to provide houses to destitute Harijans. In Palamau sixteen colonies of Adivasis and Harijans were set up where they were given lands, implements, seeds, etc. In Saran, however, houses could be built by 1958.

The implementation of these schemes left much to be desired.

However, the government was steadily marching ahead in integrating the Dalits and removing the handicaps they suffered.

The next milestone in the history of Dalit upliftment was passage of an Act in 1955 in the Indian Parliament. It outlawed untouchability. By an amendment in 1977 the Act was made more comprehensive. The government also issued booklets, so that people at large would become familiar with the new legal status of the untouchables.

The General Elections of 1967 were a landmark in Indian history. For the first time the Congress party was unable to form a government in several states in north India. A split in the Congress party as pro-Indira Gandhi and anti-Indira Gandhi factions together with an economic crisis following the war with Pakistan in 1965 disenchanted the electorate.

In Bihar Mahamaya Prasad Sinha, a former president of Bihar Provincial Congress Committee became the first non-Congress Chief Minister of Bihar. Congress had lost a big chunk of Harijan and intermediate caste votes. The intermediate castes were particularly vocal as they felt that their numbers entitled them to a bigger chunk of the political cake. Confident of their numerical superiorty, they laid claim to the highest political office—the Chief Ministership. B.P. Mandal became the Chief Minister following the resignation of M.P. Sinha.

During period of political instability and dissolution of Congress hegemony, two Dalits occupied the office of Chief Minister Bhola Paswan Shastri and Ram Sundar Das. The latter was a member of the Socialist Party; the former had been an old Congressman. Bhola Paswan Shastri became Chief Minister at the beginning of 1970s for a brief spell. He was again Chief Minister in year 1980. Later he rejoined the Congress party and served a Central Cabinet Minister as well.

Ram Sundar Das, a socialist and an acolyte of Karpuri Thakur, enjoyed a longer spell as Chief Minister in 1979.

Thus Dalits in Bihar had the privilege of reaching the highest political post for the first time in the Hindi heartland, much before Mayawati held the position in Uttar Pradesh.

During these years besides specific legislations, certain changes in the administrative goals helped to improve the socio-economic status of the Dalits.

The launching of the community development programme, the desire to develop cooprative institutions, to promote the Panchayat Raj, the abolition of the zamindari system, all contributed to bring about a change for better in the status of the

Dalits in rural areas. But the improvement was tardy. Prof. Januzzi maintains that marked changes appeared only in 1970s.

Bihar in the late 1970s also had a Dalit Governor, Shri Jagannath Pahadia.

Dalits were now holding the highest political offices in the state. This was a sign of their political clout; though nothing much could be done for their general well being.

It was clear the Congress no longer commanded the support of this cluster. Other parties were wooing the Dalits; the leadership among the Dalits became conscious of this political reality.

The visible symbol of this realization was defection of Jagjivan Ram from the Congress party soon after Mrs. Indira Gandhi lifted the Emergency in 1977. He launched a new political outfit, Congress for Democracy. Jagjivan Ram's half a century connection with Congress had ended. It signified the widespread Dalit disenchantment with Congress in north India. The results of the elections, held after the lifting of Emergency were a stark testimony to this truth; the Congress failed to win even a single Lok Sabha in Bihar.

Many leaders emerged among Dalits who were professedly anti-Congress. This was the time when Kanshi Ram founder of the Bahujan Samaj Party started an organization of Dalits with a clear cut anti-Congress stance.

In the post-Emergency scenario in Bihar a new Dalit leader in the person of Ram Vilas Paswan emerged. He was young and energetic. He won his Lok Sabha seat by a record margin. He became a minister when the first non-Congress government was formed at the Centre under the Prime Ministership of Morarji Desai.

The Dalits were becoming more assertive of their political, economic, social and legal rights because of growing political consciousness, access to higher education and government jobs at all levels. They knew about their newly acquired dignity; they resented rude behaviour on the part of upper and intermediate caste landowners for whom they worked as farmer labourers in the rural areas. They protested of misbehaviour with their women folk. They raised their voice if they were not properly reimbursed for their labour. They protested against injustices. They were not prepared to put up with atrocities anymore.

From the mid-1970s, the Dalit farm labourers became more and more vociferous about their rights and resentful of the wrongs done to them. To this day this has remained a burning issue for the Dalits. The confrontation has been marked by violence and atrocities, widely reported in the print and electronic media. These events are highly regrettable; nonetheless they have helped to draw attention of the politicians, administrators and public at large to the problems of the Dalit farm labourers and Dalits as a whole.

The Magadhi and Bhojpuri speaking areas, south of the river Ganges, have been the heartland of these violent incidents. Before these incidents are analysed, one could look at their probable causes.

The abolition of Zamindaris in 1950s, profoundly affected the socio-economic structure of rural Bihar. A large number of upper-caste people lost assured income, the source of their livelihood since the time of their forefathers. Suddenly land became the primary source of their income and livelihood. All these years they had never personally farmed the lands. The task was carried out either by farm-labourers or by giving land on lease. Some felt uneasy about farming as it was never done in their family. Others had no experience. They, if they could moved to urban areas. If they had education, they tried to find a job to support themselves. They gave their land on lease to upper caste marginal farmers but mostly to intermediate caste farmers, who were accustomed either to till their land or to get it tilled by farm labourers. Some among this new bunch of farmers soon purchased these lands as farming became more remunerative and brought them economic gains.

The new landholders were keenly interested in landownership and its production. They were dependent on farm labourers for production. They were not prepared to pay even the minimum wages because sometimes it meant substantial curtailment of their profits. For some years the situation did not result in clashes as the farm labourers had no alternative employment.

They were illiterate and in absence of any movement were not fully conscious of their rights. But in 1960s things began to change.

Socialism as an ideology became prominent. The socialists organized the industrial as well as farm labourers. Prices also were rising. The farm labourers were facing economic hardship. Education was also spreading. To contain discontent, the upper caste and the intermediate caste landowners tried to terrorize the labourers. Tensions developed. The discontent increased after the Naxal movement started in West Bengal in 1966 and reached Bihar in 1970s.

The first major clash was at Belchchi, a Harijan village near Barh in Patna district during the Janta regime. On 27 May 1977 landlords of Kurmi caste killed Dalits and some members of the Sonar caste. They also indulged in arson (Narayan Mishra, *Exploitation and Atrocities on Dalits in India*, p. 12). There was a great hue and cry. However, members of the Janta Cabinet at Delhi did not care to pay a visit to the place of incident. But Mrs. Gandhi came from Delhi. She rode on an elephant to reach the village and comfort the aggrieved Dalit families. Her visit to the inaccessible place was deeply appreciated by the Dalits. They equated it with Congress party's renewed concern for their welfare. Mrs Gandhi had won back Dalit support and sympathy. The Dalit votes also helped her to win back power at the Centre when the next elections were held.

Belchchi was a turning point in the history of Dalits in Bihar. It was a pointer of things to come. The Dalits came at the centre of concern for all the political parties. From now onwards at regular intervals both the Centre and the State governments passed legislations for the benefits of the Dalits. At the same time the powerful landlord-lobby also concluded that they could perpetrate atrocities, individual as well as collective, on the Dalits and under the current administrative dispensation get away with it. Subsequently the landlords formed caste-based armies (Ranvir Sena, Lorik Sena, Sunlit Sena, etc.) to attack Dalit villages, to burn their houses, to kill them, to rape

women-folk and to humiliate them. Of course there was occasional retaliation by the Dalits. But the Dalits by and large have
been the greatest sufferers.

An NGO has reported that in 2005 published news of atrocities on Harijan women numbered 525. Of these 150 related to
murder and 60 to rape.[41]

According to one calculation between 1981 and 1999 the
number of Dalits killed by landlords and their armies was 198.
The worst was the massacre at Laxmanpur Bathe in Jehanabad
district in December 1997 when 61 Dalits were murdered.[42]

It must be noted that simultaneously the Government both
at the Centre and at the State-level have initiated measures for
the well-being of the Dalits.

Atrocities on the Dalits and measures for the improvement
of the Dalits have had a parallel history.

The Janta government formed by a coalition at the Centre
was moved to action because of the event in Belchchi. To show
its concern for the Dalits, it launched the Antodaya Programme.
It intended to lift five Dalit families, living below the poverty
line in certain villages. They were to receive financial help
at a low rate of interest, 4 per cent. In Bihar the scheme was
implemented in the four districts of Vaishali, Palamau, Nawada
and Munger.

However, Prof. Sachchidanand who conducted a study of the
beneficiaries found that scheme had failed to deliver the desired
results.

To prevent atrocities against the Harijans, the government of
Bihar established a Harijan Police Station at Patna. It was placed
under the direct guidance of a DIG-ranked police official who
was in-charge of Harijan cell in the Home (Police) Department.
Soon the number of Harijan Police Stations rose to ten. They
were organized in Nalanda, Rohtas, Bhojpur, Gaya, Vaishali,
Samastipur, Begusarai, Bhagalpur, Munger and Ranchi.[43] But
these Harijan Police Stations failed to stop attacks and atrocities
against Harijans. The measure symbolized government's desire
to stop atrocities against Dalits.

The Government of India has been regularly floating projects aiming directly or indirectly at promoting economic improvement in the condition of the Dalits.

In the 1980s it formulated Integrated Rural Development Programme (IRDP). Like its predecessor it also failed to deliver the desired results. Nevertheless, it showed the Centre's continued interventionist role in uplifting the socio-economic status of the Dalits. Centre's intention was clear when the Sixth Five Year Plan was formulated. For the first time it separated plans for Dalit's well-being from the general plan.[44]

A Special Component Plan decreed that every department the State government had to reserve a certain percentage of its plan fund for expenditure on the development of the Dalits. A separate budget head was introduced in 1983 for the Harijan component of every department. Under the plan, Dalits would be given loans for acquiring cycle rickshaws, knitting machines, purchasing animals, etc. It was laid down that at least 14.5 per cent of plan resources were to be spent for the benefit of Dalits alone in Bihar. Later on it transpired that only 9 per cent of alocated resources were spent. Some Dalits benefited and extricated themselves and pulled themselves up from below the poverty line.

The Bihar government put in place new administrative measures to monitor the implementation of several programmes for economic and social improvement for the Scheduled Castes, now being implemented. The government established three directorates, four corporations, a number of committees and boards under the welfare department.

The Bihar State Schedule Caste Cooperative Development Corporation was established in 1979. Its task was to identify the poorest among the Dalits and to grant them financial assistance to enable them to generate income. According to the Annual Report of 1988-9 of the Department of Welfare, Government of Bihar Rs. 2,681 lakh were allotted for paying stipends to Scheduled Caste students; Rs. 236 lakh was sanctioned for payment of their fees; Rs. 16 lakh were meant for their clothes.[45]

The government had established seventy-two residential schools with an intake of more than 14,000 Dalit students. Each student was paid Rs. 500 per month for food, Rs. 500 per annum for clothes, Rs. 300 per annum for purchasing reading material, and Rs. 15 per month for soap, oil, etc. The students were accommodated in 361 hostels, which had a capacity for the intake of 11,641 students. In 1998-9, the government spent Rs. 236.45 lakh on these hostels. They gave Rs. 4.50 lakh to engineering and medical students to purchase textbooks.

The government took care to promote primary education among children of Dalits. It spent Rs. 23 lakh on progeny of those engaged in scavenging and leather work. The government also sanctioned Rs. 61 lakh from non-plan fund and Rs. 38.36 lakh from plan fund for spreading education among the children of Musahars. In addition to these sums the government further approved Rs. 17 lakh for rendering medical aid to Scheduled Caste students. It released Rs. 3 lakh for promotion of sports among the Scheduled Caste students.[46]

It transpires that no follow up action was taken after the grants were allotted. This conclusion is based on the following facts. The allotment to different districts for the improvement in the condition of the Dalits was Rs. 30 crore in 1993-9, Rs. 28 crore in 1997 and Rs. 32 crore in 1998. But by May 1998 hardly any amount was spent.[47] The districts could not submit the utilization certificates. Consequently the Centre did not release the matching grant it had promised. The inefficient local bureaucracy was responsible for depriving Bihar of substantial Central government funds which could have been utilized for the welfare of the Scheduled Castes. The data show the non-governing face of the Rashtriya Janta Dal government then in power. Lack of political vision and insensitive bureaucracy were chief hurdles for implementing welfare measures meant for the Dalits. Subsequently it transpired that senior bureaucrats had embezzled these funds by producing forged caste certificates. Kameswar Paswan, Vice-Chairman, National Commission for Scheduled Castes and Scheduled Tribes stated that complaints

were lodged against fifty-six senior administrators of Bihar
government for cornering benefits meant for the Scheduled
Castes. No heed was paid. No action was taken.

Yogeswar Paswan underlined the mismatch between government figures and claims way back in 1995. 'There is great dis-
crepancy between the official information of the government
and the actual achievements regarding the development of
Scheduled Castes.'[48]

To make matters worse, the landless and share-croppers
among the Dalits were not given land acquired under Bhoodan.
50 per cent of land received under Bhoodan remained undistributed. The government inaction was condemnable as
66 per cent of bonded labourers are Dalits.[49] It has been the
assessment of scholars that 'Land reforms, especially transfer of
surplus land, have been a complete failure in Bihar.'[50]

The importance of land for the Dalits can also be gauged
from the following data:

Though only 30 per cent of all Dalit households are landless, the vast
majority (94 per cent) of Dalit households is landless or holds less than
one acre of land. . . . Land scarcity affects non Dalits also and, hence the
intermittent and bloody struggle to increase or maintain land among
various caste groups.[51]

The sheer callousness and corruption on part of the government functionaries have prevented full benefits from percolat-
ing to the Scheduled Caste community in Bihar.

The miseries of the Dalits have been compounded by the
government's failure to introduce land-reforms and redistribute
the land among the landless. It resulted in growing tension
between the haves and have-nots in the rural community. This
was a major factor in the outbreak of violent conflicts.

The government agency in Bihar failed the Scheduled Castes
at another count as well. It did not fill up vacancies reserved for
the Dalits under Articles 16(4), 320 and 335.[52] Rajlaxmi Rath in
1995 had reported that though 14 per cent of government jobs
were reserved for the Dalits only 6.19 per cent posts had been
filled up. This was unfortunate as Rajlaxmi Rath found that

majority of those who had been employed were economically better off. 'All the respondents had a chance to free themselves of caste occupation for good.'[53] The indifference to posting Dalits to posts reserved has continued.

The Chairman of the All Confederation of SC and ST organization Ram Raj in a press statement regretted that more than one lakh government jobs, exclusively reserved for the Dalits were lying vacant in 2000.[54]

Despite the apathetic attitude of the bureaucracy, changes for the better in the status of the Scheduled Castes in the political, social and economic fields have been visible.

Dayadhar Jha has estimated that between 1962 and 1990 the number of Dalit MLAs rose from 35 to 48; they constituted 14.81 per cent the total strength of the Assembly. This closely approximated to their percentage of the total population. In the Parliament also their number was in proportion to the size of their population.

Politically the Dalits had become active and a new pack of leadership has emerged from within. They were no longer dependant upon National or Regional Political parties for voicing their grievances and securing their demands.

We have already noted the entry of Ram Vilas Paswan during the first Janata regime. After moving from one party to another, he formed political outfit, Lok Janshakti Party. But by 1990s, the most influential Dalit party came into existence through the efforts of Kanshi Ram, who had realized the need for properly organizing the Dalits. His argument was that Dalits could play a decisive role in the destiny of the nation, only if they had a well-knit organization. He first formed the Dalit Shosit Samaj Sangharsh Samiti (DS-4) on 6 December 1981. Next in 1982, he participated in electoral battle. He officially established the Bahujan Samaj Party on 14 April 1984. The new political outfit could not become the same force in Bihar as it was in Uttar Pradesh and the Punjab.

In Uttar Pradesh, Mayawati became the Chief Minister (though with the support of different political parties). This success increased the self-confidence of Dalits in Bihar. For example, Ramai Ram, a Dalit MLA, belonging to Laloo-led RJD, became the president of Bihar Rashtriya Janta Dal. When Laloo resigned the Chief Ministership of Bihar following the Fodder Scam, Ramai Ram made a strong bid to replace him. He failed but he remained a Cabinet Minister so long as Rashtriya Janta Dal remained in power in Bihar. Clearly the Dalits now knew the political value of their support and would not hesitate to encash it, whatever be the political complexion of the government in the State.

However, the government recognized the importance of earning the support and confidence of their Dalit employees. Several new laws having far-reaching significance were enacted. Earlier posts for the Dalits were reserved only at the entry level. Sometimes some posts were not filled up on the plea that suitable candidates were not available. Thereafter these jobs were given to general candidates. Under the new law posts reserved for the Dalits had to be filled by Dalit candidates. In case no qualified candidate turned up, the post was to be kept vacant till a suitable Dalit candidate turned up. In effect this meant that Dalits could not be deprived of the posts reserved for them. The second law made in 1982, allowed reservations of posts in each department of the government at all levels obligatory for the government. Armed forces and some other departments were kept out of purview of this law. This meant that higher posts now came within the reach of Dalit candidates.

Teaching and research posts in academic and research institutions were also reserved for the Dalit candidates.

In effect these enactments brought twin benefits to the Dalits. First, the number of jobs available to the Dalits increased considerably. Secondly, they did not have to compete with general candidates for promotion to superior posts within the Department. As a result the Dalit candidates occupied almost all important positions within the bureaucracy. Dalits rose to the posts of Chief Secretary and Director General of Police.

The long term effects of these measures would be that members of these families would never return to their caste occupations; members of these families would have the opportunity from childhood to acquire new skills enabling them to enter well-paid professions. Their parents would take care of their future careers; absence of right connections would not be a deterent factor.

Seen from this perspective, it would seem that improvement in the conditions of the Dalits was tangible; one could feel disappointed at their pace or the extent of spread.

How politicians take care of their family members can be seen from the fact that the younger brother of Ram Vilas Paswan has already served as a member of Bihar legislature for a number of times. Mrs. Meira Kumar, the daughter of Jagjivan Ram has also been a member of the Lok Sabha and a Minister at the Centre.

It has to be admitted that the beneficiaries among the Dalits were generally limited to certain communities in the cluster, i.e. Chamar, Dushadh, Pasi and Dhobi. The third largest numerical community of the Dalits in the state, the Musahars have considerably lagged behind.

History explains the comparative backwardness of the Musahars. Primarily agricultural laboureres, their major concentration is in the rural areas. They mostly escaped urban influences. Even in rural areas they lived in segregated areas called Musahar Toli and therefore, did not have much interaction with the rural community. Finally, economically and socially they were so depressed they hardly think of better life.

But their sheer numbers (the third largest community in the Dalit cluster) and atrocities committed against them forced politicians to pay special attention to them.

What are factors that militate against rapid changes in the improvement of the Dalits? There are some intrinsic causes. First, the Schelduled Caste politicians do not work as a team for the betterment of the entire community; they promote their family members or members of their own community.

The majority of the Dalit population still lives in rural areas. Illiteracy is widely prevalent. They are not developing any new skill equipping them for a non-caste profession. Occupational mobility is almost non-existent.

In rural areas the majority of the Dalits are mostly landless or marginal sharecroppers.

The landless are forced to work on low wages, despite government attempt to fix minimum wages. This becomes a contentious issue; upper caste and intermediate caste farmers perpetrate atrocities on these landless labourers. This is especially true in central Bihar. B.N. Patnaik has shown that between 1977 and 1989 in nine out of sixteen cases, it was the intermediate caste groups whose men killed Harijan labourers.[55]

The increasing value of land has come in the way of land re-distribution among the Dalits as upper and intermediate caste landowners resent it; they themselves covet the land owing to its increased value and scarcity. They adopt different means, including extreme violence to thwart it. Their opposition hind-ers the government from implementing its professed policy of land distribution among the Dalits and the landless.

Similar is the fate of land donations received as a part of Bhoodan movement. The upper and intermediate caste land-owners have ensured by using a variety of tactics that this land also remains undistributed among the Dalit have-nots.

The failure of the land reforms policy has caused resentment, discontent and frustrations among the Dalits. Many Dalit youths have joined Marxist organizations; they with other party members do not hesitate to use violence in intra-village feuds, be it over land, payment of wages or humiliations heaped upon them.

This explains continuing violence in the countryside. News items relating to the killing of Dalits and sometimes non-Dalits appear with unceasing regularity. They are and should be a cause of grave concern not only to the government but also to the civil society.

CIVIL SOCIETY AND THE DALITS

As the above account shows the Civil Society had become interested in improving the conditions of the Dalits much before the government took up their cause. But this was mostly confined to small groups of individuals, who owed allegiance to Brahmo Samaj, Arya Samaj or certain sects of Vaisnavism.

Mahatma Gandhi made it a national issue and integral part of his campaign to free the country from the foreign yoke. It was this commitment of the Congress party that in the post-Independence era they adopted a series of measures to alleviate their sufferings. The government integration curbed the rigours of the Dalits and opened their way to social and religious mobility though much remains to be done. For sometime the Civil Society let the government do its bit for the Dalits but soon the inadequacies of governmental efforts came to the forefront; the Civil Society again took up this issue. Several non-governmental organizations have taken up the cause of the amelioration of the condition of the Dalits. Some of them have achieved laudable success.

Samanvay Ashram was set up by Vinoba Bhave in Bodh Gaya in 1954. Its aimed at improving the condition of the Musahars in three blocks of Gaya district. The Ashram has provided residential educational facilities for Musahar boys and girls. They run a number of non-formal education centres for Harijans. They gave Harijan families a small piece of Bhoodan land along with agricultural inputs. They ensured irrigation facilities. This holistic approach aimed at improviing socio-economic condition of the Harijans.

In Bihar the most important and the most lasting contribution has been made by Sulabh International, founded by Mr. Bindeshwar Pathak. The NGO, aims at improving the lot of Bhangis, engaged in removing human excreta on their head from service lavatories. He has been successful because of his unique approach. He concentrated on replacing service lavatories by especially designed lavatories where the traditional sysem of removing excreta becomes obsolete. This resulted in loss of traditional occupations of the Bhangis. To overcome this, he simultaneously started training programmes for the members of the Bhangi community so that they would acquire new skills and go in for new occupations. During 1990-3, more than 3,000 young men and women of this caste group were trained in different crafts. They either got jobs or started their small business.

Dr Pathak began his work in 1970s and had soon moved out of Bihar. By early 1990s the Sulabh International was active in 109 towns all over the country. A fall out of this experiment was the establishment of Sulabh Sauchalay (or community lavatories) in different towns where after nominal payment one could use clean latrines, non-stinking urinals and take a bath. This has improved sanitation in towns and contributed to clean environment The Sulabh Sauchalays movement has received acclaim at both national and international levels. In this context one remembers the comments of eminent journalist Khuswant Singh after a visit to Patna in mid-1960s, '. . . every wall is a urinal.'

While the Sulabh International has been trying to improve the condition of a particular community, another NGO rose in early 1982 to cater to the needs of the entire community of the Dalits. This was the formation of Dalit Vikas Samiti by Father Kananaikil, a Catholic Christian missionary. He was attached to Indian Social Institute, New Delhi and was therefore theoretically conversant with challenges the new organization could face. Originally called Premdas Harijan Utthan Samiti, it was renamed Bihar Dalit Vikas Samiti.[56] It was concerned with general problems affecting the Dalits such as availability of safe drinking water, education, medical aid and general sanitation. Since then the Society has been very active. It has grown considerably. During the last quarter of a century, it has grown from strength to strength. It is now functioning in 15 districts. On 31 March 2004 village units numbering 7,923 were affiliated to it. The heartening fact was that 'Women's units continue to grow at a faster pace than that of men's units.' It had a membership of 1,52,897. The Samiti started Self-Help Groups on the model of Grameen Bank of Bangladesh. It had kept education of the Dalit children as one of its top priorities. As on 21 March 2004, BDVS was running 513 educational institiurions where 18,503 students were studying. Out of these 8,500, i.e. 45.93 per cent were girls. The Samiti publishes a quarterly newsletter from its Patna office. The functionaries of the Samiti pledge 'We the dalit family—mahapramukhs, youth pravaktas, pramukhs and members, prabharies, volunteers and animators, solemnly declare and promise that: We will make all the children of 6-14 age group of our families fully literate within three years, . . .'[57]

Prayas is another organization trying to improve the lot of Musahars and Harijans in Patna and Gaya during the last two decades. Sister Sudha Verghese has been the main inspiration behind this effort. Her dedication has been widely appreciated. The President of India, A.P.J. Abdul Kalam conferred upon her Padma Shree on the Republic Day.

While recounting the role of Christian missionaries we should not forget that they had started their efforts on village-level at Ossaiganj in Behea block, way back in 1930. When Jesuit Father Nicholas Pollard undertook this work among Ravidasis. He concentrated on education, medical aid, financial management, relief and rehabilitation work. He also looked after orphans. The Ravidasis mainly performed four tasks: removal of the body of dead animals, to tan leather, play musical instruments on religious and festive occasions and the female-folk worked as *Chamains*, i.e. assisted pregnant women during delivery. According to a survey in 1980, the Ravidasis of the village had a literacy rate of 60 per cent as against the general literacy rate of 13.63 per cent among the Scheduled Castes.[58]

It has been a common perception that attempts at improvement in the condition of Dalits have not fused into a movement either in Indian and especially in Bihar.

A common explanation is the Dalits have failed to throw up creative leadership. None of the leaders that emerged in Independent India could transform the Dalit discontent into an all India agitation.

All the Dalit leaders have tried to regain their regional and/or community base. Kanshi Ram was content to garner support of the Ravidasis, the community to which he belonged.

Ram Vilas Paswan has more concern for the Dushadhs and is the president of Akhil Bhartiya Dalit Sena.

It must be said that Dalits cannot escape from peculiar regional problems they face because of historical reasons. For example, Dalits in central Bihar have to face a caste war, not known in either the Punjab or Gujarat.

It is also a fact that when they rise up they behave as the upper/intermediate caste landlords towards their brethren. The most telling example of this has been the incident at Arwal (in Jahanabad district) in 1986. This was a conflict between a rich SC family whose head was a high government official and some poor Harijan families. The poor Harijan families were occupying a piece of public which the official coveted. The poor Harijan families sought the support of Mazdoor Kisan Sangram Samiti. He called the police. The police firing on the demonstrators left twenty-two persons dead. [A detailed account of atrocities perpetrated on the Dalits in Bihar can read in 'The Pattern of Abuse: Rural Violence in Bihar and the State's Response', in *Broken People: Caste Violence Against India's 'Untouchables'*, Human Rights Watch, New York, Washington, London, Brussels, pp. 42-81.]

However, even though the pace of change is slow but trans-formation is undoubtedly taking place. Internal attempts to bring about changes are also gaining strength. This is shown by an attempt of a group of Mushar women of Champaran to stop drunkenness in the community. The women, under the leadership of illiterate Girija Devi have successfully banished the evil of drinking in their area. They fought with their men-folk, they complained to the Police Station, they unitedly thwarted the efforts of intransigent men-folk to brow beat them. After succeeding in their own area, they have started to spread their message into the surrounding areas.

Girija Devi, for her tenacity to bring about reform, was invited to address the UNO session. Unfortunately she could not make the trip as her paper could not be readied within the short span of time.

All the sections of the Dalits are progressing though the pace of change varies from community to community.

For example, the Dhobis have the highest percentage of

literacy among the Dalits. They can be found in all professions and in all services. They may not have politicians of the stature of Kanshi Ram or Ram Vilas Paswan, but they have done fairly well.

The Paswans and Ravidasis have the second and third highest literacy among the Dalits. The Ravidasis are also the most numerous in Bihar among the Dalits. They occupy important position in bureaucracy, professions and politics. Currently, their political ascendancy is signified by Mrs Meira Kumar, Minister in the Central Cabinet, Kanshi Ram, the leader of the Bahujan Samaj Party and Miss Mayawati, the former Chief Minister of Uttar Pradesh.

In urban areas, many Dalits are shifting to non-traditional occupation. Those with higher education are occupying top positions in central and state services. These with professional degrees are working as doctors, engineers, etc. Many are teaching in universities, colleges and schools. Those who lack education are working as rickshaw pullers, waiters in restaurants, salesperson, etc.

But in rural areas atrocities on Harijans are still being perpetrated. Things would change when the problem is tackled at the national level by a national movement led by a national leader commanding support of a wide section of the society.

As a part of this strategy, the Dalits must be given possession of land. Farming would strengthen their economic base. It would mean that they would not completely be dependent upon the big landlords for a living. As the number of farm-labourers comes down, the big landlords would have no escape from paying them at least the minimum wages to ensure cultivation of their land.

As Bataidars the Dalit farmers are not in a position to sell paddy to the government procurement cell because at the time of the sale they are required to produce landownership papers. This means economic loss and loss of income. Since they cannot do so now, they have to sell their paddy to middle-men at lesser prices causing loss to them.

Secondly, these farmers are too poor to keep milch cattle,

another important source of income to rural landlords. It said that hardly between 1 and 2 per cent suppliers of milk to Confed are Dalits. They do not benefit by supplying milk under this scheme as it one would wish. Hence attempts should be made that Dalits have milch cattle. The government should either supply them or subsidise their purchase.

The Prime Minister's Rozgar Guarantee Yojana has promise to help the poor Dalits economically. But only effective implementation and careful monitoring can bring about the desired results. Otherwise, Dalits would benefit only marginally and the money would be embezzled by corrupt bureaucrats and politicians.

This disenchantment with the governmental has compelled the government to look for non-governmental agencies to execute developmental projects. For example, the government is planning to handover the revenue collection, maintenance and distribution of water of some canals to association of farmers with the express proviso that women and Dalits should have definite role in its functioning. If this happens things should improve the condition of Dalits.[59]

The government had been keen to promote literacy among the Dalits. Under the Sarva Shiksha Abhiyan, special effort is made to educate girls belonging to Scheduled Castes, Scheduled Tribes, extremely backward castes, minorities and those below the poverty line by opening residential girls schools.[60] This is another scheme along with thirteen other schemes through which the central government offers financial help to Scheduled Caste students. One study shows that between 1990-6, the Centre Government offered Rs. 280.7 crore. But the amount could not be disbursed to the Scheduled Caste students. The State Government was able to spend only Rs. 5.17 crore. Rs. 100 crore was either diverted to other schemes or posted in civil deposits. The Scheduled Caste students got only 8 per cent of the sanctioned amount. It is therefore clear that the government machinery has to be activated to ensure maximum benefits to Scheduled Caste students from government schemes.

The Dalits are now conscious of their rights. In the political arena they protest wherever they feel they are discriminated or neglected. In the elections to Rajya Sabha and Vidhan Parishad in March 2006 from Bihar, no Dalit was set up as a candidate by any political party. Protest voices were raised especially against the Socialist Party, Lok Janshakti Party and Rashtriya Janta Dal by Dalit activists.[61]

The Dalits have also formed Dalit Sena or Ambedkar Sena to face and retaliate against violence, perpetrated by upper and intermediate caste landlords. A combination of firm action, economic and social reformation only would ensure peace in the society.

Bihar Dalits have several achievements to their credit. They have served as Cabinet Ministers/Minister of State at the Centre. Besides Jagjivan Ram, they include Bhola Paswan, Ram Vilas Paswan, Mrs. Meira Kumar, Muni Lal, Sanjay Paswan, etc. As bureaucrats they have headed almost all departments at one time or the other. Bihar has had two Dalits as governors, Sri Jagannath Pahadia and Sardar Buta Singh.

POSTSCRIPT

It is clear that that the progress of Dalit communities in Bihar has been highly uneven. The worst sufferers have been the Musahars, the third largest community in the state. Partly, history has been responsible for this fate. As landless agricultural labourers, they were economically too poor to think of even a better fate for themselves. After all they got their name because they had to catch mice, or pick up grains from the excreta of cattle to satisfy their hunger. In 1991 their rate of literacy was 1.31 per cent. During the next ten years it rose to 2.20 per cent.[62] Another decade, the literacy rose to 3.4 per cent (Dr. A.K. Biswas, 'The Musahars of Bihar: A Neglected People'). Dr. Biswas shows that they have only 1,354 graduates out of 16,87,557 souls. There are probably no engineers or graduates among them.

The backwardness of Musahars has been graphically described in a recent write up published in *Hindustan* of 28 March 2006. The author says that Musahars living in around a dozen villages such as Siwan, Sirisian, Harerampur, Balthari, Ambalia, Jogipur, etc., still subsist on Ghoghan, Snake, Newala, Jackals, Frogs, etc. After marriage they migrate to the house of their wives. Consequently they have hardly stayed in one place from one generation to another. The women collect grains from the fields after the crop has been harvested; men collect grains from the holes of rats in the field. They hardly have time to think about change.

Dr. Rita Singh has recently published a monograph entitled *Bihar ke Musahar* from Patna.

However there is light at the end of the tunnel. Harsh Mander in his article 'Living with Hunger', published in the *Frontline* of 8 November 2002 has shown that Musahars living in adjoining district of Uttar Pradesh are migrating to the Punjab as mechanization of agriculture has robbed them of traditional job opportunities in the farm sector. They have also started working in brick kilns. Migration will definitely change their mindset as they come in contact with the wider world. Academics have started taking interest in this community. Needless to say sooner or later politicians and bureaucrats will be compelled to take notice of problems faced by the community and take specific and proper measures to eliminate their backwardness.

NOTES

1. Hetukar Jha, 'Promises and Lapses: Understanding the Experience of the Scheduled Casts in Bihar in Historical Perspective', *Journal of Indian School of Political Economy*, vol. XII, nos. 3 & 4, July-December 2000, p. 426.
2. Ibid.
3. Ibid.
4. Ibid.
5. Ibid., p. 427.
6. W.N. Kuber, 'Dalit Movements in India', in V.D. Divekar (ed.), *Social Reform Movement in India*, Bombay, 1991, p. 96.
7. K.K. Datta, *Freedom Movement in Bihar*, Patna, 1957, p. 374.
8. Ibid., p. 399.
9. Ibid., p. 628.
10. Petra Heidrich, 'Ochre Robe and Tricolour, Sanyasis and Sadhus in

social Movements in the First Half of 20th Century', in Annemarie Hafner (ed.), *Essays on South Asian Society, Culture and Politics*, Berlin, 1995, p. 63.

11. Kuber, op. cit., p. 96.
12. Braj Kishor Pandey, *Dalit Samasya ki Rajniti*, Delhi, 2003, p. 38.
13. Jha, p. 434.
14. Rajendra Prasad, *Atmakatha*, New Delhi, 2002, pp. 330-1.
15. Anugrah Narain Sinha, *Mere Sansmaran*, 2nd edn., Patna, 1961, p. 154.
16. Kishor Kunal, *Dalit-Devo Bhava*, Publications Division, 2006.
17. *Social Reforms . . .*, p. 86.
18. Ibid.
19. Sumitra Devi, *Sri Jagjivan Ram Jeevan Aur Mahanta*, Patna, n.d., pp. 111-13.
20. Jha, p. 433.
21. Jha, p. 431.
22. *Selected Works of Mahatma Gandh*, vol. 63, pp. 38-40.
23. Ibid.
24. Sinha, p. 185; and Sumitra Devi, pp. 116-17.
25. K.K. Datta, *The Writings And Speeches of Mahatma Gandhi Relating to Bihar 1917-1947*, Patna, 1960, p. 243.
26. *The Writings and Speeches . . .*, pp. 243-4.
27. Ibid., p. 26.
28. Ibid., p. 27.
29. Ibid., p. 27.
30. Jha, 432.
31. Sumitra Devi, p. 119.
32. Christophe Jaffrelot, *India's Silent Revolution*, Delhi, 2005, pp. 98, 99.
33. Ibid., p. 99, fn. 2.
34. Sumitra Devi, p. 121.
35. Ibid., p. 122.
36. *Atmakatha*, p. 689.
37. Jha, p. 432.
38. Ibid., 433.
39. Jaffrelot, p. 99.
40. Jha, 434.
41. *Hindustan*, 17 March 2006.
42. Aloka Srivastava, 'Dalit Identity in Bihar', in Fernando Franco (ed.), *Pain and Awakening: The Dynamics of Dalit Identity in Bihar, Gujarat and Uttar Pradesh*, Delhi, 2002, p. 57.
43. Jha, 436.
44. Rajlaxmi Rath, 'Social Transformation among Scheduled Castes in

Bihar: Case Study of Three Generations in Bihar', in A.K. Lal (ed.), *Protective Discrimination, Ideology and Praxis*, New Delhi, 2002, p. 101.

45. Jha, p. 435.
46. Ibid., pp. 435-6.
47. Ibid., p. 436.
48. Quoted in Aloka Srivastava, p. 117.
49. Mishra, p. 16.
50. Srivastava, p. 80.
51. Ibid., p. 79.
52. Rath, p. 102.
53. Ibid., p. 105.
54. *Times of India*, 2 April 2000, quoted – Jha, p. 436.
55. Jha, p. 438.
56. *Aryavarta*, 5 May 1999.
57. *Consolidated Annual Report 2003-2004*, Bihar Dalit Vikas Samiti, Patna.
58. Jose Kalapura, 'Challenge of Socio-Religious Structures: The Chrstianisation of the Ravidasis of Bihar', *Proceedings*, Indian History Congress, 56th Session, Madras, Calcutta, 1997, pp. 592-8.
59. *Hindustan*, 17 March 2006.
60. Ibid.
61. *Hindustan*, 18 March 2006.
62. Jose Vadasery, 'Dalit Literacy and Education in Bihar', in A.K. Lal, op. cit., p. 111.

CHAPTER 13

The Roots of Conservatism and Casteism: A Study of Social Change in Bihar in the Second Half of the Nineteenth Century

During the second half of the nineteenth century several factors emerged which challenged social norms, attitudes and customs; the response to these challenges determined the direction and extent of social change. The present study takes into account some of these forces such as new system of education and new technology and tries to study in outline the change ushered in by them.

An undeniable fact in Bihar during the period under review was the growth of literacy at primary, secondary and collegiate levels. The term 'growth' is used here in a restricted sense for the percentage was very poor. Between 1886-90 and 1904-5 the percentage of primary education remained practically static, at about 2 per cent. Patna and Chaibasa, the two districts, were often in the vanguard, though for entirely different reasons. By force of historical reasons the former was the chief administrative town in Bihar and so contained more literate persons than any other district. Chaibasa, besides bordering on Bengal, where education was more widespread than in Bihar, had an influx of Christian missionaries, who in their attempt to spread the Christian religion, supplemented the meagre official efforts to propagate literacy among the tribals. In the year 1891-2, between 3 and 5 per cent of the population was literate in Chaibasa. The Patna district had this figure during the year 1889-90. But other districts were far behind and the figure for Bihar territory as a whole in 1904-5 was about 2 per cent. Thus education, an important aspect of social change, was not playing the role it ought to have because of governmental policy as well as popular apathy.

The first Zila school was opened in Patna in 1835[1] and it was followed by schools in Arrah in 1836, Bhagalpur in 1837 and Chhapra in 1839. After 1857 all the district headquarters were covered by Zila schools but obviously the spread of English and non-English education was extremely unsatisfactory. Similarly, college education was confined to very few as, up to 1880s, there was only one college in Bihar, Patna College, which came into being on 9 January 1863. The Zila schools acted as beacons of new education. All the Bihar leaders towards the end of the nineteenth century and the beginning of the twentieth century received their education in these schools. In Patna and Chaibasa the figures of secondary and collegiate education remained constant around 0.25 per cent between 1889-90 and 1904-5.

All over Bihar the percentage slided back as the comparable figures in north Bihar were only around 0.05 per cent over the same period.

Female education began to look up only towards the end of the nineteenth century but here again the figures were extremely poor. The district of Monghyr along with Patna and Chaibasa was in the lead.[2] But the fact remained that the people had become conscious of the need for female education. The Brahmos and the Christian missionaries were striving in that direction[2] and once in a while Biharis also attempted to promote education among the girls. The *Bihar Times* in 1897 began to campaign for girls education and criticized those who found the idea of a girl school 'revolting'.[4] The Maharani of Bettiah had opened a school for the girls in Bettiah.[5]

The unevenness and poor figures of literacy in Bihar point out both to the uneven and imperceptible nature of social transformation that was overtaking it during this period.

The literacy figures included those receiving indigenous as well as Western education. Since the recipients of higher education were extremely limited in number, it was not surprising that no educated professional class consisting of doctors, engineers, etc., could emerge in the society.

In fact, the only professional education seems to have been confined to survey schools and Industrial schools. The survey and drawing classes were started in 1871 in Patna College[6] and an independent institution Patna Survey School was started in March 1876.[7] It is interesting that out of 31 students on its roll in 1880, only three were Hindus and the rest were Muhammadans. This shows the reluctance of the Hindus to go in for professional training. In order to popularize the survey school among Biharis, the government laid down that only those born or brought up in Bihar were entitled for scholarship. But even then the first fourteen students in 1893-4 were all Bengalis.[8]

Similar was Bihari response to Industrial schools. The Industrial School was opened in Patna in 1879 with 150 students[9] but by the end of the year the number had dwindled to 20.[10] A technical school opened in Dehri had to be amalgamated with that of Howrah in 1880 because of poor response from the students.[11]

The Temple Medical School was started in 1874 but the Hindus remained indifferent so much so that there was only one Bihari Hindu medical graduate in 1896[12] and there were no engineers. Nobody came forward to avail of the offer of a scholarship awarded by the Bhagalpur National Improvement Association for study in the Calcutta Medical College. There was no Bihari student in the Veterinary College.[13] In other words, in Bihar no professional class of engineers and doctors could emerge in the nineteenth century. The absence of this class contributed to the stagnancy in the society because by the nature of their professional duties, the doctors and engineers have to be rationalists and believers in truths demonstrated by logical reasoning and experimentation.

In spite of stagnancy in percentages there was a definite increase in absolute number of literate persons in Bihar, a very important fact of the social life of this period. Even this limited growth of education ushered in social changes and unleashed movements of varying intensity for social transition.

However, this hesitant growth calls for explanation. Why is it that Bihar which came under the sway of the English along with Bengal did not keep up with the latter when it took up Western education? A look at enrolment in Patna College during initial years shows that Bengali students outnumbered the Biharis, which is inexplicable when it is noted that for persons with English education jobs were going a begging in Bihar. The government had to import Bengali teachers for the schools even though it was realized that imperfect knowledge of local language was a handicap in the efficient discharge of their duties.[14]

The absence of English-educated Biharis necessitated the import of Bengalis in even petty clerical posts and jobs in the schools. In their wake also came Bengalis of independent professions, lawyers and doctors, etc. Many Bengalis also crossed over to areas of Bihar adjoining Bengal on account of deteriorating climatic conditions as a result of silting up canals and consequent increase in malaria. Thus, a sizeable number of educated Bengalis happened to live in Bihar and formed the biggest intellectual elite in the society. The Bengali teachers were especially in a favourable position to mould the thinking of the impressionable Bihari young men who were under their care. But the presence of Bengalis as governmental functionaries had caused a reaction among the Biharis even in the 1870s.

The Bihari middle-class had come to regard them as 'copressors' Bhudev Mukherjee, who was appointed Inspector of Schools in the 1870s, records that his arrival drew the comment from the local population, *'Aate hain Bengali Bihari ke dukhdai'* (the Bengalis come to oppress).[15] Thus, the Bengali-Bihari feeling, which arose at the level of middle-class towards the end of the century in an acute form, had already appeared.

While talking of education, one is struck by the fact that in the 1860s, 1870s and probably in the 1880s the Muslims were more responsive to English education than the Hindus. All the five Bihari fellows, of Calcutta University in 1899 were Muslims. Moreover, Urdu had been included in the Calcutta University syllabus, but Hindi had yet to find a place.[16] Consequently the Muslims had more of high government jobs in Bihar than their Bihari Hindu counterparts. In 1893 there were four Muslim munsifs as compared to three Hindus, and between 1895 and 1899 twelve Muslims were appointed to gazetted posts as compared to seven Hindus.[17] Practically all these Muslims belonged to aristocratic and zamindari families. Thus in Bihar at least the Muslims had not shunned Western education or governmental positions. This is, in spite of the fact, that Bihar was the storm-centre of Wahhabi movement in the post-1857 era, which called upon the Muslims to restore the primitive glory of Islam by following laws laid down by the Prophet. In fact, among the Muslims, several organizations for popularizing Western education were active. Mention may be made of Bihar Scientific Society, established in 1868 at Muzaffarpur through the efforts of Imdad Ali.[18] Though not an exclusive preserve of the Muhammadans, it published a bimonthly Urdu paper *Akhbar-ul-Akhbar* and brought out translations of sciénfic works into Urdu. It also opened eight or nine middle schools in Muzaffarpur.[19]

Among the Muslims of Bihar, two parallel developments could be observed. On the one hand serious efforts were being made to popularize Western education and, on the other hand, traditional Islamic learning was also being propagated. *Maktabs* and *madrasas* all over the state flourished where Persian and Arabic were taught to familiarize the students with Islamic theology, jurisprudence and philosophy. The crucial fact to remember is that education was not ignored and it did not lose importance. Education was a means for changing social status, for earning one's bread and also for controlling levers of power in the society. Hence, both traditional and Western education received attention. Thus, the Muslim community was not inward looking. It was casting its glances towards the new forces in the society that had come into play.

Another proof that the Muslims were becoming conscious of the changes in the world around them can be seen in the growth of Urdu journalism. According to one author the period 1857 and 1914 was the golden age for Urdu journalism in Bihar. No less than sixty journals, newspapers, etc., were started.[20] These were published from various urban centres and occasionally from villages. Among urban centres from where publications in Urdu came out were Patna, Gaya, Muzaffarpur, Monghyr, Chhapra, Bihar Sharif,[21] etc. Among the villages mention may be made of as Khujwa and[22] Phulwari Sharif.[23] Some of these *Akhbar-ul-Akhbar* (Muzaffarpur), *Chasma-i-ilm* (Patna), *Shuja-i-Meher* (Muzaffarpur), *Akhbar-i-Anjum, Mujakira Ilmiya* (Patna), *Lama-i-Nur* (Muzaffarpur), *Institute* (Patna), etc., were organs of societies aiming to promote modern knowledge and education among the Muslims. The Muslims in Bihar, despite the growth of Wahhabi movement, never shunned Western education and thus did not ignore the currents of change that were stirring the society.

In view of the above it is obvious why in Bihar bitterness between the Hindus and the Muslims was absent as compared to Bengal where the Hindus monopolized the government jobs and also surpassed the Muslims in acquisition of English education. So at the turn of the twentieth century when political consciousness against the British began to manifest itself, the Hindus and the Muslims of Bihar were found, by and large, united.

The growth in absolute number of literates in Bihar began to show its effect by the 1890s. The demand for higher education and more share in government jobs increased in Bihar. Since Bihar did not have adequate number of institutions of higher learning, Bihari youths left for adjacent areas where facilities existed. Many Bihari youths went to Calcutta; some of them were also attracted towards. Benares[24] and the newly established University of Allahabad was then emerging as another important centre of Western education in north India. The Kayastha community under the leadership of Munshi Kali Prasad had opened the Kayastha Pathshala (a college) in 1872.

In the 1890s, this was converted into a college and became the focal point for Bihari students specially from western Bihar because of easy accessibility. Simultaneously he started the publication of *Kayastha Samachar* in Urdu to carry the message of social reform to the members of his community.[25] Eventually it became an English paper and in 1900 Dr. Sachchidanand Sinha, a Bihari Kayastha, assumed its editorship.[26]

The more enterprising among Biharis began to cross the seas for studying in England. Two prominent names which stand out during this period are that of Maulana Mazharul Haque and Dr. Sachchidanand Sinha.[27] Sea voyage was an anathema to orthodox Hindus. Mahamahopadhyaya Ganga Nath Jha describes how even the Maharaja of Darbhanga had to use subterfuge before undertaking a journey to Europe for medical treatment. Eventually his courage ran out and he gave up plans.[28] Among the Kayasthas, there was a good deal of agitation against sea voyage and several of the Kayasthas who had crossed the seas were ostracized from the caste. The outcastes had to perform penance before being accepted again in the community. However, soon sea voyage was accepted by the Kayasthas.[29] Education was breaking the shackles of caste-orthodoxy.

Among Bihari Hindus the lead for English education was taken up by the Kayasthas, who were traditionally service-holders or bureaucrats and did not entirely depend upon land for their livelihood. A Kayastha, Govinda Charan was the first Bihari to have passed M.A. in English. He edited the first English journal to be published by a Bihari – *The Indian Chronicle.* His brother Mahesh Narayan subsequently became the founder-editor *of Bihar Times* in 1884.[30]

The Bhumihars and Rajputs, who formed the bulk of the landed aristocracy and landholding peasantry, followed suit. The Brahmans also took to English education although their response varied depending upon local conditions.

Demand for higher education led to the opening of a few more colleges by the end of the century by the public who also began to take more active interest in the spread of education. The Bihar National College, Patna and Langat Singh College, Muzaffarpur, among others came into existence during this phase and are still thriving. These English schools and colleges helped the formation of the Bihari educated middle class. The leaders of Bihar public life at the beginning of the twentieth century were the products of these schools and colleges. However, in Bihar, as compared to the neighbouring Bengal, public enthusiasm for English education was still less. It is difficult to explain this situation because Bihar as a whole was hardly economically better off in order to miss this chance of sharing government jobs. Actually, clamour for government jobs was made a plank for the movement of separation of Bihar from Bengal because Biharis were supposed to lose to the Bengalis in competition as a result of poor grounding in English education. A separate Bihar wound have meant greater security of government jobs and more opportunity to the lawyers—the most numerous professional class which had been brought into existence as a result of the English education in the last few decades of the nineteenth century.

The English educated Bihari middle-class became the most vocal element in society. A look at its composition explains its motivations. It was wholly upper caste and predominantly upper class. The scions of the landed aristocracy or the Kayastha community contributed to its numbers. It now spearheaded the revolt against conservatism in religious beliefs and social practices. Two of its leaders married outside the state. Shri Deep Narain Singh married a Bengali lady and Dr. Sachchidanand Sinha took as his wife a lady from the Punjab. Dr. Sinha too had already flouted the taboo against sea-voyage and refused to seek forgiveness in spite of social ostracism by his fellow caste-men.

Among the Kayasthas voices against social evils were being raised. Munshi Pearey Lall had in the 1860s opposed extravagance in marriage ceremony and the dowry system.[31] An organization Anjuman-e-Hind was set up in different towns of Bihar, Arrah, Patna, Gaya, Chhapra, Muzaffarpur, Darbhanga, Ranchi, Sahebganj, Dumraon, Buxar, Sasaram, Bhabhua, etc. in the 1870s to popularize the ideas of Munshi Pearey Lall.[32] It was, however, soon apparent that people paid only lip service to these ideals and in practice remained traditionalists.

The awareness for the need of social reform had led the Kayasthas to establish a caste-organization, the Kayastha Conference in 1887.[33] The conference met in Gaya in 1897 and besides condemning other social evils, it called upon its members to support the temperance movement.[34] Sri Gajadhar Prasad, a votary of social reform among the Kayasthas, was the president of the Temperance Society in Bihar.

Thus the outcry against social customs, which prevented the educated class from competing on equal terms with their Bengali or Christian peers in matters of governmental jobs, professional career or social intercourse, began. Educated persons among both the Hindus and the Muslims began to raise their voice against ritualism, evils of dowry system and unnecessary pomp. Some of them also supported widow remarriage. Several local associations were formed by enthusiastic young men. Mention may be made of the Muzaffarpur Dharma Sabha which brought out two magazines to propagate against the dowry system and other social evils.[35] But in comparison to Bengal these movements were comparatively weak. Even all-India reform movements like the Arya Samaj and the Theosophical Society failed to have any significant impact on the middle-class, although their branches in Bihar were established soon after they were founded.[36]

One would think that the Brahmo Samaj, which had originated in the contiguous territory of Bengal would have some worthwhile impact in Bihar, especially in view of the fact that a number of Bengali Brahmos had settled down in different parts of the province. Many of them were employed as teachers in schools and colleges and had thus ample opportunity to project their ideals and impress the young Bihari minds. As a matter of fact, the response to these movements in Bihar was curious and may be termed as somewhat unique. All the important reform movements stood against the caste system. But in Bihar, the attack on it brought it further into focus. Caste became the most important matter of concern. Caste consciousness began to develop. Several caste organizations came into existence ostensibly for changing the outlook of their caste-men but in actuality to look after 'caste interests'. This is the origin of the present-day caste consciousness in Bihar. Why this over emphasis on caste? Only a social psychologist can answer the question. To a student of history this is one of those phenomena with which human history often abound but which defy rational explanation.

Initially these caste organizations in a limited sense played a positive and progressive role by exhorting their caste men to take up English education, to disown dowry system and such other social practices. They also succeeded in breaking down intra-caste barriers to some extent. But the net result was that caste stratifications became more pronounced. Inter-caste rivalries were sharpened and jealousies fostered. Thus ostensible attempts to destroy the caste system, actually reinforced it.

This was also true of the economically well-off lower castes, especially those who were engaged in trade and crafts. They adopted the new ideologies preached by organizations such as Arya Samaj because it promised them a social status in commensurate with their economic position. Some of their social disabilities in respect of joint meals with the upper caste people were lessened. Intra-caste mobility among them was visible. But they too were unwilling to lose or submerge their caste identities. Their new caste consciousness was reflected in the setting up of caste organizations even among the so-called 'lower classes'. Failure to strike at the rest of casteism fostered social conservatism.

Together with the consciousness of caste, the consciousness of being either Hindu or Muslim made faint appearances. Violence occasionally broke out and communal polarization could be detected in political life.[37] But on the whole, Hindu-Muslim unity was preached by the leaders of both the communities. A sign of Hindu-Muslim unity was the interest taken by the Hindus in the promotion of Urdu journalism in the province during the period under review. A number of Hindus brought out journals in Urdu. Mention may be made of *Akhbar-i-Bihar* begun by Lala Binda Prasad Hasrati from Patna in 1856, *Weekly Report* from Gaya by Munshi J.J. Ram in 1856,[38] *Akhbar-ul-Akhbar* from Muzaffarpur in 1868 edited by Babu Ajodhya Prasad Maneri,[39] *Guldasta-i-Najaer,* published from Gaya in 1871 was owned by Sri Rameshchandra Sarkar. *Nadir-ul-Akhbar* which came out from Monghyr in 1872 was owned by Ram Prasad Dilshad,[40] *Majma-ul-Fawaid,* a supplement to *Nadir-ul-Akhbar* appeared in 1878. *Nasim-i-Saran* was published from Chhapra by Babu Rakhi Kumar Chatterjee. *Mushir-i-Bihar* was brought out from Patna in 1880 and was edited by Babu Govind Charan Vakil, etc.[41] It is interesting to note that among the names mentioned above, some are of Bengali Hindus.

We have dealt above mainly the influence of new education on the social transformation in the second half of the century. There were factors also, though they were less conspicuous at first glance. In Bihar the introduction of the railways in some parts proved to be significant.

The spread of the railways was the harbinger of increased mobility for the people, and it was evident in population displacement. It became easier for groups of Biharis to go out to work as labourers in the tea-plantations of Assam or jute mills of Bengal or even in the mines of Chotanagpur. In north Bihar, specially in the district of Chhapra (Saran), there was a great pressure on land because of the decline of the traditional salt-petre industry, which had formerly supported a large number of labourers. No alternate local employment possibilities had appeared. The railways siphoned off the surplus labour of the district to Assam, Bengal and Chotanagpur and other areas where unskilled jobs were available in plenty. Similarly, railway helped a large number of persons to go to Calcutta and then to emigrate to Burma, the West Indies and Mauritius, etc. Thus big fractions of the population could now go over long distances for a short period or for long periods. In certain districts of Bihar, a sizeable sector of population earned its living by working in far-off places. These job opportunities which appeared in the wake of the introduction of railways brought economic stability to some pockets specially in the district of Chhapra where, in 1901, 10 per cent of the population had gone out to earn their livelihood.[42] A complete economic breakdown of the old society was prevented.

Similarly, the railways also helped to soften the rigours of caste system in its outward form because journey in a railway compartment naturally meant the company of passengers of various castes, and the travelling person was compelled to drink water from a common well or a common tap. But in essence, caste rigidity was not modified; there was no inter-caste mobility.

The emigration of labour from Bihar, which was seasonal as well as for long stretches of time, had important repercussions on the family system. The labourers did not always take away his wife and children and needed somebody to look after them; and naturally his choice was the joint family, which instead of disintegrating because of his absence became stronger as it was called upon to perform a new function. Another consequence was that the labourer retained his bonds in the village and was not lost to his original society. He practically always returned to its fold. The emigrant labourer was unable to strike roots in new places. The Bihari labourer did not become the homeless proletariat, the antithesis of capitalists, as envisaged by Karl Marx. The population mobility did alleviate the economic distress.

The joint family thrived on traditionalism and social con-servatism, and in spite of the efforts of a section of upper classes, it had a strong tendency to perpetuate itself. In absence of any detailed study it would be hazardous to guess as to what changes resulted in attitude, norms and other habits of the labourer as a consequence of the contact with the outside world. However, in Saran, infant marriage was much less common and the growth of population was less than in other parts of Bihar.[43] The emigrant labourer hardly had any education. He was not in a position to educate his younger kinsmen and progeny who as a rule had stayed behind in the villages. This handicap along with the traditional role of the caste-system did not allow him to look forward to betterment of his material prospects and enhancement of his social status. Even the process of Sanskritization was not at this stage available to him. Hence, he hardly bothered himself about new attitudes and fresh norms of social behaviour. Bihar thus remained significantly different from Maharashtra where Jyotiba Phule at least roused the consciousness of the depressed castes and classes. Again it is equally distinguishable from Tamil Nadu where the Nadars made determined efforts to rise in the social hierarchy. In cities some erosion of caste privileges and disabilities took place, but in villages the situation hardly changed.

The growth of literacy had led to the rise of the press both English and vernacular, which also helped to accelerate the pace of social reform and national consciousness. Periodicals both in English and vernacular were printed and various pamphlets were in circulation from time to time. Most of these journals often ceased publication after a short time. We have already referred to publications in Urdu. In Hindi a number of publications brought out from 1870 onwards up to the end of the nineteenth century were mainly interested in social reform primarily of the community to which the publisher belonged.[44] The story of Hindi journalism might be said to begin from the publication of *Bihar Bandhu* in 1874 from Patna.[45] It is a sign of Hindu-Muslim amity that the first editor of the paper was a Muslim, Hasan Ali, a family friend of the proprietor. Munshi Hasan Ali tried his hand in Hindi journalism again when he started the publication of a monthly, *Motichoor.*

Patna was the main centre but Hindi journals began to be published from several other towns such as Arrah, Bhagalpur, Muzaffarpur, Chhapra, Bettiah, Motihari, Gaya, Aurangabad, etc.[46] Once in a while journals were also brought out from villages as well, for example *Vidyadharma Deepika* of Chandrashekhardhar Mishra came out from Ratanmala.[47] Hindi daily of *Bihar Sarva Hitaishi* came out from Patna in 1890 under the editorship of Babu Mahabir Prasad. The period saw a definite growth in the number of Hindi journals and periodicals, it is not therefore surprising that social reformers tried to propagate their views through the press. Hence, we have at the same time a proliferation of journals with the specific purpose of social reform and social change. However, these journals were usually the mouth-piece of a particular community. Mention may be made of *Dwij Patrika* (published in 1890 from Patna), *Kshatriya Patrika* under the editorship of Babu Ramdin Singh, the proprietor of Khadgavilas Press, *Brahman* of Pandit Pratap Narayan Mishra published in 1897, *Khatri Hitaishi, Kshatriya Samachar, Kayastha Hitaishi, Bhumihar Brahman Patrika, Teli Samachar, Rauniyar Hitaishi, Madhyadeshiya Vanik Patrika.* etc.[48] It may be noted that not many of these survived for long and even among the so-called lower castes, consciousness for introducing social change was growing. In fact the list also makes the point that removal of social disabilities always had its caste dimension and orientation.

In north Bihar, the indigo-planters formed a distinct social group by themselves. Living in an alien land, their primary concern was to earn as much money as possible and some of them may have considered the mass of humanity surrounding them merely an object of exploitation and inferior in all respects. The tales of oppression of the indigo-planters were many. It was not surprising that the local population hated them. The indigo planters felt themselves insecure. They had a corps of mounted armed volunteers who were expected not only to defend themselves against the local population but also to terrorize them.[49] Of couse they hardly made any effort to mingle with the populace. They were like islands of Europeans living in far off villages and with occasional exceptions they tenaciously tried to keep-up their European identity.[50] The behaviour of the English bureaucrats posted in the cities was not much different; the events of 1857 had further widened the chasm between the Indians and Englishmen.[51] However, there were occasional indigo-planters, who took keen interest in the welfare of the local populace. For example, Messrs Thomson and Fox established and supported an English school in Jagdishpur.[52]

Thus, in the second half of the nineteenth century, the most important social change could be said to be the formation of the English-educated middle-class, which acquired vested interest in government services and legal profession and became irritated by social taboos. This educated class had not yet entered into either business or industries nor they had taken enthusiastically to medical or engineering professions. The reason for lack of attention to industry was that the nascent middle-class still retained its ties with the villages in shape of *zamindaris* or landholdings and could always turn to them for sustenance. So it showed practically no interest in commerce and industries and the Bihari capitalist class did not emerge and the estrangement between the villages and the towns was not noticeable. Kazi Reza Hussain, a Muslim aristocrat of Patna was an exception. He believed that people should invest their money in joint-stock companies and take to commercial pursuits. Hence, when in 1880s the Patna Tramway Company was established to run trams in Patna by an Englishman he purchased shares and encouraged his friends and relatives to do likewise.[53] It may be noted that the Muslims had the vision to realize the potentiality of Joint-stock Companies. The urban-rural dichotomy was practically absent. In fact the urban elite had merely made the city another temporary and convenient halting place while he remained in service of profession. Sometimes a city residence was merely a convenience for educating the children or for looking after other interests especially if one had a zamindari because in this case litigation was virtually endemic. A facile generalization that the urban centres in Bihar were usually extended villages may not be very wide-off the mark. It explains the virtual absence of urbanization. No new city of commercial or industrial importance grew in Bihar, except in the Chotanagpur area. The traditional crafts had decayed with the advent of machine-made goods and so the cities which formerly owed their prosperity to them had lost importance. Some of the old cities continued as mere administrative centres or railway junctions, and failed to have worthwhile impact on social life.

An overview of the whole thing would therefore suggest that ripples of change had begun to appear on the surface. It would be wrong to describe the society as stagnant, just as it would be fallacious to describe it as dynamic. The ground was prepared for social changes which invaded it in the beginning of the twentieth century. The local people had begun to show concern. One example was the emergence of the Bhagalpur National Improvement Association in 1897 under the presidentship of Hariballabh Narayan of Sunbarsa.[54]

The social changes initiated in the State remained largely confined to the upper castes. Moreover, the upper castes accepted only those modifications in its social habits and attitudes which would enable them to go in for English education and land them governmental jobs or help to establish themselves as professionals. In other words, there was no attempt to challenge the basis or the basic elements of the social structure. They held back when they were called upon to challenge the caste. system, ensure equality to womenfolk and shun ritualism. Hence, the situation at the turn of the century was that reform from above was not forthcoming. Whatever new features appeared were only on the surface. At the grass-root level no serious effort was made. Bihar, therefore, entered the twentieth century with burdens of conservatism and casteism on its back and to this day, has not been able to free itself from these twin evils.

NOTES

1. K.K. Datta (ed.), *The Comprehensive History of Bihar*, vol. III, pt. II, K.P. Jayaswal Research Institute, Patna, 1976, p. 409 [henceforth cited as CHB II, pt. II].
2. All the figures have been compiled from the reports of the Director of Public Instruction Bengal for the years referred to.
3. CHB III, pt. II, Chapter XVII.
4. Satyanarain Prasad and Surendra Gopal, '"The *Behar Times* and News" and the Social Awakening in Bihar (1894-1912)'.
5. *Bhudev Charit* II, p. 157.
6. Satyanarain Prasad, 'Origins of Technical Education in Bihar (1854-1915)', *PIHC*, Jabalpur, 1970, vol. II, p. 187.
7. Ibid., p. 188.
8. Ibid., p. 190.
9. Ibid., p. 88.
10. Ibid., p. 189
11. Ibid.
12. Surendra Gopal, *Patna in the 19th Century*, Naya Prakash, Calcuta, 1982, p. 54.
13. '"The *Behar Times* and News" and the Social Awakening in Bihar', pp. 3-6.
14. *A History of the Patna College*, Patna, 1963.

15. Bhudev Mukhopadhyay, *Bhudev Charit*, vol. II, n.d., p. 122.
16. V.C.P. Choudhri, *The Making of Modern Bihar*, Patna, p. 64
17. Ibid., pp. 69-72
18. V.A. Narain, 'The Role of Bihar Scientific Association in the Spread of Western Education in Bihar', *PIHC*, Varanasi, 1969, p. 421.
19. Ibid., p. 423.
20. Dr. Muzaffar Iqbal, 'Sube Bihar ki Urdu Sahafat ke Sau Saal', *Souvenir* published on the occasion of All India Urdu Editors Conference, 1972, Patna, p. 8.
21. Ibid., pp. 8-16.
22. Ibid., p. 16.
23. Ibid.
24. *The Autobiographical Notes of Mm. Dr. Sir Ganga Nath Jha*, ed. Hetukar Jha, Allahabad, pp. 29-31.
25. Lucy Caroll, 'Kayastha Samachar: From a Caste—To a National Newspaper', *IESHR*, vol. X, no. 3, p. 281.
26. Ibid., p. 282.
27. Q. Ahmad and J.S. Jha, *Mazharul Haque*, Publications Division, New Delhi, 1976, p. 7. Mazharul Haque left for London in May 1888. B.P. Sinha, *Sachchidanand Sinha*, Publications Division, New Delhi, 1969, p. 23. He left for London in December 1889.
28. *The Autobiographical Notes . . .*, pp. 33, 35.
29. Satyanarain Prasad and Surendra Gopal, '"The *Behar Times* and News", and the Social Awakening in Bihar (1894-1912)', p. 7.
30. Lucy Caroll, 'Kayastha Samachar . . .', p. 290.
31. V.A. Narain, 'Munshy Pearey Lall and the Anti-Dowry Agitation', *PIHC*, Muzaffarpur, 1972, p. 531.
32. Ibid., p. 532.
33. Lucy Caroll, 'Origins of the Kayastha Temperance Movement', *IESHR*, vol. XI, no. 4, p. 440.
34. Ibid., p. 441; The temperance movement had appeared in north India.
35. Bihar National Improvement Association of Bhagalpur was another example. Similar Associations came into being at Bankipur and Purnea.
36. The first branch of Arya Samaj seems to have been established in 1878.
37. In the district of Saran under the influence of *Gorakshini Sabha* during 1893-5 in some villages Muslims were prevented from drawing water from the common well. *Bengal District Gazetteers, Saran*, Calcutta, 1908, pp. 39-40. Swami Dayanand Saraswati, the

founder of Arya Samaj had started the Gorakshini Sabha in 1882. J.N. Farquhar, 'The Arya Samaj'. *The Punjab Past and Present*, vol. VIII, pt. I, April 1973, p. 213.

38. Alam, op. cit., p. 8.
39. Ibid., p. 9.
40. Ibid., p. 10.
41. Ibid., p. 11.
42. *Bengal District Gazetteers, Saran*, p. 34.
43. Ibid.
44. Bishwanath Lal, 'Language Journalism in Bihar: Retrospect and Prospect', *Souvenir*, Indian Federation of Working Journalist, Patna, p. 45.
45. Ibid., p. 46.
46. Ibid., pp. 46-7.
47. Ibid.
48. Ibid., p. 47.
49. *Bhudev Charit* II, pp. 257-8.
50. *Patna in the 19th Century*, pp. 31-2.
51. Pat Barr, *The Memsahibs*, Allied Publishers, Bombay, 1978, p. 143.
52. Resolution, General Department, Education, Fort William, the 10th November 1870.
53. Syed Abdul Gilani, *Hayate Reza*, Aligarh, 1935, p. 32.
54. *The Bihar Times*, 25 February 1897.

CHAPTER 14

An Elite Group in the Second Half of the Nineteenth Century in Bihar

In the second half of the nineteenth century, a small group of people proficient in the English language emerged in several areas under British rule. This qualification enabled them to secure appointments to some top-level and middle-level jobs such as membership of the provincial civil service, non-gazetted clerical posts, etc., under the auspices of the alien government. A knowledge of English also helped them to take up a variety of professions such as law, journalism, teaching and so on. Besides, they were in a position to play another crucial role. When the British government decided to introduce a modicum of local self-government in the country, they were the persons who were initially called upon to shoulder this responsibility. In fact, this emerging class was the new middle class and it also assumed the form of an elite group.

Against this broader national framework, the role and activities of the English-educated people in Bihar deserves to be studied. The findings might show the process or processes at work in the society when it faced a challenge for change. We might also know the attitudes and the norms that developed in the colonial context.

In the second half of the nineteenth century the number of English-knowing persons in Bihar was extremely limited because of two factors. First, the efforts of the government to this end began comparatively late as compared to Bengal, Madras and Bombay. Secondly even after the government tried to promote the knowledge of English, it invested meagre financial resources for this purpose. As a result very few persons learnt English. Those who went in for English education generally belonged to upper and intermediate castes and were economically well-off. However, this small group occupied important positions in administration and various professions. They became a select, conspicuous and highly influential group.

In the colonial situation in India, this group played a significant role in politics, administration, society and in the economy of the country. In politics, they were links between the masses and the alien government and interpreters of the political will of the government to the masses. It was through them that the decisions of the government were conveyed to the people and implemented. They were the channels which provided the necessary feedback to the government so that it could assess the impact of its decisions.

Furthermore, the British had come to this country with their own set of values, norms, attitudes, behavioural pattern, dress, eating-habits, etc. As a conquering nation it was their desire that these should be disseminated among the Indians as widely as possible. They were unwilling to do it through the missionaries because they realized that such actions would be resisted strongly by Indians who were deeply attached to their centuries-old religion. They feared political implications and therefore, they decided to use the English-educated set to propagate their behavioural pattern among the Indian masses.

For this two-fold purpose, it was necessary that the government select such people who had traditionally performed this role. In India, where the people have been assigned a definite place in the social hierarchy and earmarked for certain jobs by virtue of their birth, the choice of the British government could not be any different. These were from the upper caste and the intermediate caste. Amongst them were also members of those castes which had traditionally performed these functions. By and large they belonged to the family of medium or small sized zamindars in eastern India. They pursued English education because they had the material means for the purpose and the incentive in the expectation that they would secure administrative posts. Among such castes in Bihar the lead in securing English education was taken up by the Kayasthas because of a number of historical reasons.

The Kayasthas have an old history of literacy and have worked at various levels in the administration for the past several centuries. Such service has been their traditional occupation. In return for such services, they were sometimes given zamindaris and land grants, but as a group they remained in the administration. They served the Nawabs from whom the British had conquered Bihar. They continued to do so when British rule was established. They had learnt Persian and Urdu for the purpose and now they decided to learn English, the new language of administration.

The British paid serious attention to this problem of creating an English-educated group to act as intermediaries between them and Indians only after the events of 1857, which had threatened to drive them out of this country. In fact, their minds had begun working in this direction in the 1830s when the famous Minute of Macaulay of 1835 on education had been accepted. A further indication was provided when they declared in 1844 that proficiency in English was essential for taking up jobs under the British. But they were unable to find enough men in Bihar for a variety of factors. People distrusted the British rule and feared the alien authority. There were physical and material difficulties in obtaining the new education. Even the British were lukewarm in their attitude because till the 1850s they broadly confined their functions to revenue collection and maintenance of law and order.

After the 1850s the British rulers changed policies. Certain public welfare projects such as the building of railways, canals, roads, etc., were undertaken which at once meant proliferation in the activities of the government and an opportunity for economic advancement to the masses. Suddenly the government needed men with English education for the new jobs that appeared. The people realized that the biggest obstacle in the way of using the new opportunities was their lack of knowledge of English.

From the 1860s the British increased their efforts to promote English education with the result that, by the end of 1870s, all the district headquarters in eastern India had at least one government-run and managed high school. Soon those who passed through the portals of these institutions became actively involved either in the work of administration as employees of the British or a few big zamindars,[1] or they took to professions such as teaching, journalism., etc. In Bihar, they were attracted to law more readily as a profusion of zamindari and tenancy rights generated innumerable law-suits. Also, the nature of justice was such that a civil suit once instituted, could drag on interminably, and this afforded the lawyers plenty of opportunities to make money.

The introduction and popularization of the printing press and the growth of education introduced journalism. It became possible to publish journals in Hindi, English and Urdu and other languages. Thus a number of journals appeared in Bihar in the second half of the nineteenth century.

Another avenue where the newly acquired talent in the English language could be exercised was in public activities which became popular as the English government granted the rudiments of self-government to Indians who then began participating in Municipal Committees, etc.

Thus English education had helped to bring into focus a middle-class though it was not as yet similar in form and character to the middle-class of the West. But it is significant that this middle-class constituted the elite in the society because it controlled several vantage positions in the day to day administration. Alien rule did not allow it to participate in policy-formulation and decision-making at the top-level. Secondly, as teachers at various levels, they were in a position to mould the opinion of the young, who were eventually to become citizens and the most important element in the social structure. As lawyers, again, they were the best people to uphold or reject the system formulated by the British and therefore were given importance both by the rulers and the ruled. Finally as journalists, they were required to articulate the public mood. They could interpret the rulers as well as the ruled. The English educated element thus set the pattern which the society by and large emulated. The new elite group was in the best position to find out how things were going on in the world and what should be adopted or discarded, and how far and to what extent the society should stir itself. Thus the elite did set the trend in society and in view of the circumstances described above, the task fell to the lot of the handful of English-educated persons in Bihar.

It would, therefore, be rewarding to study the values, the attitudes and the activities of a member of this class specially on the basis of his own diary that has fortunately come down to us. The diary was written in the year 1899. His book *English Poems* supplements the information that we gain from the diary.[2] It may not be a typical case but the study is bound to deepen and widen our understanding of the functioning of an important elite group in Bihar in the nineteenth century.

Avadh Behari Lall was born in a Kayastha family in the then Gaya district presumably in the year 1866, for he says he was a student of F.A. class in Patna College in 1883, aged seventeen, when he wrote his first verse in English.[3] He came from a family of zamindars[4] and his father and grandfather were both well educated. According to him his grandfather Sita Ram had written an autobiography.[5] He thus belonged to a family where education was valued and scholarship was a tradition. In view of this background it is not surprising that an attempt was made to give him an English education from the beginning, and, after passing the Matriculation examination, he joined Patna College, then the only college in the state imparting English education.[6] He tried to acquire the maximum fluency and skill in the English language. Together with this he developed a deep loyalty and attachment to the English rule. This is not surprising if we keep in view the situation then obtaining.

In the first phase the educated elite which works as the link between the rulers and the ruled and is the channel for conveying the decisions of the 'masters' to the 'enslaved masses' looks with suspicion upon the ruling race. The suspicion may turn into distrust which under certain favourable circumstances may lead to confrontation and eventually erupt into open hostility. In Bihar this phase was over by 1857. In the next phase, the educated elite, after it was convinced that the ruling power was capable of suppressing revolts, rebellions and open defiance to its authority, tries to discover areas of agreement with the sovereign power. It is haunted by a feeling that the 'masters' do enjoy some sort of superiority—moral, physical, technological, economic, social and institutional, etc. This gives rise to a two-fold attitude. There is an attempt to understand the culture as a whole of the ruling race. Inevitably the elite rushes to study this culture and hence tries to learn their language in order to become acquainted with the heritage and 'the mind' of the 'ruling civilization'. This is evident from the career of Avadh Behari Lall, who diligently applied himself to the study of the English language and literature. His heroes among his compatriots were those who had acquired great proficiency in writing and speaking English. Govind Charan who was the first Bihari M.A. in English from Calcutta University is described by him as 'guide, philosopher and friend'. He calls him, 'the first Beharee orator as he may be truly called', and he repeatedly sent his English poems to him for his opinions and eagerly looked forward for a word of approbation and advice.[7] He is similarly enamoured of his brother Mahesh Narayan, who was the first Bihari to edit an English journal.[8] His intense desire was to publish his poems so as to reach to as wide an audience as possible, both in India and England. He corresponded with journals and publishers in Calcutta and London.[9] He was hurt when the editor of an English newspaper at Calcutta refused to see him because of his busy schedule.[10] He was very happy when favourable reviews appeared.[11] The urge to learn and show proficiency in English was so great that he would write his diary in English and not in any Indian language in which he was proficient. It is against this background that we can understand voluntary efforts on the part of the English educated elite to propagate the knowledge of the English language by opening schools and colleges and by making donations.[12]

The second aspect of the desire to find accommodation with the alien ruling power was to express their deep loyalty at every conceivable opportunity. After the suppression of India's first organized and wide spread opposition in 1857 by the

English, this was inevitable. It stemmed, first from an explicit recognition of the superiority of the physical and coercive power of the alien rule. Secondly it reflected their gratitude to the alien rulers for the power and privileges that had been conferred upon them. They knew that but for the alien rule and the forces generated by it, they might not have occupied the crucial points in administration. Their economic privileges, but for the system of zamindari, would not have been such as to make them a leisured class. In Bihar, in particular, and in areas where the British had introduced the Permanent Settlement, in general, the zamindars were greatly beholden to the English for their system which gave them enough economic security. The prolongation of their privileged status was bound with the continuation of the British rule.

Avadh Behari Lall, however, justified his interest and deep love for English by invoking much nobler reasons. He writes,

It [*sic*] is this language which has enabled and still enables the Rulers and the Ruled of this vast country, a continent in itself, to understand and appreciate each other and to spread goodwill between them; it is this language by which the heterogeneous races of India, having separate dialects of their own communicate with one another; it is this language, this vehicle of thought, in which the state-education is imparted to us and which has Literatures and Sciences of the West; . . .[13]

Moreover, only a united front of the two could protect them from the discontent of the masses which was gathering fast because of increasing poverty among them. Hence, a clear expression of loyalty was necessary to enlist English support against the mass of their countrymen. Furthermore, after receiving English education, they depended upon the new rulers of the country for jobs and positions in the decision-making apparatus of the government. Thus profession of loyalist sentiments was an attempt for ingratiation so that they might be more favourably rewarded at the time of the distribution of government jobs, honours, membership of committees, etc. The desire to acquire English education and the expression of loyalist sentiments were part of the same phenomenon. The life of Avadh Behari Lall reflects both the above aspects.

On every possible opportunity Avadh Behari Lall is profuse in his expressions of sentiments of loyalty to the British rule. He bows before the symbols of British authority such as officers, the members of the British royal family, etc., on all possible occasions. He composes poems to celebrate all happy events concerning the royalty. Part I of his book carries several such poems.[14] On the death of Gladstone, an illustrious British prime minister, again his poetic feelings overpower him and he wrote a long poem which he wanted inscribed on Gladstone's Monument in West Minister Abbey.[15] He thus wrote to the Prince of Wales, the Duke of York and the President of the Gladstone Memorial Committee. His request, however, was not accepted, but he noted that his letter was acknowledged. In short, he makes no secret of his admiration for and loyalty to the British rule. He is not content merely with his expression of sentiments. He wants them to be conveyed to the appropriate quarters. Thus when he writes a poem on the occasion of the Imperial Durbar he wanted to recite it at Delhi. His hope did not materialize though he 'used the good offices of Dr. Sachchidanand Sinha, Bar-at-Law'.[17] An acknowledgement from the Secretary to His Most Gracious Majesty the King Emperor sent him into transports of joy. He preserved the letters received from His Most Gracious Majesty George V on several occasions and called it 'an inestimable treasure'.[18] Obviously these gestures were tokens of his acceptance by the Establishment and this was a matter of deep satisfaction to him.

He also participated enthusiastically in functions organized by the pillars of British rule. Thus when the District Judge of Gaya organized a party on New Year's Day in 1899, he attended it and at the same time he noted: 'This is one of the first parties of the kind as the high European officials seldom condescend to mix with the native gentry'.[19] Similarly at Patna he was present at a farewell given to the Judge Mr. Knox, who was going to England on furlough by pleaders of the Bankipore Bar.[20] Expressions of loyalty to the British rule had become a way of life with the English-educated elite. It found its crudest expression when Lord Curzon partitioned Bengal in 1905. The

Bengalis protested against this decision. Processions, rallies and public meetings were held to express opposition to the action of the English. But in Patna, the educated Bihari elite brought out a procession in support of the government measure. As a matter of fact, the Bihari elite was now assuming a somewhat aggressive posture. It still believed in collaboration with British rule because its support was needed for the protection of its economic interest and stability of its position in the administrative hierarchy. Its aid was also crucial in its fight with the Bengalis, who formed another prominent segment of the English-educated elite in the province. The Bengalis came into contact with the British first and had taken to English education much earlier and on a larger scale. The emergence of socio-religious and cultural movements such as the Brahmo Samaj and Ramakrishna Mission enabled them to get over their initial reluctance towards an alien education. Hence, when after 1844 the British needed English-educated persons to man the administrative apparatus in various parts of the country, they widely recruited Bengalis. As a consequence, in Bihar, in public services and professions the Bengalis not only outnumbered the Biharis but virtually monopolized them. When the English-educated Bihari elite was formed, it found itself in competition with the English-educated Bengali elite on its home ground. As English education spread in Bihar, the number of Biharis proficient in English increased and they started looking for positions in government and professions. This brought them face to face with the English-educated Bengali elite. The Bihari elite wanted to have as its ally the British rule with whose help it expected to displace the Bengalis from their vantage positions in jobs and professions. The support extended by the English-educated Bihari elite to the governmental decision to partition Bengal in 1905 merely reflected this attitude. It would thus seem that in the colonial context collaboration with the alien rule might emerge because of contradictions within the elite set itself. One reason for this contradiction may be rivalry and competition for jobs and other privileges.

But the collaboration did not lead to a transformation of the behaviour pattern, norms or values of this set. First, neither proficiency in English-education nor a study of English culture, nor jobs in the government nor membership of various professions or committees brought about any immediate and radical change in the world-view of the members. Their habits, kinship ties, interpersonal relationships, network of obligations, norms and values remained as of old. This is evident from the facts narrated by Avadh Behari Lall.

Almost every page in the diary contains references to some or the other kin. Whenever a name is mentioned, and if he happens to be a relation, the precise relationship is given, however, distant it might be.[21] He also writes about the interrelationship between his different relations. Thus the kinship ties remained as strong as ever. To an extent, they had been further reinforced because of facilities for quick and safe travel provided by the newly introduced railways. Kinship solidarity as it was based on caste enhanced caste-consciousness.

A further contributory cause was the British recruitment policy. Men of higher and intermediate castes were preferred. The presence of a relative in a government job was an added qualification. Most jobs, especially at clerical and ministerial levels were awarded on the basis of recommendation and nomination. Caste and kinship ties became extremely important factors in securing positions in the government.

The most popular profession amongst the English-educated elite was the legal one. As a result of more than a hundred land-tenure and occupancy types and confusion and complexity within the law, litigation was endemic. The lawyers, therefore, had plenty of work to do. But success depended on popularity and quick popularity could be had by appealing to the caste and kinship nexus. Besides reinforcing the caste-system, the situation, prevented the urban based lawyer from completely severing his ties with the rural areas from where most of his clients hailed. In fact, the lawyer approved and practised a behavioural-pattern. Which was understood by the realties. It was also meant to express his solidarity with them and win their confidence.

The elite, instead of destroying the old social structure, contributed to its further solidification. As kinship ties were retained and nurtured, inter-personal relationships maintained in its old pattern and intensity. Thus when the question for the settlement of a marriage arose, Avadh Behari Lall participated in the negotiations for settling the amount of Tilak.[22] Similarly, he shared all the joys and sorrows of his kinsmen and caste men. Traditional kinship and caste obligations did not cease.[23]

The hold of religion was not broken. The English-educated elite participated in all the rituals enjoined upon the Hindus.[24] When in Gaya, a relation arranged for a Nawah Katha of Tulsidas's *Ramcharitmanas*, he took notice of it and noted when it was completed.[25] The religiosity was reflected in his faith in astrology. When his son suffered a long illness and various doctors were unable to cure him, he consulted a reputed local astrologer and sought his advice.[26] When the temperature persisted the recitation of *Ram Sahasranam* was commenced by a Brahmin.[27] However, it must be admitted that under the impact of new ideas the elite was desirous to understand religion and so he took notice of all the prominent new religious movements such as Theosophy, the Brahmo Samaj, etc.

The Theosophical Society established a little earlier immediately struck root in Bihar, especially among English-educated members. Its branches were opened in different districts and were patronized by government officers and members of professions. Avadh Behari Lall attended lectures held under the auspices of the Dharma Sabha.[28] Similarly the Dharma Sabha, set up to defend orthodox Hinduism against attacks by modernist movements, was patronized by large numbers of these English-educated Biharis. They felt that in doing so they were upholding the traditional religion and thus fulfilling another duty enjoined upon them. To uphold tradition was considered an important aspect of their duty. They endeavoured to follow scrupulously the behaviour-pattern sanctioned by tradition. To conform to traditional religious beliefs and practices was an important part of their day to day behaviour. This aspect of the activities of the English-educated elite need not surprise us.

English education had opened up India's past before them. The researches carried out by European and Indian scholars in Indian history, religion, philosophy, art and literature placed before the Indians their glorious past. The inferiority complex which they had initially felt was now vanishing. It was not unnatural, that instead of rejecting their past unconditionally, they should start looking at it with considerable pride and attachment and stick to some of its old practices.

The English-educated elite, therefore, acted also as a conservative force in the society. As the activities of Avadh Behari Lall, one of the members of the elite class, show, they remained conscious of their traditional duties to their kinsmen, caste men, their religion and their countrymen. However, in their desire to preserve and protect the old order, the English-educated elite was forced to take a new and critical view of things. Thus they turned their attention to those social customs and practices which they thought were alien to the spirit of the times and could be shown as alien to ancient Indian tradition. These also happened to be such as to affect the smooth functioning of day to day affairs. Besides, they knew these efforts were not likely to raise the ire of the ruling power. Instead there was a possibility of ingratiation because the British were keen to see the introduction of certain social reforms. The British had from the days of Lord William Bentinck by forbidding *sati* and infanticide tried to raise the status of women. They further wanted to give them opportunities for education and legally permit them to remarry after divorce, widowhood, etc. The ruling power would have been happy to see the caste-system lose its rigour. The British did not want to take the initiative in these affairs because they feared this might arouse the suspicions and hostility of the local population and thus become a political liability. Hence, they were keen that the Indians themselves should come forward here.

Avadh Behari Lall was true to type. He expressed sympathy with the fate of young widows who had been condemned for their entire lives for no fault of their own. He wrote a long poem entitled 'A Virgin Widow's Lament'[29] but significantly enough, he disowned any radical step. He recorded his suggestion that 'a Hindu Widow's Maintenance Act is more urgently necessary than changes in laws about their remarriages'.[30] He further noted,

I think that her perfect right of separate maintenance from the estate of her children whether living with or separate from her, and even from reversioners under certain special circumstances—should be more clearly defined, legitimately allowed, and perfectly safeguarded, so that she may have sufficient and sure and independent means of support in her young and old age, diseases and death; and whatever maintenance may be expressly assigned to her by law should be made inviolate and inviolable, within her easy reach, prompt in methods of realization for, and regular in modes of payment to her.[31]

He would thus seem to favour measures only for redressal of economic hardship. In fact, he marshalled contemporary opinions both in India and abroad to plead against widow remarriage; he approvingly quoted an English poet saying 'Twice-married dames are mistresses of the trade'.[32] But it seems he was under some sort of mental conflict. English education had made him value rationality but as a member of the elite he realized he had to uphold the traditions of the society. This is clear from the following lines,

. . . so far as my individual opinion is concerned, I am at least in favour of the re-marriage of Hindu virgin-widows; and orthodox Hindu as I am and I pride upon my following the ancient Brahmanical faith of my native India—which faith, by the bye, may require some wholesome reformation but does not require wholesale condemnation—I am of this opinion since I was only 14 or 15 years of age.[33]

Moreover, the new elite set was unwilling to shed its class-character. This becomes clear when he writes about the Bengal Tenancy Act of 1885 in connection with his poem on Harbans Sahay, who was the vice-president of Bihar Landholders' Association. According to him, Baboo Harbans Sahay and Maharaja Lakshmeshwar Prasad Singh Bahadur of Darbhanga (then the biggest zamindari in Bihar), 'carried many amendments favourable to the zamindari cause though the Act is still more favourable—partially and unjustly more favourable—to the tenants and "peasant proprietors", and requires some necessary, just, useful, and equitable amendments.'[54] He further laments,

This harsh Act was followed in quick succession by other agrarian laws some of which have proved harsher still, more in working than in wordings of the statute, and various reasonable amendments and alternative proposals made by the late Maharaja Bahadur of Darbhanga and by the subject of this Elegy were simply negatived.[35]

Thus as soon as he found any encroachment in the privileges he enjoyed, he was ready to oppose it. However, he did not shirk some of his traditional duties towards his tenants. When necessity arose he constructed a bridge for the convenience of the peasantry.[36] Similarly, he built a water channel for purposes of irrigation.[37] But this was done in order to discharge an obligation which he had as a zamindar towards his tenants.

On the whole at this stage the English-educated elite in Bihar was by and large acting at cross-purposes with the masses because it had discovered that its material needs and advantages could remain secure only through the process of 'ingratiation' with the ruling power.

The English-educated elite would feel only in the early decades of the twentieth century that 'ingratiation' with the alien regime could only serve its purpose to a limited extent and then it began to make common cause with the masses against the foreign rule. The elite then added the next dimension to its activity. Besides being anti-Bengali, it became anti-British. It decided to provide leadership to the freedom movement that was gaining momentum in the country with the advent of Mahatma Gandhi as the guide of the Indian National Congress.

Avadh Behari Lall probably did not live to see that phase. But he will be certainly remembered at least as the first Bihari poet in the English language, who even carried on a correspondence with the then poet laureate of England, Lord Tennyson.[38]

NOTES

* I am obliged to Dr. Amar Nath Sinha of the Dept. of Hindi, B.N. College, Patna for having lent me Avadh Behari Lall's *English Poems* and the diary for the year 1899.

1. In Bihar because of lack of trade, no avenue for employment in commercial firms was open to English-educated persons as had happened in the neighbouring province of Bengal. The people in Bihar with insignificant exceptions also did not take to technical and scientific education.

2. Avadh Behari Lall, *English Poems,* Patna, 1918.

3. Ibid., p. 165.

4. On the title page of his book he writes after his name the word 'Zamindar'.

   In his diary for the year 1899, on the last page, he gives his address as follows

   Avadh Behari Lall

   Zamindar of Mouzah Baksunda

   Pergunnah Pachrukhi, P.O. Akbarpore

   District Gaya.

5. Diary, entry dated 21 November 1899. He had revised the manuscript and handed it over to the proprietor of Khadag Vilas Press, Patna for publication. However, it is not known whether the book was ever published. His father Babu Jagdamba Sahay was preparing for the Native Civil Service Examination, when he died in an accident in 1873. Avadh Behari Lall, op. cit., p. 186.

6. Avadh Behari Lall, ibid., p. 165.

7. Ibid., p. 175.

8. Ibid., p. 176.

9. Diary, 24 January, 4 and 8 March 1899. He visited the offices of the *Statesman* and *Amrit Bazar Patrika.* On 25 March 1899 he wrote to MacMillan & Co., London asking them to publish a London edition of his collection of poems.

10. Diary, 4 March 1899. Deeply hurt he writes, 'Inaccessibility is becoming rule of the day for every European'.

11. Diary, 29 April 1899. *Behar Guardian,* a fortnightly organ of the Temperence Society, Patna carried a favourable review of his poems.

12. B.N. College, Patna, R.D. and D.J. College, Monghyr, L.S. College, Muzaffarpur, etc., were established in the last quarter of the nineteenth century. Several schools all over the province were founded through voluntary efforts. Many persons especially English-educated ones donated money handsomely for running these institutions.

13. Avadh Behari Lall, op. cit., p. 81.
14. Ibid., pp. 1-68. The titles of the poems are as follows: (1) A Poem On The Coronation of His Most Gracious Majesty King George V. As Emperor And Of Her Most Excellent Majesty Queen Mary As Empress Of India: Or Shortly, A Coronation Poem. (2) An Ode On The Marriage Of H.R.H. The Duke Of York, Now His Imperial Majesty King George V, Emperor Of India. (3) An Ode On The Coronation Durbar At Delhi. (4) A Poem On The Coronation Durbar At Delhi.
15. Ibid., pp. 244-5.
16. Ibid., p. 245.
17. Ibid., p. 14.
18. Ibid., p. 15.
19. Diary, 1 January 1899.
20. Ibid., 22 March 1899.
21. Ibid., 19 March 1899. The entry reads, 'At morning went to Uncle Jaggernath Sahay Saheb's . . . Lodging in Mohalla Mooradpore. Came to know the grievous news of the death of B. Lachchami Pershad of Mozufferpore, the second son-in-law of Uncle Deonath Sahay. He was a F.A. student and was suffering from chronic fever. Went to my friend B. Benode Miner's at Mooradpore, close to my maternal Uncle's lodging. A little south of Benode's lives B. Mahesh Narayan, Editor of the *Behar Times*, who is now-a-days at Rajmahal'.

    His entry of 23 January 1899 reads, 'Munshi Nagwant Sahay a famous pleader of the local Bar died yesterday on account of his taking medicines for the cure of piles from a quack. . . . Munshi Nagwant Sahay's nephew (brother's son) is married to a daughter of the late Bhai Baikuntha Sahay's daughter and so he was a distantly-related samandhi of mine'.
22. Ibid., 14 March 1899.
23. Ibid., 2 August 1899. He writes, 'At 2 p.m. Munshi Sajeewan Lall, late Dewan of the . . . Tikari Raj, died today. I came to know this about 3 p.m. or even a little after and so could not join the funeral procession though I had a mind to do so from before. This gentleman was of respectable character and after all a religious person of the old orthodox Hindu type. He was a self-made man'. The entry next day, i.e. on 3 August 1899 reads, 'Went along with Bhai Kailash Nath Sinha at morning to the lodging of the late Munshi Sajeewan Lall at Mohalla Tottari. . . .'
24. Ibid., 6 January 1899. He writes, 'Sunday the 10th Poos 1281 Fasli is the date of my father's death and this day is the 25th anniversary of his death. Last year (Deer. 1897) I had performed the *Ekodishta sradh*

but though I might have performed this *sradh* this year also, I did not do so. I should be more observant of the anniversary in future'.

25. Ibid., 5 and 13 October 1899.
26. Ibid., 20 August 1899.
27. Ibid., 24 August 1899.
28. Ibid., 13 January 1899. He attended all the lectures given by a theosophist lecturer Pandit Bhavani Shankar at the Dharma Sabha.
29. Avadh Behari Lall, op. cit., pp. 205-32.
30. Ibid., p. 201.
31. Ibid., pp. 201-2.
32. Ibid., p. 203.
33. Ibid.
34. Ibid., p. 233.
35. Ibid., p. 234.
36. Diary, 12 June and 5 July 1899.
37. Ibid., 18 October 1899.
38. Avadh Behari Lall, op. cit., p. 192.

CHAPTER 15

Industrial Capitalism and Entrepreneurship in Bihar in the Nineteenth Century

The battles of Plassey (1757) and Buxar (1764) enabled the English East India Company to establish its sway over eastern India comprising the present day eastern Uttar Pradesh, Bihar, Bengal and Orissa. The political control enabled the Company to begin unabashed exploitation of the local economy. By the end of the century it had successfully eliminated its European competitors, the Dutch, the French, the Danes, etc., and reduced to insignificance Indian and local rivals.[1] The English East India Company and the British Government began to tighten their control over the local economy as the Industrial Revolution in England unfolded itself during the closing decades of the eighteenth century for the newly established textile mills needed assured supplies of raw cotton and markets for their fabrics.

In effect, the colonial economy had to be subservient to the metropolitan economy. In the early phase of the rise of industrial capitalism, such a relationship was a must for sustaining the new mode of production marked by the use of steam to run the machines made of iron and steel and a large capital investment with long gestation period. The economic intercourse between England and the newly acquired territories of eastern India followed almost the same course. There were certain superficial variations in respect of Bengal and Bihar owing to historical and geographical factors.

The economy of Bihar was primarily characterized by the export of saltpetre to Europe and opium to China and the Southeast Asia.[2] The earnings from exports of opium paid for

English purchases of tea in China and enabled them to secure silver.[3] The agricultural production of Bihar consisted of cereals which in normal years adequately met her needs and cash crops like sugar cane and cotton, which provided raw materials for the manufacture of cotton textiles and sugar. Hence, the desire of the colonial masters was to harness the production and marketing of all these commodities in the wider interest of metropolitan economy.

The government through various measures promoted the cultivation of opium; but the cultivator was paid a small amount; the profit was shared between the middle-men and the Company. The middle men were generally Europeans or traders from outside Bihar, primarily Khatris or Bengalis. Colonialism patronized comprador traders. The producers or members of the local trading community, Raoniyar, Kesarbani, Kalwar, Madhyadesiya, etc., were virtually excluded from the gains accruing from long-distance trade and export of opium. The story was repeated in the case of saltpetre.[4]

The new situation severely curtailed the chances of capital accumulation precisely at a time when it was the need of the hour since the machine-age in industries were dawning. The new land policy embodied in the Permanent Settlement of 1793 acted as a further disincentive. It strengthened the traditional *landed elite*; it buttressed the economic position of primarily upper-caste Hindus, viz., Rajputs, Bhumihars, Brahmans and Kayasthas and upper section of the Muslims. It did not give any *fillip* to the cultivator to bring about changes in agricultural productivity through improvements in agricultural techniques.

In fact the agriculturists were now subjected to greater economic exploitation. The zamindars could levy several extra legal taxes and cesses with greater impunity. The cultivator, unable to fathom the terms and twists of the new legal system was hardly in a position to seek a legal remedy for the injustices done to him. Hence, there was a general economic depression in the first three decades; the purchasing power of the masses sharply decreased. In fact, the most deprived could hardly afford even a pinch of salt. An Englishman who extensively travelled in

Bihar reported, 'Although salt is such a necessary ingredient in a vegetable diet yet poverty compels the substitution of wood ashes.' He further remarked, 'These facts . . . all demonstrative of men of wretchedness, such as no other country on the face of the earth presents; and the continuance of which is a disgrace to the British name.'[5]

It is hardly surprising that the general economic depression failed to stimulate the local populace to take any worthwhile initiative in the economic field.

The same environment afflicted the artisans of Bihar. It was significant because the artisans in England were playing a pioneering role in bringing about the Industrial Revolution.

The local artisan community was hemmed in with cultural and/or caste constraints which prevented them from getting education and which could have enabled them to learn about the theoretical aspects of the techniques of production.

Another problem also dogged their steps. The artisans especially the weavers were faced with intense competition from the increasing distribution of machine-made textiles. Some weavers found their traditional occupation totally unremunerative and had to give it up either in favour of agriculture or in favour of unskilled manual labour.

In sum, the general economic depression was responsible for the creation of an army of unemployed or severely underemployed men, prepared to move out of the state and even out of the country if there was a chance to earn livelihood. Hence, from the 1830s unskilled labour from the Bihar plains started migrating to mining areas of south Bihar, tea plantation being developed in the sub-Himalayan tracts of West Bengal and Assam and to Mauritius in the Indian Ocean where Europeans had taken up sugar plantation on a large scale.[6]

The two segments of the local population, the traders and cultivators were in no position to risk new ventures.

The local trading community virtually remained mere small grocers or at best wholesale distributors to local retailers. They neither had the capital nor the opportunity to enter into the large scale long-distance trade. This is evident from the biodata of one of the important rich traders of the nineteenth century Rai Baboo Shivghulam Shah of Chhapra. His father started as a small shopkeeper and managed to save some capital on which Shivghulam Shah prospered. He started trading in salt, sugar, saltpetre, mustard, etc.[7] Once in a while, he did participate in the timber business but could never become a big enough trader to engage in long-distance trade.

When the traders or the peasants made good, they looked forward to investing in the purchase of a zamindari, which brought in an assured and comfortable income and also pushed them up in social estimation. The same was true of a zamindar, if he saved, he would try to add to his zamindari. He would never think of investing in alternative sources of income which, thanks to colonial economic policies, were virtually non-existent in Bihar.

The social ethos still preferred a zamindar to a trader, a land-lord to an organizer of a factory.

But what made the situation for the entrepreneur still worse was his relationship vis-à-vis that of the zamindar. The English had introduced the rule of law, but in actual practice the zamindars were beyond it.

They could humiliate or misbehave with a trader, however, rich and could get away with it. For example, Shivghulam Shah was a rich and famous trader. He went to the great Sonepur fair held for a fortnight after Deepavali. While moving in a palanquin he happened to pass by Kunwar Singh, a powerful zamindar of Shahabad (later Kunwar Singh became a legendary hero for his fight against the English in 1857). He did not greet Kunwar Singh with the result that the men on the retinue of Kunwar Singh felt greatly offended. In retaliation, they broke and destroyed the palanquin of Shivghulam Shah, who had no option but to put up with this humiliation.[8] The autocracy of zamindars prompted many traders to acquire zamindari, if for nothing also, at least to escape the tyranny of zamindars. Shivghulam Shah himself invested in zamindari and became a zamindar.[9]

Another famous instance of a trader turning to a zamindar is that of Tej Narain Sinha, who, though a Jaiswal (a trading caste) had acquired a big zamindari in the late nineteenth century. He travelled with his sixteen-year old son Dip Narain Sinha to England in 1891[10] where he stayed till his death in 1896 and his son returned to India in 1897 after having been called to the Bar.[11]

The change in the attitude of the traders followed the growth of the Western system of education in Bihar in the second half of the nineteenth century.[12] But the interesting point is that the concept of modernity did not include the acquisition of the spirit of entrepreneurship or an urge for setting industries, both widely prevalent in Europe.

Another interesting case is that of K.P. Jaiswal, a famous historian, whose family originally hailed from Mirzapur in the neighbouring Uttar Pradesh. He came from a rich and prosperous trading family. He, too, was sent to England at the turn of the twentieth century to become a Bar-at-Law. On his return, after completing his education, he set up a *lucrative* law practice at Patna and remained a lawyer till his death in 1937.[13]

In fact, the new education with its emphasis on secular and scientific content, failed to promote the culture of entrepreneurship. This is evident if we take a quick look at its pattern of growth in Bihar in the last century.

The early enthusiasts of the new education were immigrant Bengalis.[14] The Bihari Hindu response was comparatively slow and came primarily from traditional literary and martial castes, the Brahmans, the Kayasthas and the Rajputs, etc. Their primary motive was to secure government employment and enjoy the attendant power and prestige. Soon there was a rush to law profession when it became apparent that monetary rewards were larger since property and land revenue related litigation were widespread owing to the complexity of the new laws and novelty of jurisprudence introduced by the English.[15] Hence these upper castes with the benefit of new education did not venture in the realm of trade or industry. White-collar jobs or professions like law or medicine or to some extent journalism were preferred. The members of trading castes, who accepted the new education after the Arya Samaj had pleaded for it in the last quarter of the nineteenth century, followed the example set by the upper castes. Thus Madhav Lal, an enthusiast of the Arya Samaj and one of its founders in Bihar, sent his son Lakshmipati to Edinburgh to study medicine.[16]

The introduction of scientific and secular education did not introduce the culture of entrepreneurship either among the traditionally literate communities or those whose caste profession was trade or some craft. Instead it fostered a reverse trend. Even those communities whose caste-ordained profession was either trade or craft, turned away from it to enter into government jobs or professions of medicine, law, journalism, etc. The traditional Indian attitudes, putting high value on non-manual and intellectual pursuits were, in fact, reinforced.

The disdain verging on total disregard for trade and industry is visible in case of zamindars as well. A few zamindars such as those of Darbhanga, Hathwa, Bettiah, Dumraon, Tekari, etc., controlled the major part of Bihar.

The zamindars at least those in the higher echelon and who had at their command sufficient capital, were immune from outside interference in their day to day activity and several of them had imbibed new education. Furthermore, they had on their pay rolls educated Europeans as well as Indians. But they also refrained from venturing into the sphere of trade and industry and could not rise above the traditional socio-economic and cultural norms.

Ostentatious consumption on occasions of birth, marriages and death remained a continuous and a considerable drain on their capital.

Several zamindaris were sold out bit by bit for meeting household expenses and paying government dues. It was not rare that a new accession to zamindari would mean prolonged family litigation and lavish grant of land and/or cash to members of the family who were earlier looked after by the deceased. Thus when Lakshmishwar Singh of Darbhanga died on 17 December 1898, his successor Rameshwar Singh had to face suits filed in the court of law by the widowed Maharanees and eventually an out of court settlement was arrived at on the intercession of the Nawab of Dacca and Maharaja of Benares, both family friends. Each Maharanee was given landed property yielding an annual income of Rs. 77,000 plus Rs. 1 lakh in cash.[17]

They could not dream of any long term investment in trade or industry which contained a considerable element of uncertainty and risk. While the above factors remained operative, certain objective factors also hindered their entry into trade and industry. The absence of the rule of primogeniture with certain exceptions also resulted in prolonged litigations involving great expense,[18] or in the increasing fragmentation of the zamindaris which considerably impaired their capital accumulation and its eventual reinvestment in trade and industry.

To top it all, minority or mismanagement was almost an endemic feature and the government had to devise the institution of Court of Wards to prevent the dissolution of the zamindaris. Under the scheme the administration of zamindaris was taken over by the government till it was convinced that the old proprietors were in a position once again to manage it efficiently. All the big and important zamindaris faced this situation at one time or other. Darbhanga, the biggest zamindari of the province was under the Court of Wards from 1858 to 1878[19] till Maharaja Lakshmishwar Singh came of age and the administration of zamindari was restored to him.[20] The next biggest zamindari Hathwa was similarly placed under the Court of Wards after the death of Rajendra Pratap Shahi.[21] Another big zamindari of the province Bettiah was brought under the aegis of the Court of Wards in 1895 and remained till India's Independence. Such situations whenever they occurred also prevented any long term planning by the zamindars to enter into trade or Industry. They therefore, preferred the familiar sphere of expansion of zamindaris as a field of further investment.

This is not to suggest that there was a total disregard for trade and industry. Some of the zamindars on the pattern of European indigo planters did set up indigo works in the second half of the nineteenth century[22] but it was this far that they ventured and no further. Here again, the intention was never to excel in this field or become an indigo planter. The intention was just to diversify a little.

Among the indigenous population, the Muslims too had a tradition of trade. But the loss of political power also unnerved them. In the nineteenth century, their primary aim seems to have been to secure government jobs. Hence when Western education was introduced the upper and middle classes accepted it too readily than their Hindu brethren of Bihar. In fact, in the early years, they outnumbered the Bihari Hindus in Western style educational institutions. They joined professional courses in medicine, engineering and law![23] A Muslim Syed Sharafuddin was the first Bihari to go to England to secure a Bar-at-Law degree.[24] Bihari Hindus emulated his example and because of sheer weight of numbers, later on, surpassed the Muslims in the legal profession.

A Muslim with Western education had a job waiting for him in the princely state of Hyderabad. Khuda Bux Khan, the founder of the world famous library, Khuda Bux Oriental Public Library served as the Chief Justice of the High Court in the princely state of Hyderabad for quite some time.[25] It is there that he imbibed his great love for books and began collecting them.

The important point is that even the Muslims found that economic opportunities existed in white-collar jobs and professions and therefore, there was hardly any attraction for entering into trade and industries. Of course, there were individuals who realized that the economic regeneration of the country was not possible without promoting indigenous trade and industry. Qazi Reza Hussain even planned a Joint Stock Company and purchased shares in the company which thought of introducing tram-ways in Patna.[26] But these individuals failed to make any worthwhile impact on the prevailing social attitude towards trade and industry.

The culture fostered by education and introduced by the colonial administration did not result in the acceptability of trade and industry as professions by the moneyed and educated segments of the population in Bihar.

The factors responsible for these attitudes must also be

sought in the policies of the colonial administration which was geared to serve the economic interests of the foreign capitalists and industrialists rather than to promote indigenous economy.

The Railways did not enter as an agent of economic change. They were support systems for the existing economic relationship. In the short run they perpetuated the colonial economic environment.

The Railways enabled a large number of traders of northwestern India, the Marwaris, the Jains, the Khatris, the Agarwals, the Gahois to move to Bihar and to compete with the local communities even in retail trading.

From the 1860s Railways were introduced in Bihar. Of course, they vastly increased the mobility of men and material. But the immediate economic consequences were negative. They helped in quicker distribution of imported goods and thus they further depressed the condition of local traders and artisans. Furthermore, food grains were carried to the port of Calcutta for being exported to England where more mouths had to be fed because of rapid industrialization and urbanization.

The British interest then lay in promoting agricultural production. But for this they were not prepared to disturb the traditional agrarian structure. The Bengal Tenancy Acts of 1859 and 1885 were designed to assuage the ruffled feelings of the peasantry so that food production might not suffer.

Even the increase in the number of European indigo planters did not mean any change in the agrarian structure although after the big zamindars they were the largest land holders. It meant the induction of a new set of exploiters for the cultivator. Besides, these indigo planters had only one aim: to make a quick buck and then to pack off to their motherland. Therefore, the capital earned was lost to the local economy.

Hence, on the whole the colonial context kept the local economy depressed because it suited the English capitalists and industrialists.

Therefore, it is not surprising that local entrepreneurship did not develop because there was no real economic opportunity waiting to be exploited.[27]

It is true, it was during this period that there was a spurt in mining activity,[28] but most of the entrepreneurs were either Europeans or Marwaris.

The Calcutta-based European businessmen had the required capital, the necessary technical expertise for exploiting the mineral resources as well as a knowledge of markets. They, therefore, rushed in as soon as they realized that mining was an area of great profit. They were followed by Bengalis, who had acquired some interest in these activities because of their long and close association with the Europeans in Calcutta. To some extent, the Gujaratis who had worked as contractors and suppliers when railway lines were being constructed decided to join the band of European and Bengali entrepreneurs engaged in mining activities. Some Marwaris also did the same but the Biharis did not bother to profit from this opportunity. Bihar was content with supplying only the labour force.

Thus it is clear that Biharis had not become conscious of entering into productive economic activities other than agriculture; Western educated citizens preferred government jobs, independent professions of law, medicine, journalism, etc. Industrial capitalism in the colonial context made a negative impact. Instead of imbuing Biharis with the spirit of entrepreneurship and inspiring them to take up trade and industry as legitimate economic activities they put more value on jobs with assured income, involving no manual labour and very little risk of total failure. Industrial capitalism in the colonial environment fostered an economic mentality, which did not prize initiative, enterprise, thrift and hard work. On the contrary, love for land and white-collar jobs became so deeply ingrained that when in the twentieth century, the economic environment began to change, the Biharis were still unwilling to come forward and profit by it. Outsiders retained the dominant say in setting up and running industries and allied economic activities.

NOTES

1 K.K. Datta and J.S. Jha (eds.), *Comprehensive History of Bihar*, vol. III, pt. I, Patna, 1976, pp. 173-4.

2. H.R. Ghosal, *Economic Transition in the Bengal Presidency*, Patna, 1960, pp. 142-3.
3. J. Kumar, *Indo-Chinese Trade 1793-1833*, New Delhi, 1974, pp. 45-6; Ghosal, op. cit., pp. 124-5.
4. Ghosal, ibid., pp. 119-20.
5. Montgomery Martin, *Eastern India* (rpt.), Delhi, 1976, vol. II, pp. XVII, XX.
6. Sir Percival Griffiths, *The History of the Indian Tea Industry*, London, 1967, p. 102; P.B. Sinha, *Development of the Mineral Industries of Bihar*, Muzaffarpur, 1975, pp. 192-5.
7. Babu Ramdin Singh, *Behar Durpan* (in Hindi), 2nd edn., Patna, 1883, pp. 249-50.
8. Ibid., p. 252.
9. Ibid., pp. 250-3. At the time of his death, he was the owner of a zamindari worth Rs. 1,50,000.
10. Sachchidanand Sinha, *Some Eminent Behar Contemporaries*, Patna, 1944, p. 167.
11. Ibid.
12. Patna College was established in 1863, in 1900 there were six colleges in Bihar.
13. Sinha, op. cit., pp. 130-1.
14. J.N. Sarkar and J.C. Jha, *A History of the Patna College*, Patna, 1963, p. 50.
15. William Tayler received Rs. 300 per month from the Raja of Hathwa as his retainers fee and was given Rs. 20,000 to argue his case. He was promised a further sum of Rs. 20,000 if he won the case. Surendra Gopal, *Patna in the 19th Century: A Socio-Cultural Profile*, Calcutta, 1982, p. 55.
16. Sarvendra Shastri, 'Bihar Rajya ke Pratham Aryasamaji Svargiya Babu Madhavlalji', *Aryasankalp* (in Hindi), vol. X, no. 9, April 1988, p. 7.
17. Ganganath Jha, *Autobiographical Notes of Dr. Sir Ganganath Jha*, Allahabad, 1976, pp. 41-2.
18. Guru Prosad Sen, 'The Aristocracy of Behar', p. 11. In the zamindari of Hathwa the first suit was brought in 1829 and then in 1848. Another litigation was carried to Privy Council and was decided in 1868, ibid., p. 78.
19. *Some Eminent Behar Contemporaries*, p. 35.
20. At the time the zamindari was restored to Lakshmishwar Singh its annual income was Rs. 21,61,885. Jata Shankar Jha, *Biography of an Indian Patriot Maharaja Lakshmishwar Singh of Darbhanga*, Patna, 1972, p. 112.
21. Guru Prosad Sen, loc. cit., p. 19.

22. Navinchandra Sen, *Navinchandra Rachnavali* (in Bengali), vol. I, p. 326. He speaks of a Bengali manager of an indigo-work owned by a Beharee zamindar in the old Shahabad district.

23. *Patna in the 19th Century*, pp. 24-6.

24. Surendra Gopal, 'Bihari Association with the Indian National Congress during its Formative Years (1885-8), '*Memorial Lecture Series*, vol. 2, 1986, p. 28. Syed Sharfuddin was followed by his two nephews Ali Imam and Hasan Imam and Mazharul Haque, 1888. It was in 1889 that the first Bihari Hindu, Sachchidanand Sinha left for England to study law.

25. *My Eminient Behar Contemporaries*, p. 3.

26. *Al Panch* (in Urdu), 26 April 1897.

27. This view was contradicted in the 1880s by the British administrators and the zamindars that the material condition of peasantry was worsening. Guru Prosad Sen, 'Is Behar Rackrented?', p. 6.

28. *The Comprehensive History of Bihar*, vol. IE, pt. I, pp. 506-13, between 1885 and 1900 the number of coal mines trebled.

CHAPTER 16

Socio-Cultural Contours of Patna at the Turn of the Twentieth Century

Developments during the decade following the victory of the English East India Company at Plassey in 1757 created a new politico-administrative and economic environment in Bihar, Bengal and Orissa which affected the future development of Patna, the second largest city of eastern India after Calcutta. The emergence of the British as masters in place of the Nawabs, altered the pattern of politics. A new administrative system, dominated in the upper echelons by Englishmen, endowed with an unfamiliar political philosophy, sprang up. This developing politico-administrative context required functionaries trained in the English-educational system. The people, at large, were faced with an unfamiliar life-style, that of their rulers. The nineteenth century was thus marked with the confrontation of the traditional with that of the English; and by the end of the nineteenth century, the local response had crystallized.

Bankipur, the new suburb which had begun to develop under colonial stimulus, emerged as a viable entity in terms of size, population density, services, conveniences and institutions, needed for modern living. The far-flung villages and habitations had been integrated through the rise of new mohallas and the constructions of roads, running from east to west and from north to south, crossed by lanes and by-lanes. The population had a fair sprinkling of professionals trained modern system of education, law, medicine, etc.[1]

The new professionals, mostly immigrants from the neighbouring province of Bengal acted as an important catalyst in the formulation of response of the local population to the new challenges. This was important because in a colonial set up, 'the effective propagation' of the policies of rulers is possible only when an indigenous group consciously accepts them and tries to convey them to their compatriots. The Bengali professionals, resident in Patna, performed this role, specially in the field of modern education.

The system of education introduced by the British had received acceptance as a result of conscious governmental and voluntary efforts. The government had set the ball rolling by opening the Patna Collegiate School, Patna College and Temple Medical School. The public had responded by setting up T.K. Ghosh's Academy, B.N. Collegiate School, P.N. Anglo Sanskrit School, Raja Rammohun Roy Seminary, Bankipore Girls School and B.N. College. Except B.N. Collegiate School and B.N. College; all the voluntary schools were set up by Bengalis.[2] Besides, even government-run institutions relied heavily on Bengali teachers, both at the school and collegiate levels. As a result of these efforts, by the beginning of the twentieth century, a group of Biharis, well-versed in English language and trained in modern professions emerged. Though small in numbers, they became the pace setter of new trends, that developed in the society.

Patna was fortunate to have been provided with a complete infrastructure of modern educational system by the end of the nineteenth century. But it is ironical that Engineering and Medicine, for long, did not attract the attention of the local Hindus.[3] The most popular professional course was Law. The attraction for law can be explained largely in terms of local factors.

First, among Hindus, the dogmas of caste enjoined a strong code of purity and pollution and therefore, any technical education was taboo, because it involved manual work. Study of allopathic system of medicine necessitated dissection of corpses and coming into physical contact with people belonging to different religions and castes and hence, militated against the caste-based notion of purity and pollution. Consequently, scientific and technical education in its early phases did not become popular amongst Bihari Hindus. The lack of enthusiasm for scientific and technical education persisted till the first two decades of the century; only the establishment of the first steel-mill of the country in Jamshedpur in south Bihar in 1907[4] and the out-break of the First World War forced upon them the realization of the importance of technical education. The neglect of scientific and technical education, on the one hand, perpetuated traditional norms, and on the other hand, inflated the importance of law as a profession.

No manual labour was involved in the profession of law and therefore, according to prevalent norms, was not *infra dig*. Secondly, physical contacts with clients were not required and hence there was no fear of pollution for the caste-conscious Hindus. Besides, certain other factors enhanced the attraction for the profession of law.

Bihar had a predominantly agrarian economy despite the development of mining industries in the Chotanagpur region[5] during the second half of the nineteenth century. The agrarian structure was highly complex; it gave rise to conflicting claims which had to be resolved in law courts. The Zamindari system established by the Permanent Settlement of 1793 had become encumbered with overlapping rights because of the growth of Pawi, Dar Patni and Se Patni systems,[6] etc. This gave rise to lots of legal complications and matters had to be taken to law courts. The British efforts to simplify laws relating to land rights and the land revenue laws through the tenancy legislations of 1859 and 1885 met with only partial success.[7] Recourse to law-courts was the only remedy for securing rights in land and undoing the wrongs done under various revenue laws. The demand for the service of lawyers was increasing and they received fabulous fees. Tayler, a British practicing lawyer earned as much as Rs. 20,000 in a single case.[8] R.K. Bhattacharya, who started his career as a lawyer in Patna in 1870 earned so much that he became one of the largest urban property-holders of the town.[9] The same was true of lawyers such as Gobind Mitra, B.M. Das and later the Imam brothers, etc. Financially, a lawyer's profession was the most lucrative and attractive for the newly English-educated Biharis.[10]

At the early stages of his career, a lawyer leaned heavily on his caste and kinship affiliation to secure legal cases and thus the popularity of law as a profession reinforced and hardened the traditional attachment to caste. The spread of new education instead of diminishing the role of caste in social life, in fact, enhanced it. By the time, scientific and technical education became popular after the First World War, caste-attitudes had hardened and they became a part of the value-system of the English educated group. Gradually, this value-system manifested itself in diverse spheres not directly related to caste ordained norms of inter-personal relationship.

Along with the English education, people slowly began to accept the technical devices relating to everyday life introduced by their colonial masters. Its consequence was an altered lifestyle. People began to use railways for their travels and printing press technology became more and more widespread.[11]

The printing press stimulated the growth of journalism; Patna became the principal centre for the publication of journals and newspapers in Hindi, Urdu, Bengali and English in the province of Bihar since mid-nineteenth century. No doubt, some of these journals and newspapers died young but never the less, some like, the *Bihar Herald* and *Bihar Bandhu* survived. The English educated class initially took to journalism as a part-time vocation.[12] But by the beginning of the twentieth century, at least some of them drifted towards it as full-time workers such as Mahesh Narain, the editor of *The Bihar Times*, established in 1894 and later on called *The Beharee*. A new profession for educated people had emerged.

The emergence of full-time journalists vitally changed the character of journalism. From being informative and descriptive it turned analytical and critical. Journalists became educators of people in socio-politico-economic affairs and also their conscience-keepers. Journalism became a powerful instrument for arousing public consciousness and contributed to the dissemination of political ideas taking shape in different parts of the country. It became a propagator of nationalism.

The Patna Press emerged as the trendsetter of public opinion all over the province.

The impact of education and printing press was visible in the day to day functioning of the society in Patna.

Public meetings dedicated to a variety of causes were regularly held. Several political, social and religious organizations, local, provincial and national in character and catering to the needs of various sections of the populations emerged. Among local level organizations[13] mention may be made of Bihar Young Men's Institute, which got a building of its own almost in midst of various educational institutions.[14] Leaders of national socio-religious organizations such as Brahmo Samaj, Arya Samaj, Theosophical Society, etc., frequently visited the city to address members of their organizations and to win new adherents for their faith.[15] But they were hardly able to win dedicated followers in large numbers. Only a handful of Biharis joined these movements with the result that the society could hardly get a radical orientation. The shell of conservatism and casteism were scratched only on surface by these socio-religious reform movements. The society remained inward-looking.

Even a strong leaven of Bengali immigrants, who constituted the largest English-education elite in the town, failed to in-culcate a sense of urgency for change. On the other hand, the English-educated Biharis adopted a course of confrontation with the Bengalis and they received support from the colonial masters, who had their own political and administrative axe to grind. A combination of English-educated Bengalis and Biharis would be a political liability especially in view of heightened anti-British sentiments then prevailing in Bengal. The two should be delinked lest Bihar should catch the nationalistic infection from Bengal. Hence when educated Biharis, primarily Muslims and Kayasthas, raised their voice against the educated, professional and employed resident-Bengalis in Bihar, they were encouraged by the Britishers. The Bihari demand for separation of Bihar from Bengal became more insistent. Till 1912, when Bihar was separated from Bengal, Bengali-Bihari contradictions dominated the public life in the city. The movement helped to crystallize the Bihari sub-nationalism.

However, one aspect of Patna society needs special attention. The Hindus and Muslims lived in harmony and the nineteenth century tradition of communal amity was carried forward. This was in spite of communal venom engulfing the surrounding countryside and the rise of avowedly communal parties such as the Muslim League and the Hindu Mahasabha.[16] It is difficult to explain this phenomenon except as a deviant case or a reflection of high degree of interdependence and mutual trust that had developed as a result of centuries of residence side by side.

The growth in the number of English-educated Biharis and their awareness that wider opportunities for employment and enhancing socio-economic status existed, contributed to the rapid growth of political consciousness. It is true that Biharis had begun participating in the annual sessions of the Indian National Congress since its very inception in 1885, yet the association was, by and large, on individual basis. But now the need was felt for giving it a wider and collective base. Hence, participation in the political life of the country became a growing concern with the educated classes, especially the lawyers, whose profession brought them enough money and left them with plenty of leisure. Thus participation of Biharis in politics on all-India level increased and it was reflected in growing politicization of the society in Patna. Patna lawyers such as Hasan Imam, Ali Imam, Mazharul Haque, Sachchidanand Sinha, Rajendra Prasad became increasingly involved in national politics. Patna became the nerve-centre of political life in the state and also carved a niche for itself in the national politics. It is, therefore, hardly surprising that the Indian National Congress was invited to hold its 27th annual session in 1912 in Patna.[17]

Under the impact of changing modes of life, the Patna School of Painting which had existed for about a century and a half withered away. After the death of its last patron Rai Sultan Bahadur in 1891, there was no one to extend patronage to the artists, who now dispersed and took up various jobs to earn a living. The development of photography at this stage dealt the final blow.[18]

As the account shows, the nineteenth century brought in significant changes in the Patna society without sufficiently undermining the traditional mode of life. However, the two were now in confrontation and this determined the socio-cultural contours of Patna in the years that followed.

NOTES

1. A sketch map of Patna appended to Hamilton Buchanan's *Journal of Francis Buchanan* (afterwards Hamilton), Patna and Gaya, 1811-12; V.H. Jackson (ed.), Patna Superintendent Government Printing Bihar and Orissa, 1925, shows that what now constitutes Patna was a cluster of far flung villages south of the main east-west road joining old Patna, i.e. Patna City and Dinapur Cantt 30 km, apart. But by the early twentieth century Bankipore or Patna had become a compact area with the integration of many of these localities because of habitations developing in the intervening areas. In 1912 when Bihar was separated from Bengal, this area became the nucleus of capital for the new province and soon developed into a distinct township.

2. Tin Kauri Ghosh after whose name the school was established was the son-in-law of Sri Baldeo Palit a promoter of English education. He had already started a school in Dinapur Cantt. The next school was opened by a Bengali lady Smt. Aghore Kamini Devi in 1892. It aimed at promoting female education among Indians. The school is now known as Bankipore Girls' School. Sri P.N. Sinha, a theosophist and a practicing lawyer opened the P.N. Anglo-Sanskrit school in 1895. Rammohun Roy Seminary was opened by a group of Bengali Brahmos in 1897. All these schools were situated within a walking distance of twenty minutes of each other.

3. During 1875-6, of 165 pupils in Temple Medical School three fourths were Muhammadans, K.K. Datta (ed.), *Comprehensive History of Bihar*, vol. II, pt. II, p. 426. In the survey school, in the same period there were 21 Muslims in the body of 37 students, idem. In the next session, out of 45 students 23 were Hindus and 22 were Muslims. *Bengal Administrative Report*, 1876, p. 359.

4. The Tata Iron & Steel Co. was registered in Bombay on 26 August 1907. P.B. Sinha, *Development of the Mineral Industries of Bihar*, Vaishali Sammat, Muzaffarpur, 1975, p. 99.

5. Sinha, ibid., Chaps. II, IV and V.

6. A.C. Guha, *A Brief Sketch of the Land Systems of Bengal and Behar*, Thacker Spink & Co., Calcutta and Simla, 1916, pp. 48-9. Types of landownership.

7. Ibid., pp. 190.

8. William Tayler, *Thirty-Eight Years in India*, W.H. Allen & Co., London, 1882, vol. II, pp. 368-70.

9. Dr. Biman Bihari Majumdar, 'Biharer Samuhik Jibane Bengali', *Sanchita*, vol. 6, no. IV, 1977, pp. 1-26.

10. *Bihar-Bandhu*, a Patna newspaper in its issue of 18 August 1881 commented upon this tendency of educated Biharis and condemned it.

11. The first Urdu journal published from Patna was *Patna Harkara*, which came out on 21 April 1835. Dr. Muzaffar Eqbal, 'Suba Bihar. Ki Urdu Sahafat Key Sau Sal (1853-1953)', *Souvenir*, All India Editorial Conference, Patna, 1972. For the growth of English and Hindi journalism in the second half of the nineteenth century see R. Balchand, 'A Century of Journalism in Bihar', *Behar Herald*, Centenary Issue, 1975 and Bishwanath Lal, 'Language Journalism in Bihar', *Souvenir*, 16th session of Indian Federation of Working Journalists, Patna, 1973.

12. The most important example is that of Guru Prosad Sen, the founder of *Bihar Herald*, the first English journal in Bihar at Patna in 1874. Guru Prosad Sen was a practising lawyer. The other example, that readily comes to mind is that of Sachchidanand Sinha, who having returned from England and after being called to the Bar, came to Patna and took active interest in the publication of *The Beharee.*

13. Other organizations worthy of mention are Bihar Student' Conference, established in 1906, which held its first session in Patna in the same year.

    Bihar provincial conference consisting of members of Congress and non-Congress men was organized in 1908 and its first session was held in Patna in early 1908 under the presidentship of Ali Imam. K.K. Datta, *Bihar Main Swatantrya Andolan Ka Itihas*, Bihar Grantha Akademi, Patna, 1974, pp. 162-5.

14. Though formed in the last century, its present premises were constructed in 1911 on the Ashok Rajpath.

15. Among Brahmo visitors P.C. Mazoomdar and Sivanath Sastri were most important. For the visits of P.C. Mazoomdar see Suresh Chunder Bose, *The Life of Protop Chunder Mazoomdar*, Nobabedhan Trust, Calcutta, 1929, vol. II, pp. 325, 332, 344.

    The Theosophical Society had been established in Patna in 1882 and Mrs. Annie Besant and Colonel Olcott first visited Patna in 1894. *Comprehensive History of Bihar,* vol. III, pt. II, pp. 13, 14.

16. Respectable liberal politicians were associated with these two political parties. Sachchidanand Sinha, who became the first president of the Indian Constituent Assembly was associated with the Hindu Mahasabha. *The Beharee,* 11 August 1911. Maulana Mazharul Haque who founded the Sadaquat Ashram, the headquarters of the Indian National Congress was associated with Muslim League. Mazharul Haque became the secretary of the Bihar Branch of Indian Muslim League when it was first established in 13 March 1908. Datta, *Bihar Mein . . .*, p. 165, fn. 3. Haque was the president-elect of the Bombay session of Muslim League in 1915. Q. Ahmad and J.S. Jha, *Mazharul Haque*, Publications Division, Govt. of India, New Delhi, 1976, p. 10.

17. Datta, *Bihar Mein . . .*, p. 167.

18. Mildred Archer, *Patna Painting*, The Royal India Society, London, 1947, pp. 1, 31.

CHAPTER 17

European Accounts of Bihar in the Second Half of the Eighteenth Century

European accounts constitute an important primary source for the study of the history of Bihar in the second half of the eighteenth century.

The post-Plassey period which witnessed the establishment of the British rule again is much better illuminated by the European accounts, especially the British accounts, rather than by the local sources. For example, the *Journal of Archibald Swinton* who was in Bihar and Bengal from the beginning of 1764 highlights the circumstances which enabled the British to score a victory at the battle of Buxar in October 1764. He writes

The Vizier (the Nawab of Oudh) crossed the Carumnassa with the most formidable army that any Nawab has commanded for many years (and) . . . surrounded Patna and our entrenchments. *Armed Boats on the Ganges saved our Army from famine.* It was very much apprehended that Sujat Doulah would detach a considerable corps from before Patna to possess even Muxadavad (Murshidabad)—but fortunately for us the retreat of our Army had elated him beyond measure. On the 3rd May 1764 he made a general attack upon all our entrenchments. Carnac wisely stood upon the defensive, and the Moors were at every stage repulsed with loss. The Vizier remained some days longer in the vicinity of Patna and the rainy season approaching, he crossed the Carumnassa and wintered in his own Dominions. . . .

He goes on to record an eye-witness account of the events which followed the battle of Buxar and culminated in the treaty of Allahabad.

As is well-known the decade which saw the establishment of the British rule in Bihar also witnessed the terrible famine of 1770—a famine surpassing even that of 1670, described earlier by Marshall. Stavorinus a Dutch traveller to India between 1768-71 writes,

the ravages of famine were there so great, that hundreds of Indians perished daily for want of food; so that our people (the Dutch) avoided going out of the lodge, in order not to beheld the misery of these wretched inhabitants, who lay dying in crowds, along the streets and highways merely for want of nourishment. The survivors began even to attempt satisfying their craving hunger with the flesh of the dead in order to preserve their own existence. In this instance, the observation, that nature overcomes precept, was forcibly verified; for these poor, superstitious heathens into whom, from their childhood an abhorrence of every kind of animal food is instilled, and more especially with respect to human flesh, on account of their belief in the transmigration of souls now sought to prolong their miserable existence a little while, by devouring the flesh of their fellow creatures.[2]

Stavorinus confirms the deep involvement of the Dutch in the opium trade of Bihar. He writes,

Opium is a very important production, both for the inland trade and that which is carried on by sea, to the coast of Coromandel and Batavia. It is not, in fact, produced in Bengal but in Bihar, which borders upon the former; but all that is exported, comes. down the Ganges, through Bengal. More than one hundred thousand pounds weight of this drug is annually shipped by our Company's vessels, and is consumed at Java, the Moluccas, and other places in the eastern part of Asia. The natives of all those countries are fond of it, smoking it together with their tobacco, or chewing it unmixed.

Opium continued to be a major commodity of export from Bihar by the Europeans. Stavorinus also speaks of the export of saltpetre. Thus we can discern the continuity of the major trends that had emerged in the economy of Bihar in the seventeenth century. The commercialization of agriculture, and the monetization of economy were progressing. But how far they benefited the common man, a question which cannot be answered. But a second question did the commercialization of agriculture and monetization of economy unleash new progressive forces can be answered in the negative. The researcher is now left to explain this phenomenon.

The British rule survived the calamititous famine of 1770 and gradually stabilized itself. Thus began a new chapter in the colonial history of Bihar.

The period is equally well-served by the European accounts and supplements a great deal of what we know from other sources. Further, the new travellers are far more relaxed: they are not merchants in the strict sense, but are now bureaucrats. They can devote more time to things which are not economic and are now better prepared to describe the sights and the scenes.

Also we have the arrival of the artist-travellers who try to capture with pencil or paint and brush what they see. Among these breed of travellers mention may be made of William Hodges who spent four years, between 1780 and 1783 in India and visited Bihar during this period. He was the first artist in the line of Danille, Robert, Homes, etc., to have painted Indian scenes and popularized them in England.

Hodges while journeying from Murshidabad by boat arrived at Rajmahal and was deeply impressed by the ruins of the old palaces and buildings. He comments,

It was the seat of the Government of Bengal, under Sultan Sujah, and it continued to be his residence untill he fell in the conflict for the empire with his brother Aurangzeb. The numberless ruins found at and in the neighbourhood, evinced his passion for building; and the great extent of many of them affords a proof of his splendour and magnificence. There yet remains a part of the place which was supported by vast octangular piers, raised from the edge of the river. The great hall yet remains, with some lesser apartments, as well as the principal gate leading to the palace: these are surrounded by Immense masses of ruins. . . .[4]

What is significant here is the fact that old urban centres had either declined or were in a state of decline. Rajmahal's fate was probably an example of the former. An early consequence of the colonial rule was probably deurbanization and the indifference of the colonial masters towards remedial measures for reversing this trend. Hodges, however, rendered a significant service by preparing a pencil sketch of the sikriguli pass for the posterity.

Proceeding up the river he noted that at Colgong (Kahalgaon) the Kosi falls into the Ganges. His comments here are interesting.

The country about colgong is, I think, the most beautiful I have seen in India. The waving appearance of the land, its fine turf and detached woods, backed by the extensive forests on the hills, brought to my mind many of the fine parks in England; and its overlooking the Ganges, which has more the appearance of an ocean at this place than of a river, gives the prospect inexpressible grandeur.

While visiting Bhagalpur, he again sketched a big banyan tree. But by now the Englishman had become imbued with a sense of mission; he was not a trader but a ruler. Hodges writes about Bhagalpur,

The care that was taken in the Government, and the minute attention to the happiness of the people, rendered this district, at this time (1781) a perfect paradise. It was not uncommon to see the manufacturer at his loom, in the cool shade, attended by his friend softening his labour by the tender strains of music. There are to be met with in India many old pictures representing similar subjects, in the happy times of the Mogul Government.[6]

Pax Brittanica now coloured the vision of the Englishmen and Hodges is the first such example. How strong this element had became can be seen from this comment. 'From Murshidabad to Patna,' he says, 'everywhere on either side of the river there are collections of villages, and the country is in high cultivation.'[7] He looks around and visits old sites, comments on the state of society, its customs, manners and conduct of the people and in brief may be said to foreshadow the academic traveller such as Buchanan, Bishop Heber, etc., of the nineteenth century whose accounts from an important basis for the study of the nineteenth century society of Bihar.

Describing the scene when the Governor-General arrived in Patna, he writes,

When the fleet arrived at the city of Patna the shores were lived with people, the windows in the houses on the banks of the river were filled, even the tops of the buildings and every wall was crowded, so that when the Governor-General went on shore, it was scarcely possible to proceed, from the multitude, which pressed as every side, to salute him. When he had passed them, all appeared struck with the simplicity of his appearance, and his ready and constant attention to prevent any injury to the meanest individual from the irascibility of his Chubdars, or other servants, who endeavoured to keep them from pressing in. They could not but contrast this appearance and conduct with that of their Nabobs, whom they had never seen except mounted on lofty elephants, and glittering in splendour with their train followed by the coldiery to keep off the multitude from offending their arrogance and pride."

Within two decades, the Indian population was reconciled with its loss of independence and the British was speaking of the peace and[8] happiness bestowed upon the common man by the new dispensation. Hodges deserves to be reread by the students of the history of eighteenth century Bihar.

I now come to the last decade of the eighteenth century.

Thomas Twining left England in 1792 as an employee of the English East India Company. As a bureaucrat-academic, he tempers his observations with philosophical musings. Seeing the ruins of Rajmahal he notes,

In India, where history is so imperfect and tradition so contradictory, it required more time than my official avocations permitted me, to devote to such researches, to trace in each case the character of the extraordinary rise and fall; to say whether the change occupied a long series of years, or was a sudden transition dependent upon the test or caprice of the reigning prince.

Impressed by Rajmahal he writes, 'the ruins of Rajmahal being the most remarkable of any that are to be found in this part of India, I never passed this city without visiting them.'[10]

When Twining reaches Bhagalpur, he showers praises on its late administrator Cleveland, whom he describes as an 'excellent administrator of the country, who considered the rights of the inhabitants committed to his care as well as the interests of the Government; a just and praiseworthy example which I hoped I might endeavour to follow if I should ever be placed in a similar situation.'

He gives another bit of significant information, 'Boglipore (Bhagalpur) was another of the places at which the tobacco plant was cultivated on its first introduction in India.'

The impression is irresistible: Bhagalpur received more attention than the neighbouring Munger from the hands of the
English and from now onwards, for the next century it became
a leading urban centre of Bihar, probably next only to Patna.

Reaching Patna, he could not resist commenting, 'The country we had entered on passing the proper limits of Bhagalpur
was not inferior to the latter in culture or population, while
for salubrity and pleasantness it was far superior.'[11] He further
notes, 'The name of this unrivalled country implies its charms.'
It is called Behar, a word signifying spring, the poetical season
of India, as of other countries:

'Come lovely spring, ethereal mildness come', is the song of
all nations.[12]

I will like to conclude this picture with another experience of
Twining, '... still farther to the north, beyond Tirhoot, are visible,
at certain seasons, and in a favourable state of the atmosphere,
the snowy mountains of Thibet. I once enjoyed, very distinctly,
this extraordinary sight; for singular it was to look upon these
snowy peaks from the sultry plains of Hindustan.'

More than two centuries ago, Peter Mundy had remarked on
the greenery, surrounding Patna, now we have a peep of the
snowy Himalayas. May our city once again enjoy this ecology.

NOTES

1. *Bengal Past and Present*, pt. I, 1926, p. 30.
2. John Splinter Stavorinus, *Voyages to the East Indies*, vol. 1, London,
   1798, pp. 151-2.
3. Ibid., pp. 474-5.
4. William Hodge, *Travels in India*, London, 1793, p. 21.
5. Ibid., pp. 25-6.
6. Ibid., p. 27.
7. Ibid., p. 43.
8. Ibid., pp. 43-4.
9. Thomas Twining, *Travels in India: A Hundred Years Ago*, London,
   1893, p. 116.
10. Ibid., p. 119.
11. Ibid., pp. 134-5.
12. Ibid., p. 135.

CHAPTER 18

Bihar in the Eyes of British Travellers and Painters, 1780-1850

When Vasco da Gama opened the sea-route from Europe to India in 1498, the primary European concern was to develop trade with India. The early European visitors were mainly Portuguese. Their observations are full of geographical information, discussion of available economic resources and descriptions of prime commercial centres. These data relate to coastal India where the Portuguese were active. The Portuguese hardly visited the interior of the country.

The first century after the arrival of Vasco da Gama in India belonged to the Portuguese. In the late sixteenth century non-Portuguese Europeans, Cesare Fredrici (Italy), Ralph Fitch (England), Linschoten (Holland), Pyard da Laval (France), etc., also came to India. They ventured because Portuguese power had declined and the myth of Spain's naval superiority had been exploded after the defeat of Armada at the hands of England in 1588; their objective was to assess trade prospects for their respective countries and suggest measures to help start trading operations in India. Their reports threw light on Portuguese activities and also on the state of affairs in areas away from the coast. Non-Portuguese Europeans decided to start trading operations in Mughal port of Surat in Gujarat.

From the beginning of the seventeenth century European accounts of India undergo a qualitative change since the Dutch, English, French, etc., actively pursued trade in the plains of north India. They had fanned out in almost all parts of India. As the European employees were answerable to Directors of the Company back home, we learn about their day to day activities. The searchlight was on economic affairs but some of them such as Mandelslo (German), Tavernier, Bernier and Thevenot (French), Fryer (Englishman), etc., wrote about India at great length. They pointed out the ills that beset it; they noted social practices such as *sati* and/or female infanticide. The behaviour of ruling circles was not ignored. They commented on Hindu, Islamic and other religions, followed by masses in different parts of the country. They described the trading communities, both indigenous and external, with whom they interacted. They mentioned the prominent social groups. However, the European accounts were still primarily concerned with Indian economy, politics and focussed on mainly urban areas.

The dawn of the eighteenth century witnessed increase in European visitors as new European trading companies arrived and the old ones expanded their activities. They discerned that the Mughal Empire was weakening; local leaders paid lip service to the Emperor while they successfully defied Emperor's diktat and declared independence. Regional kingdoms emerged. European visitors portray the politico-economic situation and tell us how they exploited the situation to their advantage. The Indian sources talk of fragmentation that had set in, but are unable to shed light on the future political design of Europeans.

Intra-European political rivalry led military confrontation among them. Success in war would also make them dominant traders. The European accounts discuss wars they waged on the Indian soil.

The Mughal Empire suffered a significant blow after the invasion of Nadir Shah, ruler of Iran (1739) and a decade later of Ahmed Shah Durrani of Afghanistan. The latter also defeated the Marathas in the third battle of Panipat; this defeat destroyed the chances of the Marathas to replace the decadent Mughals in Delhi.

The greatest beneficiary of the decline of the Mughal power was the English East India Company. They were the first European powers to become politically dominant in Bengal, Bihar and Orissa after they had defeated the forces of Siraj-ud-Daulah in the battle of Plassey in 1757. They turned into *de facto* rulers when they emerged victorious against the combined army of Bengal Subah, Nawab of Oudh and Mughal Emperor Shah Alam in the battle of Buxar in 1764. The Mughals lost the first full-fledged war they had fought against the English. The Company cemented their position in administration by obtaining the grant of Diwani of Bengal Subah from Shah Alam in 1765. Very soon they set aside the Nawab of Bengal and became the rulers of a territory extending from Benares (Varanasi) to the eastern borders of Bengal.

The English East India Company was called upon to govern an extensive territory for the first time. They found that administration was more profitable than trade; the receipt of land revenue and other taxes far exceeded their profits from commercial ventures. This was the situation even after they had successfully ousted their European trade rivals the Dutch, French and Danes. The Company's primary task now was to create a viable administrative structure, which would ensure regular and maximum receipt of various taxes, they were entitled to collect.

The administration was now concerned with gathering information relating to crafts, agriculture, social stratification, religious and social rituals and practices, etc., so as to formulate policies which would bring maximum revenue, preserve social and political peace and prevent opposition to their rule. Now, they had to *understand* India. So far they were content to *know* India. It was imperative for them to be familiar with the historical heritage of the area, its culture and social mores. The Company and Governor-General Warren Hastings initiated a series of measures for this.

One dimension of this policy was to assess the Indian artistic achievement by well established European artists. To this end the Company invited eminent artists from England; they travelled across the land and prepared sketches and paintings of monuments which were landmarks in the architectural history of the area. They were also told to prepare visuals of people as they celebrated different socio-religious festivals. A new class of European visitors emerged.

The English East India Company also brought some experienced administrators. With them came their family members. Some of these women were close witnesses to the social life of the Europeans. They had the opportunity to observe the working of the British administrative system at close quarters. They could experience and assess the reaction of indigenous population to British innovative administrative measures.

European accounts following the establishment of the British during the later half of the eighteenth century had a distinct aim and functional utility; the writings of new observers (who were overwhelmingly Englishmen) were product of a changed politico-administrative and social environment.

The two visitors to Bihar, William Hodges and William Daniell were artists. Hodges had been recruited by the Company to visit the area under its rule and prepare sketches of important monuments. W. Daniell, a celebrated artist, came with his uncle. He was seeking his fortune. Both not only prepared drawings and paintings, but also wrote about their experiences.

Emma Roberts accompanied her sister whose husband was recruited by the Company during early decades of the nineteenth century. She was a highly talented intellectual and an accomplished writer. She had published essays, poems and fictions and was well-known in literary circles in England. She was among early women-writers to pen her ideas on India; undoubtedly she was the best.

We have also included an Englishman, Sir Charles D'Oyly, born in India in 1783. He spent his childhood in England but came back in 1797. Hodges, whose description has been given, met his father Sir John D'Oyly, who was then posted in Murshidabad. (Willian Hodges, R.A., *Travels in India During The Years 1780, 1781, 1782 and 1783,* The Second Edition, Corrected, London, 1794, p. 43). He noted, 'The liberality and attention of this gentleman to every person travelling this road are well known; and his home, I may truly say, reigned the very spirit of old English hospitality' (Hodges, p. 43).

D'Oyly served the English East India Company in various capacities, in Bengal and Bihar. He was also an artist; his talents were variously employed by his contemporaries. We were unable to get a copy of his book *The Europeans in India* (London, 1813) but we are happy to give some details about him so that he is not forgotten and ignored by the coming generation of historians of nineteenth century Bihar.

D'Oyly established Behar Litho Press and printed several booklets for circulation among new learners of English and Hindi. The books, illustrated by D'Oyly won praise of those who were concerned with the task of spreading literacy. Finally, his Press ensured that paintings done in Company style were preserved for posterity and also that they were circulated so that people would recognize this distinctly new school.

WILLIAM HODGES

After the British established their administration in Bengal, they realized that collection of land revenue was more profitable than trade. Hence, administration's attention was focused on this particular aspect. Invariably, it meant that they should better know the country, i.e. what the land produced, where the fertile land lay, what was the culture and craft of the people. They also wanted to learn about social customs, practices and ideologies. In fact, an indepth knowledge of the process of historical evolution of the people was a *sine qua non* for running the administration. Warren Hastings, the first Governor-General appointed by the Company enthusiastically promoted these activities. He supported the establishment of the Royal Asiatic Society of Bengal in Calcutta in 1784 and encouraged the publication of results of inquiries by those interested in familiarizing themselves with Indian society and culture.

The Company sent trained and well-known artists to India. Their mandate was to prepare paintings of different monuments, Hindu, Buddhist and Islamic, which they came across in course of their travels. William Hodges was one of the earliest artists chosen for this task.

William Hodges had been trained in William Shepley's drawing school from 1758 to 1765. He had also received formal training in sculpture. He accompanied Cook on his second voyage to South Africa and the Pacific Ocean. The admirality became the owner of his paintings, prepared during this trip. He was posted as an artist in the service of the Admirality. In 1779 he sailed to India. He travelled extensively and painted a lot and won the admiration of Warren Hastings. He returned in 1783 and his book of paintings *Select Views in India* consisting of 44 prints came out in 1788. He was elected Royal Academician in 1789. He published his Indian memoirs in 1793.

As a trained artist, he had an unparalleled sense of detail. He was appalled at the ignorance of his countrymen about India's artistic heritage. He noted 'it is only a matter of surprise, that, of a country so nearly allied to us, so little should be known'. He went on to say,

The public is, indeed, greatly indebted to the learned labours of gentle-men, who have resided here for the information which they have afforded concerning the Laws and the Religion of the Hindoo tribes; as well for the correct and well digested details of the transactions of the Moghul government. But of the face of the country, of its arts, and natural pro-ductions, little has been said. . . .

He wrote, 'To supply, in some slight degree, this hiatus in the topographical department of literature, is the immediate object of the following pages.' He went on to add,

It will, not be disagreeable to my readers to be informed, that they consist of a few plain representations of what I observed on the spot, expressed in the simple garb of truth, without embellishment from fiction, or fancy. They were chiefly intended for my own amusement, and to enable me to explain to my friends a number of drawings I had made during my residence in India, some of which accompany the present publication. (R.A. William Hodges, *Travels In India During The Years 1780, 1781, 1782 and 1783*, The Second Edition, Corrected, London, 1794, Preface)

It should also be noted that the drawings were made on the spot (Hodges, Preface). Hence, they were as good as modern photography and faithfully recorded the details.

In Bihar Hodges visited Rajmahal, Bhagalpur, Munger and Patna and their surrounding regions.

Before coming to India, Hodges familiarized himself with Indian history and culture. Hodges was acquainted with historical details of the region, especially from Mughal times onwards, and his observations are well-informed. When he commenced his journey from Calcutta, he passed by the battle-field of Plassey; he remembered the role played by Lord Clive whose victory at the battle fought here placed the foundation stone of Company's rule in Bengal (ibid., pp. 16-17). When he reached Uduahnala, he saw a bridge and commented that it was built by Shah Shuja, the second son of Shah Jahan, then the Governor of Bengal. He also mentioned that Company's forces obtained a victory over Mir Kasim, the Bengal Nawab, whose defeat enabled the Company to establish unhindered sway over the subah (ibid., p. 20).

He was now around 2 miles distant from Rajmahal, situated on the banks of river Ganges, capital of Bengal and Bihar in the late sixteenth century.

He visited the local ruins and remarked that 'numberless ruins' indicate Shah Shuja's 'passion' for building and 'the great extent of many of them affords a proof of his splendour and magnificence'. He noted the architectural feature of the palace in the following words:

There yet remains a part of the palace which was supported by vast octangular piers, raised from the edge of the river. The great hall yet remains, with some lesser apartments, as well as the principal gate leading to the palace: these are surrounded by immense masses of ruins. The palace, in the time of Sultan Sujah, was nearly destroyed by fire: the *zananas*, or that part inhabited by the females of his family, was totally destroyed. (ibid., p. 21)

He also comments on the institution of *zenana* or the female quarters as they existed in the Muslim society.

Near Rajmahal was the Sikrigali pass, the gateway to Bengal from Bihar. He saw the ruined fortification and the gate and observed that they were useless in preventing a huge army to pass as was shown by the passage of an army of 50,000 Mahrattas in 1742-3 (ibid., p. 22). He, therefore, supported British policy of not bothering to repair them since the citadel and the gate could not stop the enemy from entering Bengal.

He noticed the two falls nearby, which taken together were

105 feet high. He found the water falling in a cave. When he entered the cave, he found pieces of coal. He carried some and showed them to knowledgeable persons (ibid., pp. 23-4).

Proceeding further, he found that the

road continues by the river side, opening in extensive glades, covered with a fine turf, and only interspersed with woods, consisting of timber trees of considerable magnitude, which from the great heat and moisture in this part of India (like all other vegetable productions of the country) continue verdant through a great part of the year. (ibid., p. 24)

He noted, 'After this the road skirts the woods, and under great trees, which are filled with a variety of birds and beautiful colours, peacockes in abundance, which sitting in the vast, horizontal branches, and displaying their varied plummage to the sun, dazzle the eyes of the traveller as he passes' (ibid., pp. 24-5).

He notes the rivulets, the impact they had on terrain and tries to present a faithful picture of the topography of the land through which he was passing. He writes,

The country about Colgong is, I think, the most beautiful I have seen in India. The waving appearance of the land, its fine turf and detached woods, backed by the extensive gauts on the hills, brought to my mind many of the fine parts in England; and its overlooking the Ganges, which has there the appearance of an ocean at this place than of a river, gives the prospect irrepressible grandeur.

The author had promised to give a true picture of the topography of the land; he remained true to his word. He did not miss any significant change in the terrain during his journey. He continued in this vein while describing Sultanganj. He says,

. . . opposite to which [Sultanganj], in the river, is the small island of Jangerah, or according to some authors, Jehanguerry. The island is a rock, with a few trees growing from its interstices, and on the top is a small hermitage, inhabited by a Hindu monk. . . . This rock is considered by the Hindoos as a sacred place, and on many parts of it are sculptures relative to their mythology. . . . Considering these works as I do with the eyes of an artist, they are only to be paralleled with the rude essays of the ingenious Indians I have met with in Otaheite, and or on other islands in the South Seas. (ibid., pp. 25-6)

While entering the town of Bhagalpur, he saw a big banyan tree. He immediately drew it because, 'This is one of those curious productions in nature which cannot fail to excite the attention of the traveller. The branches of this tree having shoots depending upon them, and taking root, again produce, and become parents of others' (ibid., p. 27).

Like a true Companywallah, the author also positively assessed the impact of British rule. He wrote of the town of Bhagalpur, 'The care that was taken in the government, and the minute attention to the happiness of the people, rendered this district, at this time (1781), a perfect paradise' (ibid., p. 27).

While going from Bhagalpur to Munger, he remarked, 'The roads are good, the country highly cultivated, and the villages neat' (ibid., p. 28). He is careful to indicate where agriculture flourished.

Looking around, he found burial places of Muslims. His observations are interesting.

Along the side of the road are the burial places of Mussulmans; for they, like the ancient Greeks, always bury by or near the highways; those of the common people are mounds of earth, . . . , with a small column at the head, about three feet high, and another, not more than eighteen inches, at the feet: those of superior rank have mausoleums, decorated in proportion to the wealth or munificence of the family. It is a custom with the women of the family to attend these tombs of their friends, or nearest and most valued relations, after sun-set; and it is both affecting and curious to see them proceeding in groups, carrying lamps in their hands, which they place at the head of the tomb. . . .

He painted the scene (ibid., p. 28).

Reaching Munger, he described the fort; he informed the reader that Shah Shuja had built it. About the proof of the antiquity of the city, he tells the reader that a Sanskrit inscription on a brass plate dating to fifth century AD was found here. Currently the place was used to house a section of the Company's army, with a house built by General Goddard for the residence of the Commanding Officer (ibid., p. 29).

He wrote about the weather.

The heat in the months of March, April, and May is immoderate; and, until it becomes tempered by the rains that constantly fall in June and July, it is dreadful to the bearers of the pallankeens to travel in the middle of the day: the dust and heat are then, indeed, so intolerable that they are frequently under the necessity of putting down their burthens, and sheltering themselves beneath the shade of the banyan trees, many of which are found on road, particularly by the side of wells, or some little chaltry on the borders of a tank.

He appreciated the system and complimented both the Hindu and Muslim rulers. 'The number of these rural accommodations for travellers reflect the highest credit on the care of the old Hindu and Moorish governments' (ibid., pp. 29-30).

He indicated the various travel groups usually seen on the road. They included Company's soldiers, peasants, merchants, and most interestingly, *fakirs* (ibid., pp. 30-1). He also noted that Serais built by rulers or charitable persons provided accommodation to travellers. He described one serai located in Rajmahal (ibid., p. 32).

At this point he remembered the Indian ruler Sher Shah who had provided these facilities for the travellers. His strong sense of history lends authenticity to the information he conveyed.

He returned from Munger to Calcutta by the riverine route. He sailed on a boat on the river Ganges. This provided him with an opportunity to discuss another aspect of Indian landscape.

After sun-set the boats are moved close to the banks, where the shore is bold, and near a gunge or a market, for the accommodation of the people. It is common, on the banks of the river, to see small Hindoo temples, with gauts or passages, and flights of steps to the river. In the mornings, at or after sun-rise, the women bathe in the river; and the younger part, . . . continue a considerable time in the water. . . . To a painter's mind, the fine antique figures never fail to present themselves. . . . A surprising spirit of cleanliness is to be observed among the Hindoos: the streets of their villages are commonly swept and watered, and sand is frequently strewed before the door of the houses.

From the landscape, he shifted to a description of people.

The simplicity, and perfectly modest character, of the Hindoo women, cannot but arrest the attention of a stranger. With downcast eye, and equal step, they proceed along, and scarcely turn to the right or left to observe a foreigner as he passes, however, new or singular his appearance. The men are no less remarkable for their hospitality and are constantly attentive to accommodate the traveller in his wants (ibid., pp. 33-4).

The author cited his personal experience to support his statement. 'During the whole of the journey in my pallankeen, whether I wanted, as boiling water for my teas, milk, eggs, etc. etc. I never met imposition or delay, but always experienced an unreadiness to oblige, and that accompanied with manners, the most simple and accommodating' (ibid., p. 34).

He described Muslims as 'haughty', 'insolent', 'irritable' and 'ferocious'. But then he qualified his statement. These were attributes of Muslims of 'lower classes'. According to him, '. . . a Moorish gentleman may be considered as a perfect model of a well-bred man.'

He wrote about the occupations of both Hindus and Muslims.

The Hindoos are chiefly husbandman, manufacturers, and merchants, except two tribes—the Rajpoots, who are military, and the Brahmins, who are ecclesiastics. The Mussulmans may be classed as entirely military, as few of them exercise any other employment, except collecting the revenues, which under the Moorish governments have always done by military force. (ibid., p. 34)

The author is well read about both India and British rule. He quotes Shakespeare (ibid., p. 35). He is aware of Indian history and also of the events, which took place in the recent past. He spoke of Sir Eyre Coote.

When he was not able to observe anything worth recording he admitted it. 'My former passage down the river to Calcutta was too rapid to allow of more observation that what related to the general appearance of the village and towns on its banks' (ibid., p. 41).

He travelled to Patna in the retinue of Governor-General. He described the scene at Patna on the arrival of the Governor-General and his party. When the fleet arrived at the city of Patna the shores were lined with people; the windows in the houses on the banks of the river were filled; even the tops of the buildings and every wall was crowded; so that when the Governor-General went on shore, it was scarcely possible to

proceed, from the multitude, which pressed on every side to
salute him. When he had passed them, all appeared struck with
the simplicity of his appearance, and his ready and constant
attention to prevent any injury from the irascibility of his
chubbdars, or the servants, who endeavoured to keep them
from pressing in. They could not contrast this appearance and
conduct with that of their Nabobs, 'whom they had never seen
except mounted on lofty elephants, and glittering in splendor
with their train followed by soldiery to keep off the multitude
from offending their arrogance and pride' (ibid., pp. 43-4).

He described the city of Patna and remembered important
events in its history. He also travelled to nearby Maner – the
seat of a well-known Sufi shrine. He looked at the building from
an architect's point of view.

This building, though not large, is certainly very beautiful: it is a square
with pavilions rising from the angles; and in the centre is a majestic dome,
the top of which is finished by what the Indian architects call a cullus:
the line of the curve of the dome is not broken, but is continued by an
inverted curve until it finishes in a crescent. I cannot but greatly prefer
this to the manner in which all great domes are finished in Europe, by
erecting a small building on the top, which, at the point of contact with the
dome, has a sharp angle. The outer surface of this dome is ornamented by
plantane leaves cut in stone, covering the whole; the lines intersect each
other in great lozenges, and form altogether a beautiful ornament. The
great entrance to the mosque is familiar to many of the doors to our large
Gothic Cathedrals, having columns diminishing as it were in perspective
to the inner door. (ibid., pp. 44-5)

Hodges sailed up the Ganges, touched Buxar, the last point in
Bihar and moved on to Ghazipur and Benares (Varanasi).

The author was in Benares when the camp of Governor-
General Warren Hastings started on his journey to Calcutta; he
joined him. At Bhagalpur, where the party reached in January
1782, he decided to stay back. With the help of Cleaveland, the
Collector of Bhagalpur, Hodges was able to see the life of the
tribesmen living in the area called 'Jungle Terai' which extended
up to Rajmahal as the author had already stated (ibid., p. 86).

Hodges got the chance to visit a village of tribesmen when

Cleaveland was invited by villagers to attend their annual sacrifice ceremony. The author accompanied Cleaveland.

The local landscape was different from what he had seen earlier.

The appearance of this part of the country is very singular, having immense masses of stones piled one on other; from the interstices of which grew very large timber trees, in some places overshadowing the whole of the rocks; the trees are of various kinds. In many of these rocks I found the teek, a timber remarkable for its hardness and size; and these accompanied with the mango, no less remarkable for its softness, and which produces the fine fruit of that name. The tamarind and other trees are also produced here. On some of the highest of these hills I observed durgaws, or burial places, with little chapels annexed belonging to the Mussulmans. (ibid., p. 87)

We have here a fine description of local flora. The author noted that the local people were different from inhabitants of the plain.

It has been conjectured by some (how well founded I know not) that this people are the aboriginal natives of the country. They have manners certainly different from the Hindoos, being neither divided into caste nor tribes, and eating of every species of provision which the followers of Bramah cannot, as they are limited in this article according to their caste. (ibid., pp. 87-8)

Hodges knew that these tribesmen occasionally came out of their jungle dwellings and caused depredations in plains, forcing the government of the day to take punitive action. Cleaveland, however, decided to convert them into peaceful citizens. He evolved a plan which would ensure that the tribesmen did not cause any law and order problem. In pursuit of his plans, he entered the area, called a meeting of principal chiefs and convinced them of his good intentions.

By a variety of attentions, by little presents, and acts of personal kindness, he so subdued their ferocious spirits, that they promised to desist entirely from their usual depredations; and returning to their families and their people, the whole body became earnest to be personally introduced to this humane and benevolent stanger. (ibid., p. 89)

After Cleaveland had assured himself that the tribesmen had a change of hearts, he tried to bring them into the mainstream. They were inducted into a specially raised battalion of sepoys; they were disciplined and trained 'for the express purpose of preserving from injury the very country that had for centuries before been the scene of their depredations.' Cleaveland thus achieved, 'in the face of little more than two years, more than could even have been hoped so from the utmost exertions of military severity' (ibid., p. 90). The tribesmen greatly appreciated the gesture of Cleaveland; they all loved and respected him.

The ceremony of sacrifice was performed in the presence of Cleaveland. The author gives a graphic description of rites that accompanied the ceremony (ibid., pp. 91-3).

Cleaveland left after the ceremony was over. Hodges started for Bhagalpur by a different route. He reached Deoghar. There we have the earliest description of this place of pilgrimage for Hindus by an European.

Hodges writes,

. . . on the following day arrived at Devgur [Deoghar now in Jharkhand], a small village, famous for the resort of Hindoo pilgrims, this being a sacred spot, there are five curious pagodas here, of perhaps the very oldest construction to be found in India. They are simply pyramids, formed by piling stone on stone, the apex is cut-off at about one seventh of the whole height of the complete pyramid, and four of them have small ornamental buildings on the top, evidently of more modern work, which are finished by an ornament made of copper, and of gilt, perfectly resembling the trident of the Greek Neptune. These pagodas have each a small chamber in the centre, of twelve feet square, with a lamp, hanging over the Lingham. The passage to it is exactly of a height and width sufficient to admit one person. This chamber can have no light from without, but what enters from the door and through the passage.

At Deoghar multitude of pilgrims are seen, who carry the water of the Ganges to the western side of the peninsula of India. The water is carried in large flasks or bottles, holding nearly five quarts each, suspended at either end of a bamboo, which rests upon the shoulders. A considerable trade is carried on by these people, and the price of the holy water bears a proportion to the distance of the place where it is sold from the river.

The practice of carrying Ganga's water to worship the holy

lingam, especially in the Hindu month of *Sravan* (July/August) continues to this day.

Since Hodges always had his ears to ground, he noted that the territory from Deoghar to Bhagalpur was sparsely populated even though the land was fertile and was capable of supporting far larger number of people. His observation was correct. 'The silence that reigns here, owing to this de-population, spreads a melancholy over the mind of the traveller, and for miles together, nothing is heard but the screams of the cormorants, nor is the trace of any footsteps found but those of the wild elephant' (ibid., p. 95). This was the result of the famine of 1770 which had wiped out half the population of Bengal Presidency. The author was also told that certain important persons in the famine-affected districts, indulged in corrupt practices and accummulated a large fortune. He took up the matter with Cleaveland, the Collector of Bhagalpur district. The Collector listened to him carefully and told him that he had personally investigated the matter, talked to affected persons and concluded that there was no truth in the accuzations. Cleaveland showed to Hodges relevant official documents. Hodges was convinced that the rumour was an exercise in character assassination and the accused persons were innocent (ibid., p. 96).

Hodges not only reported what he saw but tried to under-stand the forces that had shaped the present state of affairs. Behind the exotic India, for him, there was an India with milennia of history, culture and artistic achievements. The country's landscape varied; it consisted of fertile fields, forests, hills, rivers and rivulets. The people talked in several languages and dialects. Within a common history, there lurked many histories. To rule over the country, the Company needed special administrative policies, taking into account the sentiments, aspirations, psychology and plurality of the people. Hodges had correctly identified the core problem before the Company's administrators.

Such accounts as prepared by Hodges and subsequent officials and travellers helped the new rulers to understand the unique problems facing them. The Company slowly and steadily, built-up an administrative structure, which took into account peculiarities of Indian situation. This helped them to rule over the country for around a century and a half.

WILLIAM DANIELL

Hodges was followed to India by other artists; one was a team of uncle and nephew, Thomas and William Daniell in 1786. The Company did not send them; they came to seek their fortune and succeeded. Their talent as artists was recognized on all hands; they received orders to draw; they were never short of work. They made a fortune by sketching and painting; they returned home in 1803.

In England, they published engravings of their paintings. These were immediate hits.

The Daniells' magnificent views of Indian landscapes and antiquities in both oil and aquatint made an immediate impact on British elite . . . their magnitude and novelty charmed the romantically inclined for whom the Greeco-Roman culture was effete. Motifs were freely borrowed from Oriental Scenary to decorate wall papers and ceramics, while the flamboyant domes and minarets of the Royal Pavilion extravaganza at Brighton were directly inspired by the Daniell's accurate depiction of Indian architecture.

A critic remarks, 'The Daniells gave the people of Britain their first accurate look at the exotic subcontinent.'

The popularity of their work prompted William Daniell to publish *The Oriental Annual Scenes in India.* The first volume published in 1832 dealt with Madras Presidency. The second, which came out in 1835, dealt with Bengal Presidency (including some parts of Bihar).

The volume, *The Oriental Annual, Or Scenes in India Comprising Twenty Two Engravings from Original Drawings* by William Daniell, R.A. and *A Descriptive Account* by The Rev. Hobart Caunter, B.D. was published in 1835 by Bull and Churton, Holles Street, Cavendish Square, London.

William Daniell was different from Hodges. He painted the monuments and scenes and supplemented them with information, which could be considered exotic by his European readers. He was not concerned with understanding the dynamics of the Indian society, culture, social customs and rites. These were noticed either incidentally or if they appeared exotic.

He started his account of Bihar with the description of a person who ate one whole sheep weighing thirty-two pounds. (William Daniell, pp. 201-3). He also added that an earlier visitor had reported a person, who ate a *live* sheep! Continuing the tale, he discussed the wide-spread belief that Hindus were mostly vegetarians.

Rev. Caunter who supplied the write up rightly affirmed that Hindus could be non-vegetarians in accordance with their religious laws. Only the Jains were strictly forbidden to kill anything (ibid., p. 204).

While crossing the forest, he caught a black monkey. He intended to send it to England, but the monkey escaped.

When he reached Sasaram, he sketched the tomb of Sher Shah. He noted, 'The country round exhibits some noble specimens of oriental architecture, both Mahomedan and Hindu' (ibid., p. 206).

Continuing his journey, he reached the fort of Rohtas. He noted that Sher Shah had captured it from a Hindu ruler. He had destroyed several idols; for this act, he was hated by Hindus even to this day (ibid., p. 207).

The ascent to the fort was very difficult. When he arrived at the first gateway, the guides barred the visitors' entry by extending their turban. They wanted them to pay something, as was the convention. Otherwise they warned 'mischief' might occur to them. He complied with their wishes (ibid., p. 208).

After a trying ascent, the party entered the fort

At length we entered the fort, which is gained by a flight of winding steps through a gateway, flanked on either hand by a wall of vast thickness that abuts each side upon a precipice. This wall is built of large masses of a most durable stone so strongly cemented together, that there is not the slightest appearance of decay. The masonry is entirely without ornament, but is still very imposing from its stern simplicity and massive strength; it is a fine specimen of ancient military architecture. (ibid., pp. 208-9)

Describing the fort, the author says,

The fort of Rohtas, . . . stands upon the summit of a table hill, but is much
more extensive, embracing a circumference of many miles, within which
are several villages, and a moderately numerous population. . . .

Beyond the gateway which leads immediately to the principal
formation, are several plain but handsome structures. There are temples,
palaces, granaries, besides village and single houses. The bazaars are
furnished with everything necessary to supply the domestic wants of the
people, of whom many never descended to the plains. (ibid., pp. 210-11)

Looking around the land from the summit, the author, for
once, thoughts about the impact of Company's rule on Indian
society.

The distant plains lay extended before the eye, . . . There were several
towns and villages scattered over the extensive scene, and to a superficial
observer, bespoke a happy and thriving population. But these appearances
in India are too often fallacious: for while the country round you seems
to promise a plentiful harvest to the husbandman, the ryot, or the farmer
of the soil, having, from the urgency of immediate want, been obliged
to mortgage the produce to the more wealthy zemeendar, . . . In India,
the social condition of husbandmen is one of extreme privation and
pitiable endurance. The taxes upon the produce are very heavy, and being
moreover levied before there is a return upon the sale of the crop, the
farmer is almost reduced to the hard necessity of selling it as it stands
to the zameendar, who generally contrives to grind him down to a hard
bargain and he has no choice left between acceptance or starvation. Thus
he sells the labour of months for little or no profit, all but giving it away,
in order to meet the demands of a prince under whose government he
lives, and the rapacity of the zameendar through whose covetousness he
starves. (ibid., pp. 213-14)

The author concludes,

The agriculturists in India are pre-cisely in the same state they were
centuries ago, nor can there be any substantial improvement until there is
a change in the social system. Until, in short, the condition of those who
raise the crops is ameliorated and brought nearer to that of those who
enjoy the fruits of the harvest. (ibid., p. 214)

The author's view on the state of agriculture, agriculturists
are completely at variance of those, who believed the Permanent
Settlement of 1793 ushered in an era of economic prosperity

and well-being in the Bengal Presidency. The artist not being a servant of the Company, fearlessly wrote something which reflected badly on Company's administration.

During the stay in the village, he witnessed the cremation of the dead body of a Hindu. He rightiy observed that the 'pariah;' whose touch was avoided by other Hindus, played an important role in the last rites.

The corpse was now laid upon the pile by four pariahs, who alone touch dead bodies in India; for the contact with a corpse is held by all other castes to be a pollution from which no one can be purified but by undergoing the severest mortifications. It is on such occasions only that the poor pariah is tolerated, and thus because his services are indispensable; though even then no rigid Hindoo will approach him so near as to run the risk of coming even within the reach of his shadow. (ibid., p. 217)

The author's sensibility prevented him from overlooking the pernicious system of untouchability and Hindus. He pointed out the 'interdependence' aspect of the caste system prevalent among the Hindus.

He informs that he did not witness *sati* or widow-burning, then practised among some sections of Hindus (ibid., p. 219).

Daniell confined himself to exposing certain facets of Indian society; they are, however, informative and well-grounded.

The observations became philosophical when he visited a temple. Rev. Caunter, with his theological background raised doctrinal issues, philosophical, ethical and moral.

After reaching Gaya, he went to a temple in the village of Madanpur (a village close to Gaya, near the Grand Trunk Road, now in the district of Aurangabad), in the neighbourhood of the town. Although in ruins, the temple was majestic. He sketched it. It belonged to the Hindu Vaishnav sect. Simultaneously he wrote about Hinduism. He insisted that its teachings '. . . inculcate a highly pure morality, and whenever this is infringed . . ., it is a violation of the pure Hindoo creed (ibid., pp. 223-4). He quoted Christian scholars who affirmed that it contained 'doctrines so pure and wise, as to be second only to the oracles of inspiration' (ibid., p. 224). To buttress his point, he quoted the following extract from *Bhagvat Geeta:*

Let the motive be in the deed and not in the event. Be not be me whose motive for action is the hope of reward. Let not thy life be spent in inaction. Depend upon application, perform thy duty, abandon all thought of the consequence, and make the event equal, whether it terminate in good or evil, for such an equality is called *yoga*. (ibid., p. 224)

He followed it with another quote from *Geeta*. He is one of the earliest European scholars to go to Hindu religious texts to bring out its philosophical and ethical essence.

About the Hindu sculptures he noted, '... they are masterpieces of ancient oriental art. The anatomical proportions are such as show that those masters by whom they were executed had studied the human figure with no common attention. These sculptures have all the reality of life in the attitude and action which they represent, having more grace than the Egyptian, and more action than the Greek, nor are they much inferior to the latter in beauty of proportions and vigour of outline . . .' (ibid., p. 231).

Very few Englishmen then spoke of Hinduism or its artistic heritage in such appreciative terms. He knew Hinduism and Buddhism were different creeds and they existed side by side.

Daniell, then moved to the nearby Bodh Gaya, one of the holiest places for Buddhists all over the world since 'there is one of the most celebrated Buddhist temples to be found in Hindostan, . . .'.

On the basis of the architectural features of the temple of Buddha, he attributed a much earlier date to the temple than tenth century held by Tod (ibid., p. 232).

He found it 'deserted'. 'The priest is no longer there to receive and console the pilgrim; no devotees throng its aisles— no offerings are made at its shrines. It has become a scene of gloomy desolation, a forsaken sanctuary, a shelter for the fox-bat and the serpent' (ibid., pp. 232-3).

He was deeply impressed by the stone carvings. He says, '... so great is the knowledge of art displayed in these carvings and the adaptation of that knowledge to the subjects they exhibit, that it would be difficult to find a specimen of modern sculpture of a similar character that could surpass them' (ibid., p. 233).

The sight of Hindu and Buddhist temples in Gaya and Bodh Gaya inspired him to mull over the fate of these two religions.

He rightly held that Buddhism emanated from Hinduism and 'borrowed' its mythology, its philosophy and a part of rites and ceremonies. It 'substituted' for an hereditary priesthood, an organized hierarchy and monastic institutions (ibid., p. 235).

A detailed discussion of Buddhism, its founder, its ethics, philosophy, etc., follows. There are certain minor factual errors since West was just beginning to appreciate Buddhism and its close connection with India. He finally raised the question, that still worries scholars. Why did Buddhism disappear from India?

Daniells reply is predictable. 'Assailed by the Mahomedans on one side, and the Brahmins on the other, few, if any Buddhists are to be found in India' (ibid., p. 242). According to him, the Vaishnavists, the 'ancient adversaries' made Buddha an incarnation of Vishnu (ibid., p. 242). Hinduism permitted 'men of every class' to embrace 'a monastic life' (ibid., p. 243). 'Hence it is probable that the remnant of the Buddhists may have been lost in the Jains and Vishnuvites' (ibid., p. 243).

The artist eventually turned a philosopher and a student of religious history.

We do not have any idea when Daniell came to Patna and what did he do. Did he sketch anything in Patna? His narrative is silent at this point. He was one of the earliest Europeans to throw light upon Bihar's contact with Buddha and Buddhism and to point out that it had disappeared from Bihar and India.

BRITISH PAINTERS IN BIHAR IN THE FIRST HALF OF THE NINETEENTH CENTURY

SIR CHARLES D'OYLY (1781-1845)

Among Englishmen who contributed to the development of Company or Patna School of Painting, the name of Sir Charles D'Oyly is widely known. D'Oyly was one of those civilians who experimented with Indian paintings. He painted numerous pictures taking India as the subject matter.

He was born in India on 17 September 1781. His father, Baron Sir John Hedley D'Oyly, was the Resident of the Company at the Court of Nawab Babar Ali of Murshidabad. D'Oyly went to England with the family in 1785 and received education there. In 1798, he returned to India and joined as the Assistant to the Registrar in the Court of Appeal in Calcutta. In 1803, he was appointed as the 'Keeper of the Records' in the office of the Governor-General.

D'Oyly got his first important post in 1808 when he was appointed as the Collector of Dacca (now Dhaka). In the subsequent years, the posts he held were the Government and City Collector of Customs in Calcutta (1818), the Opium Agent of Bihar (1821), the Commercial Resident of Patna (1831) and lastly the Senior Member of the Board of Customs, Salt, Opium and of the Marine (1833). After serving the Company for forty years, his shattered health compelled D'Oyly to leave India in 1838. After the death of his father, D'Oyly was conferred the Baronage and he also received knighthood. The greater part of the rest of his life, he spent in Italy and died there on 21 September 1845 leaving behind no son.

D'Oyly was the Collector of Dhaka from 1808 to 1817. During that period, he drew various types of pictures, especially the Mughal ruins. He decided to publish the drawings relating to Dhaka in the form of a folio. After engraving, the drawings of D'Oyly began to be published in the form of folios from London since 1823. In the first folio, there were four, in the second, four, in the third, five, and in the fourth folio, five drawings. A short historical account of Dhaka was also appended to each folio. James Atkinson wrote these accounts and these were engraved by Landsear. The folios are known as *Antiquities of Dacca*. Added together with these is an account relating to the history of Dhaka, which is entitled *Some Account of the City of Dhaka*. It is for this reason that very often the *Antiquities* is mentioned as a book. It is an important source for the writing of the history of Dhaka. These drawings are the witness to the politico-socio-economic adversity of Dhaka during a particular period of time.

D'Oyly's stay at Patna was the most creative period in his life.

D'Oyly was a prolific amateur artist who was greatly admired by the European community. He set up and ran a lithographic press, the 'Bihar Lithography' and also formed an amateur art society the 'United Patna and Gaya Society' or 'Bihar School of Athens' for the promotion of Arts and Sciences and for the 'circulation of fun and merriment of all descriptions.'

He himself was a prolific painter and encouraged other painters too by printing their works. He published several collections of paintings on various themes from his press. A lot of paintings have survived till date and are valuable sources of information on socio-cultural aspects of India in general and Bihar in particular.

Bishop Heber during his visit to Patna found his host Sir Charles D'Oyly, the Opium Agent, keenly interested in painting. He was an amateur artist himself. After looking through Sir Charles's drawing books, he noted, 'He is the best gentleman-artist I ever met with.' Mrs. D'Oyly was of the opinion, 'India is full of beautiful and picturesque country, if people would but stir a little way from the banks of the Ganges.'

Heber remarked, 'and his own drawings and paintings certainly make good her assertion.' Patna had become a centre of Euro-Indian art.

When D'Oyly opened the first lithographic press in Patna, he employed an artist Jairam Das as his assistant, whose cousin Hulas Lal was a noted artist of the period. D'Oyly published a number of books from this press. The notable among them are the *The Bihar Lithographic Scrap Book, Indian Sports, Costumes of India*, and *The Bird Book*. These publications helped to popularize paintings of local scene and won new European customers, which encouraged local artists to devote themselves single-mindedly to painting as a profession. European patronage created a fashion for local paintings and hence, rich Indians also decided to extend their patronage to these artists. Undoubtedly, the background for the development of the next phase when the local artists achieved new successes was well-prepared.

In the second period which extended from 1830 to 1850, two names Hulas Lal and Jairam Das from the old period continued. Hulas Lal's (1785-1875) sketchbook with autograph is available. It appears that he was also employed as a draughtsman. His style and choice of subjects resembled that of Sewak Ram. His paintings were in *Kajli Siahi*. Some of his famous paintings are 'Gambler's Den' and 'Ladies Drinking Party' (Surendra Gopal, *Stepping into Modernity: Patna in the 19th Century,* Patna, 2008, pp. 151-2.)

D'Oyly's services were available to Englishmen who were keen to promote their social norms and values among Indians through small booklets. We learn this from *The Calcutta Christian Observer,* vol. 111, January to December 1834, printed at the Baptist Mission Press, Calcutta, 1834.

On 12 September, it reported,

. . . It is truly gratifying to see the admirable talent of Sir Charles D'Oyly employed in such a noble cause as the education of the people; his beautiful illustrations may be expected to give attraction and charm to every book of native instruction. It seems very desirable to keep all the books small and cheap, instead of putting much matter into larger volumes at a price beyond the purses of the people; for a poor man cannot afford to give a rupee for a book, though he will buy many at different times for one, two, or three annas. Those with Sir Charles D'Oyly's spirited illustrations may be expected to be in great demand, and to convey into thousands of family's the soundest instructions and purest morals. What a sad mistake to throw away so much money and time upon useless Arabic books. . . .

The report dated 14 September, says,

. . . I have been much gratified to read your correspondence with Sir Charles D'Oyly about illustrations for the 'Native Library of Useful Knowledge, and Library of Entertaining Instruction'. It is delightful to see such an undertaking: may every success attend your efforts! Most happy shall I be to lend my humble aid. Sir Charles' illustrations have indeed got ahead of the printing and composition of the books, and I had a hearty laugh at your observation, that all your efforts were unable to produce books fast enough 'to be married to the sketches!' like captivating damsels the latter have only to exercise a little patience, and they will be happily married by thousands, and go forth to the delight of all the people, . . .

It is singular that two days ago I should have written to you about the sketches for Aesop's Fables, and by your dispatch of to-day, I see that by the kindness of Sir Charles it has already been determined upon that they shall have illustrative sketches: this is most gratifying intelligence. . . .

The fables hitherto printed are very good, but the *morals, the object for which all fables are written,* are so brief, that they cannot be expected to fix in the native reader's mind. Now when he is fully interested by the entertainment of the sketches and fable, it seems a pity to let the opportunity *slip of pointing home the moral with full force to his mind.* With this view I prepared new and more full morals to all the fables of the '5th Volume of the English Reader', and sent them down in *English and Hindusthani.* Let me therefore recommend these fables for Sir Charles' sketches.

As a volunteer of *talent* here has kindly offered to prepare sketches for the fables: 'pray let me know those for which Sir Charles intends to propose illustrations, that others may be selected here. It is delightful to see such abilities applied to so noble a purpose as the moral elevation of the people—Let us hope this is the beginning of a great work for India. . . .'

List of works by Sir Charles D'Oyly

1. *Tom Raw, the Griffin: A Burlesque Poem, in Twelve Cantos,* 1825;
2. *The Costume and Customs of Modern India,* 1813;
3. *Views of Calcutta and Its Environs,* 1848;
4. *Oriental Ornithology,* 1829;
5. *Antiquities of Dacca,* 1828;
6. *Behar Amateur Lithographic Scrapbook,* 1828;
7. *Indian Sports,* 1828;
8. *The Leathered Game of Hindostan: With Birds Introduced in Pairs, Covies, or . . . ,* 1828;
9. *Costumes of India,* 1830;
10. *Sketches of the New Road in a Journey from Calcutta to Ejah,* 1830.

The drawings and sketches of D'Oyly attracted attention of one and all interested in Bihar.

Emma Roberts, a contemporary writer noted, 'The beauties of the province of Behar have been extensively known from numerous drawing and lithographs by the pencil of Sir Charles D'Oyly, whose views of this part of India and Dacca are in possession of those who have the means of gratifying a taste for the splendid scenes of our Indian territories' (Emma Roberts, *Scenes and Characteristics of Hindostan and Sketches of Anglo-Indian Society,* vol. III, London, 1835, p. 304).

Emma Roberts concluded, 'The establishment of lithographic press, through the spirited exertions of Sir Charles D'Oyly, to whose taste for the fine arts the scientific world is so deeply indebted, is alone sufficient to render Patna a place of no ordinary interest to travellers in search of information' (Emma Roberts, 1837 edn., p. 133).

OTHER PAINTERS

Many painters were hired by the Company itself to accompany the officials on their journey and make paintings of the places they visited, e.g. Seeta Ram. Marquess of Hastings, the Governor-General of Bengal and the Commander-in-Chief (r. 1813-23), was accompanied by the artist Seeta Ram (flourished *c.*1810-22) to illustrate his journey from Calcutta to Delhi in 1814-15. He was a prolific painter and his works were compiled in several volumes. A few of them related to Bihar are in 'Views by Seeta Ram from Moorsheedabad to Patna.' Individual officers also tried their hand on making painting of places where they were posted.

There is a painting by an anonymous artist of a single-storeyed European house at Chhapra in Bihar, in the Patna style, *c.* 1796. Inscribed on the back: 'East View of Chuprah.'

The British residential quarter lay to the east side of Chhapra where the civil courts and public offices were situated. This drawing shows a European couple standing at the door to a house, which is standing in a large grassy compound, done in the Patna style of painting, part of the company school. Company painting is a style of miniature painting that developed in the second half of the eighteenth century in response to the tastes and influences of the British serving with the East India

Company. The style first emerged in Murshidabad in West Bengal and subsequently spread to other British centres, the most notable being Patna, Benares, Delhi and Lucknow.

Out of many paintings done by Robert Hyde Colebrooke, only one painting has survived. It is dated 1796-7. 'An Invalid Village near Sicrigully. Indian Scenery by R. Colebrooke 1796. Sakrigali, along the river Ganges, was situated at the foot of a pass into the adjoining hills and it was a favourite spot for boats to anchor. Around there the artist drew the view of a native village.

JAMES CROCKATT (1755/6-1804) made several paintings but the one that has survived is of Mahabodhi Temple at Bodh Gaya. 'East View of the Hindoo Temple at Bode-Gya, in the Neighbourhood of Gya in Behar', taken by Capt. Crokatt. *c.*1800 is inscribed on the back in ink.

ROBERT SMITH (1787-1873) was another amateur painter of the era. He made a few paintings of important sites of Patna. His water-colour painting of Golghar made in 1814-15, is remarkable. He describes Golghar as 'the granary (gola) at Bankipur, near Patna in Bihar, seen from the river with European officials' houses near by. The inscription on the original mount is: 'Grain Golah at Bankipoore near Patana'. He further describes,

Throughout the 1770s and early 1780s there had been a number of years during which crops failed and led to disastrous periods of famine. This huge granary was built by Captain John Garstin in 1786 and was intended to store grain for those times, but unfortunately the building was found to be unsuitable for its purpose. (It has been functioning as granary in the twentieth century, ed.) The design, based on indigenous storehouses for grain and salt, consists of a series of concentric circles forming the thick walls of the large globe, which has two symmetrical spiral staircases winding around it leading to the central opening at the top.

JOHN NEWMAN (fl. *c.*1795-1818), made a beautiful painting using water-colour of the island and tomb in the Ganges at Sultanganj on 9 February 1814. Inscribed on the front in ink is: 'A View at Dusk at 5 in the Evening of Sultangunje. Ichageerah with the Mausoleum on a Rocky Point of Land behind the Island. 9th February 1814. Newman.' Sultanganj is a village in the Bhagalpur district of Bihar famous for two huge granite rocks in the river one of which is crowned by a Siva temple, the other by a mosque. It is thought that Sultanganj was the abode of the sage Jahnu. The hill that contained the Ashram of Jahnu is still sited in the middle of the Ganges and at present the famous Shiva temple of Ajgaivinath is situated on the summit.

H.H. WILSON did several paintings collected in *The Oriental Portfoli*. Describing the fort of Munger, Wilson wrote:

The remains of the fortress of Monghir (Munger) rise from a high bank, on the south side of the Ganges, and present a long line of parapeted walls, of the elevation and construction of similar strong-holds, before the skilful employment of artillery rendered such exposure a source of weakness rather than defence. . . . The Fort of Monghyr is in the shape of an irregular square, occupying a considerable extent of ground, at a spot where the Ganges forms an angle, so as to wash two sides of the Fort. The point of the angle is in the rainy season a place of perilous navigation, from the great body of water, and rapidity of the current boats are frequently lost. . . . The walls of the Fort are built of brick but the gateways are of stone, bought from the neighbouring Kurukpore (Kharakpur) hills. The view here taken is that of the western gateway, as being probably less familiar than that of the river front. . . . The town of Monghir, situated on the west and south of the Fort, is a thriving and industrious place . . . famous for its gun and pistol barrels, cutlery and other hardware.

COLIN MACKENZIE (1754-1821) joined the East India Company as an engineer at the age of twenty-eight and spent the majority of his career in India. He used the salary he earned from his military career as a captain, major and finally a colonel to finance his research into the history of Indian and Javan culture. During his surveys he collected and recorded details concerning every aspect of Indian history, architecture, language, life and religion, resulting in thousands of drawings and copies of inscriptions.

He made several paintings of Mahabodhi Temple at Bodh Gaya and Barabar Hill Caves of Gaya. Describing them, he wrote,

The Mahabodhi Temple complex is one of the holiest sites related to the life of the Buddha as it is the place where he attained enlightenment. The present temple dates from the 7th century with later additions, and was built on the site of a previous temple erected by Emperor Ashoka in the 3rd century BC. The temple consists of a central sanctuary with a tall pyramidal tower that is over 50 metres high and houses a large gilded image of the Buddha. The temple is built in front of the Bodhi Tree, the tree under which the Buddha obtained enlightenment, which is surrounded by a quadrangular stone railing that dates to the 2nd century BC.

He wrote about Barabar Caves,

The Barabar Hills are home to a group of cave temples which date to the Maurya period or the third century BC. They represent some of the earliest examples of rock-cut architecture in India and were used by Jain monks as a retreat. This drawing depicts the Lomas Rishi cave which has a very elaborate doorway imitating the elevation of a hut with sloping timber supports, curved eaves and a pot finial. The curved architrave is sculpted with a frieze of elephants proceeding towards stupas. The interior of the cave consists of an oval chamber with a dome roof entered through a rectangular vaulted hall.

HENRY SALT (1780-1827) made a beautiful painting of Fakir's Rock in Sultangunj on 22 September 1803. His companion Viscount Valentia (George Annesley) wrote, 'September 22. . . . The river then turning to the south, and the wind falling, we got on by six to the celebrated Faquir's Rock at Janguira. It rises in the river near to the right shore, and has deep water all around.'

HARRIOT MARY WOODCOCK was born in Calcutta in 1807, the daughter of Colin Shakespeare of the Bengal Civil Service. She married William Woodcock, also of the Bengal Civil Service, in Calcutta, 1828. This is one of twelve drawings of views and architecture made between 1831 and 1833 while William Woodcock was Assistant to the Magistrate and Collector of Tirhut, 1828-32 and Head Assistant to the Magistrate and Collector of Mirzapur, 1832-4.

She made a sepia wash drawing of the entrance to the mosque at Hajipur, dated November 1831. Inscribed on the reverse is: 'Ruined Mosque – Hadjipore.'

A number of paintings have survived to this day and are reported to be private collection of individuals and libraries across the world.

* * *

Though we are commenting some of these excellent pieces of art done by the painters mentioned above, we would be examining in detail the works of art as well as travelogues of only three, viz., William Hodges, William Daniell and Emma Roberts. Except Emma Roberts, others have left paintings as well as their experiences, and observations which they published in form of travelogues.

EMMA ROBERTS

After the Englishmen established their rule in Bengal defeating Nawab Siraj-ud-daula at Plassey in 1757, they needed admintrators and experts in different walks of life to run the administration. Well-educated persons with families came to India. Some of these, women, who accompanied their husbands/relations/especially if posted outside the metro cities of Calcutta, Madras and Bombay, had plenty of time and practically no distractions to observe the local society, people, festivals, social customs, religious rites, etc. As a result in the opening decades of the nineteenth century, they put their findings in articles and /or books and published them. Thus a new dimension was added to literature produced by the visiting Englishmen.

Among these early women writers mention may be made of Lady Mary Nugent (*Journal of a Residence in India* (*1811-15*), 2 vols., London, 1839), Fanny Parkes (*Wandering of a Pilgrim in Search of the Picturesque*, London, 1850), Maria Graham (*Journal of a Residence in India*, 2nd edn., Edinburgh, 1813), Emma Roberts (*Scenes and Characteristics of Hindostan with Sketches of Anglo Indian Society*, 1st edn., 1835; 2nd edn., 1837), etc.

The account of Emma Roberts is the best.

Born c. AD 1794, she was keenly interested in studies. She published a two-volume book of history, *Memoirs of the Rival Houses of York and Lancaster, or the White and Red Roses* in 1827. She had emerged as a sensitive writer who had the capacity to describe accurately the minutest details and keep the reader engrossed.

On the death of her mother and the marriage of her sister to an officer of the Bengal army (Captain R.A. M'Naghten), Miss Roberts accompanied Mrs. M'Naghten and her husband to India in February 1828, taking her passage in the *Sir David Scott,* to Bengal. From Calcutta she proceeds with them to the Upper Provinces, where she spent the years 1829 and 1830, between the stations of Agra, Cawnpore, and Etawah' (*Notes of An Overland Journey Through France And Egypt To Bombay By The Late Miss Emma Roberts,* London, 1941, p. XV).

'Her sister passed away in 1831 (ibid., p. XVI). Around this time she shifted to Calcutta. Here she found a fertile field for her creative activities. She came in contact with a wide-range of British society and Anglo-Indians. She contributed to different magazines and journals especially *Asiatic Journal* (which first appeared in 1832)' (ibid., p. XVIII).

During her stay she carefully observed the society, acquired as much knowledge as she could and wrote articles. Nowhere she allowed her fancy to override her observations.

She won a place among the British intellectual elites. She was given the difficult task '. . . of editing a newspaper, and the *Oriental Observer,* while under her direction, was enriched by some valuable articles written by herself, indicating the versatility of her talents, the extent of her resources, and the large area of knowledge over which her active mind had ranged' (ibid., p. XVII). She earned a great reputation for the informative articles she wrote.

Unfortunately her health was shattered due to hard work. She decided to quit Calcutta and sailed back home in 1832.

The voyage restored her health. She wrote at a feverish pitch. In 1835 she published a collection of her articles in three volumes (ibid., p. XVIII). Her book was an instant success. It was remarked, 'Of the many attempts which have been made in this country to furnish popular draughts of Indian "Scenes and Characteristics", that of Miss Roberts is the only one which has perfectly succeeded' (ibid., p. XIX).

Soon there was a second edition in 1837. The extracts relating to Bihar furnished here have been mostly taken from the second edition.

Miss Roberts realized that since her return from India, vital changes had taken place as the English East India Company by the Charter Act of 1833 had given up commerce and was concentrating upon administration alone. It was now actively promoting modern education. It had introduced new technology in the shape of steam engine. Means of communication and transportation became faster. Indian studies dramatically prospered.

Miss Roberts decided to acquire the knowledge of these changes at first hand. She proceeded to India by the overland route. Her intention was to study western India, as during her previous trip she had seen only eastern India.

She was the guest of the Governor Sir James Carnac at Bombay (ibid., p. XXI). She started her work in real earnest. The Government allowed her to consult official records. Locals, both Europeans and Indians, brought to her source-material for her studies. She also became the editor of *Bombay United Service Gazette* (ibid., p. XXIII).

Her health again broke down. Hoping a change of place and weather would help her, she went to Poona. Unfortunately, she died suddenly the next day after her arrival in the house of Col. Campbell.

After her death, the *Calcutta Literary Gazette* wrote:

Nothing can be more minute and faithful than her pictures of external life and manners. She does not, indeed go, much beneath the surface, nor does she take profound or general views of human nature; but we can mention no traveller, who has thrown upon the printed page such true and vivid representation of all that strikes the eye of a stranger. Her book, entitled *Scenes and Characteristics of Hindostan,* is the best of its kind. Other travellers have excelled her depth and sagacity of remark, in extent of information, and in mere force or elegance of style; but there is a vivacity, a delicacy, and a truth in her light sketches of all that lay immediately before her, that have never been surpassed in any book by travels that is at this moment present to our memory (ibid., pp. XXVII-XXVIII)

Another writer remarked, 'Miss Roberts had previously accompanied her sister, Mrs. M'Naghten, to India, and resided in the country sometime; but on her death returned to England, and employed her pen assiduously and advantageously illus-trating the condition of our Eastern dominions . . .' (Sylvanus Urban, Gent, *The Gentleman's Magazine*, vol. XV, New Series, 1841, London, p. 544).

Coming from the pen of such an astute observer, Emma Roberts' account gives us an intimate glimpse of society in Bihar in the 1830s.

She described important urban centres of Bihar and begins with Patna. She says, 'Patna is the first native city of wealth and importance passed by voyagers of the Ganges, on their way to the upper country' (*Scenes*, p. 130). Speaking of its importance to the British, she remarks, 'The annexation of Patna to the Company's territories rendered the subjugation of the upper country comparatively easy, . . .' (ibid., p. 131).

About Europeans living in Patna, she noted, 'The houses of the numerous civil servants of the Company . . . are built in the style of those of Calcutta, and are chiefly *pukah;* many are very stately edifices, having broad terraces overlooking the Ganges, and being surrounded with luxuriant plantations' (ibid., p. 132).

Europeans in Patna were never intellectually starved. Easy communication with Calcutta helped Patna residents obtain books and English newspapers, '. . . and the inhabitants, keeping up a more regular intercourse with Europe, are not so entirely dependent upon the Indian press for intelligence from home as these attached to more remote stations, . . .' (ibid., p. 132).

The local European society had continuous intercourse with their fellow countrymen as they 'proceeding up or down the river, and their appointments, though clipped and curtailed, being comparatively liberal, they are enabled to keep up a portion of the ancient hospitality. . . . It is not, therefore sur-prising that the headquarters, Bankipore, should always be distinguished for the intellectuality and elegance of its principal residents' (ibid., pp. 133-4).

The writer commends the efforts of Charles D'Oyly through his lithographic press to encourage knowledge about its flora and fauna. She feels that the step promotes drawing skills among Indians (ibid., p. 134).

Miss Roberts is one of the earliest to dwell at some length about Europeans, stationed in Dinapur Cantt, a few miles distant from Patna. A feature was European addiction to smoking cheroots. She noted. 'Ladies have also been known to retreat *en masse* from a dinner party, to be succeeded by dancing, offended by cheroots proceeding from a neighbouring apartment. . . . This highly-esteemed preparation of tobacco has nearly superseded the use of the far more elegant hookah' (ibid., p. 134).

The writer correctly evaluated the role of Muslims in the local society. She says, 'Patna is a strong-hold of Mohammedans' (ibid., p. 136).

Patna had become prosperous. The enormous wealth of Patna was probably the chief cause of the pride and insolence of the inhabitants.

Many of the great men of the city are exceedingly rich; and at a *durbar* held by Lord Amherst, on his way to the upper provinces, one of them offered, and it is said, a lac of rupees to have his name inserted at the head of the list of native gentlemen who paid their respects to the Governor-General on that occasion. (ibid., pp. 138-9)

Writing further, the author remarked, 'It (Patna) also possesses very expert worksmen in every department of mechanical art (ibid., p. 139).

But the properous and well-populated urban centre was not beautiful. The author noted,

The streets of Patna cannot be traversed on horse-back, or upon an elephant, being too narrow to admit any wheel-carriage superior to the native *ruth,* a creaking, nodding, non-descript vehicle, in which the ladies of the country, concealed from public view by thick curtains, huddle themselves when they travel or pay visits. (ibid., p. 140)

The housing pattern came under the author's scrutiny. The rich inhabitants took advantage of the city's location on the bank of the river Ganges. 'The best houses face the river; . . .' 'The houses tenanted by the middling classes are exceedingly crazy, and have somewhat of a cruise air, each story lessening in size, and standing in the verandah of the below' (ibid., p. 141).

Although not impressed, the author candidly admitted some positive points.

Amid much that is unsightly, there is a great deal to admire in the long avenue which stretches from gate to gate of the city, every few yards bringing some picturesque object to view, lofty open cupolas, in the most elegant style of Moghul architecture, surrounding handsome mosques, are contrasted with solid towers of dark-red stone, which seems to have been the favourite material in former times. The houses built for accommodation of the English residents on the first occupation of the city, now long deserted and falling into decay, have a singular and melancholy appearance.

The city actually came to life in evening.

The shops are all lighted up, and as the evening advances, the dusky buildings which near themselves against a dark blue sky studded with innumerable stars, have a solemn and imposing appearance . . . Patna at this time assumes a gorgeous aspect, presenting a succession of temples and palaces worthy to have been abode of the luxurious Moghuls. (ibid., pp. 142-3)

The Englishmen, however, remained aloof. The author noted, 'The gracious example of a few distinguished individuals, whose courtesy has endeared them to all ranks and classes, is unfortunately disregarded by the majority of British residents in India' (ibid., p. 143). The racial divide remained a permanent fixture.

The author turned her eyes to the neighbourhood of the city. She described in great detail the annual fair held at Hadgeepore (Hajipur) at the commencement of the cold season. (The fair has been now shifted to the nearby Sonepur and is famous as Sonepur Fair.) She noted extensive European participation but says '. . . natives and Europeans of course occupying places distinct from each other' (ibid., p. 144).

The author pointed out,

A description of Patna, however, slight and superficial would be exceedingly incomplete unless some mention should be made of . . ., Deegah Farm, the extensive establishment of Mr. Havell, who conducts his business upon a scale of magnificence which is unequalled throughout India. . . .

Mr. Havell's boats go down to the Sand-Heads, at the mouth of the Hoogly, to catch the mango and hilsa fish, which, after being properly cured, are despatched to every part of India; his humps, his chetney, and his sauces, form a portion of exports from Calcutta to London; and hams, bacon, and hung beef, prepared at his farm, are highly esteemed even by those who are apt to fancy that nothing of this kind can be excellent which does not come from England. (ibid., p. 148)

The author voiced concern over the durability of this establishment.

During a great part of the year, there are a thousand persons employed in the different departments of this concern, and the wages of these people must amount to an enormous sum. . . . There is very little encouragement for trade in a country where so few persons possess incomes large enough to allow them to indulge in the luxuries of life, and there is but too much reason to apprehend that, at the death of the present spirited proprietor, Deegah will dwindle and fall into decay. (ibid., p. 150)

The author discussed other urban centres in Bihar such as Munger (Monghyr), Bhagalpur, Arrah, etc.

Munger, before Company conquered almost the whole of north India, was 'one of the principal military stations of the British army' (ibid., p. 294). Currently 'A few invalided soldiers garrison the dismanded citadel, which has been turned into an asylum for lunatics belonging to the native army, and a depot for military clothing, the tailors in the neighbourhood being considered particularly expert' (ibid., p. 296). Some of the European residents had erected palaces like houses 'which give

a regal air to the splendid landscape of Bengal' (ibid., p. 295).
These European veterans were mostly pensioners of the
Company, who had abandoned all plans of returning home
(ibid., p. 299).

Emma Roberts gave a detaded description of crafts practised
in Munger.

> A considerable trade is carried on at Monghyr, from the manufactories
> of the place; the workmen possess considerable skill, and construct
> palanquins, European carriages, and furniture, in a very creditable manner.
> Under the inspection of persons well acquainted with these arts, they can
> produce goods of a very superior description, and at astonishingly low
> price. . . . The clothing of the army is made here; and it is celebrated for its
> shoes, both of the native and European forms. But the most famous of its
> manufactures is that of the blacksmiths, who work up steel and iron into
> a great variety of forms; these goods are coarse, and not of the very best
> description; but they are useful, especially to the natives, and remarkably
> cheap. Double-barrelled guns are sold for thirty-two rupees each, rifles at
> thirty, and table knives and forks at six rupees per dozen. . . . (ibid., p. 296)

Furthermore, the writer advised that, 'It is perhaps safest to
confine purchases to iron goods of native construction; spears,
which are necessary articles in the upper country, are of the
best kind, and are sold at twenty annas (about 1s. 4d.) each;
and the *ungeethas*, iron tripods in which charcoal is burned, are
excellent.'

The author is conscious as to what was lacking. She opined,
'The only things that are wanting to improve the quality of the
steel are a superior method of smelting, and a higher degree of
labour bestowed on the anvil; the guns are not warranted not to
burst, and it is not very difficult either to break or to bend die
knives . . .' (ibid., p. 297).

The craftsmen were receptive to new ideas. 'There would
be no difficulty in rendering native workmen quite equal to
those of England; . . .' (ibid., p. 298). The author was certain,
'The excellence of the workmanship of those employed in the
service of Europeans, show how easily they can be trained to
any mechanical employment when under the superintendence
of scientific persons' (ibid., p. 298).

'Since the importation of European fashions, a vast number of new articles have been introduced into the shops of the natives; tea-kettles, tea-trays, toasting-forks, saucepans, and other culinary vessels unknown in the kitchens of the Muslem or Hindoo, are exhibited for sale, . . .' (ibid., p. 297).

The author provided an interesting account of 'Seeta-coond', the well-known hot water spring, famous for the 'purity of its water'. She noted 'Persons travelling down the country, with the intention of returning to England, generally provide themselves with several dozens of bottles of water from Seeta-coond, to serve as sea-stock' (ibid., p. 301).

Munger was surrounded by forests and hills, where lived 'numerous tribes of savage animals'. Among these were tigers and bears, which often attacked passersby and entered the local houses (ibid., p. 203).

The fields around Munger were fertile. The author informs us that cash crops such as poppy, cotton, indigo and sugar cane, etc., were cultivated (ibid., pp. 313-14).

Coconut trees also grew in abundance. It was very useful, 'It affords nutritious food and several kinds of beverages. When green, its fruit is excellent stewed, and when not eaten alone, slices enter into the composition of kaaries, and . . . made dishes. . . . Vinegar is manufactured, and spirits distilled, from the juice of palm-tree; the oil it yields is unrivalled in excellence; its leaves plaited are employed in making the walls and covering in the roofs of native cottages, and fibres are twisted into cables, or, used for stuffing matteresses, . . . The coco-nut, either whole or in slices, always enter into offerings made to the deities. (ibid., p. 314)

It seemed agriculture was flourishing but we do not have idea if the prosperity reached the common peasant. The author in his chapter on Munger also described other areas in the state, which had been neglected by most of the European writers. For example, she talks of the district of Saran, situated north of the river Ganges. 'The zillah or province of Saran, during many ages, enjoyed the reputation of being one of the most fertile tracts in the British territories, having had the name, common to all fruitful places, of 'the garden of India', bestowed upon it' (ibid., p. 312). The district gradually lost its fertility as Gandak River encroached upon it; many villagers quit as land became unfit for agriculture. The government decided to take measures to stop Gandak water flooding the district in early 1830.

Captain Sage, the executive officer of the division was directed to construct a dyke, or bund for the security of the adjacent country. He personally designed it. He commenced his operation in the middle of April in the same year, and on the 19th of the following June had completed his undertaking along a distance of ninety-two miles, two furlongs and fifty-seven yards. The bund is in its average dimensions forty-five feet wide at the base, ten in width at the top, and nine feet in height, forming an elevated road, on which carriages of any description may safely be driven. Another cross-bund, supplied with sixteen sluices for the purpose of irrigation, was completed after the rains by the same indefatigable officer, who, under a burning sun, in the hottest season of the year, accomplished a work which would have done credit to the genius of Holland.' 19,489 men were employed daily. It was stated that the 'solidity of the construction is such as to defy the utmost force of the river for many ages to come. (ibid., p. 313)

By now European indigo planters had settled down in rural areas. They were keen that indigo and / or opium crops did not suffer due to draught or floods. Some of them motivated the government to undertake construction of dykes and bunds in their areas to prevent the ravages of floods, draughts and / or siltage.

Emma Roberts' concern with urban centres away from Patna was geniune. She devoted full chapter to Ara. It had developed because the Company government located district offices (first edition of *Scenes and Characteristics* published in 1835). It was a 'civil' office (p. 105). The British presence as the author noted, seldom consisted of 'more than five families—those of the judge and the Collector, their respective assistants, and a surgeon.' The official residence of the Collector was grand.

Emma Roberts was one of the earliest authors to describe the 'mansion' or the house of the Collector.

Whilst perambulating the numerous chambers of this spacious mansion, I could fancy myself in the situation of a heroine of a fairy tale, following

. . . through the laybrinths of some enchanted castle. . . . Long suites of lofty and beautifully-furnished apartments extended on every side; in the Verandahs hung numerous cages filled with brilliantly-plumed birds, from the ranges of Nepaul, rare even in neighbouring plains. (p. 106)

She was so overwhelmed that she wrote, 'I had arrived at the end of my pilgrimage, and that I was destined to pass the remainder of my life in a retreat so well adapted to my taste, and presenting so many objects of attraction—books, pictures, flowers, and birds—to a mind already shrinking from the turmoils and troubles of the world' (p. 109).

She found out, 'During a long series of years, the domestic quietude of Arrah had not been disturbed by brawls or blood-shed; its inhabitants appeared to be quiet, inoffensive, indu-strious race, removed from all temptation to commit outrages on the persons or purses of their fellow creatures' (p. 112).

Little did she know, within four decades the place would become the centre of freedom fighters under the leadership of Kunwar Singh who sought to end the Company's rule. Despite all her praise for Arrah, she did not gloss over a sad aspect of the place.

She has narrated in detail the presence of *thugs* in the neigh-bourhood and their working. So far we thought that *thugs* were mostly confined to Central India (pp. 112-29). She also mentions a local tradition that the Mughal ruler Shah Jahan adopted strong measures to eliminate the *thugs* after one of his officers was murdered by a man of their clan (pp. 113-24).

She ended her chapter on the city on a positive note. 'I quitted Arrah with an indelible impression on my mind; but can never hope to convey to my readers the effect produced by its wild tales and gorgeous scenery.'

Emma Roberts devotes a chapter to one of the most colourful characters of eighteenth century India, Begum Sumroo.

Originally Muslim, she married a German mercenary and adventurer, commonly called Sumroo. Her husband at one point of time served Nawab Mir Kasim of Bengal. He massacred all Englishmen at Patna, after the place was occupied by Mir Kasim.

The Company's army retaliated; Mir Kasim quit Patna and took shelter at the Court of Awadh (Oude), Sumroo transferred his services to other Indian rulers and materially prospered. He was offered the Jagir of Sardhana (Seerdhuna) near Meerut in western Uttar Pradesh; he himself become a minor ruler.

After Sumroo's death, his Muslim wife, who had converted to Catholicism, continued to rule. She (Begum Sumroo), survived the turmoils of eighteenth century politics. She had enlisted the support of Company's government.

Excerpts from these visitors, Hodges, William Darnell and Emma Roberts deepen our knowledge of late eighteenth-century and early nineteenth-century Bihar. Hodges while sketching the monuments presents a graphic picture of its terrain. He throws light on rural Bihar. Daniell painted the monuments, especially the temples at Gaya including the Bodh Gaya temple associated with Lord Buddha. His colleague, Rev. Hobart Caunter discusses the theology and principles of Buddhism and tries to answer the question why Buddhism disappeared from India. Emma Roberts has a beautiful style. She combines erudition with a keen sense of observation. She is the only author who discussed urban centres other than Patna in Bihar.

We have presented data available to us about the contribution of D'Oyly, a practitioner and a protagonist of Company or Patna School of Painting in the hope that someone is inspired to write a monograph about him in near future.

NOTE

A few lines about how the idea of preparing the present volume emanated:

The publication of a revised version of my earlier book *Patna in the Nineteenth Century* recently published by Khuda Baksh Oriental Library rekindled my interest in nineteenth-century Bihar. A conversation with Sri Tejakar Jha further motivated me to examine European sources on the topic. He had downloaded from internet the accounts of Hodges, Emma Roberts and some information on D'Oyly's works. He also showed digital copies of the paintings as well as the travel accounts of William Daniell available in the library of Maharajadhiraja Kameshwar Singh Kalyani

Foundation, Darbhanga. We then decided to bring together extracts relating to Bihar from these accounts so that future historians of Bihar can have easy access to them.

The observations are remarkable; they have details of rural life and supplement our information on Bihar in the late eighteenth and early nineteenth centuries. When the manuscript was ready, we showed it to Prof. Hetukar Jha. He was delighted and offered to publish it. We also thought it appropriate since he has published several volumes under Bihar Heritage Series. We take this opportunity to thank him heartily for publishing the work on behalf of the Maharajadhiraja Kameshwar Singh Kalyani Foundation under the Bihar Heritage Series.

We also thank M/s Vigyapan for its help in preparing the manuscript right from the time of first draft to the press copy.

CHAPTER 19

Aniruddha Ray on European Discourses on Bihar

Bihar created the first pan-Indian Empire and simultaneously hosted the first recorded foreign envoy, Megasthenes, who has left behind in his *Indika,* a brilliant description of society and polity of Pataliputra (modern Patna), then and now the capital of Bihar. For more than a century, students of Indian history have repeatedly studied Megasthenes' work to reconstruct a picture of ancient India's socio-economic, cultural and administrative life.

Under Magadhan ruler Ashoka the Great, Buddhism spread beyond the borders of India and became the religion of masses extending from the Caspian to the Pacific. Bihar came into lime-light on the international scene.

The Buddhists flocked to India to pay homage to the places associated with Lord Buddha. The Chinese Buddhists and their rulers felt they needed to know the teachings and philosophy of the Lord at first hand. Therefore, among Chinese pilgrims came scholar monks who stayed for long years in India. For them a visit to Bodh Gaya where the Lord gained enlightenment was a must. They studied Buddhist scriptures for several years in the Universities of Nalanda and Vikramshila. Some of them owing to their prolonged stay in Bihar became well acquainted with the local society and on their return wrote about Bihar and other parts of India. The most famous Chinese monk-scholars were Fa-hian, Hiuen Tsiang and I-tsing. Once the Chinese had completed the translation of Buddhist scriptures, the flow of Chinese monk-pilgrims ceased around the eighth century AD.

For the next eight centuries with certain exceptions, such as Dharmasvamin, a Tibetan who came in the thirteenth century,

Bihar remained unreported by foreign scholars. The Arab geographers and Europeans who visited India between the eighth and the sixteenth centuries mostly wrote about the coastal areas and peninsular India.

The situation changed after Vasco da Gama discovered the sea route between India and Europe towards the end of the fifteenth century. The number of Europeans coming to India went on increasing, but they still visited mostly coastal areas and journeyed up to the Mughal capital Agra; Bihar was still the backwaters.

There was a reversal in this trend after Ralph Fitch, an Englishman passed through Patna in the closing decades of the sixteenth century. As the seventeenth century dawned, the picture changed. With the arrival of European trading companies from England, Holland, etc., and their decision to visit markets in north India including Bihar ensued a regular flow of Europeans. Soon the trickle became a regular stream as they realized that they could get saltpetre, a sought after commodity of the very best quality in Bihar cheap and in plenty. They studied the market conditions carefully and report their observations home. Hence from the 1620s onwards for the next two centuries the flow of European travellers to Bihar continued unabated. Their accounts, both published and unpublished preserved in the archives of various European countries are a mine of information on socio-economic and administrative system of Bihar, more particularly on its capital Patna.

For historical reasons, European accounts available in English have been used but those in French, Dutch or German, or in other European languages have been largely left unexplored.

Prof. Aniruddha Ray, highly knowledgeable about French language sources on Indian history, has assiduously scanned some unused, both published and unpublished, French sources from the seventeenth century onwards to prepare a profile of Patna from the late sixteenth century to mid-nineteenth century. He has supplemented his data from English-language accounts and prepared a story which shows a picture of Patna in the seventeenth century, how it thrived in the eighteenth century when Agra decayed and Delhi stagnated. As the colonial grip over Patna tightened its prosperity went downhill; it gradually lost its glamour from the beginning of the nineteenth century when the British consolidated their rule over the province of Bihar.

To substantiate his thesis, Prof. Ray carefully traces the physical expansion of the town; its growth was linear-geography had ordained it. On the north flowed the Ganga; towards the east, outside the eastern gate, the low lying areas were inundated during the rainy season; towards the south, the Poonpoon River overflowed during the rains and people, therefore, settled towards the west, outside the western gate in almost a straight line along the bank of the river Ganga. The linear character of the city was further accentuated.

Prof. Ray speculates who were the people who occupied the areas outside the western gate. There is no easy answer: the immigrants came from all strata, craftsman, traders, labourers, etc., from the surrounding areas as well as from outside the province. The thriving economy invited people to come to eke out a living, to add to their wealth.

The English and the Dutch had their regular establishments as soon as they realized that the city was to be their scene of operations. They crossed the Ganges and procured saltpetre from north-west of the province, from Lalganj, Chhapra, etc. Luckily all the places, Chhapra, Singhia, etc., were connected by water route to Patna. As a result, the transportation of this bulk commodity to Patna did not pose much of a problem, except when the administration obstructed and managerial difficulties intervened. From Patna, the saltpetre would be loaded on big boats and sent to the port of Hughly before Calcutta came up in AD 1690 for transmission to Europe. We had known this from English language sources but Prof. Ray unravels another not so-well known European export from Bihar in the seventeenth century.

The Dutch found opium growing in plenty and they started sending it to Batavia in Indonesia, their headquarters in North-East Asia. The Patna opium also found a market on

the Coromandel and Malabar coasts. The English also became
interested in the export of Patna Opium and as history tells us
and Prof. Ray collaborates, opium exports outlasted saltpetre
exports. The later ceased towards the end of the eighteenth
century but opium remained on the export-list till the end of
the nineteenth century.

Export of saltpetre and opium should have monetized Bihar
economy but did it? No historian so far satisfactorily answered
this question and Prof. Ray is no exception. But Prof. Ray has
rightly noted three things about Patna's flourishing commerce
in the seventeenth century.

First, Patna was the emporium for goods produced in the
hinterland. They included textiles and other items produced by
craftsmen; agricultural produce such as minor spices meant for
export were also brought to Patna. Secondly, up county traders
arrived here in increasing numbers not only to get locally produced items but also to procure what the Europeans brought
from their home. He correctly argues that this was an additional
reason for upswing in Patna's commerce. Thirdly, Patna was also
the emporium of Himalayan and trans-Himalayan products,
such as medicinal herbs. This added to the importance of Patna
as a commercial hub. The Himalayan connection was perceived
by Europeans as an opportunity to penetrate into Tibet. They
desisted; but the Armenian traders did go to Tibet; European
missionaries also used this route to reach Tibet. Prof. Ray
narrates attempts by Patna based missionaries to propagate
Christianity in Tibet. His is a useful addition to what we had
known from Seth's book on Armenians.

The Mughal state collected its taxes in cash. The tax collection exceeded that of Bengal. Aurangzeb recognized Patna's
importance for the Empire's financial health and therefore,
deputed men of confidence as officers and Governors; his
grand-son Azimus-shan served here as a Nawab; he gave his
own name to the city. In medieval chronicles Patna is referred
to as Azimabad.

Azimabad or Patna continued to prosper in the eighteenth
century even after it became an appendage of Bengal suba

after the death of Aurangzeb in 1707. Murshidabad became the capital and the House of Jagat Seth left Patna to be relocated in Murshidabad.

Delhi was languishing as its links with Gujarati port towns became tenuous on account of uprisings on the Surat-Delhi route. Delhi's loss was Patna's gain. Traders from north-west India had earlier frequented Delhi to secure European goods. As this became difficult they travelled to Patna as it maintained a steady link with the port of Calcutta, which had gradually replaced Surat as a centre of European trade in India. European goods were brought to Patna from Calcutta and the upcountry traders had no difficulty in securing their choice of European goods. This was another incentive to Europeans to gather in Patna as they had a good market for commodities they brought from Europe and other parts of Asia.

The French who had been coming to Patna but had not opened a Factory as the Dutch and the English had done, decided to set up their own establishment in the 1730s. The initiative was taken up by the French Governor of Chandranagar (the French headquarters in Bengal) Dupleix, the most illustrious French Company official in India. Dr. Ray on the basis of French documents had delineated the problems and constraints faced by the French Company in opening their factory and also in carrying out their business. They mainly purchased saltpetre and opium and tried to sell even coffee.

Groiseele established the first Factory of the official French East India Company at Patna in 1734. Simultaneously both Dupleix and Groiselle formed a private Society for carrying on personal trade in Patna. Corruption was endemic in European trading companies and the French were no exception.

From now onwards the documents of the French East India Company shed light on various aspects of life in Patna and Bihar.

It is clear, in the light of trade statistics, that at his stage the French and the Dutch competed with the English and other Asian traders such as Indians from north India, Central Asians, Armenians for the products of Bihar. As an important player in the game, the French experience helps us to reconstruct a truer picture of Bihar's commercial life and Patna as a urban centre.

The French documents show that within three years the situation changed drastically and dramatically. The English East India Company emerged as the dominant political force in the Eastern region after their victories in the battles of Plassey and Buxar; they used their political clout to further their commercial, financial and political interests. When English policies hurt Dutch and French business interests, they lodged their complaint but they failed to check the onward march of English domination. Before the century was out the English were seated as a colonial power and the French and the Dutch had been marginalized.

The road to political supremacy and their emergence as number one player in the commercial life of Bihar is well documented in the accounts of contemporary French visitors, Gentil, Madec and Modave, who happened to come to Bihar in the 1760s. Gentil writes of the massacre of English by the Bengal Nawab, Mir Qasim Ali from firsthand knowledge.

The Anglo-French correspondence from 1765 onwards reveals joint efforts of the Dutch and French to safeguard their business interests in face mounting encroachment by the English East India Company. They were keen that they be allowed to procure saltpetre and opium, the most profitable local commodities as in the days of the Bengal Nawabs. The English managed to satisfy them but both the Dutch and the French knew they were playing a losing game. On the basis of data put forward by Prof. Ray one can write a history of opium and saltpetre trade of Bihar during the seventeenth and eighteenth centuries.

Prof. Ray has presented to the English-speaking world for the first time the narratives of German Tieffenthaeler (from the French translation of his book in German) and the French Modave on Bihar.

Tieffenthaeler writes about the whole of Bihar even though it is certain he did not visit all the places he mentions. After reading this one gets the impression that Patna was not Bihar and there was more to Bihar than opium and saltpetre. He extensively writes of north Bihar, neglected by preceding Europeans. He calls Darbhanga as the 'capital' of Tirhoot. He speaks of Janakpur where 'lived Raja Janak, the father of Sita'. The problem with his account is that it is not structured. He mentions places without any fixed plan. It is a picture when the colonial rule had just been established.

Modave is different from Tieffenthaeler because he describes his journey through Bihar meticulously and describes the different places in the order in which he passed through from September 1774 onwards on way to Delhi. At Patna he learnt that the English did not view with favour 'visits' by Europeans, especially places beyond the British territory, i.e. to Oudh and Delhi. He therefore hid his intentions, entrusted his luggage to a friend, refrained from visiting the French Factory so as not to attract British attention, and took a boat to Hajipur, a town on the opposite bank of the Ganges, facing Patna. He travelled on foot and boats through north-west of Bihar and reached Faizabad, then the capital of the suba of Oudh.

The French visitors also speak of the physical features of Patna and thus contribute to our knowledge of the historical geography of Patna.

To round up the picture, Prof. Ray culls facts from Hamilton Buchanan and Bishop Heber, both Englishmen, who passed through Patna in the early decades of the nineteenth century. He also brings facts from the account of Jacqumont, a French anthropologist who travelled through the province in 1820s. These travellers help us to understand the transformation that had come over Patna as a colonial city. It had lost its character as a thriving commercial centre. The official class was from England and so the city was now just one of the cities, bereft of the houses that belonged to native officials as in the days of the Mughal Empire or in the time of the Nawab. People were steeped in poverty and would serve anywhere for a pittance, as Jacquemont found out. Little wonder, in 1830s, Bihari labour was forced to migrate to Mauritius in search of a living.

Prof. Ray has thus brought before us a profile of Patna from the late sixteenth century to the first half of the nineteenth century. It will remain an important contribution to the study of urban life in Bihar and also for the study of economic activities going on in the province. It goes without saying that European accounts constitute an important primary source for the study of the history of Bihar in the period beginning from the late sixteenth century.

I would like to point out to some more European accounts in the post-Plassey period which contribute to the study of urban and economic life in Bihar. As the British rule stabilized, more and more British travellers passed through Bihar and they noted their observations.

For example, the *Journal of Archibald Swinton* who was in Bihar and Bengal from the beginning of 1764 highlights the circumstances which enabled the British to score a victory at the battle of Buxar in October 1764. He writes

The Vizier (the Nawab of Oudh) crossed the Carumnassa with the most formidable army that any Nawab has commanded for many years (and) . . . surrounded Patna and our intrenchments. *Armed Boats on the Ganges saved our Army from famine.* It was very much apprehended that Sujat Doula would detach a considerable Corps from before Patna to Possess even Muxadavad (Murshidabad) but fortunately for us the retreat of our Army had elated him beyond measure. On the 3rd May 1764 he made a general attack upon all our intrenchents. Carnac wisely stood upon the defensive, and the Moors were at every stage repulsed with loss. . . . The Vizier remained some days longer in the vicinity of Patna and the rainy season approaching, he crossed the Carumnassa and wintered in his own Dominions. . . . (*Bengal Past and Present*, pt. 1, 1926, p. 30)

He goes on to record an eyewitness account of the events which followed the battle of Buxar and culminated in the treaty of Allahabad.

As is well-known the decade which saw the establishment of the British rule in Bihar also witnessed the terrible famine of 1770—a famine surpassing even that of 1670, described earlier by Marshall. Stavorinus, a Dutch traveller to India between 1768 and 1771 writes,

. . . the ravages of famine were there so great, that hundreds of Indians perished daily for want of food; so that our people (the Dutch) avoided going out of the lodge, in order not to beheld the misery of these wretched inhabitants, who lay dying in crowds, along the streets and highways merely for want of nourishment. The survivors began even to attempt satisfying their craving hunger with the flesh of the dead in order to preserve their own existence. In this instance, the observation, that nature overcomes precept, was forcibly verified; for these poor, superstitious heathens into whom, from their childhood an abhorrence of every kind of animal food is instilled, and more especially with respect to human flesh, on account of their belief in the transmigration of souls now sought to prolong their miserable existence a little while, by devouring the flesh of their fellow creatures. (John Splinter Stavorinus, *Voyages to the East Indies*, vol. I (London, 1798), pp. 151-2)

Stavorinus confirms about the deep involvement of the Dutch in the opium trade of Bihar. He writes,

opium is a very important production, both for the inland trade and that which is carried on by sea to the coast of Coromandel and Batavia. It is not, in fact, produced in Bengal but in Bihar, which borders upon the former; but all that is exported, comes down the Ganges, through Bengal. More than one hundred thousand pounds weight of this drug is annually shipped by our Company's vessels, and is consumed at Java, the Moluccas, and other places in the eastern part fond of it, smoking it together with their tobacco, or chewing it Unmixed. (Ibid., pp. 474-5)

Opium continued to be a major commodity of export from Bihar by the Europeans. Stavorinus also speaks of the export of saltpetre. Thus, we can discern the continuity of the major trends that had emerged in the economy of Bihar in the seventeenth century. The commercialization of agriculture, and the monetization of economy were progressing. But how far they benefitted the common man is a question which cannot be answered. But a second question did the commercialization of agriculture and monetization of economy unleash new progressive forces can be answered in the negative. The researcher is now left to explain this phenomenon.

The British rule survived the calamitous famine of 1770 and gradually stabilized itself. Thus began a new chapter in the colonial history of Bihar.

The period equally well-served by the European accounts and

supplements a great deal of what we know from other sources. Further, the new travellers are far more relaxed: they are not merchants in the strict sense, but are now bureaucrats. They can devote more time to things, not economic and are now better prepared to describe the sights and the scenes. Also we have the arrival of the artist-travellers who try to capture with pencil or paint and brush what they see. Among these breed of travellers, mention may be made of William Hodges who spent four years, between 1780 and 1783 in India and visited Bihar during this period. He was the first artist in the line of Daniell, Robert, Homes, etc., to have painted Indian scenes and popularized them in England.

I now come to the last decade of the eighteenth century.

Thomas Twining left England in 1772 as an employee of the English East India Company. As a bureaucrat-academic, he tempers his observations with philosophical musings. Seeing the ruins of Rajmahal he notes,

In India, where history is so imperfect and tradition so contradictory, it required more time than my official avocations permitted me to devoted to such researches, to trace in each case the character of the extraordinary rise and fall; to say whether the a sudden transition dependent upon the test or caprice of the reigning prince. (Thomas Twining, *Travels in India a Hundred Years Ago*, London, 1893, p. 116)

Impressed by Rajmahal he writes, 'the ruins of Rajmahal being the most remarkable of any that are to be found in this part of India, I never passed this city without visiting them' (ibid., p. 119).

When Twining reaches Bhagalpur, he showers praises on its late administrator Cleveland, whom he describes as an excellent administrator of the country, 'who considered the rights of the inhabitants committed to his care as well as the interests of the Government; a just and praiseworthy example which I hoped I might endeavour to follow if I should ever be placed in a similar situation.'

He gives another bit of significant information, 'Boglipore (Bhagalpur) was another of the places at which the tobacco plant was cultivated on its first introduction in India.'

The impression is irresistible: Bhagalpur received more attention than the neighbouring Munger from the hands of the English and from now onwards, for the next century it became a leading urban centre of Bihar, probable next only to Patna.

Reaching Patna, he could not resist commenting, 'The country we had entered on passing the proper limits of Bhagalpur was not inferior to the latter in culture or population, while for salubrity and pleasantness it was far superior' (ibid., pp. 134-5). He further notes, 'The name of this unrivalled country implies its charms. It is called Behar, a word signifying spring, the poetical season of India, as of other countries: 'Come lovely spring, ethereal mildness come, is the song of all nations' (ibid., 135).

I will like to conclude this picture with another experience of Twining, '. . . still Farther to the north, beyond Tirhoot, are visible, at certain seasons, and in a favourable state of the atmosphere, the snowy mountains of Thibet. I once enjoyed, very distinctly, this extraordinary sight; for singular it was to look upon these snowy peaks from the sultry plains of Hindustan'.

More than two centuries ago, Peter Mundy, had remarked on the greenery surrounding Patna, now we have a peep of the snowy Himalayas. May our city once again enjoy this ecology.

CHAPTER 20

Science College, Patna, 1927-1947

Modern education was introduced in Bihar by the British when they opened a school at Patna in 1835. In content and object, it differed radically from the two major streams of education prevalent in our country, the Hindu and the Islamic. The new system emphasized secularism, and stressed the teaching of science, technology and professional subjects. It had well-defined courses for all the stages, ranging from the lowest to the highest. The assessment system was well-defined. The candidate was awarded a certificate, diploma or degree after he/she successfully passed a public examination at the completion of the course. The school was accessible to all, irrespective of race, religion or gender. It acquired popularity when people found that the new education was a gateway to employment in the colonial administration and entry into the professions. As the government extended its functions, its need for trained people increased. Indians decided to enhance their career prospects, and so an ever-increasing number of Indians opted for modern education, including science and professional courses.

The government set up Patna College in 1863, the first in Bihar. It conducted courses on humanities, social sciences, sciences, professional and technical courses samultaneously for four decades. First, the engineering school was separated in 1900 and then law classes were introduced in the newly established Law College in 1908.[1] Science subjects taught in colleges including physics, chemistry, mathematics and biology. At the turn of the twentieth century, graduate and postgraduate teaching a science subject was confined to Patna College. Some of the teachers who taught science subjects in the 1860s and 1870s[2] were A.L.V. Ewbank[3] (mathematics and chemistry).

Hutchinson[4] (zoology), Simpson[5] (chemistry), J. Wilson[6] (chemistry and botany). Dr. Prasanna Kumar Roy,[7] D.Sc. (all science subjects), Nanda Krishna Basu[8] (mathematics), Abinash Chandra[9] (lecturer in science), George Watt[10] (chemistry and botany), and Narendra Nath Basu[11] (mathematics, chemistry, botany and logic)

SCIENCE EDUCATION IN BIHAR IN THE EARLY PART OF THE TWENTIETH CENTURY

In 1909, a need was felt to expand science education. A project to build up and equip new laboratories on the campus of Patna College was suggested. Till 1912, nothing came of it. The number of students willing to take up science subjects in their college study programme forced the government to upgrade the laboratory facilities. In the meantime, First World War began, and the government faced problems in procuring equipments. However, it managed to implement the project.[12] Social awareness about the importance of science education was seeping in when Patna University was established in 1917. The general feeling was that an institution imparting education exclusively in science subjects would be a positive step towards popularizing science education. The establishment of Patna University was a turning point in the history of science education in Bihar. Its commitment to science education can be deduced from several measures it adopted to promote higher education in the science subjects.

A scheme drawn up for the establishment of a Science College by a subcommittee of the Syndicate of Patna University was forwarded to the government in May 1918. Nothing came of it.[13] Despite being unsuccessful in this endeavour, the university continued its efforts to expand and promote science education. It introduced B.Sc. Honours and M.Sc. courses in physics, chemistry and mathematics in Patna College. At that point in time Patna College was the only institution in Bihar teaching honours and postgraduate courses in science subjects. A positive beginning had been made.

Patna University conducted its first examinations in 1918,
At the Intermediate in Science (I.Sc.) examination 830 students
appeared; 421 students were successful. Out of the 34 students
who took the B.Sc. examination, 22 passed.[14] The university's
desire to promote higher education in science continued. In
May 1919 it appointed Dr. K.S. Caldwell.[15] He was appointed
the first reader in chemistry. When he resigned in December
1919, the university' conferred this honour upon Sir P.C.
Ray,[16] a great patriot and a distinguished chemist.[17] Under this
scheme the university brought eminent scientists to Patna to
speak on important topics on science, like Dr. C.V. Raman.[18]
He came as the University Reader during the 1924-5 session,
and spoke on 'Diffraction of X-rays'.[19] The university appointed
Ashutosh Chatterjee[20] and Ashutosh Mookerjee[21] as lecturers
in mathematics and physics, respectively, during the session of
1924-5.[22]

Despite these measures, the number of students opting for
science education was still small. The following figures reveal
this: 12 candidates appeared in the B.Sc. examination in 1921-
2, and only eight passed. Next year, only four students out of
the nine who took the B.Sc. examination were successful.[23]
Postgraduate classes in physics, chemistry and mathematics
were started in July 1921;[24] the first M.A. examination in
mathematics and the first M.Sc. examination in physics under
the auspices of the university were held in 1921 and 1922,
respectively;[25] the number of students was low due to the Non-
Cooperation movement led by Mahatma Gandhi,[26] which had
gripped the country in 1920. Gandhiji called upon students in
government institutions to give up their studies and join the
freedom struggle. A large number of students heeded his call.

The university was not deterred. It rightly believed that
unless the number of students admitted to I.Sc. classes
increased, it could not expect an increase in the enrolment
for B.Sc. and M.Sc. classes. It tried to introduce I.Sc. teaching in
more colleges. The university viewed science teaching in schools
as an overture to increase enrolment in I.Sc. classes; it could do
so because it controlled school education as well at that point

in time. It laid down the syllabi of different subjects taught, conducted the matriculation or school final examination, and granted certificates to candidates who passed the examination. Only a matriculate was entitled to pursue college education. Science was being taught in nine government schools. There was a proposal 'to open classes of science' and offer 'annual training' in all schools.[27]

By this time, public interest in the promotion of science education had increased. A private endowment sponsored Sukh Raj Rai[28] as reader in the natural sciences.[29] The university was asked to use the money donated under this endowment to invite a distinguished scientist to Patna to deliver lectures on science subjects. The university would subsequently publish those lectures. This was in addition to the already existing scheme in the university for inviting distinguished scientists. The guest lecturer was paid an honorarium of Rs. 100 per lecture, besides travel and daily allowances for his journey. An environment in favour of science studies had been created in the province. The university responded suitably.

In 1922-3, a committee examined a scheme prepared by the university Vice-Chancellor V.H. Jackson[30] for the development of science teaching within the Patna College.[31] The university had become deeply concerned with the establishment of an institution to impart science education exclusively. The government put forward a proposal before the Legislative Assembly for promoting science education at all levels. During the discussion, there was a general consensus in favour of opening a college devoted exclusively to the teaching of science subjects. The Legislative Council, at its meeting on 19 August 1924, considered a resolution to construct a new building at Patna University. After a thorough debate the Council recommended 'an expenditure of twenty lakhs of rupees for the improvement of Patna College itself'. The director of public instruction (DPI), following up this resolution, suggested measures for the separation of 'Arts teaching and science teaching altogether, reserving Patna College for the one, and building a new College for the other'. The provision of additional accommodation to the students and facilities for higher teaching were also suggested. This recommendation paved the way for the establishment of an institution far imparting science education exclusively. The government now moved swiftly.

Towards the end of 1924, the Chancellor, His Excellency Sir Mortimer Wheeler,[32] assisted by G.E. Fawcus,[33] DPI, V.H. Jackson, Principal of Patna College, and K.S. Caldwell, professor of chemistry at Patna College, started planning new laboratories. It was through their effort and the thrust placed on this by Sir Sultan Ahmad,[34] then Vice-Chancellor of Patna University, that new, well-equipped laboratories were built near Patna College within three years.[35] The laboratories were designed for teaching 20 postgraduate students, 168 degree students and 240 underganduate students.[36] The cost of building and equipping laboratories in physics and chemistry came to Rs. 13,78,851.[37] the government accepted the proposal and sanctioned the opening of a Science College at Patna from July 1927, vide the government letter 4675-E of 27 December 1926.[38]

ESTABLISHMENT OF SCIENCE COLLEGE

On 15 July 1927, science teaching was shifted from Patna College to the newly built institution named the Science College. Principal Jackson of Patna College was the principal of this college on the opening day. The next day, on 16 July, Science College got its own principal. Dr. R.K. Caldwell, who served the college till his retirement in 1935. Under his stewardship, the college developed rapidly. All the science teachers of Patna College were transferred to the Science College. At the beginning, Science College had no playgrounds. By 1930 it had a gymnasium and a common room—a very fine building beside the play-field. The College grounds were also laid out. It was difficult to believe that these playing fields had been covered by a dense cluster of houses till recently.[39] Besides science subjects, provision was made for the teaching of English, Hindi and Urdu to I.Sc. students. Two lecturers were appointed in English. Teachers from Patna College taught Hindi and Urdu. A teacher for mechanical drawing was also attached to the college. In the 1930s, there was no provision for teaching biology in the Science College.

Although the new college started functioning in July 1927, its formal opening was performed on 15 November 1928 by Lord Irwin,[40] then Viceroy and Governor-General of India, at a gala function held on the campus of the Science College within a *shamiana* put up in front of the Chemical Laboratory. The Vice-Chancellor Sir Sultan received the Viceroy and the Chancellor (Governor of Bihar) in front of the *shamiana*. The Vice-Chancellor then presented the registrar and members of the Syndicate to His Excellency. A procession was formed with the registrar at the lead, followed by members of the Syndicate in rows of two in order of seniority. The Vice-Chancellor, the Chancellor and the Viceroy came after them. The staffs of the Viceroy and the Governor were at the near end of the procession.

The Viceroy, His Excellency Sir Hugh Lansdowne Stephenson[41] as the Chancellor, the Vice-Chancellor Sir S. Sultan Ahmad, and the honourable minister of education of Bihar. Khan Bahadur Saiyid Muhammad Fakhruddin[42] took their seats on the dais.[43] The function commenced with a welcome address by the Vice-Chancellor, who while, extending a warm welcome to the distinguished guests, spoke in detail about the state of science education in Bihar during the preceding half a century. He threw light on how the idea of establishing a Science College was conceived; he mentioned the amount spent in constructing and equipping the different laboratories and buildings. The physics laboratory, a two-storeyed building, with a plinth area of 26,430 sq ft, was built at a cost of Rs. 3,25,000. The following facilities were available in the college:

The ground floor has accommodation for workshop, machinery, cells, research rooms, M.Sc. laboratories, two large lecture theatres, one tutorial room, a common preparation room, a museum for apparatus, a library and reading room. The first floor provides accommodation for B.Sc. Pass and Honours laboratories, ISc laboratories, X-ray, store and photographic rooms. There is an electric lift designed for the transportation of assembled apparatus, transformer and delicate apparatus from one floor to the other.

There are three spacious staircases for communication between the two floors. The roof of the building contains a small observatory for recording the transit of stars, a laboratory for the transmission and reception of wireless work, with necessary storeroom for chronometers, telescopes, etc. There is a separate block for radioactive work. Another separate structure contains instruments for Meteorological work.[44]

The chemistry laboratory was equally well planned, the Vice-Chancellor noted:

The Chemical laboratory, a two-storied building with a plinth area of 34,495 sq ft and a total floor space of 19,709 sq ft was constructed at a total cost of Rs. 4,13,107. It has been so designed that all the main practical rooms have north light and thorough ventilation. The south wing contains the general laboratories for the undergraduate and postgraduate work. The north wing contains laboratories for special branches of the subject, rooms for research work and a reference library. The centre block connecting these two wings contains the lecture theatres on the first floor and store rooms on the ground floor, a lift giving direct communication between store rooms and the lecture-preparation rooms.[45]

The viceroy, while thanking the Vice-Chancellor for inviting him to formally open the Science College, said, 'No University to-day in a scientific age is complete without its equipment for scientific research, as one of the many branches that go to make the whole tree of human knowledge, and it gives me great pleasure to declare open these buildings which are to form so important part of this great University. Continuing his speech, the Viceroy noted, 'And to those who of you who are going to pursue this side of study I would say that, if you take all that a scientific training has to give to you, you will find that besides having much to give to others, you will gain much that will be of use to you in wider life that will open for you when you have left this university.[46] After the speeches ended, the Viceroy, accompanied by his wife, the Chancellor and his wife, the Vice-Chancellor, the DPI and the Principal of Science College, visited the chemistry and the physics laboratories.

By 1935 the college buildings and grounds were all in use. The inspectors wrote.

The buildings are the finest of their kind in the province and better than those in many other provinces in India. They cost over 19 lakhs, not an inconsiderable sum. It is evident that much careful thought was expended on the design, and considerations of efficiency, and convenience were paramount. Physics and Chemistry are each housed in a large self-contained block. A third block accommodates Mathematics, English, the Library, and Administrative offices. A small compact fourth block consists of gymnasium downstairs and the students' Common Room on the upper floor. . . . The buildings stood very well to the earthquake.[47]

The college tried its best to create conditions that would enable the students to develop well-rounded personalities. Several 'societies' emerged to aid students to follow their hobbies. By 1935, there were nine societies functioning in the college for the students. These were the Chemical Society, Physical Society, Mathematical Society, Bazme-Sokhan, Debating Society, Athletic Society, Hindi Literary Society and the Photographic Society.[48] A college journal was also published. The public appreciated the contributions of the college. They instituted prizes and scholarships to inspire the good students; these also ensured monetary support to needy students. In 1931, Rai Bahadur Surendranath Mukherjee[49] set up an endowment of Rs. 1,500 with the instruction that out of its income, a medal should be awarded 'to a candidate securing the highest aggregate at the B.Sc. examination.' In 1933 Ali Hasan[50] gave the university a sum of Rs. 965, and asked the university to use its income to give the Macpherson Gold Medal to students 'standing first in Chemistry (Honours) at the B.Sc. examination.'[51] Some Muslim intellectuals made a determined effort to popularize the study of science among the Muslims, and instituted scholarships and prizes for them in Science College. In 1933 the following scholarships were available for Muslim students: two 'Saiyid Kazi Reza Husain Scholarships' for those studying in the B.Sc. and those studying in the I.Sc. classes. The scholarships were worth Rs. 12 and 10 per month for B.Sc. and I.Sc. students respectively. 'The Saiyid Kazi Reza Husain Scholarship' of the Science College every alternate year by the Director of Public Instructions of Bihar and Orissa. The 'Saiyid Lutf Ali Scholarship' of Rs. 8 was to be awarded 'annually' to Mohammedan students by the Director of Public Instruction, Bihar and Orissa.[52]

TEACHING OF STATISTICS

After Second World War ended, a new phase of expansion began in Patna University with the introduction of new subjects. The Science Faculty also benefited from these developments. Post-graduate classes in Statistics began in 1947 under the headship of Professor D.N. Lal.[53] The department was initially an autonomous unit affiliated to Patna University, but was not connected with the Science College. However, when undergraduate teaching began, a department of Statistics was opened in Science College.[54]

TEACHING OF BIOLOGY

Biology was not taught in the Science College in the 1930s. At the meeting of the Patna University Syndicate held on 30 March 1936, a committee was set up with Lt. Col. Mahany as the Convener. Other members were A.T. Mukharji,[55] P.K. Parija,[56] A.S. Khan,[57] S.S. Choudhury[58] and S.P. Prasad.[59] The committee was to draw up courses of study in biology and organic chemistry for premedical studies, and suggest measures to introduce biology as a part of the I.Sc. course.[60] However, nothing was done to start the teaching of biology till 1941. A new building, the Biology Block, was built to accommodate biology till 1941. A new building, the Biology Block, was built to accommodate biology classes and laboratories. In 1944-5 there were five biology teachers and teaching of biology up to the I.Sc. level began.[61] In 1946, biology was split into two subjects, zoology and botany. Zoology courses up to the B.Sc. Pass and Honours standard were started in 1945 and 1948 respectively.[62] this provided the basis for starting postgraduate classes in botany and zoology in 1948.[63] before biology teaching was shifted to the Science College, it was taught at the P.W. Medical College to students for the first six months after their admission to the college.[64] S.S. Choudhury was the professor of biology in Science College.[65] When the zoology department started teaching at the postgraduate level, it had only three teachers.[66]

TEACHING OF GEOLOGY

In 1946, an important event took place. The House of the Tatas established a Tata professorship in geology in Patna University through a magnificent grant. The Vice-Chancellor of Patna University, Dr Sachchidananda Sinha,[67] had pleaded for this during the university's silver jubilee celebrations two years earlier. In the beginning, the department was housed in the ante-rooms of the Wheeler Senate Hall. It shifted to the Science College campus after Patna University became a teaching-cum-residential university in 1952.[68] Dr. L.A.N. Iyer,[69] an eminent geologist working with the Geological Survey of India, became the first professor of geology and the first head of the postgraduate department of geology. He was assisted by two lecturers, A.P. Jain and Stephanski,[70] a Pole (belonged to Poland). Earlier, St. Xavier's College at Ranchi had introduced geology as a subject for I.Sc. students in 1944.[71] The undergraduate teaching of geology began in Science College in 1949 under the stewardship of Raghuji Varma,[72] who was among the first batch of six students to be admitted to the newly established department, these six students were chosen by a committee headed by the Vice-Chancellor.

ACHIEVEMENTS

The above account shows that Science College fully lived up to public expectations, both in terms of teaching and scientific research. Its several alumni served as science teachers wherever science teaching was introduced. The college also provided the largest number of qualified candidates for various professional and technical instructions' established in the state, aimed at producing qualified engineers, doctors and then supporting them. They accelerated the processes of industrialization and modernization, and helped to carry a modern system of medical care to an increasingly greater part of the population. Bihar's industrial growth or health-care system was no longer dependent on qualified technical hands educated in other parts of the country.

CONTRIBUTIONS TO SCIENTIFIC RESEARCH

Soon after the establishment of the college, the faculty realized that their responsibilities did not end with teaching students. They should actively pursue research and explore the frontiers of knowledge in their disciplines. Simultaneously, they deemed it their duty to popularize the study of science and inculcate a scientific spirit in society, so that it could lift itself out of the morass of social superstitions and modernize. The teachers went about their chosen task with zeal. One of the ways they took to increase public interest in science and its application in everyday life was organizing lectures on different aspects of the three disciplines—physics, chemistry and mathematics. Later, when the department of biology was created in 1941, lectures in both botany and zoology were also organized. Credit must be given to Principal Caldwell for making the college a renowned institution within such a short period. He set high standards for both teaching and research in the college. Under his guidance, the college soon became the standard bearer of quality teaching and research in science. The reputation of the college as a fine institution of teaching and research soon spread within a academic circles in India and abroad.

Caldwell's contribution was recognized at all levels. When he was leaving the college after retirement, all the university bodies showered praise on him. At the Patna University Convocation on 30 November 1935, the Vice-Chancellor said in his speech, 'At the Annual Convocation I paid tribute to the services of Dr. Caldwell. In him the university lost an eminent and capable, administrator.'[73] The Chancellor's address, which followed the Vice-Chancellor's speech, echoed the same sentiments. He said, 'We have lost Caldwell who I believe, had put in the whole of his service in Patna and was largely responsible for planning our modern Science College and bringing it to its present state of efficiency. . .'.[74] Fellow teachers, in appreciation of Caldwell's services to scientific researches, dedicated the January 1935 issue of the *Bulletin of the Patna Science College Philosophical Society* to him. The cover page earned the inscription, 'Dr. Caldwell

Commemoration Number'. The First page of the journal had a photograph of Caldwell with the caption: 'Dedicated to Dr. K.S. Caldwell, President 1930 to 1935'.

I.Sc. Results

The results of the I.Sc. showed that the students of Science College formed the majority of those passing in the first division. In 1933, out of 12 students who secured a first division, seven belonged to Science College.[75] In 1934, six out of the 14 students who passed the I.Sc. in the first division were from the Science College.[76] In 1938, out of 12 students securing a first division, 8 were from the Science College.[77] Science College students often occupied the first rank among the successful candidates. In 1934, Ajit Kumar Ghose was ranked first in the first class,[78] and subsequently joined the Indian Police Service. The holder of the second rank, Bishnupada Mukhopadhyaya,[79] became an internationally famous orthopaedic surgeon. In 1936, Sudarshan Prasad Sinha[80] of the Science College stood first in the first divisions.[81] He subsequently rose to be the Vice-Chancellor of his *alma mater*. In 1938 Jagdish Narayan Kohli[82] repeated this feat.[83]

B.Sc. Results

Students from Science College excelled in the B.Sc. (Honours) examination. In 1934, out of five students who secured an Honours in physics, three belonged to Science College. In the same year, all the five students who passed the B.Sc. with Honours in Chemistry belonged to the Science College.[84] B.Sc. (Honours), Sailaja Prasad Ghose[85] of Science College stood first in the second class.[86]

Recruitment of Teachers

The excellent performance of students in various examinations ought to be attributed to good teaching. Teachers with excellent academic records and a proven aptitude for research were recruited. The government cast its net wide in search of capable teachers. The selection of Dr. G.P. Dubey[87] is an example. He had acquired his Master degree from Allahabad, and was working with Prof. Meghnad Saha[88] when the Bihar Public Service Commission advertised for the post of a professor in physics, Prof. Dubey applied and was selected.[89] A look at the teaching staff during the 1933-4 session would show that the teachers were highly qualified. Candidates with postgraduate qualifications began their careers as demonstrators in their respective disciplines. Some of them, such as Prafulla Chandra Sinha,[90] demonstrator in chemistry, and Mahendra Narayan Verma,[91] demonstrator in physics, later became professors and heads of their departments.

The largest number of teachers came from the Bengali community, both from those domiciled in Bihar as well as immigrants from Bengal. A breakdown of the composition of the science faculty has been given. This situation arose because very few Bihar students took admission in the M.Sc classes. In 1936, M.Sc, examinations were held in the three subjects of physics, chemistry and mathematics. Out of the six candidates who appeared for the M.Sc. examination in mathematics, only one passed. In physics, there were five candidates, of whom three were successful. In chemistry, ten out of the eleven students who had appeared for the examination passed.[92]

According to one calculation, Patna University candidates passing the B.Sc. examination numbered 1,212 between 1917 and 1942. During that same period, 188 candidates got M.Sc. degrees.[93] It should be remembered that the jurisdiction of Patna University extended over Bihar, Orissa and Nepal. The reason why so few Bihari students studied in M.Sc. classes was the absence of B.Sc. courses in the colleges. However, Bihari students registered their presence in each subject. It was only a matter of time before they became the largest group amongst the teaching staff.

PATNA SCIENCE COLLEGE
PHILOSOPHICAL SOCIETY

The teachers formed the Patna Science College Philosophical Society on 1 August 1930 with the principal as the ex-officio president. The other office bearers were the treasurer, vice-president and secretary. Rai Sahib K.N. Banerjee[94] was selected as editor. An executive committee was established, which included all the office bearers along with six members. The committee was empowered to decide the topics on which popular lectures were to be organized. Membership of the society was open to all in the province interested in the study of science and scientific researches. The election of an editor showed that members were keen to communicate their researches to a wider audience. Hence, almost simultaneously, it was decided to bring out an annual publication known as *Bulletin of the Patna Science College Philosophical Society* to publish their research work. Some enlightened citizens of Patna welcomed this initiative. They extended their patronage by becoming life members of the society. Mention may be made of Dr. S. Sultan Ahmed, a former Vice-Chancellor of Patna University and a leading lawyer of India, Rai Bahadur R.K. Jalan, a philanthropist, and Justice Manohar Lal, Bar-at-Law.[95] People were conscious of the importance of scientific researches and the need for a wider circulation of their results.

The expenses of the society were met through grants from the government, the Patna University, and an income from the Trust created from a donation of Rs. 1,225 and 9 paise received from the Local Secretaries of the Indian Science Congress held at Patna in January 1933.[96] During the session of 1938-9, the DPI Bihar sanctioned Rs. 230 and the Syndicate of Patna University gave Rs. 200 to the society.[97] The society decided that it would do its very best to infuse the masses with an appreciation of the utility of the results of scientific researches. For this purpose, it decided to organize popular lectures.

Lectures Organized by the Society

In 1938-9, the department of mathematics was asked to select topics for popular lectures. N.N. Chatterjee[98] and V. Rangachariar[99] spoke on topics titled 'Our nearest neighbours in the heaven' and 'On Cornets', respectively,[100] and during the 1939-40 session, on 'Low Temperature Coal Carbonisation'. The former lecture was illustrated by lantern slides.[101] Radio was becoming popular, and the people were interested in knowing more about the technical marvel. The society organized a lecture on it so that people would know that it was a work of science, and not a miracle. Another lecture was on 'Vegetable Oil', which was then gaining popularity as a substitute for ghee or clarified butter made from cow's or buffalo's milk, and used for cooking Indian meals. These lectures helped to serve another purpose as well. By bringing together specialists in different subjects, they also hoped to encourage multidisciplinary and joint together specialists in different subjects, they also hoped to encourage multidisciplinary and joint researches. For that purpose, they decided to organize a symposia and colloquia.

Paucity of funds was a handicap; the society was always forced to look to the university and government for funding its activates. During the next session, the Syndicate of Patna University sanctioned Rs. 200. The grant of the DPI was a meagre Rs. 30. However, being a publication of a government-run institution, the report termed it 'a generous grant'.[102] There were times when the government failed to offer any money; however, the Syndicate consistently sanctioned money for the purpose, which ranged from Rs. 200 to 350.

Research Publications

The real service rendered to the academia was the society's decision to publish an annual journal, the *Bulletin of the Patna Science College Philosophical Society* (hereafter, *Bulletin*) to publish the research papers of its members. The Patna gentry sensed that the publication would involve financial transactions, and therefore donated money. Raja Raghunandan Prasad Singh donated Rs. 300 for the publication of the first issue, which came out in January 1931.[103] This issue contained 10 papers; the faculty members of Science College contributed nine. Some of these were reprints of papers published earlier in journals like *Nature, Proceedings of the Royal Society, Philosophical Magazine, Transactions of the Faraday Society, Journal of the Indian Chemical Society, Proceedings of the London Mathematical Society*, etc. These papers covered three disciplines—physics, chemistry and mathematics. It is interesting to note that one of the contributors was P.K. Kichlu,[104] who was already a D.Sc. and worked as a demonstrator in the physics department. It is clear that the teachers of Science College were actively pursuing research, and were communicating their results through internationally acclaimed journals.

The activities of the society aimed at keeping teachers informed of the latest developments in their disciplines, and inspired them to explore the new branches emerging in their subject. To inculcate a spirit of research among new appointees, the society invited them to speak on any subject under its auspices.[105] Research scholars were asked to present research results before the members of the society. A teacher who joined Science College in 1948 and served the institution for four decades remarked. 'The Philosophical Society of the College was unique of all societies'.[106] Another research scholar presented a paper titled 'Franck-Condou Principle and its Application' on 6 December 1943. Yet another read his paper, 'The Optical Properties of Metals', on 22 December 1943. Sudarshan Prasad Sinha, a demonstrator in the physics department, spoke on 'The Absorption Spectra of Sodium and Potassium Vapours' on 11 and 12 April 1944. He went on to become the Vice-Chancellor of Patna University later. On all these occasions, senior teachers of physics discussed the paper threadbare and suggested modifications and improvements. Another researcher read his paper 'Hydrides of Metals with special reference to Iron, Cobalt, and Nickel' on 23 February 1944. Members of the chemistry and physics departments were present and participated in the discussions. Physicist Professor Kamta Prosad[107] reported that the subject was of interest to students of both physics and chemistry.[108]

The *Bulletin* of January 1945 was dedicated to Principal Kamta Prosad. The Preface carries the statement, 'The present volume is being dedicated to Mr. Kamta Prosad, B.A. (Cantab); O.B.E.; I.E.S. in appreciation of the valuable services rendered by him to the Society since its very start.'

A symposium on 'Surface Phenomena' was organized from 1 to 3 November 1944. Seven papers were read by physicists, chemists, botanists and zoologists.[109] It was a convention that newly appointed teachers, were invited to speak before the society on any subject of their choice. The society concentrated on promoting serious scientific researches. Here, the strategy was clear—to enthuse both the young and the seniors.

Teachers of Science College dominated the Boards of Studies in different science subjects because of their knowledge of and familiarity with the latest advances in their discipline. This is evident from the list of the Boards of Studies constituted in different science-subjects in the 1930s. They were also nominated to the Board of Governors of prestigious research institutes, such as the Indian Institute of Science, Bangalore, and Indian School of Mines, Dhanbad. The senate elected Dr. K.S. Caldwell in November 1933 as its representative on the Court of the Indian Institute of Science.[110] After his retirement, his successor at Science College was given the same honour.

The college's fame as a centre for advanced research had spread far and wide. Researchers abroad sought the advice of teachers of the college. In one instance, the British (Government asked 'whether the Patna University would accept the offer of the Department of Scientific and Industrial Research for the supply of apparatus for receiving measurements of national illumination at various times of the day on the payment of the initial cost (about 20 pounds sterling). The University Syndicate asked the Principal of the Science College 'to consider the offer', and 'inform the Educational commissioner' of the action taken.[111] The university also showed a keen interest in promoting and facilitating research in science subjects by giving financial incentives to teachers. In March 1930, the Senate set apart a sum of Rs. 10,400 for providing research scholarships to students in the university. From the interest of this sum and amount of Rs. 75 per month was to be given to a student of Science College for carrying on research under the guidance of a 'Senior Professor'. The intention was to promote research in science subjects. In 1931 Swami Sharan[112] of Science College received a scholarship of Rs. 75 per month for working as a research scholar.[113]

The Patna University Syndicate, in its meeting of 16 January 1936, appointed Sudhangsu Kumar Chakravarti[114] to conduct research in physical chemistry under P.B. Ganguly. He was asked to submit a report in July so that his scholarship could be extended.[115] Amritansu Sekhar Chakravarti[116] got a Ph.D. degree in 1941. The subject of his thesis was 'Studies in the Viscosity of Solutions of Strong Electrolytes'. Bishwanath Prasad Gyani[117] was awarded a Ph.D. degree in chemistry for writing a thesis on 'Physical Chemistry—Studies in Absorption Relation to Constituencies' in 1944.[118] World War II had shown that the Allied Powers had won because of their superior industrial-power and firm base in scientific researches. This contributed to a deepening of interest in the development of science education. The government introduced newer disciplines, as stated earlier. They felt that teachers needed to upgrade their qualifications in order to guide the students properly. They should be sent abroad to get acquainted with the latest researches. The government encouraged teachers to go abroad for higher studies by granting them study leave. In 1946, several teachers from Science College proceeded to go abroad, and returned after obtaining Ph.D. degrees.

THE 20TH ANNUAL SESSION OF THE INDIAN SCIENCE CONGRESS

This session was being held at a time when there was a controversy raging between the acolytes of Sir C.V. Raman and the scientists of Bengal. The latter had publicly accused the former of 'Dravidisation' of the scientific academic life. A teacher of physics of the Science College, D.K. Bhattacharya,[119] wrote in Raman's defence in the *Amrita Bazar Patrika*, a leading English daily of Calcutta.[120] Patna University was asked to host the 20th Annual Session of the Indian Science Congress in 1933. A reception committee was formed with his Excellency the Governor of Bihar[121] as patron, and the Maharajadhiraj of Darbhanga[122] and the Chief Justice of Patna High Court[123] as vice patrons. Sir S. Sultan Ahmad, who had been instrumental in the establishment of Science College during his tenure as Vice-Chancellor of Patna University, was the Chairman of the Reception Committee. Principal K.S. Caldwell and Professor Kamta Prosad of the physics department were made Local Secretaries. The office of the reception committee was set up on the campus of the Science College.

An information bureau was set up in a room adjoining the office of the committee. The reception room was situated on the first floor of the students gymnasium; members were asked to collect stationery and writing materials from there. It was planned to hold the meetings of the sectional committees in the buildings of the Science College and Prince of Wales Medical College. The sections of medical and veterinary research, zoology and psychology were to meet in the buildings of P.W. Medical College. The team went about *its work meticulously. A report in the Amrita Bazar Patrika* of 30 December 1932 stated that 'preparations for the ensuing Science Congress have been completed'. It mentioned that the local secretaries were 'arranging for an exhibition of scientific instruments' for the public.

The Congress session opened on 1 January 1933. It was inaugurated by Sir Courtenay Teller, the Chief Justice of Patna High Court. Dr Fermor[124] was the elected president of the session. Sir Courtenay Teller was an appropriate choice. He was keen to take science education to the common masses. While addressing the convocation of Patna University some-time back, he had suggested, '. . . you would be well advised to spend your money on efficient scientific polytechnics more especially elementary education in agriculture, agricultural management and accountancy'.[125] In his inaugural address, Sir

Courtenay said, 'The abstract of papers for your consideration is of imposing size and serves to illustrate the vast expanding universe of knowledge. You who live over the periphery of a mighty development where the field for any single man is rapidly diminishing, fraction of the outer area must feel the ever increasing difficulty of integrating that area for human comprehension.' He added,

We rejoice that you have chosen Patna for your deliberations. We cannot offer you the amenities which you have found in big cities; but we claim to be more representative of the real India and we furnish a wider field for scientific research than any other province. From Nepal to the seas, from Santhal Parganas to Palamau, from Champaran to Balasore, from Purnea to Kalahandi, you will find more variety in social conditions, language, races, geological and biological features that can be presented in any other province in India. We are a great agricultural people and yet we possess the greatest mineral resources—sugar and lac are ours and thriving fisheries. With all these we suffer maladies of a peculiar intensity and variety. In fact anthropology, engineering, geology, chemistry, both inorganic and organic, botany, zoology and medicine offer an enormous field for investigation.[126]

THE ISSUE OF 'INCREASING POPULATION'

A part of the presidential address of the medical and veterinary section was dedicated to the problem of 'Population and Birth Control' Lt. Col. Stewart spoke of the primary effort of the scientist, which was directed towards 'the enlargement of life and the increase of human capacity, physical and mental, which we seek to ensure.' To buttress his point, he put the question. 'What evidence is there that numbers alone are the cause of economic distress?' He stated, 'We might bear in mind the example of England, where human life has been rendered extremely tolerable to a population of 40 million in an island where a century ago 14 million had found it hard to earn a livelihood.' He deprecated birth-control measures. He said,

Those who strongly advocate the wide adoption or such measures are probably activated by a sense of apprehension of personal or class calamity, calamity owing to increasing numbers of the so-called lower classes or races and by a desire for personal, class or race security. This apprehension is psychological phenomena, much commoner in the educated middle aged adult than in youth or in the more elementary human masses.

It is worth noting that three-quarters of a century ago, Patna had provided a forum to debate the issue of birth control.

In the psychology section, Lt. Col. O.N. Burkley[127] of Ranchi gave an interesting account of his own experiences in learning 10 different foreign languages. In the same section, Prof. Rangin Haldar[128] of B.N. College, Patna, presented a paper on the psychological aspects of Hindu aesthetics. Researchers in Patna University contributed research papers and also actively participated in discussions that followed the presentation of the papers. Several steps were taken during the sessions to promote public interest in science. The physical and chemical laboratories of the Science College remained open for visitors from 10 a.m. to 5 p.m. during the Congress. The visitors could also consult doctors at the P.W. Medical College during these hours. During the Congress session (3-5 January), exhibits from various farms, instrument makers and chemical manufacturers were open to the public. Popular lectures were also organized in the I.Sc. Lecture Theatre at 6:30 in the evening. Prof. A.T. Mukharji of Science College delivered a lecture on 'Electrical Measurement' in the Physics Lecture Theatre. On the evening of 4 January, Dr. W.D. West[129] spoke on 'Movements of the Continents which have Produced Present Features of the Earth's Surface'.[130]

The local committee organized excursions to the Agricultural Research Institute, Pusa, and the ancient University of Nalanda. Pusa visitors proceeded by the midnight steamer and returned at midnight. The trip to Nalanda was a one-day affair. The delegates were entertained at a garden party thrown by Rai Bahadur Radha Krishna Jalan[131] at the Qila House in Patna city. Several High Court judges, high government officials, and almost the entire elite of the two were present. The guests were deeply impressed by the antiquities collected by the Rai Bahadur. Sir Sultan Ahmad, Chairman of the reception committee, also invited all the delegates to a party. From all accounts the

Congress seemed to have been well-organized. It certainly gave a boost to science education in the province by motivating intelligent Bihari students to go in for studies and researches in science and technology. The reception committee managed to save some money, which was donated to the Philosophical Society, Science College. The society deposited the sum, and out of its interest met the expenses incurred in connection with the publication of the journal and the organization of scientific programmes.

ANNUAL SESSION OF THE INDIAN SCIENCE CONGRESS OF 1948

In January 1948, within a decade and a half, the Patna Science College had the privilege of hosting the Annual Session of the Indian Science Congress again, it was a memorable event. This was the first session of the Congress after India had attained Independence. It was being held at a time when the new government had firmly committed itself to the cause of promoting science and technology. Prime Minister Jawaharlal Nehru[132] chose the two distinguished scientists Homi Bhabha[133] and Shanti Swarup Bhatnagar[134] as his chief scientific advisors. The Prime Minister was to inaugurate the session, but had to cancel his visit at the last moment. The President-elect Sir Ramnath Chopra,[135] who was head of the School of Tropical Medicine, Calcutta, also could not come. Among the distinguished scientists present on the occasion were Sir C.V. Raman, Meghnad Saha and P.S. Gill.

The first Governor of Bihar in Independent India, Jairamdas Daulatram,[136] inaugurated the Congress. Since the President-elect was absent, Sir C.V. Raman presided over the deliberations.[137]

The Question of Atomic Weapons

Meghnad Saha gave a popular lecture in the evening of 2 January on the uses of atomic energy. Dr. Saha pleaded for researches in the field of atomic weapons and advocated the manufacture of the atomic bomb. C.V. Raman expressed the view that the huge expenditure on atomic researches was a waste; he was opposed to the manufacture of an atom bomb. P.S. Gill favoured a middle course. He sought a ban on experiments leading to the manufacture of atom bombs, but wanted research in atomic energy to continue. Raman remained firm in his opposition to the manufacture of atomic weapons. He gave a public lecture on 'Infra-red Spectrum' at the Wheeler Senate Hall. This was because he had already become so popular that no lecture hall in the college could accommodate the public that was expected to come to listen to him.

For scientists in Bihar, the session was made memorable because two members were elected fellows; Dr S.C. Chatterjee[138] was given this recognition for his work on Basic and Ultra-basic Rocks in Bihar, and Dr K.R. Krishnaswami Iyer,[139] Director of Industries, Bihar, was honoured for his work in industrial chemistry. This was the last time that Bihar hosted an annual session of the Indian Science Congress. However, the successful organization of the Indian Science Congress had sent a strong message to the people of Bihar early on. Even the political parties sought to play a part in the promotion of studies in science. Mahamaya Prasad Sinha,[140] then president of the Bihar Congress Committee and a future Chief Minister of the state, announced the formation of the Patna Institute of Science 'with a view to assimilate scientific knowledge and spreading of education in science . . .'.[141] However, the institute never functioned. But science education in Bihar was poised for a spectacular leap in the 1950s, which coincided with a development that considerably lessened the role of the Science College.

Honouring Eminent Scientists of India

Science College had, within a short span of two decades, instilled a consciousness regarding the dissemination of scientific studies in Bihar. Patna University never lost sight of its mission to widen and deepen this sentiment. A major step was taken during the silver jubilee celebrations in 1944. On this occasion, it conferred upon eight eminent scientists and technologists of India the degree of D.Sc. (*Honoris Causa*). They were Sir M. Visvesvaraya, Sir Chandrasekhara Venkata Raman, Sir Zia-Uddin Ahmad, Sir A. Lakhmanswami Muddaliar, Mr. P.K. Parija, Dr. Birbal Sahni, Dr. Homi Jehangir Bhabha and Sir Shanti Swarup Bhatnagar.[142] On 2 January 1952, Patna University was made a teaching-cum-residential university vide the Patna University Act, 1951.[143] Its jurisdiction was confined to the municipal limits of Patna. The conduct of the matriculation examination was no longer its responsibility. Postgraduate departments in all disciplines were converted into autonomous departments and placed directly under the control of the university. As a result, M.Sc. classes were withdrawn from the Science College. Science College, after almost quarter of a century, became an undergraduate college. Its reputation as a first-rate institution survived, and it continued to attract the best students from all over Bihar.

CONCLUSION

The Patna Science College fulfilled its mission. It gave a push to science education in Bihar. Several institutions sprang up to teach up to the B.Sc. (Honour.) level. Many of the Science College alumni became teachers in these institutions, and thus helped in the spread of science teaching and the promotion of a scientific temperament in the society. It provided scientific personnel in Bihar, and prepared students for technical education in different branches of engineering. The alumni entered into the medical profession and rendered treatment in accordance with latest scientific researches. They improved the quality of life. Some alumni became top administrators. In pre-independence India, C.S. Jha and T.P. Singh (Junior) were selected for the Indian Civil Service (ICS). During this period, seven alumni joined the Indian Police Service. Many of its alumni have served the State of Bihar as chief secretaries.[144] The achievements of the Science College alumni have been well summed up in the following words:

Of the eleven First Class Firsts in physics, between 1922 and 1942, seven are . . . College teachers, one is in ICS, one in the Provincial Executive Service, and the first gentlemen to secure a first class first in the subject died before the publication of the university results. Between 1922 and 1942 of the eight first class first in chemistry, three became college teachers, three were Deputy Magistrates, and one was a Research Scholar.[145]

NOTES

1. Jagdish Narayan Sarkar and Jagdish Chandra Jha, *A History of the Patna College*, Chs. II, III, IV.
2. Ibid., pp. 45-7. I.Sc. classes were introduced in other colleges in Bihar in the 1890s.
3. A.L.V. Ewbank: Taught mathermatics and chemistry and was principal, Patna College, 1880-7.
4. Hutchinson: Taught zoology at Patna College in the 1870s.
5. Simpson: Taught chemistry at Patna College in the last decades of the nineteenth century.
6. J. Wilson: Taught chemistry and botany at Patna College.
7. Prasanna Kumar Roy, D.Sc.: Was the first Indian teacher of science subjects at Patna College from 1870 onwards.
8. Nanda Krishna Basu: Taught mathematics at Patna College from 1870 onwards.
9. Abinash Chandra: Served as lecturer in science at Patna College in the last decades of the nineteenth century.
10. George Watt: Taught chemistry and botany at Patna College in the late-nineteenth century.
11. Narendra Nath Basu: Taught mathematics, chemistry and logic at Patna College at the beginning of the twentieth century.
12. *Science College Old Boys' Association Souvenir* (hereafter, *Association Souvenir*), pp. 6, 7.
13. *Patna University Silver Jubilee Souvenir Volume* (hereafter, *Silver Jubilee*), p. 40.
14. *Patna University Golden Jubilee Souvenir Volume* (hereafter, *Golden Jubilee*), p. 12.
15. K.S. Caldwell: Was professor of chemistry at Patna College. He was transferred to Science College after it was established in 1927. He was the Principal of Science College from July 1927 to February 1935.
16. *Golden Jubilee*, p. 12.
17. Sir Prafulla Chandra Ray (1861-1944): Indian chemist, educator and entrepreneur.

18. *Patna University Calendar*, 1933-4, p. 22.

19. Chandrasekhara Venkata Raman (1888-1970): Conducted research on light scattering (Raman Effect), for which be received the Nobel Prize in 1930.

20. Ashutosh Chatterjee. Was appointed by Patna University soon after its establishment in 1917 as a teacher of mathematics.

21. Ashutosh Mookerjee. Was appointed to teach physics by Patna University when it decided to strengthen the teaching of science soon after it was set up.

22. *Golden Jubilee*, p. 12

23. Ibid., p. 13

24. Ibid., p. 25.

25. *Silver Jubilee*, p. 55. Nine students appeared and four passed. *Golden Jubilee*, p. 13.

26. Mohandas Karamchand Gandhi (1869-1948): Indian political leader and freedom fighter.

27. *Patna University Calender*, 1925-6, pp. 20, 58.

28. Sukh Raj Rai. An endowment was made in the early 1920s in his name for an annual lecture on science subjects.

29. *Calendar*, 1925-6, p. 59.

30. V.H. Jackson: Taught physics at Patna College at the turn of the twentieth century. He served as principal, Patna College, twice (1914-19 and 1924-7), Principal, Science College (1927) and Vice-Chancellor, Patna University.

31. *Golden Jubilee*, p. 13.

32. Sir Mortimer Wheeler: Was twice the Governor of the province of Bihar and Orissa (1922-5 and 1925-7), and ex-officio the Chancellor of Patna University.

33. G.E. Fawcus: Was member of the Patna University Syndicate for seventeen years in the 1920s and 1930s.

34. Sir Sultan Ahmad (1880-1965): Was a legal luminary and the first Indian Vice-Chancellor of Patna University. During his term as Vice-Chancellor, Science College came into existence. He was the first Indian to be awarded the degree of Doctor of Laws (*Honoris Causa*) by the Patna University in 1931.

35. *Association Souvenir*, p. 7.

36. Ibid.

37. *Calender*, 1935-6, p. 85.

38. *Silver Jubilee*, p. 112.

39. *Golden Jubilee*, p. 44; Jagmohan, *Bihar and Orissa in 1929-30*, p. 48.

40. Lord Irvin (1881-1959): Was the Viceroy and Governor-General of India (1926-31).

41. Sir Hugh Lansdowne Stephenson: Was thrice the Governor of the province of Bihar and Orissa (1927-9, 1929-30 and 1930-2). He was ex-officio the Chancellor of Patna University.
42. Khan Bahadur Saiyid Muhammad Fakhruddin (1868-1933): In the 1920s, he was the Education Minister of the province of Bihar and Orissa.
43. Radhanandan Jha, *Origin and Development of Bihar Legislature*, pp. 65, 68.
44. *Association Souvenir*, p. 7.
45. Ibid.
46. Ibid., p. 9.
47. *Silver Jubilee*, p. 113.
48. *Patna University Calendar*, 1935-6.
49. Rai Bahadur Surendranath Mukherjee: Was a member of the Bihar and Orissa Judicial Service.
50. Ali Hasan: Was a leading lawyer in the 1920s and 1930s in Patna, and actively promoted modern scientific education.
51. *Silver Jubilee*, p. 47.
52. *Patna University Calendar*, 1933-4, pp. 140, 141.
53. D.N. Lal Originally taught mathematics. He retired in the 1980s as professor and head. Department of Statistics, Patna University.
54. N.C. Ghose (ed.), *Souvenir of the Department of Geology*, Patna University, 1946-96 (hereafter, *Souvenir*), p. 1.
55. A.T. Mukharji: Was Principal, Science College (1935-8).
56. P.K. Parija: Taught botany at Ravenshaw College, Cuttack, in the 1930s and 1940s.
57. A.S. Khan: Was Principal, Science College (1938-41).
58. S.S. Choudhury: Taught biology at the Prince of Wales Medical College, Patna, in the 1930s.
59. S.P. Prasad: Taught biology at the Prince of Wales Medical College, Patna, in the 1930s.
60. *Proceedings of the Syndicate*, 1936, p. 275.
61. *Silver Jubilee*, pp. 113-14.
62. *Association Souvenir*, p. 20.
63. *Golden Jubilee*, p. 25; *Association Souvenir*, p. 20.
64. *Silver Jubilee*, p. 10.
65. Ibid., p. 110.
66. *Association Souvenir*, p. 27.
67. Sachchidananda Sinha: Was Vice-Chancellor, Patna University, 1936-46.
68. *Association Souvenir*, p. 1.

69. L.A.N. Iyer: Was the founder-head of geology at the Patna University, 1946-50.
70. A.P. Jain: Served as a lecturer in geology when the department of geology was first established.
71. *Souvenir*, p. 42.
72. Raghuji Varma: Was Principal, Science College, 1975.
73. Patna University Proceedings of the Convocation and Minutes of the Senate, Syndicate and Faculties, p. 17.
74. Ibid., p. 26.
75. *Patna University Calendar*, 1933-4, p. 455.
76. Ibid., p. 416.
77. *Patna University Calendar*, 1939-42, pt. I, p. 261.
78. Ajit Kumar Ghose (1918-2004): Headed the Bihar Police in the rank of D.G-cum-IG Police, *Patna University Calendar*, 1934-5, p. 416.
79. Bishnupada Mukhopadhyaya: Became an eminent orthopaedic surgeon and served as Director, Health Service, Government of Bihar, in 1973.
80. Sudarshan Prasad Sinha: Served as Vice-Chancellor of Patna University in the 1980s.
81. *Patna University Calendar*, 1936-7, p. 470.
82. Jagdish Narayan Kohli: Joined the Indian Revenue Service in the 1940s.
83. *Calendar*, 1939-42, pt. I, p. 261.
84. *Patna University Calendar*, 1934-5, pp. 414-15.
85. Sailaja Prasad Ghose: Served as the head of chemistry, Patna University and also as Principal of Science College.
86. *Patna University Calendar*, 1936-7, p. 467.
87. G.P. Dubey (1914-73): Served as DPI, Government of Bihar, Principal, Science College, Patna, and head of physics, Patna University.
88. Meghnad Saha (1893-1956): Physicist and educationist.
89. From an interview with Professor V. Dubey of the department of geology, Patna University Professor. Dubey is the son of the late Prof. G.P. Dubey of Patna Science College.
90. Prafulla Chandra Sinha: Was a professor of chemistry in the 1950s.
91. Mahendra Narayan Verma: Stood first with a first class at the M.Sc. examination of Patna University in 1938. He served the Science College and retired as professor of physics.
92. *Patna University Calendar*, 1936-7, p. 623.
93. *Silver Jubilee*, p. 55.
94. Rai Sahib K.N. Banerjee. Taught physics in the 1930s and 1940s.
95. Justice Manohar Lal: Served as a judge at the Patna High Court in the 1950s.

96. *Annual Report of Philosophical Society*, Session 1938-9, pp. 5-6.

97. Ibid., p. 6.

98. N.N. Chatterjee: Taught mathematics at Science College in the 1930s and 1940s.

99. V. Rangachariar: Topped the list of successful candidares in the Master's examination of Patna University in mathematics in 1927, and served the Science College as professor of mathematics.

100. *Annual Report of Patna Science College Philosophical Society*, 1938-9, pp. 3-5.

101. *Annual Report*, 1939-40, p. 4.

102. *Annual Report of Philosophical Society*, p. 5.

103. *Bulletin of the Patna Science College Philosophical Society* (hereafter, *Bulletin*), I, Preface.

104. P.K. Kichlu: Taught physics in the 1930s and was the first president of Bazmal-Sakhan.

105. *Annual Souvenir*, p. 27.

106. Ibid.

107. Professor Kamta Prosad: Taught physics at Science College. He was the Principal of Science College at the time of his retirement in 1945.

108. *Bulletin*, 1945, pp. 106-16.

109. Ibid., pp. 116-20.

110. *Calendar*, 1933-4, p. 18.

111. *Patna University Minutes of the Syndicate*, 1935-6, p. 45.

112. Swami Sharan: Served the Bihar College of Engineering, Patna, in the 1950s.

113. *Patna University Calendar*, 1934-5, p. 105.

114. Sudhangsu Kumar Chakravarti worked as a research scholar in the Science College in the 1930s.

115. *Proceedings of Syndicate*, p. 275.

116. Amritansu Sekhar Chakravarti: He was the first research scholar in science in Science College to receive a Ph.D. degree from Patna University.

117. Bishwanath Prasad Gyani: Served as Director of Public Instruction in Bihar in the 1970s.

118. *Silver Jubilee*, pp. 50-1.

119. D.K. Bhattacharya: He taught physics in the 1930s.

120. *Amrita Bazar Patrika* (hereafter cited as *Patrika*), 23 December 1932.

121. His Excellency the Governor of Bihar in 1933.

122. Kameshwar Singh, Maharajadhiraj of Darbhanga: He was one of the richest zamindars in India. He donated large sums of money to educational institutions in India, including Patna University.

123. Sir Courtenay Teller: Was the Chief Justice of Patna High Court from 1928 to 1938.

124. Dr L.I. Fermor: He was the President of the 22nd Session of the Indian Science Congress as well as President of the inaugural session of the National Institute of Sciences of India, held at Calcutta on 7 January 1935.

125. *Patrika*, 1 December 1932.

126. Ibid., 3 January 1933.

127. O.N. Burkey: Was Director of the Institute of Mental Health at Ranchi.

128. Rangin Haldar: Taught psychology and Bengali literature at B.N. College (Patna University) from the 1920s to the 1950s.

129. W.D. West: Wrote the Report of the Geological Education Committee in 1946; the Committee was set up by the Government of India in 1945.

130. *Patrika*, 5 January 1933.

131. Rai Bahadur Radha Krishna Jalan (1882-1954): Was a leading trader of Patna and an enthusiastic collector of art objects and antiques.

132. Jawaharlal Nehru (1889-64): Was the first Prime Minister of Independent India (1947-64).

133. Homi Bhabha (1909-66): Indian nuclear physicist; he played a major role in the development of atomic energy in India.

134. Shanti Swarup Bhatnagar (1894-1955): Chemist and science administrator.

135. Colonel Sir Ramnath Chopra (1882-1973): Hailed as the 'Father of Indian Pharmacology', he was elected President of the 35th Session of the Indian Science Congress.

136. Jairamdas Daulatram: Was the first Governor of the province of Bihar in Independent India (1974-8).

137. *The Searchlight*, 3 January 1948.

138. S.C. Chatterjee: Headed the department of geography in Patna College in the early 1940s, and then the department of geology in the 1950s.

139. K.R. Krishnaswamy: Was the Director of Industries, Government of Bihar, in the late 1940s.

140. Mahamaya Prasad Sinha: Was Chief Minister of Bihar (1967-8).

141. *The Searchlight*, 23 January 1948.

142. *University of Patna Calendar*, 1952-5, p. 468.

143. Ibid., p. 73.

144. *Silver Jubilee*, p. 56.

145. Ibid.

CHAPTER 21

Munshi Binayak Prasad: A 'Native' History-writer

Tawarikh-i-Ujjainia of Munshi Binayak Prasad is the most comprehensive historical work, written in Urdu by a Bihari Hindu writer. It runs into four volumes and covers over 817 pages, written over a period of twenty-two years (1883-1905).

The work was sponsored by the ruling house of Dumraon who belonged to the Parmar clan of Rajputs. They are popularly known as Ujjainia, since their ancestors came from Ujjain (Madhya Pradesh) in the fourteenth century and settled down in the western part of Bihar, south of the Ganges adjoining the borders of Uttar Pradesh.[1]

So far our knowledge goes, this is the first case of sponsored history writing in Urdu in Bihar though we know that the Lt. Governor of Bengal encouraged Shad Azimabadi to write *Tawarikh-i-Suba Bihar* in 1870[2] to be presented to the Prince of Wales who was to visit Bihar during his tour of India. In case of *Tawarikh-i-Ujjainia*, an employee, Munshi Binayak Prasad was asked to write the history. The estate of Dumraon set up a full-fledged office named as History Office and appointed a supporting staff. We learn about this from a letter of the author dated 21 January 1891 published at the beginning of the second part of the book.[3]

In this letter addressed to Maharaja Radha Prasad Singh, the Chieftain of Dumraon, Munshi Binayak Prasad pleaded for granting rewards to staff members who had helped him in preparing the first two volumes of the *Tawarikh*. He first mentions Lala Thakur Prasad of Jagdishpur, himself a historian. He had narrated a number of facts told to him earlier by Babu Kunwar Singh. Munshi Binayak Prasad averred that the present work 'had immensely benefited' from this information. He recommended that a consolidated sum of Rs. 500 be granted to him. Next he pleaded the case of Lala Gopilal, the Head Clerk of the Record Office who had supplied to the author documents for writing the present history. He recommended that he be granted Rs. 7 per month as pension. After his death the amount be reduced to Rs. 5 per month to be paid as pension to his eldest son. Thereafter he requested consideration of his proposition regarding Lala Madhavlal, another employee in the History Office, who knew English, Persian and Hindi and was working at a paltry salary of Rs. 7 per month. Madhavlal regarded this as inadequate and was always looking for a better job. The author suggested that the wife of Lala Madhavlal be paid a life-long pension of Rs. 5 per month. The two peons Govind Panda and Kanun Rai should be given a reward of Rs. 100 and 75 respectively. He wanted that the sum to be given to Govind Panda might be deposited in the Charity Office and 25 *dam* be given daily to a poor person for twenty years. Govind Panda had joined the History Office at the age of seventy-five and had served it diligently for five years. It is not clear why Munshi Binayak Prasad was making this type of recommendation. Finally, he recommended Lala Bulaki Ram for a reward of Rs. 75. He had prepared a genealogical table of the House of Dumraon, now preserved in the Record Office in beautiful handwriting.[4]

I have given these details to stress the fact that the history-writing project was considered to be an important venture by the Dumraon estate. It placed all physical facilities at the disposal of the author for accomplishing this task. The Chief's desire was prompted by a new concern for reconstructing the past to discover one's heritage under the influence of modern education. It was also fuelled by family tradition. A century back *Udwant Prakash*, a history of Ujjainiyas had been prepared by Kavi Chandra Mauli in 1747 at the behest of Udwant Singh, the grandfather of Kunwar Singh.[5] I have not been able to get hold of a copy of *Udwant Prakash* and am in no position to say how much the present work owes to its predecessor.

STRUCTURE OF THE STUDY

The task entrusted to Binayak Prasad was not exactly the history of the estate of Dumraon. It was to be the history of the community of Parmar Rajputs (or Ujjainias as they were locally known) to which the house of Dumraon belonged. As such the period covered stretched from antiquity, i.e. from their origin to their arrival in this region and from thence to the present (the beginning of the twentieth century). The book also narrates the process whereby they succeeded in carrying out a principality and preserving it for around seven centuries. Over this vast period the scions of the royal house established a number of estates, all of which except the estate of Dumraon disappeared by 1850s. Munshi Binayak Prasad traced the fortunes of leading Ujjainia families, their emergence into prominence and then their decline. The description narrated intercommunity inter-action and their relationship with the local communities and the surrounding political powers. The work could not be an exclusive history of the estate of Dumraon: it had to be the history of the Ujjania clan from the fourteenth century on-wards when they arrived in the area from central India and transformed themselves into the ruling and dominant political elite by a series of wars. The story could not be begun abruptly.

It is preceded by an account of the origin of Parmars, their history up to the fourteenth century to show that they were a part of Indian society and creating an estate in a new territory was no usurpation; it was an assertion of a legitimate ancient right. The history of the clan, the estate and the region was intertwined; the account had to be a chronicle of all the three at one and the same time. This realization dictated the structure of *Tawarikh-i-Ujjainia*. The author was therefore faced with a challenging task: he had to present a complex narrative where several strands had to be interwoven.

Since this was a commissioned history, the author had to walk on a tight rope; he had to ensure that the Ujjainias, their political activities and their role in the region always remained in focus even during their interactions with other segments of local population. The author ensures that the account he presents remains firmly rooted in the soil of Shahabad. Content wise the *Tawarikh* is a history of Shahabad from the time the Ujjainias made it their home and the chief area of their activities.

As an author of a sponsored history, Binayak Prasad enjoyed certain privileges, normally not available to a scholar, who is writing on his own. He was given unhindered access to the records and documents preserved in the office of estate. The estate functionaries and other dignitaries were asked to extend all help, by showing to him their family papers or by narrating to him what they had heard about various events from their elders. The author of *Aina-i-Tirhut* published in 1883, another monumental work, did not have this privilege.[6]

ABOUT THE AUTHOR

Munshi Binayak Prasad does not seem to have been a trained historian. But then why was he selected? His one qualification was that he knew Persian and Urdu and therefore could read documents preserved in the estate archives and could consult the correspondence that passed between the estate, the imperial power and the agents of the imperial power stationed at Patna, the capital of the province of Bihar.

Secondly, he hailed from a family, which had served the estate for several generations as *mir munshi*,[7] a high administrative post. His father Munshi Ganga Prasad was in the retinue of Raja Janki Prasad Singh when he went on a pilgrimage to Jagannathpuri and was at his bed-side when he passed away during his return journey.[8] He remained an estate employee under the successor of the late Janki Prasad Singh. It was presumed that probably he would know many facts about the estate and its chiefs from his family-members.

Munshi Binayak Prasad tried to get over his handicap of not being a trained historian by going through well known Persian chronicles of the medieval times, written between the thirteenth and the eighteenth centuries, depicting the history of the Sultans and Mughal rulers of Delhi.[9] The study of medieval

Persian chronicles enabled him to glean data about the Ujjainias and also to trace the relationship evolving between the Ujjainia chiefs and the surrounding political powers and paramount rulers in Delhi. It also helped him to get a feel of what history was and how it was written.

The medieval Persian chronicles mostly dealt with the court, wars and political and military intrigues. The *Tawarikh-i-Ujjainia* gives a vivid picture of the diplomatic and military relationship between the Ujjainia chiefs and the provincial and the imperial powers. The later after seeing Ujjainias subjugating the hill tribes in armed conflicts and establishing domination over the surrounding plain's people concluded that it would be easier to carry on local administration with the active support of the Ujjainias and so arrived at a compromise with them.

The Ujjainias, aware of their capacity to harass the imperial power and its agents if their will was totally ignored, also knew that they could not defeat the imperial power with its vast military and financial resources in a prolonged armed confrontation. This constraint fashioned their political, military and economic policies: politically it was desirable to tolerate each other and never let the differences create an unbridgeable gulf. The Ujjainias would enjoy a share in the land revenue collected from Shahabad for the imperial treasury. In case they defaulted, the Mughal arms would chastise them but at no point the Mughals would try for their total ruination. In fact, during Mughal rule, from Akbar to Aurangzeb, the Ujjainia chiefs rose in rebellion during the reign of each Mughal ruler; the imperial army was sent to subdue them but eventually both made peace.

The author portrays armed skirmishes, the operating land revenue system in the area and against this background he etches the role of the Ujjainia chiefs at various points of time.

METHODOLOGY

The study of medieval Persian chronicles helped Munshi Binayak Prasad to familiarize himself with the tradition of Perso-Urdu historiography. He was aware that a new school of historiography had also appeared in the country. Europeans, mostly Englishmen, and following them Indians had been publishing works on different aspects of Indian history in English and other European and Indian languages.

Our author attempted to understand the salient features of the new historical writings; where possible he tried to collect data for his own work from their books. He refers to Todd's *Rajasthan*, W.W. Hunter's *History of India* and *Statistical Account of Bengal* in English. In Urdu he mentions works such as *Balbantnama*, *Tawarikh-i-Marhatta*, *Riaz-i-Tirhut* and *Tawarikh-i-Suba Bihar*, etc. In Hindi among the histories he consulted were *Chinargarh Itihas*, *Kasiraj Darpan*, *Bihar Darpan*, *Vashin Vamsa*, etc.[10]

But it must be said at the outset that these data appeared to him peripheral and supplementary. He missed the core of their methodology, i.e. to compare and contrast the evidence he had gathered from different sources and to critically discuss them before coming to a final conclusion about the veracity of the facts he was putting forth.

The Ujjainia chief Radha Prasad Singh, sponsor of the work was keen that this work should be modern, authentic and authoritative. He was familiar with *Udwant Prakash*, written by Kavi Chandra Mauli in the eighteenth century at the instance of the then Ujjainia chief Udwant Singh. We do not know for sure if Binayak Prasad knew of Bodhraj of Pugal[11] but was certainly aware of *Udwant Prakash* as he mentions that some of the Ujjainia chiefs loved to hear the recitation of *Udwant Prakash* and at least, one chief could recite it by memory. Probably this tradition of reciting and hearing recitals of *Udwant Prakash* was an added stimulus for the preparation of a new version of the history of the Ujjanias. The new history, the Raja felt, should not be the replica of the old one; it should incorporate the elements of new history writing without forsaking the Perso-Urdu tradition.

Raja Radha Prasad Singh of Dumraon, the sole surviving Ujjainia chief after the upheaval of 1857, he set about the task of preparing a new history of community methodically. He opened History Office, a new department, for the purpose and entrusted Munshi Binayak Prasad with the task.[12] He was provided with a staff, paid by the Estate. We may pause here a little and try to speculate about the credential the author had for undertaking this task. In the book we have no indication what formal training Binayak Prasad had for writing the history except that he seemed to have been well versed in Urdu and probably had a working knowledge of Persian. He might also be familiar with a smattering of Arabic and English as well because in the list of works consulted he refers to English language books. But probably the major consideration in selecting Munshi Binayak Prasad for writing the proposed history was that the family of the author was connected with the Dumaraon Raj for generations as *mir munshi*, a high administrative post. Before the work began several scholars were invited to Dumraon to suggest guidelines for Binayak Prasad.

Among the invitees was Bhartendu Harishchandra, the famous litterateur and the father of Hindi prose. Bhartendu had published a number of books on history in Hindi and was eminently suited for this task.[13] The author writes that Bhartendu suggested eighteen points and emphasized the use of oral history. To him it was the best source for establishing facts about local history. He also recommended visits to villages to collect local traditions. The opportunity could be used to put on record important buildings, such as temples, ponds and gardens and also to note the inscriptions on them. The name of the builder and other details about the structures should be collected.

The names of the villages should be noted to find out if it was coterminus with the name of its founder. If possible other details about the founder should also be collected. The names of the local rich and the famous were to be found out and the stories current in the villages about the past events should be recorded. Bhartendu also insisted that data about the local economy, local agricultural produce and crafts should be recorded. Details of local trade were to be incorporated. Bhartendu was keen that the work should not degenerate into a genealogy of the Ujjainia chiefs, their wars, victories and defeats. The work should reflect the life as it was and as lived today in the area.[14]

Bhartendu had no desire to minimize the importance of written sources. Apart from the documents the Raj could furnish, Bhartendu was sure that more papers would be available in the villages. His advice was that during field-visits they should be collected and used in history writing. Bhartendu was keen that the proposed history should be based on a wide range of sources, official and non-official, written and oral. Undoubtedly, Bhartendu's advice reflected the new trends that had emerged in history writing in India in the second half of the nineteenth century. He was an avid promoter of local history.

It seems that Bhartendu's suggestions found favour with the author, Munshi Binayak Prasad, who in the opening pages of the first volume gives a bibliography of the works he consulted in different languages, Hindi, Urdu, Persian and English. Of course, the author had no idea about the difference between the primary and secondary sources. Family documents were collected and local inquiries were made, however, the main strength of the book lies in the use of documents available in the Record Office of the Dumraon Raj. We must appreciate this fact as the Record Room of Jagdishpur, the erstwhile estate of Kunwar Singh had been destroyed during the upheaval of 1857. A little earlier the Buxar estate, another stronghold of the Ujjainias, had ceased to exist. The records of the Dumraon estate were the only available official records to him; he was able to secure documents of some of the Ujjainia families, scattered in different parts of Shahabad. It would be fair to say that the work is based primarily on documents he was able to lay his hands upon in the Dumraon Raj Record Office and some papers of different families. These documents belong to the period of the Mughals, the Nawab of Bengal, the English East India Company and British Crown. He did not consult British official records in the possession of Government of India.

The work of writing extended to well over two decades, between 1883 and 1905 when the fourth volume was completed. The first volume was finished on 1 October 1888, the second on 14 September 1891 and the third on 15 January 1899. The author says the work remained suspended between 1892 and 1898. He does not give the reason for suspension of the work. He says that Mr. Fawcus, after he took over as the Manager of the Dumraon Raj in 1897 ordered the completion of the work.[15] We learn of these dates as the author records them at the end of each volume.

CONTENT

The first volume begins with a brief account of the geography of India as it was understood by the Hindus in the ancient period, followed by the mention of provinces in which India was divided when the Muslims ruled over the country. He emphasizes the linguistic diversity by recounting the different languages spoken in various parts. He lists provinces under contemporary British rule.[16] But the most important fact is that he gives the geography of Bihar under the Muslim rule with which this history is primarily concerned. He has given the different revenue divisions of Shahabad so that later on, the reader has no difficulty in following the historical developments in the region because not all the readers are expected to be familiar with these minute details of the revenue geography of Shahabad. He also narrates the political and revenue divisions under the British rule.[17] This is methodologically an important contribution of the author.

We have a special description of the district of Shahabad, its geographical boundaries, its terrain, its rivers and rivulets and its administrative structure as well as a description of the areas attached to the Dumraon Raj. The author also mentions those areas, which were formerly in the possession of Ujjainia families of Jagdishpur and Buxar but had been taken over by the British government or had come in possession of different individuals. The exercise is in strict conformity with the practice, which was then followed under the influence of British inspiration that local histories must begin with a clear idea of the geography of the place, the focus of the historical narrative.[18]

At the outset he also draws our attention to the fact that the region came to be known as Shahabad under the Mughal ruler Shah Jahan;[19] earlier the river Ganga flowed nearby but over the centuries it had shifted towards the north and the land which had come out of water is popularly known as Tal Shahabad. The author has given a brief description of the township of Dumraon, its ecology (including the type of soil, temperature, etc.), the headquarters of the estate. Dumraon was formerly known as Horilnagar.[20]

The advantage of this exercise is that while reading the text one frequently comes across references to these names. The reader having read about these names at the beginning will feel familiar with them.

The author has also given the dates according to different calendars that were popular in the country in different times.[21]

In fact, the reader after going through the opening pages is well equipped to follow the text, where local names occur frequently and also different calendars are mentioned.

Munshi Binayak Prasad starts by tracing the history of Ujjania or Parmar Rajputs. He adds a brief account of the history of ancient India. For the present day reader all this is pedestrian. He connects the Ujjainias to King Vikram of Ujjain in central India after whom the Hindu calendar *Vikram Samvat* is named.[22] He does this on the basis of a genealogical table, prepared in 1847 in the time of Maheshwar Baksh Singh and preserved in the family. A Court of Law had accepted it as genuine. He includes a detailed genealogical table of the important Ujjainia families of Shahabad, which may be helpful to the present generation in tracing its roots. Of course the ancient history he puts forward is all confused and cannot stand the scrutiny of our present knowledge. However the effort indicates the desire of the author to connect the local with the regional as well as the national.

The first volume prepares the reader to appreciate what the author would say in the next three volumes which concentrate on the history of Ujjainias, the different estates they established from time to time and the course of events which saw the survival of only one estate, Dumraon in the post-1857 period.

The second and third volumes narrate the history: a Parmar prince, Sanatan or Santan Sahi came to Gaya to perform the funerary rites of his ancestors from central India in AD 1329. For Hindus Gaya is the holiest place for this purpose. Having performed the rites, he decided not to go back and captured a part of the region of Shahabad. The author has advanced an interesting reason for his decision to stay.[23]

In ancient times the Parmars had ruled over Magadh and Mithila (probably he got this idea from the history of Mithila depicted in either from *Riaz-i-Tirhut* or from *Aina-i-Tirhut*). He cites the former in the list of books he consulted but surprisingly ignores the latter though it was a history in the genuine sense. The Parmars had left the area in ancient times; it was then filled with forests; tribes such as Kol and Bhils dwelt there. Sanatan Sahi was only trying to reclaim the land of his forefathers and therefore, he began clearing the forest, driving away the tribes and occupying the land vacated by them. From the point of view of the author, Sanatan Sahi was no usurper. Of course, the author has got the names of the tribes wrong. The newcomers, the Parmars, were not immediately successful as the tribes put up a determined resistance. Nevertheless Sanatan Sahi carved out a principality and asked his followers who had come from central India to settle down and invited others to come and stay in his dominion.

A valuable piece of information brought before us is that the tribes considered themselves to be the masters of the land and were known as *Bhuians* or *Bhupal* or rulers of the land. Munshi Binayak Prasad now gets the correct name of the tribe residing in the area, i.e. Chero.[24] He admits that Sanatan Sahi continued to exterminate the tribesmen to establish his sway. He set outposts to prevent the Cheros from attacking and trying to regain the lost land. They still considered themselves as the real master of the land and the newcomers as usurpers: a protracted struggle ensued. The Ujjainia ruler realized the intensity of their feelings and did not lower his guard. He made Korwar, 14 *kos* (around 30 km) south of Rohtas the first capital of the Ujjainias.

This was the age when Delhi was ruled by Muhammad bin

Tughluq, who at least in theory, ruled over the whole of India. The author points out that the Delhi Sultan had imposed a heavy land tax which the people were unable to pay; they left the areas under imperial rule and began to settle down on the newly cleared land by Ujjainias. Sanatan Sahi welcomed them. The people were happy that they had found a new means of livelihood and were no longer exposed to the tyranny of the Delhi Sultans. They were determined to defend the newly acquired land. Sanatan Sahi had thus secured additional manpower in his fight against the Cheros.

For the next two centuries, the Ujjainia chiefs followed the policy of settling plains people on the newly cleared land. This brought them additional land revenue, made them economically prosperous and also placed at their disposal extra manpower to face the repeated risings of the tribes as the new settlers were mostly upper caste Hindus, Brahmins, Rajputs and Bhumihars. Of course Ujjainia Rajputs were given land on favourable terms to show community solidarity and ensure community support in the event of any conflict. The settlers were happy on being allotted land and became loyal to the Ujjainia ruler. They swelled Ujjainia contingents whenever the Ujjainia rulers went to war either to defend themselves against an external invader or to conquer land held by the tribes or had to supply armed retainers for the imperial army of Delhi.

Munshi Binayak Prasad refers to another reason for the success of the Ujjainia rulers. The Hindus of the plains shifted to newly cleared areas to escape the growing power of the Muslims in the plains and also to avoid Muslim domination. The Ujjainias provided a safe haven to these migrant Hindus and therefore, more and more Hindus came to live in the area controlled by the Ujjainias, which increased their manpower as well as contributed to their economic prosperity.

The author in an aside mentions the fact that Pradhan Darshan Rai, a Shrivastava Kayastha was an important collaborator of Sanatan Sahi; thereby he indicates that the Shrivastava Kayasthas were present at the foundation of the Ujjainia estate and constituted to be the chief pillar of the bureaucracy. They held the post of *diwan*. We do not know the truth. Probably the author was legitimizing the role of the Kayasthas in the bureaucracy of Ujjainia estate because they were the chief functionaries at the lower, middle and the higher rungs of the Ujjania official hierarchy.[25]

Having made these preliminary remarks, the author proceeds to present a long genealogical table in which we come across trees representing the various branches of the Ujjainias. He then briefly narrates the history of Ujjain and the Parmar Rajputs to which clan the Ujjainias belonged. It is interesting that while writing out the history of the Parmars of Ujjain from where the Ujjainias had emigrated, he quotes *Riaz-i-Tirhut* which says that the dynasty of Nanyadev, the ruler of Mithila was that of Parmar lineage and that the Parmars ruled over the land of Magadh and Mithila in ancient times. In fact, in his enthusiasm to establish the antiquity and the legitimacy of the Parmars, he gets both his chronology, and facts jumbled up. For example, in chapter three when he writes about the history of Parmar kings, he makes the astounding statement that on behalf of the then ruler, the famous Sanskrit poet and dramatist Kalidas wrote to Prophet Muhammad and along with other presents from India, he sent him betel leaves!

In his desire to present a complete history of the Parmars, he even writes about some of the Parmar rulers of the nineteenth century such as the ruler of Dewas in Malwa. This attitude on the part of the author at first sight makes the work look like a hagiography of the Parmar Rajputs and not their history.

THE HISTORICAL CONTENT

From then onwards the author narrates the history of the Ujjainia rulers who succeeded Sanatan Sahi after his death in AD 1360 in chronological order. Sanatan Sahi was followed by his son Hunkar Sahi on the throne. Before Hunkar Sahi could settle down he had to face a fierce attack by the tribesmen who decided to attack on hearing the news of the death of Sanatan Sahi. The subsequent chapters show that the estate had to fight regularly with the tribes for several centuries and therefore the idea that the tribes submitted without a fight to the intruders in their area is a myth. Of course, the tribes eventually had to submit to an army possessing superior arms but this was a long and tortuous process and the victors were forced to make concessions to those whom they had subdued. This is very clear when Sanatan Sahi died in AD 1360 and was succeeded by his eldest son Hunkar Sahi.

The author says on hearing the news of the death of the ruler, tribals who were hiding in the forest again rose in revolt. It appears to have been a powerful uprising as the new ruler was forced to send his brothers with armed forces to quell them. He personally took the field. Eventually the tribes were defeated; Cheros the dominant tribe of the area lost 10,000 men and the 'king' also lost a large number of soldiers. Some of the Cheros as the author says 'still inhabit the area but were steeped in poverty'. They (the Cheros), however, still claim that they were the original masters of the land. This remark shows that the author did make field enquiries and incorporated the results in his narrative.

The Ujjainias had successfully warded off the challenge. This shows the intensity of opposition the Cheros offered to their new rulers.

Here Munshi Binayak Prasad gives a detailed description of the life-style and the polity of Cheros, probably based on his personal observation. The description is extremely valuable for students of history of tribes as well as their interaction with people from the plains.

A significant piece of information is that the tribes did not pay taxes; they were secretive about their whereabouts; they did not reveal them to the outsiders. There were four centres of powers of the tribesmen; Bihia was one of their strongholds. It is clear that the fourteenth century Shahabad was covered by dense forests and dominated by tribes. From the fourteenth century onwards, tribesmen started retreating when the plainsmen cleared the forests to settle down and to engage in farming. We have a mix of history, of the tribes and of the environment.

Here the author introduces a myth, which serves as a justification for the conquest of Bihia forest from its ruler, Mahipal-
dev, a Kshatriya. The Ujjainias established contacts with intermediate caste Hindus, such as Chaulai Gowala and sought
accommodation with the Muslims (now rulers of the region)
in order to strengthen their position. Hunkar Sahi and Chaulai
Gowala saw Hazrat Sharafuddin Maneri performing a miracle
and announced their deep devotion to him. 'The news rapidly
spread. Devotees started paying obeisance to the Saint whose
popularity increased.' At this point the author says that the
Saint told Hunkar Sahi that he had become the ruler of Bihia
and should rule over the area. He also gave him a special jacket
to wear. In this way the author legitimizes the ousting of a co-
religionist by Hunkar Sahi and justifies his strategy to secure
Muslim support.

The success of Hunkar Sahi against Bihia also demoralized
the tribes who stopped offering resistance to him. To ensure
supervision over the newly occupied area, Hunkar Sahi made
Bihia his new capital and constructed several buildings. Thus
began regular contacts of Ujjainia chiefs with Muslim rulers.[26]

This account shows that Munshi Binayak Prasad did not
simply chronicle wars of Ujjainiya chiefs; he was perceptive
enough to write about the life-style of indigenous population,
the Cheros. He depicted the process of the ousting of the locals
and the settlement of the plainsmen in spaces vacated by the
Cheros.

With the passage of time the Ujjainias also tried to accommodate the interests of the Cheros as they found the ongoing
conflict with them ruinous.

It may be safely said that *Tawarikh-i-Ujjainia* is a valuable
source for the study of the dynamics of relationship between the
tribesmen and plainsmen.

Hunkar Sahi died in 1410. His eldest son Dev Sahi, a minor,
succeeded him. His uncle, Ishwar Sahi was appointed regent.
Dev Sahi is said to have fought with the Ahir ruler who was
defeated and ousted. He constructed a *Chabutra* or platform to

commemorate this victory. The step was aimed at placating the non-Ujjainias. This remained a major plank of Ujjainia policy— to give due respect and honour to the non-Ujjainias residing on the territory ruled by them.

According to the author Dev Sahi lost his mind and was replaced on throne by his younger brother Dullah Sahi who continued to fight with the tribes. Dullah Sahi adopted a new policy. When he defeated the Cheros, he appointed them to look after the security of the conquered area; they were given a part of the forest land cleared by the orders of the king. The Ujjainia chiefs consciously tried to expand the social base of their support by offering land, jobs and recognition and acceptance to non-Ujjainias. He transferred his capital to Dawan; the family of Pradhan Darshan Rai (a Kayastha) also became a resident of this place. This is another proof that from the very beginning the Ujjainias leaned on the Kayasthas (the traditional community supplying officials among the Hindus) for filling the various administrative posts.

Dullah Sahi died in 1484 at the age of eighty-five after a long reign. Ram Sahi, a younger son succeeded him because his eldest brother, Badal Sahi was blind.

It should be noted that though legally and socially the eldest son had the right to throne but this was generally not followed; whoever among the king's son was capable was anointed as the ruler. Probably this deviation from the accepted rule of primogeniture helped Ujjainias to deal successfully with political and military problems they had to face in course of their history.[27]

Ram Sahi like his predecessors faced opposition from the tribes but he continued to expand. He, however, changed his tactics with regard to safety from the warring tribes. They were asked to live in groups and were not to bear arms except when they went for hunting in the jungle. They were not to mingle with compatriots staying in other areas except for purposes of marriage. His idea was to insulate them from other tribes. Ram Sahi ensured that they had enough for meeting their day-to-day expenses. They were given jobs at the court and were provided with food and other necessities on the occasion of marriage or death from the royal-store.

Ram Sahi's policy was successful only to a limited extent. The tribes no longer in a position to offer armed resistance, took to brigandage and the law and order problem deteriorated. Ram Sahi established police outposts on the banks of the river Karmnasa and strengthened the old ones. The author admits that the measures were not very successful.[28]

The Muslim rulers allowed Ujjainias a freehand because they did not want to deal with the tribes living in the forests. War with the tribes would be costly and economic gains of victory would not justify the expenses. They let the Ujjainias suppress and drive out the tribes and clear the forest land and start settled agriculture and set up an administrative machinery. At this point the Muslims would intervene and demand a share in the land revenues the Ujjainias would collect.

While describing the ongoing conflict between the Ujjainias and the Cheros, the author also writes about the court etiquette among the Ujjainias and also their construction activities. He mentions buildings, both secular and religious built during the reign of each Ujjainia chief. This information is useful for reconstructing local history. For example, he says that the Chero leader Phoolchandra established the market at Jagdishpur. The latter became an important seat of Ujjainia chieftains.

The Ujjainia chiefs did not neglect agriculture. Two brothers Kanu Singh and Meenu Singh looked after it.[29] Ujjainias had realized that agricultural prosperity alone would fill estate coffers and attract more men to areas they controlled. Increased manpower would enable them to put more men on the battle-field in case of war, then always round the corner. Most of the Ujjainia chiefs paid great attention to the development of agriculture.

A sacred spot of the area for the Hindus, the temple of Brahmeshwar Sthan was established during this period. The *lingam* worshipped there was discovered during the cutting of the jungle. The author narrates a miracle associated with the temple. In the seventeenth century in the reign of the Mughal ruler Aurangzeb, orders were issued for an investigation into the affairs of the temple. It is said that when inquiries started, the temple door facing eastwards turned westwards. The Mughal emperor impressed by this issued a *firman* in favour of the temple. The author claims that he had seen the origin all *firman* of Aurangzeb given to the temple in possession of the priest.

In *Tawarikh-i-Ujjainia* political narrative is replete with valuable social, economic and cultural data. This is what makes it more than a political or dynastic history. The streak is present to the end.

The death of Ram Sahi took place in 1519. Gajpati Sahi alias Gajan Sahi succeeded him.[30] He was preferred in place of Dalpati Sahi, the son of Badal Sahi, the elder brother whom Ram Sahi had replaced. The rule of primogeniture never became a fetish with the Ujjainias.

BEGINNINGS OF MUGHAL-UJJAINIA RELATIONS

From now onwards the Ujjainia family comes in the mainstream of north Indian history. The Mughal rule was established in 1526; soon afterwards Mughal-Afghan contest for supremacy over eastern India began. An Afghan who enjoyed the jagir of Sasaram on the borders of Ujjainia-held territories was the principal adversary of the Mughals. The Ujjainias had no option but to participate in the struggle and try to safeguard their interest to the best of their abilities. From now onwards the history of the Ujjainias becomes inextricably linked up with the history of the Delhi rulers.

Gajpati Sahi established his capital at Jagdishpur where he built a fort. Gajan Sahi had to face opposition from Dalpati Sahi who felt frustrated at being deprived of the chieftainship. Many of the functionaries did not obey him. Simultaneously several of the tribes probably enthused by the internecine rivalries of the Ujjainias revolted. Gajan Sahi in order to get out of this position decided to join hands with Sher Shah, the *jagirdar* of

Sasaram, who had defied the Mughal rulers of Delhi and who was the major hurdle in the establishment of the Mughal rule in eastern India. He fought the Mughal ruler Humayun as an ally of Sher Shah on the banks of Karmanasa River in which Sher Shah routed the Mughal army and eventually drove out the Mughal from Delhi. For the services rendered to him Sher Shah conferred upon Gajan Sahi the title of kingship and also gave him the Sarkar of Rohtas and a *firman*.

Our author laments that the Ujjainias thus lost their independence but then he admits that this was the period when Islam was prospering in India and its fortunes were on the ascendant.

Dalpati Sahi now staked his claim to Ujjainia chieftainship. He found important support from the Mughal ruler Akbar who had not forgotten that Gajan Sahi had helped Sher Shah in defeating his father Humayun. According to the chronicler of Akbar's reign, the Mughal forces in 1575 attacked Gajan Sahi and sacked Jagdishpur and captured Gajan Sahi.[31] We do not know whether the statement is true or false. However, Dalpati Sahi took advantage of the problems faced by Gajan Sahi and attacked him in 1577. In the battle which was fought, Gajan Sahi lost his life and Dalpati Sahi became the chief of the Ujjainias. The new ruler Dalpati Sahi transferred his capital to Bihia.[32]

From now onwards the history of the Ujjainias for the next two centuries is closely linked with that of the Mughals. No other chief of Bihar had such an intense relationship with the Mughal rulers.

The reason is clear. Darbhanga, Bettiah and Hathwa, etc., the other major estates of Bihar were created by the Mughals. Only the estate of Ujjainias and Gidhaur existed prior to the establishment of the Mughal rule. They could therefore, to some extent behave like independent chieftains and challenge the Mughal rule. All the Ujjainia chiefs almost without exception, at some point or other defied the Mughal ruler or his agent in Bihar.

The relationship did not proceed in a straight line. The Ujjainias conceded supremacy to the Mughals; but at every possible opportunity challenged it. The love-hate relationship is to be seen in the reign of every Mughal ruler.

The close Mughal-Ujjainia relations are referred to in Mughal chronicles. The Ujjainia chiefs were recipients of many Mughal *firmans* and communications. A number of them were preserved in the record office of Dumraon, the last Ujjainia House to survive until the mid-twentieth century. Munshi Binayak Prasad has made full use of these Mughal documents in writing the present history. Sometimes he quotes the documents in full.

For example, in vol. II of the Urdu edition of *Tawarikh*, the author has quoted in original the letters, *nishans* and *sanads* issued by the Mughal princes to Ujjainia chiefs in 1657.[33] At another place Munshi Binayak Prasad cites a Mughal *sanad* of 1720 which permanently assigned the revenues of *parganas* of Bihia and Danwar to Horil Singh. Another document shows that in 1771 Raja Bikramajit Singh agreed to pay a sum of Rs. 1,70,000 to the English East India Company.[34]

Munshi Binayak Prasad has thus rescued primary source material; otherwise they would have been lost forever. The Dumraon estate had also created a full-fledged record office and many of the orders issued by the Dumraon Raj were also available. Munshi Binayak Prasad made full use of Dumraon Raj documents as well. Therefore from the time of Gajanan (Gajan) Sahi onwards, the author is able to write his account on the basis of documentary evidence. This is a major strength of *Tawarikh-i-Ujjania*.

The account of Dalpati Sahi is valuable for a number of reasons. From now on Mughal-Ujjainiya interaction became a permanent feature of the history of the Ujjainiyas. The unfolding of Mughal-Ujjainiaya relations gives us an insight into the organization and structure of an autonomous principality, its ethics, its strategies for survival in the face of imperial bid for military take-over, its role in the regional politics and finally, its interaction with the imperial power.

Dalpati Sahi kept his capital in Bihia but Jagdishpur remained his principal military stronghold. The cavalry was the elite section of the army and enjoyed superiority over the infantry. The capital was enclosed by a forest of a special type of bamboo tree, which remained unharmed by bullets. The approach to the capital was so difficult that one could enter only on horseback.[35]

The historian tells us that from now onwards intrigue among the leading Ujjainia families became a common feature and many of the so-called advisors fanned the fires of distrust and promoted conspiracies against each other. Munshi Binayak Prasad opines that so long a major cause of Ujjainia success was their unity and closeness to each other. Now this was lost. As the narrative advances it is evident that Ujjainia chiefs had to, simultaneously, fight their family intrigues and also to fend off the imperial power. The imperial and regional powers were always ready to exploit inner family tensions for their own benefits.

The Mughal ruler Akbar who hated Gajan Sahi threw his full weight behind Dalpati Sahi. He conferred upon him the title of a king and returned to him his confiscated holdings. In return Dalpati Sahi had to promise military support to the Mughal ruler. The Ujjainia army contingent was a part of the Mughal army when it campaigned in different parts of the country. All were impressed with their bravery and fighting qualities. The Mughal ruler made Dalpati a *mansabdar,* i.e. he was awarded a place in the elite Mughal bureaucracy. He was entrusted with the task of looking after the security of the royal household. The carrot of a place in the Mughal bureaucracy was frequently dangled to keep Ujjainiya chiefs on the Mughal side.[36]

The author gives us a glimpse as to how the military contingent was readied when the Mughals asked them to report for duty. All the armed Ujjainias assembled at Karisath before proceeding to the battlefield.

It is clear that the alliance did not mean that the Mughal ruler implicitly trusted the Ujjainia chief. This is clear from the manner in which the downfall of Dalpati Sahi was manipulated.

The author has given both the versions of the death of Dalpati Sahi after he fell from the grace of Akbar. One version says that due to the intrigue of the progeny of Gajan Sahi, Akbar arrested Dalpati Sahi and later on released him. Another version says that Dalpati Sahi was killed in Allahabad where he had gone to meet the Mughal ruler.

Munshi Binayak Prasad does not pronounce his judgement. He is satisfied with merely recounting the different available versions of the event. This is another feature of the history presented in the present work.

After the death of Dalpati Sahi, one of his nephews assumed the name of Ram Sahi II and proclaimed himself as the new ruler. He appointed his advisor Barkumar Mandan Sahi, a collateral from the family of Dilip Sahi; he ensured that the members of other distinguished Ujjainia families did not feel antagonized. They were given adequate respect and land for their livelihood.[37] He was trying to consolidate his position. But Akbar had other ideas.

Though Dalpati Sahi was dead, his son Mukutmani looked to Akbar for support and royal honours. He was physically very strong and had pleased Akbar with his feats of strength. He had uprooted an old banyan tree, which others had failed to do. Akbar had therefore allowed him to enjoy the same *mansab* rank his father Dalpati Sahi had been assigned. Obviously, Akbar's intention was to play the two major factions against each other so that he could have a balancing role. Thus for a time, there were two claimants for the chieftainship among the Ujjainias.[38]

When Akbar died in 1605, Mukutmani quietly left the Mughal court and came back to Shahabad. He lacked administrative ability and was unable to provide a clean administration. Anarchy and confusion prevailed. Local officials took advantage of the situation and stopped payment of rent. The Cheros rose again and a Chero leader Hukumchandra captured a large chunk of territory held by the Ujjainiyas. The king was unable to put down the defiant Cheros. He sat along with the chief in open court and replied to questions put to the king. He dominated Mukutmani. All this created discontent against his rule. People stopped paying land revenue with the result that the salaries of soldiers remained unpaid. There was an all-round gloom among the Ujjainias.

Informal consultations were held among community elders and the leading Ujjanias. They resolved that Mukutmani ought to be replaced. Their choice fell upon Narayan Sahi, a distant nephew of Mukutmani.[39]

Narayan Sahi was young and was keen to end the anarchy that had enveloped the Ujjainia territory. It seems he wanted to unite the Ujjainias and so he freed the family members of Gajan Sahi, who had been arrested by the agent of the imperial power. In the process he killed the imperial agent and thus provided a proof of his military prowess. This won the esteem of his community members and when he reached the capital Bihta, Ujjainias persuaded Mukutmani to quit and anoint Narayan Sahi as his successor.[40] Mukutmani left the throne after a rule of only four years.

Munshi Binayak Prasad has revealed the story how he won the royal favour and governed for thirty-four years with tact and diplomacy and left a mark on the Ujjainia polity and history.[41]

Narayan Sahi as the chief of Ujjainias was not acceptable to the Mughal ruler because he had killed a Mughal commander and was therefore, dubbed a rebel. The new Ujjainia chief decided to woo the Mughal ruler and secretly went to Delhi. He realized that he could rule peacefully only if he was able to secure imperial approval for his chieftainship. He enrolled in the Mughal contingent under the assumed name of Zarar and by dint of meritorious service steadily rose in the official hierarchy and became a favourite of the ruler. Meanwhile, in Shahabad there was no news about the whereabouts of Narayan Mal (Narayan Sahi) and anarchy continued to increase. Everyone proclaimed himself a king.

Some people seated a minor son of Mukutmani on the throne and hailed him as the new ruler. In Dawan family members of Gajan Sahi asserted their claim to be the ruler. In Jagdishpur the family of Devasahi became self-proclaimed rulers of the Ujjainias. In Dalpatpur the family of Dalpati Sahi did not lag behind in staking their claim to chieftainship. Other Ujjainia families also assumed the mantle of chieftain though they hardly controlled a piece of land outside their village.

The Cheros also took advantage of the situation. They overthrew the authority of the Ujjainias, whom they considered to be their arch enemies. They stopped paying taxes.

When the situation was reported to the imperial court, Emperor Jahangir was deeply concerned and he felt that Zarar, an inhabitant of Shahabad and a dashing officer could be entrusted with the task of suppressing the unruly elements. Zarar was summoned and he immediately accepted the proposal. He marched to Shahabad along with 500 infantry and 500 cavalry. This was precisely the time when Raja Man Singh had been sent to Bihar as Governor with a contingent of 20,000 Rajputs.

When the news leaked out that Narayan Mal was proceeding towards Shahabad with an imperial contingent, all Ujjainias proceeded to the banks of Karmanasa River to welcome him. The Ujjainias had come to this decision because they considered Narayan Mal as a powerful military commander and that is why when he was in Shahabad no one had dared to challenge his authority as the chief. The second reason was that the Ujjainias felt that Narayan Mal alone could get rid of the vexatious Chero problem.[42]

As the Ujjainias flocked to the banner of Narayan Mal his military strength increased considerably. The Ujjainias were not mistaken. As soon as Narayan Mal reached Shahabad he was called upon to face the armies of Cheros under the leadership of Kughar, Anandichak, Bolonja, etc. The hill-tribes opened a front from Toran to Son River while Narayan Mal stationed his forces at Buxar on the banks of the river Ganga. The two armies faced each other for twenty-one days without opening hostilities. On the 22nd day the Chero archers opened the attack and for twelve days a severe battle was fought. The Ujjainias laid siege to the Chero fort of Toran but before the Ujjainias could capture it, Cheros received unexpected replenishment from the arrival of Raja Magha Mudhara. Fierce battle commenced and all efforts of the Ujjainias to capture Toran fort came to a naught. In the battle more than half of the Ujjainias lost their lives and they left the battlefield, hotly pursued by the Cheros, who surrounded Pratap Rudra Sahi, thinking him to be Narayan Mal. At this point of time, the Bakshi of the royal forces Rai Kalyan Singh arrived and the Cheros became disheartened. The rumour that additional royal forces were being sent to help Narayan Mal, further disheartened the Cheros. Nevertheless, it was a closely fought battle in which Narayan Mal showed his military skill and succeeded in achieving victory. Everyone among the Ujjainias sang praises of the valour of Narayan Mal and his brother. The royal Governor wrote a letter to the Emperor extolling the bravery of Narayan Mal.[43]

I have no idea if any other history book has gone in such details in depicting the resistance offered by the tribes to the people of the plains. The details furnished by Munshi Binayak Prasad enable us to understand the history of the Cheros with great clarity.

After this defeat the Cheros dispersed and Narayan Mal strengthened his position by establishing a firm administration. The Mughal ruler did not confer the title of king upon him, probably because Mukutmani, who had been earlier designated as king was still alive. Or it might have been a diplomatic ploy on part of the Mughal ruler to keep Narayan Mal on tenterhooks and to ensure that he continued to look up to him for favours.

Internal strife, which had become a part of Ujjainia psyche, did not end here. Dharu Sahi was emboldened by the fact that the Mughal ruler did not recognize Narayan Mal as a king and therefore he was amply justified in challenging his authority. He declared himself as a king in his village Ariyanv and declared his intention to fight with Narayan Mal. Before he could march, his co-villager Mukund Ray collected a force and challenged him. In the ensuing battle Dharu Sahi was killed. Mukund Rai then took some blood of Dharu Sahi and anointed Narayan Mal with this blood. Such were the ethos of the age.[44]

The Mughal ruler conferred upon Narayan Mal *mansabdari*;

he rose quickly in the bureaucratic hierarchy. On his part Narayan Mal lavishly granted land and villages to different Ujjainia families. We have details of land with their area as well as the name of the villages gifted by him. The author also mentions the areas controlled by Narayan Mal. We have therefore data for reconstructing the historical geography of Shahabad and also an idea about the villages controlled by Ujjainia families. One can also try his hand at reconstructing the social geography of Shahabad in medieval times.

Incidentally the author also mentions the beginning of certain social practices current among the Ujjainias in his time. For example, Ujjainias never called back married girls to their parent's house. This practice began in the time of Narayan Mal. It is not clear why and how this custom began.

The Mughal ruler asked Narayan Mal to keep watch over the royal palace. On one occasion, as a guard employed to keep watch over the royal palace, Narayan Mal tried to stop a person entering the royal harem disguised as a eunuch. Narayan Mal challenged him but when he did not respond, he killed him. The king was pleased and told him to seek something. Narayan Mal requested that henceforth Ujjainias should be freed from performing guard duties at the royal harem. Secondly, he should be given back the sword with which he had killed the intruder. Both these wishes were granted.

Other Ujjainias became jealous of Narayan Mal's popularity with the Mughal ruler. They conspired against him. On his return disaffected Ujjainias forged a coalition, ambushed Narayan Mal and in the ensuing fight, killed him.

Mughal-Ujjainia relations were never again so cordial.

After the death of Narayan Mal the Ujjainias did not seat his son upon the throne. Instead his younger brother Pratap Mal, who had distinguished himself in the war with the Cheros, became the new chief.

It was argued that Pratap Mal or Rudra Pratap by virtue of his experience and talents was better suited to guide the destinies of the Ujjainias than the inexperienced son of Narayan Mal. It is probably this trait of the Ujjainias to handover the leadership of the community to the ablest and deviate from the law of primogeniture that probably saved them from extinction.[45]

The reign of Pratap Mal or Raja Rudra Pratap Narayan Singh who ascended the throne in 1621 was again full of ups and downs in its relation with the Mughal Governor of Bihar and the Mughal central authority.

Under Emperor Jahangir, Islamic orthodoxy raised its head; a group of fundamentalist Muslims started a campaign against Hindus, who were dubbed as *kafirs*.[46] These Muslims razed temples to ground and broke idols of Hindu gods and goddesses and hurt the religious sentiments of the Hindus in a variety of ways. People reported the matter to Pratap Mal who decided to resist Muslim vandalism. For this purpose he collected an army. Before going to war Pratatp Mal wrote a conciliatory letter to the leader of this fanatic group, asking him to desist from these activities. Instead of responding positively, the Muslim leader cut the hands of the bearer of the letter and haughtily replied that it was a sin to treat leniently those who worshipped idols and he would proceed to destroy the Siva temple of Brahmpur and the temple of Chaturbhuj Devi near Jagdishpur. The king marched to Brahmpur to confront the enemy. He, however, decided to use a stratagem to defeat the enemy. He wrote a secret letter to Askari Hussain, a Shia Muslim, informing him that he was waiting with a contingent of 500 soldiers 'to help the Muslims destroy the temple as well as the Ujjainias'. The Rajputs disguised themselves as Muslims and when the Muslim contingent arrived they greeted them warmly. But as soon as the Muslims came within striking distance, to lull their suspicions, the Rajputs shouted 'Ali' 'Ali' and started killing them. Many Muslims were killed and those who survived fled from the place.

The author remarks that the event took place in 1627; since then the Ujjainias started participating in the Tazia procession taken out by the Shias during the month of *Muharram*. The practice of wearing a special type of jacket by the Ujjainias dates from this time.[47]

Shah Jahan after he ascended the throne remembered the

distinguished services rendered by Narayan Mal. He, therefore, honoured his successor, Pratap Mal by conferring upon him a contingent of 500 infantry and 1,000 horses. Probably he was assigned a *mansab* as well.[48]

Pratap Mal decided to leave Jagdishpur and set up his capital at Bhojpur, the land of his ancestors. He built here a number of buildings whose detailed description is furnished by Munshi Binayak Prasad.

We should note here two things: under the Mughals the craze of building palaces, forts and other structures had reached its apogee in the reign of Shah Jahan. It also affected the local chiefs, who tried to emulate the lifestyle of the imperial rulers of Delhi. The details cited by Munshi Binayak Prasad help us to understand the style of architecture developing in places far off from the imperial capital. Artisans who had participated in the construction of imperial buildings were employed in construction work. It took two years to build the Nauratna Bhavan and the fort of Bhojpur.[49]

The expenses incurred in constructing buildings emptied the coffer of the estate. The salaries of soldiers remained unpaid. Pratap Mal did not pay the revenue to the royal treasury for three years. He remained unconcerned with the administration of the estate and oblivious to the discontent brewing among the soldiers, the estate officials and the common man. The *kanungos* of Bhojpur, Gosain Mal and Abal Singh requested the imperial capital to help them to collect the dues from Pratap Mal. They also conveyed the state of affairs to the Mughal Governor of Bihar, who summoned Pratap Mal to Patna. He dilly-dallied but agreed to go to Patna on the request of his nephews. While on way to Patna his advisors told him that he would be put into prison by the Governor. He cancelled the journey and returned. He committed more atrocities; and his officials hated him more. His *diwan* also distanced himself from the administration. At long last Sundar, the *kanungo* wrote about his incompetence, maladministration, oppression to Abdullah Khan, the Governor of Bihar at Patna. The *nazim* immediately sent a force against him. Discontented Ujjainias and soldiers whose salaries were in arrears joined the imperial forces. Pratap Mal was arrested, taken to Patna and executed after some time. The soldiers looted the Nauratna Bhavan and got more booty than the pay they were entitled to.

The queen committed *sati* and Nauratna Bhavan was razed to the ground. The estate was confiscated and the Mughal ruler appointed Baimat Khan as royal officer to look after the administration of the estate.[51]

We have a detailed account of how the estate was managed on behalf of the Mughal ruler. This gives us a very good idea about the management practices followed by the Mughals after they took over an Estate. For the first time the leader of the Ujjainias had lost his status as an independent chieftain. This was galling to Ujjainias even though some Ujjainia families like Akola Singh of Basudhar continued to serve the Mughals. As time passed the Ujjainias became more and more bitter. Kakolat Sahi was asked leave Shahabad and his property in Basudhar was confiscated.

Kakolat Sahi and other Ujjainia families reached an understanding whereby the Mughal officials were to be forced to leave Shahabad. A campaign to oust the Mughals was started.[52] The Ujjainias began killing Muslims. They killed the Mughal *amaldar*.

It is said in this period the houses of the Ujjainias did not have doors for the simple 'reason that they could escape quickly if attacked by the Mughal forces.'[53]

Although the Ujjainias were united outwardly, there were strong undercurrents of differences among them. Many of them did not want Amar Singh, the son of the late Narayan Mal to become the chief. However Amar Singh called a meeting of Ujjainias in AD 1648 in Bahadurpur and requested them to support his case. In return he agreed to reward them with the grant of *jagirs* and land. A written agreement was arrived at. He went to Delhi to plead his case but was unsuccessful. He left Rai Narayan Bhakra to espouse his cause and eventually Shah Jahan issued a *firman* conferring the chieftainship on Amar Singh and asked him to attend the royal court. Amar Singh in view of the prevailing anarchy in Shahabad decided to stay back and help the royal forces. He sent his younger brother Prabal Singh to the court, who obtained another confirmatory *firman*.

Kakolat Sahi who was leading the anti-Mughal forces faced Amar Singh and his forces in the battlefield. When Kakolat Sahi fell down, Amar Singh chivalrously spared his life. Eventually both agreed that the fratricidal war should be ended and Amar Singh was allowed to exercise administrative rights denied to him earlier.[54]

Amar Singh moved his capital to Mathila located at Chitrasen Pur. He recalled the members of the Kayastha caste who were the principal employees of the estate and who had become alienated in the time of Pratap Mal. He then allowed his caste men to keep the land they had in their possession; they also became his supporters. Finally, he again called a meeting of the three main families of the Ujjainias in a garden extending over 20 acres. All this helped him to win over the support of a large section of the community. He also won the affection of the other sections of the society, such as Kurmis, Koiris, Vaishyas, Muslims, etc. A large number of Muslims were appointed in army as well as in the court and as *mahawats*. He also tried to promote agriculture by constructing irrigation channels and bunds. He tried to reorganize the bureaucracy; estate officers were stationed permanently in a number of places. We have a list of these places. An officer was in charge of two *parganas* and each *pargana* had a Kayastha *kanungo*. A representative of estate known as Vakil was appointed to the court of the Governor in Patna. He was required to visit Patna every month It shows that the Mughal rulers were still not confident of the loyalty of the Ujjainia chieftain.

He lent his armed contingent to the Mughal state whenever its services were required. He participated in the battle of Makwanpur near Janakpur in Nepal. Probably on this visit to Makwanpur, he came in touch with Maithil pandits. He invited them to his estate and granted them land in Makandpur, Jamsohi, Lilari, Jagdishpur, Hinganthi, Malegaon, Athwan, Kohil, etc.

Amar Singh, like some of his predecessors, tried to give a broad base to his rule to ensure wide social support.

Amar Singh died in 1665[55] and was succeeded by Rudra Singh. The new chief continued the conciliatory policies pursued by Amar Singh. He invited the members of the Vaishya community to settle down, in his estate. They dispersed to Arrah, Buxar, Shahpur, etc., in course of time but continued to call themselves as Rudranagari.

Amar Singh's succession was disputed. His uncle Prabal Singh staked the claim to chieftainship, which Rudra Singh refused to entertain. Prabal Singh left for Delhi where he was arrested and converted to Islam.[56]

Rudra Singh's relations with the Mughal court did not proceed on an even keel. A major irritant was the policy of Shaista Khan, the Governor of Bihar, who imposed *jiziya* on Hindus in pursuance of the directive of the Mughal ruler Aurangzeb. This united all the Ujjainias who considered it as grossly unfair and deeply humiliating. Unity was forged between Kunwar Dhir and Rudra Singh. The former was a militant Ujjainia chief whose military skills were well known. The combined strength of the two scared the imperial *amaldar* in Shahabad. Kunwar Dhir incited rebellion against Muslim functionaries of the Mughal Empire and made life extremely difficult for the Mughals in Bihar. In Delhi Prabal Singh was released and he returned. The Ujjainias were not pacified. The movement against the Mughals did not cease. Aurangzeb recalled Shaista Khan and replaced him by his son Azam as the Governor of Bihar. He and his successor Governor Said Khan tried to wean away Rudra Pratap from Kunwar Dhir. He did succeed and Rudra Pratap became a trusted friend of the Mughal Governor of Bihar. This naturally caused a rift between Kunwar Dhir and Rudra Pratap. Rudra Pratap received a reward when the Mughal Emperor refused to endorse the claim of Prabal Singh as the Ujjainia chieftain even though he had become a Muslim and had been sent to Shahabad. It must also be said to the credit of Prabal Singh that he realized that Rudra Pratap enjoyed wide popularity; he could also fathom the disgust of the community towards the Muslims.

He now refused to stake his claim. He also turned down the advice to reconvert to Hinduism and lived like a Muslim saint. The estate looked after all his material needs and paid respect due to an elder member of the family.

The Ujjainia-Mughal alliance infuriated Kunwar Dhir and a new civil war was unleashed. Kunwar Dhir was unsuccessful and an outward peace between the two prevailed. Kunwar Dhir crossed the river Ganga and created principalities in north Bihar. As a reward for these services all the rights earlier enjoyed by Ujjainia chiefs were restored to Rudra Pratap in 1683 by Mughal authorities. He also shifted his capital to Buxar on the banks of the river Ganga.

These rights included the right to policing, to try criminal cases, the right to collect land revenue on behalf of the Mughal state. As a further mark of royal favour, Rudra Pratap was given a *mansabdari* rank, i.e. he was assigned a rank in the imperial bureaucracy and consequently the size of the military contingent that he was expected to send to the royal army was fixed. For meeting the expenses of the contingent he was given an additional *jagir* and by a royal order his possessions in Shahabad region were defined. This certainly added to his prestige and status in society as well as in politics.

The increased power of Rudra Pratap Singh was unpalatable to Kunwar Dhir and some other Ujjainias. They plotted for his downfall.

Rudra Pratap was childless and Kunwar Dhir persuaded him to marry the younger sister of his wife. After the wedding was performed, both Rudra Pratap and Kunwar Dhir were returning to Buxar by boat. Kunwar Dhir conspired with a royal servant to add poison to the betel-leaf,[57] which Rudra Pratap consumed. In mid-stream Rudra Pratap realized the foul play and felt that his death was near. He however did not speak a word about it to anyone and returned to the palace in Buxar as quickly as he could. He told his queen about the treachery of Kunwar Dhir but at the same time ordered that in the interest of the estate and to foil the ambition of Kunwar Dhir, all should keep quiet. He also had all the gates shut down and told the queen to send someone to fetch Mandhata Singh and Sujan Singh. A runner brought the two brothers from the backdoor to the palace.[58] Meanwhile Kunwar Dhir had surrounded the palace with his men in the hope that as soon as the king was dead he would declare himself to be the new Ujjainia chief. When the two brothers arrived, Mandhata Singh was hastily anointed as the new Ujjainia chief. The news was announced that Rudra Pratap was dead and that Mandhata Singh had been appointed as the new Ujjainia chief. Kunwar Dhir had lost the game; he had no option but to accept Mandhata Singh as the new Ujjainia chief.

An important role in the whole affair had been played by the *diwan* of the estate who had thwarted Kunwar Dhir's plans and had ensured that the new Ujjainia chief would be acceptable to the family of the late chief Rudra Pratap. As a mark of gratitude, from now onwards, the *diwan* was traditionally the first person to offer his greetings to the new chief on his installation.[59]

The period occupied by Rudra Singh was important in more than one way for the Ujjainias. Rudra Singh, helped by able advisors such as Dewan, Haldhar, Parthaman Rawat and Purandar suppressed anti-social elements. In one incident Haldhar and the son of Parthaman Rawat lost their lives. We get a very vivid picture of how Shahabad developed in this period and how the Ujjainia community rallied round him and strengthened the Ujjainia estate.

The author throws additional light on the dispersal and ethnology of the Kayastha community. We are informed how the title Akhouri used by the Kayasthas came into vogue. Originally a commander of one lakh contingent was known as *lakhori*. In course of time the letter L was dropped and they were called *akhouri*. He also writes about various Kayastha families and some of the Kayastha readers may be able to trace their family roots to the late seventeenth and early eighteenth centuries. The account also shows that the Kayasthas had a firm grip on the administrative machinery of the Ujjainia estate.

Kunwar Dhir continued to incite opponents of Mandhata Singh and succeeded in attracting his brother Sujan Singh to his side. Both succeeded in killing Mandhata Singh in 1708. Sujan

Singh's dream of becoming the chief did not materialize. An employee of Mandhata Singh killed him. Horil Singh became the new chief of the Ujjainias.[60]

This was the period when an intense struggle for the Mughal throne was going on among the successors of Aurangzeb. Horil Singh threw his weight on the side of Farrukhsiyar and fought in his army against his rival Jahandar Shah. Farrukhsiyar was victorious. Pleased with the valour and assistance of Horil Singh, Farrukhsiyar asked him to go back to Patna to look after the security of royal family, which he had left behind. After some time Farrukhsiyar called back his family to Delhi; he did not forget the services rendered by Horil Singh. The Emperor recalled Horil Singh to the royal court at Delhi to receive rewards. Three royal *firmans* were issued in his favour: one granted him the revenue from certain parts in *sarkar* Rohtas; the second increased his rank among the *mansabdars* and the third gave him the *jagir* of Bihia Danvar, Dev Markande and Harivanshpur. Mughal-Ujjainia alliance had been once again cemented.[61]

Normally the Governor of the Province mediated the relationship between the Centre and the Province. We have a graphic description of how this relationship could be soured by local officials. Mir Jumla, the Governor of Bihar was opposed to the Syed brothers who controlled the levers of administration at Delhi. He started sending false report against Horil Singh who had helped Syed brothers and was in their confidence. As a result small zamindars in Shahabad rose against Horil Singh. They occupied a part of his property. Taking advantage of the breakdown of the royal authority bigger zamindars started preying upon the smaller zamindars. For example, Durant Singh the zamindar of Jagdishpur wanted to incorporate the zamindari of Dawan in the possession of Bahadur Singh. This started a conflict, which continued for several years and in which different Ujjainia zamindars took sides. Eventually Horil Singh exercised his right as the Chief and through the mediation of Pahalwan Singh and Bhavani Singh put an end to the hostilities. Dina Rai Kanungo and two others signed an agreement written in Bhojpuri language. By now the Mughal rule in Bihar had become shaky.[62]

The real power now rested in the hands of the Nawab of Bengal. The book gives us a close look at how Bihar's polity changed and its fortune was tied to the apron strings of the Nawab of Bengal, now the real arbiter of the destinies of the zamindars of Bihar. For example, one of the Deputies of the Nawab of Bengal took an intense dislike for Udwant Singh, the Ujjainia zamindar of Jagdishpur. He attacked Jagdishpur in alliance with Horil Singh. On the successful conclusion of the campaign, Horil Singh's reward was a grant of Rs. 2,000 from the income of taluka Bihia.[63]

When the Afghans became turbulent and killed Haibatjang, the deputy of the Nawab of Bengal in Bihar, Mahabatjang proceeded towards Bihar from Murshidabad with a powerful army. He was supported by the leading Hindu zamindars of Bihar, Raja Sundar Singh of Tikari, Horil Singh and Pahalwan Singh, etc. The Afghans were defeated and Mahabatjang rewarded both Horil Singh and Pahalwan Singh. He asked his deputy in Bihar to recognize the status and position of Horil Singh and Pahalwan Singh. It was obvious that disunity prevailed among the leading Ujjainia zamindars and fraternal relations among the Ujjainias were deeply strained. Udwant Singh threatened to attack Horil Singh at Mathila. Bodh Singh asked Horil Singh to give him Chausa. It was clear that Bodh Singh and Udwant Singh were bent upon forcing a war upon Horil Singh.[64] As Horil Singh was not ready for a battle, he quietly left Mathila and when Udwant Singh reached Mathila, he did not find Horil Singh. Horil Singh then sought the help of Pahalwan Singh and was victorious at Nokha.

Malik remarks that in the first half of the eighteenth century the revenue settlement in Sarkar Shahabad was made with Ujjainia zamindars; despite this friendliness, it is also a fact that this was also the period when the Ujjainias were continuously at loggerheads with the governors of Bihar, especially after Bihar was attached to Bengal Nawab in 1734.[65] They were placed under the category of *zamindaran-i-zortalab*, i.e. 'zamindars who paid revenue only under military threat and their general behaviour towards the government was marked by defiance and hostility.[66]

At this point Munshi Binayak Prasad gives us a glimpse of life-style of Ujjainia chiefs. He describes the function held to celebrate the birth of a grandson to Pahalwan Singh of Nokha. It is interesting to note that Bodh Singh, Udwant Singh and Horil Singh were all present at a dance performance in the evening. It seems that despite strained and even inimical relationship, Ujjainias customarily visited each other whenever social functions were organized. Of course a protocol was observed for seating the guests. Zamindars not belonging to the Ujjainia community including Muslims were also invited. The Muslims were seated on one side in the *pandal*. The author also narrates a story whose veracity is suspect.[67]

According to him among those present were Siraj-ud-daula and Mir Kasim Ali. Some illiterate Ujjainias offended Mir Kasim Ali by throwing *gulal* over him. Eventually Mir Kasim Ali took revenge for this when he became the Nawab of Bengal by sacking and pillaging Nokha and the adjoining areas.[68]

The celebrations continued for seven days and Pahalwan Singh spent Rs. 1 lakh over it. Horil Singh received as present 18 horses, 651 *asharfis* and several other things on this occasion.[69]

The author tells us that belief in astrology among the Ujjainias was very strong. Horil Singh was a staunch believer in astrology. He was told to leave Mathila and shift the capital to Horil Nagar near Dumraon. The place was almost uninhabited except for three or four families of Ujjainias, two houses of Gowalas and one of Jolaha. Horil Singh built his palace in 1745. The new capital came to be known as Horil Nagar. Soon other functionaries of the estate settled down and others were also invited to reside here.[70]

Horil Singh died in 1746 at the age of 58. He was succeeded by his son Chhatradhari Singh who looked after administration in the time of his father and was experienced in administrative affairs.[71] The ceremony of installation was conducted according to Hindu religious rituals and member of all communities were invited to attend it. Among those present included the Deputy of the Nawab of Bengal in Patna. He constructed new buildings and more and more people including members of the trading community came to stay here.[72]

Fratricidal wars did not cease. Taking advantage of the death of Horil Singh, Digvijay Singh, son of Bodh Singh of Buxar captured Chausa and the adjoining areas. This was very painful to Chhatradhari Singh, who complained against it to the Mughal ruler Muhammad Shah. On learning about it Digvijay Singh incited Nawab Ahmad Khan, a local officer to attack Horil Nagar. Ahmad Khan led an armed contingent of 900 men. The Ujjainias resisted the attack and Ahmad Khan was forced to sign an agreement; he agreed to hand over *pargana* Danvar Bhojpur to Chhatradhari Singh.[73]

In line with his penchant for including non-political matters while describing political and administrative events, the author has deviated here and given a description of the ecology of Horil Nagar. He has also described the dress worn by the Ujjainias and their Chief.

The author refers to Dayal Narain Mishra, an astrologer who correctly predicted the birth of a son to Chhatradhari Singh and was given a grant of 200 *bighas* of land.[74]

There was no end to internal strife among the Ujjainias. Chhatradhari Singh tried to reacquire Chausa from Digvijay Singh by forming an alliance with Raja Balwant Singh of Ram-nagar (Benares). Balwant Singh attacked Chausa in 1172 AH and occupied it. In this attempt Balwant Singh had enlisted the aid of Raja Ram Narain, the Deputy Governor of Bihar and the English forces as well. He plundered the fort of Buxar.[75]

This was the period when the politics of north India was undergoing a sea change. After the battle of Plassey, the English acquired a decisive say in the affairs of Bengal and Bihar. The Ujjainias like other powers in Bengal, Bihar and Uttar Pradesh did not realize the significance of these new developments. To them politics was a matter of opportunistic alliances, a handmaid to serve immediate personal interests, an instrument to satisfy personal whims and fancies. The larger interests of the community or the region or the state did not matter.

In the changed political context when the English wanted to familiarize themselves with the land revenue system of Shahabad, they asked the *kanungos* about the whole affairs. The author says the *kanungos* were persuaded to write that since the beginning of the Islamic rule, the House of Dumraon had been collecting the land revenue from the local zamindars and had been sending it to the imperial treasury. In return for this service they were given *malikana* rights. The English thereafter fixed 12 per cent as *rajgi* right for the House of Dumraon. In addition, in each *pargana* of Sarkar Shahabad, the House of Dumraon was given one village as *nankar*.[76] The administrative understanding arrived at between the English and Dumraon further cemented the political alliance between the two.

As a result when the battle of Buxar was fought between the Mughal Emperor Shah Alam II, the Nawab of Oudh and the Nawab of Bengal Mir Kasim Ali Khan on the one hand and the English East India Company on the other in 1764, Bhavani Singh Ujjainia was on the side of the latter.[77] The English victory ensured the continuation of the British rule. In honour of the victory over the Mughal Emperor, Buxar was renamed as Fateh-garh and the Ujjainias handed over Buxar to the English. Buxar became a part of the territory ruled by the English.

According to the author, in 1768, the responsibility for collecting the revenue of Shahabad was entrusted to the House of Dumraon. Here the author has made a mistake. He says that the responsibility was entrusted to Bikramajit Singh but this would not be correct since Chhatradhari Singh handed over to him, his elder son, the reins of administration only in 1770 after his return from a pilgrimage to Vindhyachal. He had obtained the prior consent of the English for this change.[78]

The times were difficult for the new chief. The whole of Bengal and Bihar was visited by a terrible famine in 1770. Crops had failed and the people were penniless. The land revenue could not be collected. No payment was made to the Company

government. Under this situation, the English Collector William
Augustus Brooke in 1777 *Fasli* withdrew the right of Dumraon
to collect land revenue in Shahabad. It may be noted that
Munshi Binayak Prasad uses dates according to his own fancy:
Vikram Samvat, Hegira, Fasli and the Christian era. This puts
additional strain on the reader in understanding the chronology
of events. Probably this was due to lack of proper training as a
historian.[79]

Bikramjit Singh died in 1805. It was during his time that
the relation between the house of Dumraon and the English
were finally put on an even keel. First, owing to the famine
the ruler of Dumraon was unable to pay the Government its
share of revenue. The Estate was encumbered in debt. The
English wanted to take over the Estate; a meeting was called
for this purpose in Bihia and documents were prepared for the
purpose. The author laconically informs us that the Mir Munshi
of Estate, Pahalwan Singh intentionally delayed the matter and
the deed could not be prepared in time. Finally, the paper lapsed
and the Estate remained intact.[80]

When the Governor-General Warren Hastings attacked
Benares to punish Chait Singh, Bikramajit Singh personally led a
contingent of two thousand men and pursued Chait Singh up to
fort of Chunar. In appreciation of these services, the Company
wrote off the debt of the Estate.[81] It is to be noted that not all the
Ujjainia community leaders supported Bikramajit Singh's move
against Chait Singh. But they were forced to give in writing
that they extended full obedience to him. The agreement is
dated 21 *Asarh* 1186 *fasli*. It is written in Bhojpuri language in
Devanagari script.[82]

Dumraon also received zamindari rights of 77 villages in
eastern Uttar Pradesh.

He also reorganized the estate bureaucracy by appointing a
Council in which besides members of the family, others were
also inducted. For example, Prem Banda, a Bhumihar by caste
was asked to look after the affairs of the estate in Balia in Uttar
Pradesh. Other members were Gajraj Rai and Sharda Singh.[83]

It was in the time of Bikramajit Singh that the English East India Company introduced the Permanent Settlement and it seems there was no problem with regard to its implementation in Dumraon. The area under the control of Chhatradhari Singh was recognized as constituting the Dumraon Estate under the Permanent Settlement and accordingly the rights and obligations of the holder of the Estate were fixed. Bikramajit Singh went to Calcutta and stayed there for some years. The author does not give us any idea as to the purpose of this visit and what he did there. It may be presumed that he had gone there to smoothen whatever ambiguities might have remained in the settlement because the formal notification was issued on 30 May 1797, when the English East India Company sent an order to the Estate whereby the ten-year settlement was made perpetual; the land-revenue to be paid by the Estate was the same as it was fixed in the ten-year settlement. The zamindari was made hereditary.[84]

The author describes in detail how the new relationship evolved.

First, the existing system of administration by the Council was found unsatisfactory and it was disbanded. Santosh Rai, a Srivastava Kayastha was appointed chief *diwan*.[85] Mukhtars were appointed to look after the interest of the Estate in different areas. They were placed under the *diwan*. However soon it was discovered that owing to certain ingrained constraints the income of the Estate could not be raised. For example, no new land could be settled without official sanction and new areas could not be populated. The Company decided to modify its policies as the expenditure of the Estate exceeded the income. The Company also addressed itself to other administrative problems.

In the time of Bikramajit Singh the rights of the Estate in respect of criminal justice were defined. The occasion was provided by the case of Gowalas of village Kindar who had been sentenced to goal in a case of rioting by an Estate functionary Diwan Lalit Rai.[86] The Company Government pointed out that in criminal cases accused should not be arrested by the officials of the Estate. Whenever the zamindars heard a case, they were asked to send full details to the Company's government.

After some time excise cases were also taken away from the jurisdiction of the zamindars.

The English East India Company by an order of 1198 *Fasli* allowed traditional practice of *tauzy*, i.e. the practice of tenants coming to Dumraon on the Dussehra day and presenting the chief with a gift; in return the estate renewed their contracts and/or granted them fresh contracts for continuing cultivation.

The zamindars were asked to promote the cultivation of potato because it was a good safeguard against famines and food shortages. We have no idea what steps the Estate took to promote its cultivation.[87] The order was a positive sign that the Company was taking the task of governance seriously; collection of revenue was its major objective but concern for the well-being of the subjects was also considered a duty. It was keen to shed its image as a revenue collecting and territory grabbing agency.

In AD 1799 the first police station was established in Dumraon.[88] Bikramajit Singh died at Benares on 28 June 1805.[89] His death occasioned a new tussle for succession. The dowager queen eventually agreed to accept Jai Prakash, son of the youngest brother of the late chief as the new successor. After the news was announced opposition to Jai Prakash soon died out.[90] It should be noted that the wish of the widow in absence of a direct male heir prevailed in the Dumraon estate. This had happened when Kunwar Dhir poisoned Raja Rudra Singh.

From the time of Bikramajit Singh onwards, Munshi Binayak Prasad is able to give more details about administration and other allied matters in the Estate of Dumraon because armed conflicts with the Central or Provincial authority were a thing of the past; the Estate concentrated on administration. Secondly, the chiefs taking lesson from the Company's administration, reorganized the bureaucracy and developed the practice of recording administrative decisions on paper on a much larger scale for future reference. Documentary sources were available to Munshi Binayak Prasad in plenty; he was in a better position to glean more information about administrative measures and administrative practices.

With Jai Prakash Singh the Dumraon Estate stepped into a new era of its history: the primary concern of the Estate was to run the administration on modern lines and to ensure the economic health of the Estate. Jai Prakash Singh had earlier shown his reluctance to assume power as the Estate was under heavy debt. But Diwan Pratap Singh had assured him that things would change once he became chief. The *diwan* was eminently successful in his endeavour; the debts were wiped out and surplus accumulated.[91] When the *diwan* resigned from the post for personal reasons, his nephew Raghubar Dayal Singh became the new *diwan*. It seems that by and large the post of *diwan* even if not hereditary ran into the family. Only in rare cases exceptions were made.

The focus on economic well being of the Estate is reflected in the decision in AD 1811 to invest Estate's capital in money-lending, banking and commerce. For the purpose, Har Prakash Singh, a brother of the ruler Jai Prakash Singh constructed a new building known as *Mahajani Kothi* from where the banking and commercial operations of the Dumraon Estate were conducted. The *kothi* was still functioning eight decades later when the author completed this manuscript.[92]

A major event of the time of Jai Prakash Singh was the participation of the Dumraon contingent under the leadership of Wali Daud Khan in the Anglo-Nepalese War of 1814-15. The English were victorious; they rewarded Jai Prakash Singh by conferring upon him the title of Maharaja Bahadur. The English East India Company had adopted the Mughal practice of conferring titles on Indian chiefs in order to flatter their vanity and to retain their loyalty. Jai Prakash Singh in turn rewarded Daud Khan by empowering him to spend Rs. 1,000.[93]

It is clear that the Chiefs had to be very careful about proving their loyalty to the English East India Company. In 1827 it was alleged that Jai Prakash Singh was in league with the Sikh ruler Maharaja Ranjit Singh. Jai Prakash Singh had to go to a Court of Law to disprove the charge. The case was filed in Benares and Jai Prakash Singh stayed there till a verdict of 'Not Guilty' was pronounced. Then he returned to Dumraon. The Estate incurred an expenditure of Rs. 50,000 on this lawsuit.[94]

Economic prosperity and peace brought affluence to the Estate. The ruler and other members of the family spent money in constructing new buildings, ponds, temples; they planted gardens and orchards, etc.; they also patronized scholars and traditional learning. Shiv Prakash Singh, a brother of Jai Prakash Singh wrote books, *Satsang Vilas Bhajan*, *Rasaorno*, *Bhagwatras*, *Itihas Lahari*, etc. Maybe this piece of information will add new data to the history of Hindi literature.[95]

After the death of Jai Prakash Singh, his grandson Janki Prasad Singh (age 14 years) though still a minor became the Head of Dumraon Estate under the guardianship of Maheshwar Baksh Singh. He could become the chief because during his lifetime, Jai Prakash Singh in a registered Will had nominated him as his successor. Other aspirants for the honour did not question his succession.[96]

It seems that Maheshwar Baksh Singh the guardian, took good care of the finances of the Estate. He had accumulated a surplus and had invested Rs. 2 lakh in the purchase of additional zamindari, which boosted Estate's income.[97]

Janki Prasad Singh adopted a new life-style. He was a Vaishnav by conviction; he visited the temple of Bihariji in the town every day. He fasted on the *Ekadashi* day and ate mostly fruits. All the servants put on sandal paste on their foreheads; he banned the sale of fish and meat outside the town. The most influential person in the Estate was Gokulji, the temple priest who stayed with him most of the time.[98]

He started on a pilgrimage to Jagannath Puri. During the journey he fell ill but he did not postpone the trip. At Calcutta he paid a courtesy call to the Governor-General who conferred upon him the title of Maharaja Bahadur. He gave a party to the local English officials and every participant was given a gift. Entertaining the British officials was a part of the social etiquette observed by the top zamindars.

At Jagannath Puri excessive crowds thronged the temple. The womenfolk in the entourage could not worship the deity. After some persuasion and intervention of the Raja of Puri, the doors of the temple from three sides were closed and the ladies performed the *puja*.

On return journey Janki Prasad Singh was taken ill; he passed away at Mednipur on 13 May 1843. He was cremated on the bank of the local river Kasia.[99] He was succeeded by Maheshwar Baksh Singh, who was installed on 29 June 1843. He was a choice of the mother and the widow of the deceased ruler, Janki Prasad Singh. Women thus repeatedly played a major role in the installation of a new Chief among the Ujjainias.[100]

The details provided by Munshi Binayak Prasad help us to appreciate the difficulties and perils associated with long distance travel in the days before trains started transporting men and material. It is important to note that the chiefs would proceed on pilgrimages involving inter-provincial travel only after obtaining prior permission of the authorities of the English East India Company. Despite their wealth and power and prestige their actions were circumscribed by restrictions imposed on them by the orders of the Company.[101]

However as there was no Will, several other family members advanced their claims to the chieftainship. As armed conflict was ruled out; they filed their claims in the Law Court. The first person to challenge the elevation of Maheshwar Baksh Singh was his cousin Rameshwar Baksh Singh, who instituted a suit. Maheshwar Baksh Singh also put in an application intimating the Court that he been installed as the chief of the Dumraon Estate. All the ladies also wrote a letter to the Governor-General of India informing him about Maheshwar Baksh Singh's assumption of chieftainship of Dumraon.[102]

Another cousin, Lal Parmeshwar Baksh Singh, the son of Harprakash Singh, the brother of the Maharaja Jai Prakash Singh also filed a case against the Estate and claimed lakhs of rupees as his dues. The Maharaja stayed in Arrah during the pendency of the case. Ultimately he was victorious and Lala Parmeshwar Baksh Singh sought forgiveness. He was not only forgiven but also brought to Dumraon and all the earlier grants of land and villages were restored to him.[103]

It is clear that the Estate spent a substantial sum of its income on litigation. The author cites a number of lawsuits in which Maheshwar Baksh Singh was involved; he managed to emerge victorious in each one of them. Besides, he was able to increase the area of the Estate by purchasing additional zamindaris.

At this point the author briefly describes the career of Diwan Ram Nath Singh who had worked under three chiefs for thirty years. The lavish life-style of the *diwan* can be inferred from the food he consumed. His daily diet consisted of fish, brought from the Sone River, situated at a distance of 40 miles from Dumraon. It was said that he always had Rs. 1 lakh with him and 'spent lavishly on festivals, he celebrated'. After his death the post was given to his son Ram Jiawan Singh. The step followed the tradition that *diwanship* was either hereditary or ran in the family.[104]

Ecological consciousness was a part of the life-style of the chiefs. Maheshwar Baksh Singh planted Jamun and Mango trees along the road running from Buxar to Dumraon.

The trait of religiosity was deeply ingrained in him. The author says there was hardly a day when no *yajnas* or *havans* were performed. He appointed priests in important temples and granted them land for their upkeep and maintenance. Illiterate Brahmins were attracted by his munificence. They took up the study of Sanskrit and religious texts.[105]

Despite his deep religiosity and inclination towards trad-itional learning, Maheshwar Baksh Singh was forward looking. He had established on 7 July 1856 a school imparting English education. The ruler consciously promoted modernity through new education.[106]

On 30 January 1868, Maheshwar Baksh Singh voluntarily installed Lala Radha Prasad Singh as the new chief of Dumraon; he stopped taking interest in the administration of the Estate and shifted his residence to Ayodhya.

Maheshwar Baksh Singh left a number of guidelines for the new chief.

The author concludes the second volume at this point. This was logical because while writing the history down to the time of Maheshwar Baksh Singh, the author described a number of Ujjainia personalities who played important roles from time to time; it was not possible for the author to discuss them in detail because that would have affected the continuity of the narrative and prevented the reader from having a clear idea as to when the present house of Dumraon emerged and flourished.

To satisfy the reader and make the history of the Ujjainias more intelligible, the author sets out in the third volume to write about some of them at length so that their role could be better appreciated. The third volume is a necessary and welcome supplement to the second volume. We must thank the author for undertaking this task.

The author has followed a simple methodology; he writes about different Ujjainia chiefs and their seats of power, the history of each reign, the main political events of the period and the role of Ujjainias in them. Once again, he takes care to dilate upon major administrative, economic and cultural features of the period.

In the eighteenth century three power centers of the Ujjainias under different families had emerged in Shahabad: Dumraon, Buxar and Jagdishpur. Their relationship was complex; each tried to promote self-interest. There were policy clashes resulting in bruised egos. Conflict was endemic despite community solidarity. Before the English acquired the *diwani* of Bihar and Bengal, these conflicts were exacerbated by the inability of the imperial power to keep the contending zamindars in check. The author therefore, rightly decided that the histories of the three estates should be treated separately.

UJJAINIA PERSONALITIES OF THE 18TH CENTURY

The author begins the third volume with a detailed account of the career of Kunwar Dhir in two chapters. He fought a number of wars not only against the members of his own community but also against other zamindars. The sheer number of wars waged by him made him a legendary figure amongst the Ujjainia community. He crossed the Ganga River and attacked the zamindari of Bettiah. Kunwar Dhir's activities made him notorious towards the end of the seventeenth century and the beginning of the eighteenth century. He did not hesitate to defy the imperial Mughals; he refused to obey the Mughal governor of Bihar; he looted the boats of the European trading companies on the river Ganga. Finally, he made a desperate bid to capture the chieftainship of the Ujjainia community. Subsequently Kunwar Dhir fled to Gorakhpur where he built a fort at Barhaj in the impenetrable forest and remained a source of anxiety and concern for the surrounding zamindars, the employees of the imperial power and of course, his own community in Shahabad.[108]

The zamindar of Bettiah, unable to protect himself from attacks by Kunwar Dhir complained to the Governor of Bihar but was unable to receive any relief. He then requested Raja Rudra Singh Ujjainiya to help him. Raja Rudra Singh wrote a letter to Kunwar Dhir in Urdu poetry (*Jangnama*) in which he chided him for being arrogant.[109] He advised him to go back to his village and live in peace. Otherwise he threatened him with a war. Kunwar Dhir paid no heed to it.

Raja Rudra Singh attacked Kunwar Dhir; a bloody battle was fought. A detailed description of this battle shows that Kunwar Dhir had cultivated a base amongst non-Ujjainia sections of the society as well. Those who fought on his side included 'Nima Seema, Rawat (by caste Kurmi Jaiswar), Basawan Rawat, Toshkhana Bardar, Bechu Rai Bahelia (caste-bird catcher) (it is interesting that he was in-charge of the treasury and occupied this high post), Inayat Dhuniya (a Muslim carder), Bala Thakur Hajam (barber), Dhanhu Baitha Dhobi (washerman), Genda Rawat and Puru Rawat (probably by caste Kurmi)'. All of them were recognized as leaders of their respective communities. They had sided with the Kunwar in many of his victorious battles. The Kunwar had then rewarded them with land, *jagirs* and money. The Kunwar now exhorted them to join the battle and they readily followed him.[110]

The author has graphically described the battle of Siritaur
or Haldi. It is clear that in those days sometimes the result of
a war was by mutual agreement decided by individual combat
among leading members of the two sides. Here the Raja of Haldi
managed to overcome Shiv Ram, a cousin of Kunwar Dhir, sent
to fight him. Five peasants also joined the battle. Dheka Rawat
(by caste Kurmi Jaiswar) was also a participant.[111]

Indeed the account is valuable as it shows intense intercommunity rivalry, which often resulted in war and violence.
Across the Ganga River Kunwar Dhir raided parts of Saran as
well. On the borders of Shahabad he occupied parts of Gaya. The
Mughal ruler Aurangzeb knew Kunwar Dhir's reputation as a
turbulent element. The author quotes a *firman* from Aurangzeb
in which he asked Kunwar Dhir to rectify his conduct since 'his
impudence and behaviour was inconveniencing a lot of people.
If he did not heed Emperor's orders he should be prepared
for a fight with the imperial army.' Kunwar Dhir accepted the
sovereignty of the Mughal ruler but told him that 'the masses
were fed up with his religious fanaticism'.[112]

Finally, the Mughal authorities in Bihar in AD 1712 were
directed to suppress Kunwar Dhir. They managed to win over
Kunwar Dhir's nephew Udwant Singh to their side. Kunwar
Dhir was seventy-seven years old and was ailing. When he
received the news he organized his army and tried to give battle
to invading forces. He was unable to properly assess the strength
of the invading forces. As soon as he emerged on the battlefield
he fell and died. This demoralized his army and the invaders
were victorious without a fight. Udwant Singh captured his
magazine and the *parganas* of Piro and Nanaur.[113]

Kunwar Dhir's family ended when his son Sudhist Narayan
Singh died in 1719 after a paralytic attack. Sudhist was childless.[114]

Munshi Binayak Prasad presents the most comprehensive
and coherent account of Kunwar Dhir, a household name
among the Ujjainias.

The author devotes a chapter to a description of the House
of Jagdishpur. Students of history will find it instructive; this

was the House which produced Kunwar Singh in the nineteenth century, undoubtedly the most widely known name amongst the Ujjainias.

THE HOUSE OF JAGDISHPUR

Sujan Sahi the son of Prabal Sahi Singh (who had accepted Islam and was the brother of Raja Rudra Singh) took up residence in Jagdishpur in AD 1702.[115] He settled new areas around Jagdishpur. Rai Purandar who was the *tahsildar* of Rudra Singh left Mathila because of some differences with the ruler and settled down in Jagdishpur. Sujan Sahi lost his life when a fight broke out between him and the retainers of the Governor of Bihar. He had three sons Udwant Singh, Baudh or Budh Singh and Shubh Singh. All the three were well trained in the use of arms, horse riding and archery.

Udwant Singh became the chief at Jagdishpur after the death of his father Sujan Sahi in 1701.[116] He invited all Ujjainias to Jagdishpur and held a public function to commemorate the occasion.

From the very beginning he liked war. At the age of seventeen he invaded the village of Kunwar Dhir.

In 1723, the Governor of Bihar Fakhrauddaula attacked Jagdishpur. Udwant Singh defeated him.[117] The victory made Udwant Singh more daring. He decided to play an active role in the affairs of the Ujjainias and regional politics. He began organizing them under his own banner. He seems to have persuaded the Ujjainias to start eating pork. The idea was to prevent them from converting to Islam. This became important for him because one of his military officers Naubat Singh had converted to Islam. There was the example of his own grandfather. The Ujjainias also remembered the conversion of Prabal Singh. He argued that pork-eating Ujjainias would not be acceptable to Muslims as co-religionists. The Muslims when they came to know about pork eating habit of Ujjainias also stopped converting them.[118] Since he was always waging wars or starting fights, he was afraid of attacks by his enemies. To forestall them he stationed his forces at three places.

When the Afghan Mustafa Khan fought against Haibat Jang, Udwant Singh sided with Mustafa Khan. Haibat Jang was forced to retire and Mustafa Khan was killed. A separate chapter (4th chapter) is devoted to this battle.[119] Sardar Singh Marhatta was an important ally in this battle. Another participant from the side of Udwant Singh was Gorwar Rawat (by caste Kharwar). He killed Jan Baksh Khan, a Mughal commander. His brother Budh Singh killed another Mughal commander Izzat Baksh Khan. The death of two commanders disheartened the Mughal army, which left the field. Udwant Singh knew well that he had won a battle. The realist in him could not expect win the war against the Imperial Mughals. So after a week or so, he went to Azimabad. After worshipping Patan Devi (the guardian goddess of Patna) he presented himself at the court of Fakhrauddaula, the Governor of Bihar. He apologized for his behaviour and accepted the sovereignty of the Nawab. He agreed to come to his help with his contingent whenever required. The Nawab formally accepted his apologies and as a mark of his forgiveness gave him a *khillat*. [120]

In conformity with the ethos of the age, Udwant Singh extended patronage to scholars. In his court three books were compiled and each author was rewarded by the grant of a *jagir*. Among the books was *Udwant Prakash*, read by Ujjainias with great interest.[121]

Udwant Singh died in 1765 at the age of seventy. He was succeeded by his eldest son Gajraj Singh who, like his father, refused to share the inherited property with his other brothers.[122] It is said that one of his brothers Umrao Singh sought the help of Faizullah Khan, son of Abdullah Khan, the Nawab of Ghazipur against Gajraj Singh. The army of the Nawab of Ghazipur invaded his territories. Gajraj Singh made peace with his brothers and divided the property. The invaders withdrew. When Dumraon was invaded by an army of the Muslims he went to the support of the chief of Dumraon. He established a market known as Gajrajganj in the vicinity of Karisath. He had studied Persian. In an aside the author gives information about Kayasthas settled in the region.

The internecine wars among the Ujjainias and their wars with the forces of the Nawab of Bengal and Bihar ended when the English rule was firmly established in the region after the battle of Buxar in 1764.

The zamindars no longer took recourse to war either to settle a dispute or to satisfy a whim. Instead, they went to a law-court and instituted a suit for the redressal of their grievances. This altered the life-style of the zamindars.

Property rights were now won in law courts and not on battle fields. Sahebzada Singh staked his claim over the zamindari of Jagdishpur but lacked financial resources to fight a long legal battle. To secure money, he married his two sons Kunwar Singh and Dayal Singh to the two daughters of Fateh Narain Singh, the holder of the zamindari of Dev Moga. Fateh Narain signed an agreement according to which he consented to meet all the expenses of the law suit. Sahebzada Singh was going to file a case against the zamindar of Jagdishpur, Babu Ishri Prasad. The mediator was Nagachand Chikandoz of Azimabad. Nagachand may have been a cloth merchant: it shows again that zamindars in those days accepted non-Ujjainias as advisers.

Eventually Sahebzada Singh won the legal battle and became the head of the Jagdishpur estate. His victory was contested. Tej Bahadur Singh claimed a part of the property and on refusal of Sahebzada Singh instituted a lawsuit. Ultimately the judgement was pronounced in favour of Sahebzada Singh.[123]

Litigation became endemic in the society and especially in the life of zamindars. As the new system of justice unfolded itself, people realized it was not an unmixed blessing.

Even in the early days of the institution of British system of justice, litigation was a harassment. The author points out that Sahebzada Singh because of lack of money was forced to walk to the law court in Patna when Ishri Prasad Singh instituted a case against him. The author informs us that once Sahebzada Singh became angry when there was a hot exchange of words between the *mukhtar* representing the opposite side and the clerk of the presiding judge. Sahebzada Singh took out his sword and attacked the *mukhtar*.[124] Fortunately the *mukhtar* escaped death but Sahebzada Singh was arrested and sentenced to jail for six months. After he had spent three months in jail, he heard that a tiger had entered the forests around Bankipur (modern Patna). He expressed his desire to kill the tiger by his sword. He was permitted to do so. He proceeded to the forest accompanied by a number of Europeans. The tiger was sleeping. Sahebzada Singh shouted; on hearing the noise the tiger sprang on him. Sahebzada Singh dexterously avoided him and cut his waist by his sword. The tiger fell down half dead; the Europeans praised his bravery. On their recommendation, the remaining period of imprisonment was suspended and a certificate of bravery was issued to him.[125]

The story brings out the fact that at the turn of the nineteenth century Patna still had a forest cover where ferocious animals roamed.[126]

In the time of Sahebzada Singh, the Pathans dominated the administration of Jagdishpur.[127] His eldest son Kunwar Singh resented this. Kunwar Singh's younger brother Dayal Singh, however, was very obedient to his father. Sahebzada Singh made him the chief administrator of the Estate.

Sahebzada Singh was an eccentric. It is said that he bathed only thrice; first, when he was born, second when he was to get married and third when he was dead. The author sarcastically remarks only two of his wishes were fulfilled in his lifetime![128]

His other eccentricities were: every night he was massaged by mustard oil with a pot with burning fire wood placed in front of him; even in summer he would sit in the sun till 10 or 11 in the morning and no one was permitted to leave the place without his orders! Some English officials believed that he was mad.

The financial affairs of Estate were mismanaged. Often he would not deposit the government share of revenue in the treasury. If anyone spoke to him about this state of affairs, he would be sharply rebuked. Once he was told that Rs. 10,000 had not been deposited in the treasury. He found out who was the person concerned in the treasury.[129] While the employee was walking back to his house, Sahebzada Singh caught him and did not let him go till he agreed to write that there were no dues against him. He rewarded him with 10 *bighas* of fertile land. The author remarks that an orchard could still be seen on this piece of land.

ACTIVITIES OF KUNWAR SINGH

Sahebzada Singh never enjoyed good relationship with his eldest son and successor Kunwar Singh, who would loot the revenue being carried to Jagdishpur. Once Sahebzada Singh was so annoyed that he pursued Kunwar Singh and his group for 3 miles. A fight ensued in which some followers of Kunwar Singh were killed.

Kunwar Singh was unhappy at the extravagance of his father and filed a petition against him in the court. The Judge then called both, father and son to his chamber and succeeded in patching up their dispute.[130]

Sahebzada Singh, through a registered Will had divided the property among his four sons. Kunwar Singh was given 75 per cent of the property. The zamindari inherited by Kunwar Singh was worth Rs. 6 lakh out of which he was required to pay to the government Rs. 1,66,000.[131] But Kunwar Singh did not respect his father's wishes. He confiscated the lands granted in favour of his brothers by his father. As a result there was a prolonged litigation among the brothers. The court at Calcutta decided the matter. According to the court's order Kunwar Singh was entitled to all the property held in the name of the late Sahebzada Singh but his brothers must also be given sufficient property for their maintenance; the revenue collection was to be deposited in the Government treasury.

How costly litigation was can be inferred from the data furnished by the author. Kunwar Singh had spent Rs. 8 lakh; his brothers had spent Rs. 5 lakh. By all accounts a huge sum of money![132] British justice was expensive.

Kunwar Singh could be profligate. To celebrate his victory he granted land to his lawyer in Arrah which yielded an income of Rs. 50 per month. He distributed 1,000 necklaces and pashmina dresses to dancing girls.[133]

Kunwar Singh also spent lavishly on constructing fortresses, gardens, ponds, temples, etc. The marriage of his grandson Harbhajan Singh was an occasion when excessive expense was incurred.

The author gives a graphic description of the marriage procession, which went from Jagdishpur to the estate of Gidhaur near Munger. Since it was summer time the procession would start at eight in the night and stop at seven in the morning. It consisted of eight thousand men and had a moving market where shopkeepers sold groceries. It also included ten *hakims* and twenty-five *vaidyas.* There were one hundred servants. The marriage procession returned from Gidhaur in twenty-five days. The author admits that at several places, the members of the procession indulged in looting. An advance party would ensure that wild animals were not lurking in the way. Two parties were held: one at Patna and the other at Arrah. The English officials were invitees to these parties.

In the marriage procession no brother of Kunwar Singh participated. Even the father of the bridegroom did not go. This shows how strained Kunwar Singh's relations were with his family members.[134]

Kunwar Singh could not create an efficient machinery for the collection of land revenue. As a result government dues were always in arrear. The estate was saddled with debt. The author says that Kunwar Singh never went to law court for recovering his dues from any tenant. When he needed money, he plundered the tenants. No one ventured to lodge a complaint or institute a case against him with the local police.[135]

Despite his faults, Kunwar Singh's character had some traits which endeared him to the people.

Kunwar Singh built a market place Mahadeva Bazar in Arrah, later known as Babu Bazar.[136]

Kunwar Singh spent a lot of money on constructing bunds in villages of Nagar and Angara. They helped to irrigate an area of '5 *cos* around'.

Kunwar Singh was also conscious about providing forest cover. He tried to protect the forests and planted a lot of trees in the forest around Jagdishpur. He beautified Jagdishpur. He constructed 'twelve ponds, fifty pukka wells, four canals and a bund around the perimeter of the town'. He built two additional markets and started two fairs on the occasion of Sivaratri (an important festival of the Hindus). He 'prohibited traders from going to Brahmapur fair', the traditional fair in the area.[137]

As a result of arbitrary behaviour of Kunwar Singh, his mother and brothers left Jagdishpur and settled down in Dilippur. As soon as the brothers quit Jagdishpur, Kunwar Singh had their houses razed to the ground. He ordered a pond to be dug on the spot! As a result when Kunwar Singh's mother died at Dilippur, all the four brothers performed her *shradh* separately. Kunwar Singh confiscated the property and villages granted to his deceased mother for maintenance.[138]

All the brothers, unmindful of the humiliations heaped upon them, observed the traditional etiquettes prescribed in the Estate of Jagdishpur. They offered the required courtesies to Kunwar Singh on meeting; Kunwar Singh continued to be 'cruel' to them.[139]

The detailed portrayal of Kunwar Singh helps a reader to understand how much self-willed and authoritarian a zamindar could be even though the English East India Company had introduced the rule of law. Sustained development and progress was hardly on their agenda.

Politics in such an environment could not but be a pursuit of self-aggrandisement and ego clashes. Alliances even based on commonality of caste would be fragile. This comes out clearly when Munshi Binayak Prasad traces the relationship between two prominent Ujjainia houses, i.e. of Dumraon and Jagdishpur.

We have a detailed account of the manner in which the rift between Dumraon and Jagdishpur became formalized.

Munshi Binayak Prasad also traces the different branches

into which the family of Udwant Singh (founder of the House of Jagdishpur) split up. Many contemporary Ujjainia Rajput families would certainly discover their roots.

A chapter is devoted to the House of Buxar as well. We have the story how the Estate came into possession of Budh Singh who was denied his share in family property by his brother Udwant Singh.[140]

Budh Singh like other Ujjainia chiefs of the day spent lavishly on the occasion of the marriage of his granddaughter. The bridegroom was the son of Pirthipant Shah, the Raja of Pratapgarh who was a great favourite of the Nawab of Oudh. The Nawab of Oudh had undertaken to meet the expenses of the marriage party and permitted his grandees to travel to Buxar in the marriage procession. It is said the Nawab also came to Buxar in disguise.[141] A stray piece of information but quite significant. Alliance between Hindu and Muslim ruling elites would be so intense that one would incur the marriage expenses in the family of the other.

The Estate of Buxar came under heavy debt and a legal battle ensued between the Estate and the lender. The exchequer became bankrupt and the Maharaja of Dumraon had to meet the expenses of the House of Buxar.

Finally, the author describes the events of 1857 in which Kunwar Singh, the Head of the House of Jagdishpur played a major role. His bravery and determination to oust the British from India made him an unforgettable hero of Indian freedom struggle. The story is well known, thanks to a full-length work on the life of Kunwar Singh by Professor K.K. Datta.[142]

The third volume was completed on 15 January 1899.[143]

THE SECOND HALF OF THE 19TH CENTURY

The Indian uprising of 1857 in which Shahabad under the leadership of Kunwar Singh played a leading role serves a proper milestone to end the third volume. The post-1857 period was an era of restructuring and rethinking on the part of the colonial power as well as the ruling Indian elite. The foreign as well as the indigenous powers felt the urgency of the need to modernize and transform the existing socio-economic system though their motives were contradictory.

The fourth and the final volume takes up this theme and discusses the role the Estate of Dumraon played in it. The author employs the method of explicating history through a biographical study of leading personalities. The influence of Perso-Urdu historiography is also visible; a section specifically describes the administrative structure of the Estate.

The final volume has three parts: the first is devoted to the period of Radha Prasad Singh, who was knighted by the British Government.

The second part details the administrative structure of the Dumraon Raj. After the event of 1857, the House of Jagdishpur had ceased to exist and the Estate of Dumraon was the sole representative of the Ujjainias. We discover here shades of Abul Fazl, who at the end of *Akbarnamah* where he details the political history of the Mughals appended *Ain-i-Akbari*, a treatise on administrative structure.

No other historical work has so meticulously described the administrative structure of a big zamindari. It is interesting to learn that continuous innovations were being made. A printing press under the Raj was opened so that forms relating to administrative matters could be printed. Since several parts of the estate were far away from Dumraon, a system for receiving and sending communications from and to these from the headquarters was developed. In other words, a parallel postal system to that introduced by the English was put in place for administrative convenience.

Radha Prasad was elevated to the chieftainship of Dumraon after Maheshwar Baksh Singh decided to relinquish it and lead a life of religious contemplation. He had groomed Radha Prasad well for the job and taken care to educate him through private tutors.

He was taught Persian and English by separate teachers[144] and had been trained in the use of weapons by his uncle

Parmeshwar Baksh Singh. Besides he had been taught music and religious matters. He was by all standards a well-educated and liberal gentleman.[145]

From the age of sixteen he was inducted into administration and during the upsurge of 1857 he regularly informed the Company's authorities about the situation in Shahabad. The British officials advised him to remain loyal.[146] He cultivated contacts with the British authorities. The author tells us that Radha Prasad Singh unfailingly paid his respects to the Governor-General in person whenever the latter stayed at Sasaram during his journeys after 1859.

It may not be off the mark to speculate that these frequent contacts with the high colonial functionaries convinced him about the usefulness of the various elements of modern civilization and persuaded him to put them into practice in his estate.

The rapport thus established helped him to keep the British authorities in good humour and at the same time he was able to analyse and understand the causes that had contributed to British success and prosperity and the creation of a worldwide empire. When he assumed the reins of power he was already determined to turn a new leaf in the history of the estate by introducing measures, leading to harmonous relations with the British government, economic prosperity of the masses and modernization of Dumraon.

The government also appreciated the attitude of Radha Prasad Singh; as a mark of appreciation it conferred upon him the title of Raja during the life-time of Maheshwar Baksh Singh in 1875.[147] Sir Richard Temple, the Lt. Governor of Bengal personally came down to Dumraon and honoured him with this title in a *darbar*, attended by all the leading zamindars of Bengal and Bihar.

It is against this background that we can understand the policies which he adopted after he was installed as a ruler on 1 January 1869 for the socio-economic and cultural uplift of his Estate. With Radha Prasad Singh the Estate commenced its journey on the road to modernization. He knew that the first step should be the introduction of a secular and scientific system of education.

The Estate established a school where English was taught and in 1882 its headmaster, Prayag Singh was a graduate.[148] The school was developed into an Intermediate College. The Estate also awarded scholarships to students who went to Calcutta to study medicine and engineering. The school produced English-educated young men who were expected to man the administrative posts in the Estate and also to go for higher studies in modern subjects. The forward-looking policies of the ruler nurtured the school.

Radha Prasad Singh reorganized the administrative structure by instituting a stratified bureaucracy where the lower functionary was responsible to the next higher authority; the chief *diwan* or manager exercised overall supervision.

Of course what he could not curb was ostentatious extravagance. For example, the festivities associated with his installation ceremony continued for one week.[149]

When the Lt. Governor of Bengal Sir Ashley Eden decided to confer upon him the title of Maharaja Bahadur at Dumraon personally, the festivities continued for three days, from 7 to 10 February 1882. On 7 February horse-racing was organized in the afternoon and a Ball Dance was held in the evening. On 8 February Lt. Governor held the *darbar* where he read out the communication concerning the decision of the government to confer the title of Raja on Radha Prasad Singh.

All the Englishmen were invited to a special party. The evening closed with a display of fire-works. On 9 February a deer hunt was organized in the forests of Dumraon from 11 a.m. onwards. In the afternoon the distinguished guests were treated to a spectacle of horseracing. The palace in the evening was lighted and decorated with electric bulbs for welcoming the Lt. Governor. Dumraon must be one of the earliest places where electricity was used for lighting purposes in Bihar. In the evening a Ball Dance was held for the entertainment of the English and a drama was staged for the local crowd.[150]

The guests and visitors (Hindus, Muslims and Europeans) invited for the occasion stayed in special tents (fully furnished) put up for the purpose. The list of guests includes all important officials and non-officials in Bihar (including Bengal) and Uttar Pradesh. A cross-section of the Press headed by Bhartendu Harishchandra was also present. Media representatives were Munshi Newal Kishore of Lucknow, Munshi Diwan Chand (ed. *Rifai-i-Am*), Munshi Sirajuddin Ahmad Khan (ed. *Waqai-i-Alam*, Ghazipur), Pandit Chintasmani Ray (ed. *Kavi Vachan Sudha*, Benares) and editors of *Pioneer* and *Amrita Bazar Patrika*. The cost of ceremony was Rs. 4 lakh.[151]

Another example of lavish expenditure was the marriage ceremony of the daughter of the Maharaja to a scion of the royal house of Rewa in February 1892. The Estate spent approximately Rs. 7 lakh on this occasion.[152]

The chapter is revealing for it turns out that these marriage alliances needed the approval of the British government. In this case the British Political Agent to Rewa state to which the bridegroom belonged was all long consulted. When the marriage ceremony was completed at Dumraon, the Political Agent opined that the bridegroom was still a minor and a student. The bride should not accompany him, as it would interfere with his studies. He suggested that the bride should come to Rewa after a year and a detailed plan was drawn about the ceremonies connected with the departure of the bride in February 1893.[153]

This is an indication of the nature of power, enjoyed by British Residents.

The ceremonies would start with the arrival of Maharaja Rewa on 10 February and would continue up to 15 February although the bridegroom, Maharaja of Rewa would leave with his wife by a special train on 14 February.[154]

The advance planning included a description of entertainment to be organized for the guests.

The entertainment on this occasion consisted of the following: horse-racing, wrestling, sword-playing and tennis competition (which would continue from 11 to 14 February), opening of an agricultural exhibition with a special section for animals, Ball Dance by the English, a show of magic and a flower show. After the bride had left, prizes would be distributed on 15 February. The function would conclude with a Ball Dance for the English guests in the evening of 15 February.[155]

It is clear that the game of tennis had come to Dumraon by now and the festivities were aimed at catering to the taste of the guests as well as the common man in Dumraon.

These extravagances apart, the Estate remained committed to the economic well being of its tenants. The economic policies of Radha Prasad Singh were in tandem with the economic policies of the government of India, i.e. to promote the commercialization of agriculture and insulate it against the vagaries of monsoons by providing facilities for artificial irrigation.

In 1884 the Maharaja happened to visit an exhibition organized at Calcutta. Many exhibits had been sent to Calcutta from the Estate. He organized an agricultural exhibition in Dumraon in 1885 with the help of English officials in which thirty-six exhibits concerning agricultural operations, productivity and its allied crafts were shown.[156]

The exhibition ran for five days and cost the Estate approximately Rs. 20,000. The Commissioner of Patna Division Mr. Halliday opened it. In the welcome speech the Maharaja underlined the fact that in the modern context development was possible on the basis of prosperity of agriculture. The idea was to create awareness among the peasantry about proper time for sowing seeds and about irrigating the field. This would result in less investment and more production. There was a counter where doubts and queries of peasants were satisfied.

Mr. Halliday advised the Estate to continue this good work and exhorted other zamindars to follow the example.[157]

The exhibits included improved plough, British machines being used in agricultural operations, different varieties of grains, animals used in agricultural operations, improved breeds of cows and buffaloes, etc. The cow shown in the exhibition produced 10 litres of milk in one milking. An implement for refining sugar was also shown.[158]

Mr. Thomson, the Lt. Governor of Bengal came to open the third exhibition in 1887. The Dumraon Municipality accorded a reception to him and the welcome address requested him to pay more attention towards the growth of technical education and female education. It is clear that people were becoming conscious of the need for social development in which education had to play a decisive role.

There were around 150 guests, most of them were Europeans. Some of the guests were Mr. A.B. Pana, Mr. W. Barlow, Lt. Col. Neal, Mr. J. Bose, Mr. S.S. Hussain and A.C. Sen (Burdwan). The Great Eastern Hotel of Calcutta looked after catering.

The formal opening of the Exhibition took place at 3 p.m. Jai Prakash Lal read a written speech in which he stressed the fact that agricultural production had improved with the extension of canals, roads, and railways. He also assured the Lt. Governor that they would try to promote female education in cooperation with government officials.[159]

Subsequently we learn that the Estate had opened an Agricultural Department, established a Demonstration Farm as well as an Economic Museum. The Farm demonstrated to the peasants the use of latest agricultural techniques. This showed the great concern the Maharaja had for the economic development and economic prosperity of the residents of Dumraon Estate. In fact, with a view to ensure economic well being of the people of Dumraon, the Maharaja had acquired 15,000 acres of land in Myanmar (then Burma) and was keen that people of Shahabad went there and earned a living for themselves. The Estate spent Rs. 25,000 annually.[160]

It was estimated that such visits by high government officials cost the exchequer between Rs. 30,000 and 40,000. It was therefore decided to shift the venue of the Exhibition to Brahmapur where a fair was traditionally held during the Shivaratri festival. Hence the exhibition in 1888 was held at Brahmapur.

The rulers believed that the basis of economic prosperity was increase in the agricultural productivity.

Hence, when in 1870s the British government mooted the

construction of the Sone canal to provide irrigational facilities in Shahabad district, the Estate provided the required land either free or at a nominal rate to the British government. For example, the alienated land was worth Rs. 4 lakh at market price but the Maharaja charged only Rs. 1 lakh. The canals were constructed in 1879.[161]

The Sone canal was conceived as a part of ameliorative measure the British adopted when general famines struck most of British India during 1866-70 and caused an estimated 1.4 million deaths.[162] The Sone Canal Irrigation Project became fully operational in the year 1876-7 though water was also supplied from the canals while they were under construction during drought in 1873-4. The navigational use of canals started in 1876 and the Arrah canal was opened for navigation in September 1876 and the Buxar canal in 1880.

As a result the district escaped the ravages of subsequent famines, which repeatedly affected other parts in north Bihar. In pursuit of the policy for providing irrigation facilities to the peasants, the estate in 1881 give a large chunk of land to the British government for constructing a bund over the river.[163]

In 1873 and 1874 famines devastated Bihar. Radha Prasad Singh instituted prompt relief measures to alleviate the sufferings of the people. Charitable kitchens were opened at several places where free food was provided. The produce of fields at Pamper, measuring 2,000 *bighas* was distributed among the poor. Land revenue worth Rs. 3 lakh was excused. Tax collectors were asked to be lenient while collecting land revenue. The Estate also distributed cash among the needy. Public work was started to provide purchasing power to the distressed. Wages were paid both in cash and food grains. All these measures won the appreciation of the Bengal government, which expressed its gratitude in its letter dated 24 April 1874.[164]

All the Lt. Governors of Bengal commended the progressive socio-economic policies of the Maharaja.

The most interesting piece of information that emerges is that the Maharaja had opened a school for girls in 1882. In August 1887 Lady Bailey visited Dumraon along with her husband Stuart

Bailey. She was requested to lay the foundation stone of the building of the Girls' school where 200 students were currently studying. The girls came from both Hindu and Muslim families. The Hindu girls belonged to Brahmin, Kayastha, Vaishya castes, etc. After laying the foundation-stone of the new building amidst great fan-fare, Lady Bailey asked some girls to read from a book. The girls read the passage successfully. Lady Bailey was immensely pleased.[165] The Estate spent money for the good of the public. In February 1887, Queen Victoria completed twenty-five years of her accession to the throne. The silver jubilee of this event was enthusiastically celebrated in Dumraon. A public meeting was held to commemorate the occasion. The Maharaja ordered the construction of a Dharamshala. He also contributed Rs. 10,000 for the establishment of a hospital in Balia.[166]

He had already established a public hospital in Dumraon in 1871. Qualified doctors and para-medical staff were appointed and the Estate spent Rs. 4,000 on maintaining it.

Another example of his public charity was a donation of Rs. 10,000 to the Zoological Garden at Calcutta. He also sent there a number of rare birds and animals.[167]

In the interest of public good, the Estate gave land to the government gratis to establish police outposts, thanas (police-stations) and post-offices.

As the nineteenth century progressed the Estate upgraded its bureaucratic structure; they knew that running the Estate was a matter of management; violence and terror would not ensure inflow of revenue to the Estate's treasury. In course of time the Estate administrative apparatus emerged as a mini replica of the government's administrative system.

The administration was divided into different departments, each specifically dealing with a particular subject. The department was manned by officials arranged in the hierarchic order with a clear order of precedence. The work procedure was well defined. Orders were written and obtained in writing and files were maintained for each case. This meant that literate persons were employed except for the menial posts. At the head of the administration stood the *diwan*, who was answerable to the Estate's proprietor. The changeover to modern system of management brought in stability and prosperity to the Estate.

Subsequently, the author writes a detailed note on the administrative structure of the Estate and the functions performed by each department. To my knowledge, we do not have any contemporarily account giving a graphic picture of the administrative system of the Estate.[168]

There was a Survey Office that prepared maps of villages and agricultural land by using three methods, Prismatic Compass, Plane Table and Theodolite. The department employed surveyors and draftsmen.

The Estate had established its own Press where Estate stationery was printed. Of course an elaborate arrangement was made to collect taxes, to grant land to different tenants and to give contract for the collection of land revenue of certain portions.[169]

A special building housed the office of the *diwan*, office of the members of the council, correspondence department (again divided into English and Persian). The department of English correspondence had chairs and tables and was provided with a telephone as well. The department of Persian correspondence was furnished with carpets and the staff sat on the floor.

The literate personnel in the administration mostly belonged to the Kayastha caste among the Hindus. The author has advanced an interesting reason for this. He says that the Kayasthas had come along with the ancestors of Ujjainias from Malwa (in central India); the Ujjainias and the Kayasthas were closely allied. For this reason since then seven Kayastha families had provided the key personnel of the administration such as *diwans* and managers of the Estate.[170]

We have another instance of modern element in the system of administration. The Estate had decided that an employee would superannuate on attaining the age of fifty-five. Earlier there was no such restriction; the employees served at the pleasure of the Maharaja. Now the retired employees were entitled to pension as well.[171]

The secular and non-sectarian and pro-people nature of the administration was underlined by the tasks to be performed by the Charity Department, functioning since the time of Maharaja Jai Prakash Singh. This department helped poor and needy students, widows, met marriage expenses of girls whose parents were short of money, helped religious personalities who visited Dumraon irrespective of their religion, helped people by donation when they constructed religious buildings, subsidized persons who were proceeding to Mecca for performing the Hajj, etc.[172] The pro-people administration of the Estate took care of the spiritual needs of the people as well.

Finally, we have a list of courtiers who were normally summoned for consultation on important matters of the Estate. We learn of the etiquette, prescribed for the occasion.[173]

URBANIZATION OF DUMRAON

A valuable part of the book is the description of Dumraon through which we can track the process of urbanization that was taking place there.

The author begins by giving a description of the geographical boundaries of Dumraon. He distinguishes between the land surrounding the town, mostly used for agricultural purposes and the land where most of the residents resided. According to the Census Report of 1891 its population was 18,384 of which Muslims numbered 3,384. Earlier there were 16 mohallas in the town but they now numbered 49. We have a detailed description of the various mohallas.[174]

People with special skills and expertise resided in these mohallas. They were needed to render various services to the different segments of the population. It was a mixed population, staying in close physical proximity and engaged in mostly non-agricultural pursuits for a living.

The author has also described the residential areas occupied by the ruling family. Afghan guards were posted at the main gate of the palace. There were three clocks, water clock, sand clock and a clock of *ashta dhatu*. When one-hour was completed the person appointed to look after it (*ghanta pande*) sounded this watch.[175]

This description is also valuable as we get a peep in the urban architecture. The author writes about the buildings inside the fort where the Maharaja lived; he mentions the uses of the building. He has noted how things inside the palace were managed.[176]

Finally all the major temples in Dumraon have been mentioned along with the important festivities associated with them.[177]

MAHARANI BENI PRASAD KUNWARJI

The concluding part of the work is a note on the Estate under the stewardship of Maharani Beni Prasad Kunwarji, the wife and the successor of deceased Radha Prasad Singh. She assumed control after the death of her husband on 5 May 1894. Her accession was symbolic of the times. Earlier when the chief died without leaving a direct male heir, the widow would play a decisive role in choosing the successor. Now the widow herself assumed power. There might have been murmurings but there was no overt opposition and the British government also immediately extended its recognition. She was anointed on 24 May 1894.[178]

Differences developed between the new chief the Maharani Sahiba and the *diwan*. But the matter was sorted out.[179] When the *diwan* died on 7 February 1897 he was replaced by Charles Fox who had also earlier served the Estate as its manager.

Maharani celebrated the Diamond Jubilee of the coronation of Queen Victoria with great pomp in order to show her loyalty to the colonial power, the upholder of the zamindari system. A public meeting was held and a report was sent to the Governor-General. She led a special prayer for the Queen's well being inside the temple. She also gave a feast to 600 Brahmins; the poor and needy were fed.[180] In the evening Englishmen were given a dinner party and after its conclusion there was a display of fire-works.

On the occasion the Maharani laid the foundation stone of a veterinary hospital and arranged for meeting its expenses from the Estate exchequer.

The tradition of following a pro-people policy continued.

It was clear that the liberal outlook of the late Radha Prasad Singh was missing in the Maharani. Under the former ruler, the Estate had consciously opened up and developed contacts with the outside world; it had integrated new concepts and ideas into the polity. The Maharani was insular. This is evident from the measures she adopted in the name of economy.

A bungalow had been rented at Calcutta at Rs. 150 per month. This was given up. In Dumraon a Guest House was constructed for accommodating European guests. The Estate spent Rs. 25,000 annually on its maintenance. The Guest House was closed. The Estate subscribed to a number of Hindi, Urdu, Bengali and English newspapers and journals. The list was drastically curtailed. The telephone was also disconnected.[181]

The practice of the Estate to provide relief measures for the people in distress was continued. When a famine visited in 1897 relief operations were promptly set in motion. The needy and the widows were given money and food grains. A special cell was created for this purpose.[182]

The author describes the full solar eclipse of 25 January 1895. Lord Elgin, the Viceroy and Governor-General of India came to Buxar to see it. The eclipse started at 12.05 hours and ended at 15 hours. Scientists and photographers had assembled besides a host of other persons. Owing to complete solar eclipse, there was a complete darkness and a lamp was lighted where the Viceroy was staying.[183]

On 24 January the Lt. Governor of Bengal came to visit Dumraon. He inspected the hospital and the school.

Towards the end of the work, the author has described religious festivals organized by the Estate throughout the year.

Finally the author speaks of torrential rains which hit Dumraon on 24 July 1899. Many houses collapsed and a bridge over the river was also destroyed.

The fourth volume was completed on 9 February 1905.[184]

CONCLUSION

The work indeed is massive. It is not surprising, it took around two decades to write it. Being an untrained historian, the author suffered from certain constraints, which he could not overcome. By and large, the author has not cared to collate the data he had collected from other sources. In light of recent researches on the history of Bihar in the seventeenth and eighteenth centuries, it seems some of the facts adduced by him regarding political history, need further collaboration.

Normally the author does not pass an ethical judgement. But when once in a while he does so, he is very penetrating. After describing the treacherous murder of Raja Rudra Pratap Singh by Kunwar Dhir, he comments, 'One should not let his guard down and be mislead by the flatteries of enemies; one should never consider an enemy as a friend.'[185]

In terms of style it has to be admitted the work is not very readable. The author has laced his work with Persian and Arabic words liberally. He has also used Sanskrit words without any indication with the result that the reader is often bewildered about what the author wants to convey.

The style is very dense, the author has a penchant of using very long sentences and therefore, one is left to his own devices to find out its meaning or to make a sense out of it. This has prevented the work from getting the popularity, which *Riaz-i-Tirhut* enjoyed during the nineteenth century. Though it might also be true that by the time the work was published, Urdu language was no longer the language of the literati who had shifted to English. As a result of Hindi *vs* Urdu controversy in the late nineteenth century, Hindus were turning to Hindi and were ordinarily not interested in reading a voluminous work in Urdu.

Besides, the work was constrained by its narrow focus: it was the history of a community and not even the whole of the region. Developments in the region receive attention insofar as they throw light on the history of the community. Hence, the author allows many important events to let pass by without even throwing a hint. For example, it was a period of enlightenment in Shahabad and the Dumraon Estate contributed significantly towards this. But the author is unable to appreciate this fall out. Sachchidanand Sinha, a Bhojpuri and the first Bihari Hindu to go to England to study law in the late nineteenth century is not named even once. The author does not tell us the names of the students from Dumraon who had gone to Calcutta to study medicine and engineering and we cannot state who was the first full-fledged doctor and fully qualified engineer from this district.

Radha Prasad Singh was particularly keen to usher in modernity in Dumraon and like all liberal chiefs acted as patrons to scholars and social reformers. The author has skipped this aspect. Siva Nath Sastri, the famous Brahmo leader writes in his autobiography that he had stayed for a month at Dumraon at the invitation of the chief and had completed one of his novels there. The author ignores this important fact.

Some of the neighbouring zamindars in the time of Radha Prasad Singh like the zamindar of Surajpura were equally influenced by the new wave of Enlightenment. Raja Rajeshwari Prasad Singh, the zamindar of Surajpura had invited Rabindranath Tagore to his place. Unfortunately this vital piece of information is not mentioned in the voluminous history.

He is extremely brief about the period of Maharani under whom he completed this history. He simply chronicles the events and history here is reduced to just a chronology of dates and events.

Despite some of the shortcomings mentioned above, the significance of the work cannot be minimized. It ranks among the few histories of any community in any language written on the basis of contemporary documents. By quoting several documents in original he has saved them for use by future generation of historians who might someday get interested in micro-history.

The book is also important because it suggests that even small chieftains could survive the onslaughts of the mighty Mughal Empire if they followed a correct mix of policy of competition, conflict and collaboration and use each of the elements at the proper time and place. Of course, such a course of action would also require wide community support.

Credit must be given to the Ujjainia chiefs that they were able to win over non-Ujjainias, both Hindu and Muslim by their economic and social policies. The Ujjainia chiefs consciously promoted agriculture; for the purpose, they cleared forests, settled people to cultivate these lands. They provided agricultural facilities by constructing irrigation channels, ponds, wells, etc. Malik has also noted this trait of the Ujjania chiefs. Referring to the seventeenth century, he asserts,

Narain Mal, like his predecessors, took keen interest in the development of his holdings and welfare of the tenants. More and more lands were brought under tillage, the yield increased, population became large and dense, raising the *hal-i-hasil* (actual proceeds) to Rs. 14,71,000. Nevertheless, the rent was assessed at the same old rate, i.e. Rs. 5 lakh.[186]

The surplus of more than Rs. 9 lakh throughout the seventeenth century enabled the Ujjainia chief to raise a loyal armed contingent, to be used for maintaining law and order within the territory under his jurisdiction and also to defy the Mughal authorities, if need be.

The Ujjainia chiefs consciously tried to promote agriculture even in the eighteenth century when colonial rule of the British replaced that of the Mughals. Malik advances additional reason for this.

After the British take over the economic reforms had acquired a new urgency because a section of their followers who earlier got employment in the army the Ujjainia chiefs organized or were parts of the Baksaria contingent serving the Mughal army were left without any remunerative job. Their economic needs had to be met and they had to be kept busy.[187]

Throughout the nineteenth century the Ujjainias followed the policy of promoting agriculture. The acquisition of thousands of acres land in Burma was another dimension of this policy; those who could not be given economic opportunities in Shahabad had a chance to earn their livelihood in Burma.

The Ujjainias won local support because they believed in freedom of faith. In matters of religion their governance was non-discriminatory. At the same time they refused to condone the policy of conversion to Islam whenever it was tried under the Mughals. They defeated such attempts from Jahangir to Aurangzeb either through force or through stratagem or through both. They did not give up their opposition to forcible conversion when Prabal Singh, a member of the ruling Ujjania family was converted to Islam. Prabal Singh was allowed to follow Islam. He was shown all due respect but the Ujjanias refused to buckle in. They opposed conversion. This won the esteem of the local population. And hence, they hardly faced any local rebellion worth the name.

Munshi Binayak Prasad has lucidly described the introduction of modern political and administration institutions, such as the establishment of Municipality and bureaucratic governance. People were ready to welcome them when they were made aware of the likely benefits that would accrue to them.

The work also helps to write an ecological history of the region since the author is very particular about pointing out the forests that were planted by the Ujjainias and also about the forests that existed around Ujjainia settlements. It is true he does not list the flora and fauna as the author of *Aina-i-Tirhut* does it but nevertheless we get a clear glimpse into the ecological situation in Shahabad.

Another advantage of reading the *Tawarikh- i-Ujjainia* is that we get a good idea of the land-revenue system in operation. We learn about the amount that was collected and the amount that was to be sent to the imperial treasury. The book is a history of the revenue system from the days of Akbar to the establishment of Permanent Settlement in 1793.

It is clear that of all the zamindars of Bihar, the Ujjainia chiefs from the time of Akbar down to the defeat of the Mughal Emperor Shah Alam II and his allies at the battle of Buxar in 1764, always remained in limelight and their services and support were often solicited by the Mughal rulers and the

Nawabs of Bengal. No history of Bihar from Akbar down to the Nawabship of Mir Kasim would be complete without reference to Ujjainia chiefs who flourished during this period.

Hence the book has attracted the attention of prominent researchers on the history of Shahabad: Prof. H.S. Askari, Dr. B.P. Ambashthiya, Prof. K.K. Datta, Prof. Rajiv Nayan Prasad, Prof. Z.U. Siddiqui; a host of other scholars have also used it.

The book is a must for those scholars who intend to research the history of Shahabad in the medieval and early modern periods. Those interested in tracing the interaction among the tribes and the plains people will find here a mine of information.

NOTES

1. Munshi Binayak Prasad, *Tawarikh-i-Ujjainia* (henceforth cited as *TU*), 4 vols., Newal Kishore Press, Lucknow, not dated, vol. I, pp. 100- 9

2. Ali Muhammad Shad (also known as Shad Azimabadi), City Press, Patna, 1893; *TU* II, pp. 6-9. The author has given the names of persons appointed by the estate to assist him in writing this history.

3. *TU* II, pp. 6-9.

4. Ibid., pp. 7-9, Letters exchanged between the author and Mathura Prasad are printed here.

5. R.N. Prasad, *History of Bhojpur (AD 1320-1860)*, K.P. Jayaswal Research Institute, Patna, 1987, pp. 134, 164.

6. Biharilal 'Fitrat', *Aina-i-Tirhut*, revd. edn., Darbhanga, 2001, pp. 6-7. The author, Biharilal 'Fitrat' was a pleader by profession. He took up this task as a labour of love.

7. *TU* I, pp. 3-4.

8. *TU* II, pp. 191-2.

9. *TU* I, pp. 7-8. He also mentions books written in Hindi and English.

10. Ibid.

11. Bodhraj of Pugal in Bikaner in Rajasthan wrote *Bhojpur Main Parmaro Ka Itihas 1577 Tak*, R.N. Prasad, p. 164.

12. *TU* I, pp. 3-4

13. Ibid., p. 5; Hemant Sharma (ed.), *Bhartendu Samagra*, Varanasi, 1987 pp. 583-803.

14. Ibid., pp. 5-7.

15. *TU* IV, *Kamama*, p. 37. The author says he finished the writing of the final volume on February 1905. *TU* I, pp. 8-9 informs us that the writing work remained suspended between 1892 and 1898 and was

resumed on 21 February 1898 after Charles Fawcus revived it. *TU* IV, p. 13.

16. *TU* I, pp. 1-6.
17. Ibid., pp. 6-8.
18. Ibid., pp. 8-15.
19. *TU* II, p. 50.
20. *TU* I, p. 15.
21. Ibid., pp. 15-25.
22. Ibid, pp. 26-42. He bases himself mostly on Tod's *Rajasthan*.
23. *TU* II, pp. 1-4; To establish the legitimacy of Santan Sahi's seizure of power, he brings to our notice the fact that Mithila in ancient times was ruled by Parmar Rajputs.
24. Ibid., p. 3.
25. Ibid. We do not know the authenticity of this information. Probably this was an attempt to legitimize Kayasthas as the traditional occupants of the post of *diwan* in the estate.
26. Ibid., pp. 4-10.
27. Ibid., pp. 10-13.
28. Ibid., p. 14.
29. Ibid.
30. Ibid., pp. 14-15.
31. Ibid., p. 16.
32. Ibid., p. 17.
33. *TU* II, pp. 51-68.
34. Ibid., pp. 148-56.
35. Ibid., pp. 17-20.
36. Ibid., p. 18.
37. Ibid., pp. 20-1. Munshi Binayak Prasad has published the original order issued by Raja Ram Sahi. This should be one of the earliest specimens of written Bhojpuri language.
38. Ibid., pp. 21-5.
39. Ibid., p. 23.
40. Ibid., p. 25.
41. Ibid., pp. 26-42.
42. Ibid., p. 29.
43. Ibid., p. 31.
44. Ibid., 33.
45. Ibid., p. 43.
46. Ibid., pp. 40-4.
47. Ibid., p. 44.
48. Ibid.
49. Ibid., pp. 45-6.

50. Ibid., p. 49.
51. Ibid., p. 50.
52. Ibid., pp. 52-3.
53. Ibid., pp. 53.
54. Ibid., pp. 54-60. It mentions a numbers of *sanads,* issued by various Mughal officials in favour of Amar Singh.
55. Ibid., p. 84.
56. Ibid., pp. 86, 88-95. The author prints the letter which Prabal Singh wrote from jail in Delhi.
57. Ibid., pp. 101-2.
58. Ibid., pp. 84, 100, 102.
59. Ibid., p. 101; The queen immolated herself on the pyre of her husband Rudrapartap Singh.
60. Ibid., p. 103.
61. Ibid., p. 112.
62. Ibid., pp. 115-17.
63. Ibid., pp. 118-19.
64. Ibid., p. 122.
65. Ibid.
66. Zahiruddin Malik, *Agrarian System in Medieval India,* Rawat Publications, Jaipur and Delhi, 2001, pp. 15, 36.
67. Ibid., p. 15.
68. *TU* II, p. 127.
69. Ibid.
70. Ibid., p. 128.
71. Ibid., p. 129.
72. Ibid., p. 131.
73. Ibid., p. 133.
74. Ibid., p. 136.
75. Ibid., p. 137.
76. Ibid., p. 138.
77. Ibid., pp. 146-7.
78. Ibid., 145.
79. Ibid., p. 147.
80. Ibid., pp. 147-8.
81. Ibid., p. 148.
82. Ibid., p. 152.
83. Ibid., pp. 152-3.
84. Ibid., p. 154.
85. Ibid., p. 158.
86. Ibid., p. 154.

87. Ibid., p. 156.
88. Ibid., p. 158.
89. Ibid.
90. Ibid., p. 160.
91. Ibid., p. 161.
92. Ibid., p. 162.
93. Ibid., p. 166.
94. Ibid., p. 167.
95. Ibid.
96. Ibid., p. 168.
97. Ibid., p. 169.
98. Ibid., p. 171.
99. Ibid., p. 186.
100. Ibid., 187.
101. Ibid., p. 189.
102. Ibid., p. 191.
103. Ibid., p. 195.
104. Ibid., p. 189.
105. Ibid., pp. 196-8.
106. Ibid., p. 203.
107. Ibid., pp. 208-10.
108. Ibid., p. 217.
109. *TU* IV, pp. 39-40.
110. Ibid., p. 7.
111. *TU* III, pp. 2-64. The chapter is devoted to a detailed study of the career of Kunwar Dhir.
112. Ibid., pp. 54-6.
113. Ibid., 56-8.
114. Ibid., pp. 58-64.
115. Ibid., pp. 14-15.
116. Ibid., p. 38.
117. Ibid., p. 39.
118. Ibid., p. 65.
119. Ibid., p. 66.
120. Ibid., 68.
121. Ibid., p. 69.
122. Ibid., pp. 129-41.
123. Ibid., p. 141.
124. Ibid., p. 72.
125. Ibid.
126. Ibid., p. 84.

127. Ibid. p. 85.
128. Ibid., pp. 85-6.
129. Ibid.
130. Ibid., p. 86.
131. Ibid., p. 87.
132. Ibid.
133. Ibid., p. 90.
134. Ibid., pp. 92-3.
135. Ibid., p. 97.
136. Ibid., p. 98.
137. Ibid.
138. Ibid., pp. 100-1.
139. Ibid., p. 103.
140. Ibid., p. 104.
141. Ibid., pp. 104, 105.
142. Ibid., p. 108.
143. Ibid.
144. Ibid., pp. 142-58.
145. Ibid., p. 143.
146. Ibid., pp. 190-252.
147. Ibid., p. 252.
148. *TU* IV, pp. 2-3. The teachers were Pandit Dwarkanath Kashmiri, Kalikant Bhattacharya.
149. Master Jai Prakash Lal, a local resident was also his teacher.
150. Ibid., p. 4.
151. Ibid., pp. 4, 12, on p. 12 we have a copy of the government order conferring the title of Raja on Radha Prasad Singh by Northbrook, the Victory and Governor-General of India.
152. Ibid., p. 19.
153. Ibid., p. 6.
154. Ibid., p. 32.
155. Ibid.
156. Ibid., p. 75.
157. Ibid., pp. 73-5.
158. Ibid., pp. 75-7.
159. Ibid., p. 77.
160. Ibid., pp. 32-3.
161. Ibid., pp. 36-8.
162. Ibid., p. 40.
163. Ibid., pp. 40-2.
164. Ibid., p. 67.
165. Ibid., p. 16.

166. Abhay Kumar, 'Irrigation Policy of the Raj and Agrarian Society, Patna, Gaya and Shahabad Districts of Bihar, 1850-1900', Ph.D. thesis, Department of History, Patna University, 2001, p. 137.
167. *TU* IV, p. 16.
168. Ibid., pp. 9-10.
169. Ibid., p. 61.
170. Ibid., p. 53.
171. Ibid., p. 15.
172. Ibid., *Ain-i-Katcheri,* pp. V, 106.
173. Ibid., p. 17.
174. Ibid., p. 26.
175. Ibid., p. 36.
176. Ibid., p. 38.
177. Ibid., pp. 67-8.
178. Ibid., *Ain-i-Katcheri,* pp. 1-10.
179. Ibid., p. 12.
180. Ibid., pp. 44-51.
181. Ibid.
182. Ibid., pp. 71-6.
183. *TU* IV, *Karnama,* p. 5.
184. Ibid., pp. 10-11.
185. Ibid., p. 18.
186. Ibid., p. 20.
187. Zahiruddin Malik, p. 11.

Bibliography

Ahmad , Q. and J.S. Jha, *Mazharul Haque,* Publications Division, New Delhi, 1976.

An Old Planter, *Reminiscences of Behar,* Thacker Spink & Co., Calcutta, 1857.

Annual Report of Patna Science College Philosophical Society, 1938-39, Patna, 1939.

Annual Report of Patna Science College Philosophical Society, 1939-40, Patna, 1940.

Anon, *Keshub Charit* (n.d.).

Antonova, Bongard-Levin and G. Kotovsky, *A History of India* I, Progress Publishers, Moscow, 1979.

Archer, Mildred, *Patna Painting,* The Royal India Society, London, 1947.

Askari, Syed Hasan and Qyamuddin Ahmad (eds.), *The Comprehensive History of Bihar,* vol. II, pt. I, K.P. Jayaswal Research Institute, Patna, 1983.

Askari, S.H., *Islam and Muslims in Medieval Bihar,* Khuda Bakhsh Oriental Public Library, Patna, 1989.

Balchand, R., 'A Century of Journalism in Bihar', *Behar Herald,* Centenary Issue, 1975.

Barr, Pat, *The Memsahibs,* Allied Publishers, Bombay, 1978.

Beames, John, *Memoirs of a Bengal Civilian,* London, 1961.

Bengal Administrative Report, Calcutta, 1876.

Bihar Herald (Centenary Number), Patna, 1975.

Buchanan, Francis, *Journal of Francis Buchanan Kept during the Survey of the District of Shahabad in 1812-13,* Patna, n.d.

———, *Journal of Francis Buchanan Kept during the Survey of the Districts of Patna and Gaya in 1811-12,* Patna, 1925.

———, *An Account of the District of Bihar and Patna in 1811-12,* vol. II, Patna, n.d.

Buckland, C.E., *Bengal under the Lietenant Governors,* vol. I, Deep Publications, Delhi, 1976.

————, *Bihar under the Lieutenant Governors*, vols. I & II, Delhi, 1976.

Bulletin of the Patna Science College Philosophical Society, 1, January 1981.

Carroll, Lucy, 'Kayastha Samachar: From a Caste–To a National Newspaper', *IESHR*, vol. X, no. 3.

Census of India 1901, VII, Bengal, pt. II.

Chaudhury, Sushil, 'Saltpetre Trade and Industry in Bengal Subah', *Proceedings, Indian History Congress (IHC)*, Chandigarh, 1973.

————, *Trade and Organization in Bengal, 1650-1720*, Calcutta, 1975.

Chaudhary, P.C. Roy (ed.), *District Gazetteer, Monghyr*, Patna, 1960.

————, *Muzaffarpur Old Records*, Patna, n.d.

Chaudury, P.C. Ray (ed.), *District Gazetteer – Bhagalpur*, Patna, 1962, 119-20.

Choudhari, V.C.P., *The Making of Modern Bihar*, Patna, n.d.

Consolidated Annual Report 2003-04, Bihar Dalit Vikas Samiti, Patna, n.d.

Datta, K.K. and J.S. Jha (eds.), *Comprehensive History of Bihar*, vol. III, pt. I, Patna, 1976.

————, *The Writings and Speeches of Mahatma Gandhi Relating to Bihar 1917-1947*, Patna, 1960.

————, *Selection From The Judicial Records of The Bhagalpur District Office 1772-1805*, Patna, 1968.

————, *History of Freedom Movement in Bihar*, vol. II, Patna, 1957.

Datta, K.K., *The Comprehensive History of Bihar*, vol. III, pt. II, K.P. Jayaswal Research Institute, Patna, 1976.

District Gazetteer, Champaran, Patna, 1938.

Diwakar, R.R. (ed.), *Bihar through the Ages*, K.P. Jayaswal Research Institute, Patna, 2001.

Ecclesiastical Proceedings, 1-8 (June 1872) (hereafter referred to as Eccl. Progs.), Oman, 120.

Farquhar, J.N. 'The Arya Samaj', *The Punjab Past and Present*, vol. VII, pt. I, April 1973.

Farminger, W.R. (ed.)., *The Fifth Report from the House of Commons on the East India Company*, Calcutta, 1917.

Ghose, N.C. (ed.), *Souvenir of the Department of Geology, Patna University, 1946-1996*, Patna, 1997.

Ghoshal, H.R., *Economic Transition in the Bengal Presidency (1793-1833)*, Patna, 1960.

Gopal, Surendra, 'Endeavour and Persistence: Brahmo Samaj in Bihar in the Second Half of the Nineteenth Century', *Indica*, nos. 45 and 47.

———, 'Jains in Eastern India in the Seventeenth Century', in D. Tripathi (ed.), *Business Communities in India*, Delhi, 1984.

———, 'The Roots of Rural Poverty in Bihar', *Current Studies*, Patna, 1984.

———, 'Bihari Association with the Indian National Congress during its Formative Years (1885-88)', *Memorial Lecture Series*, vol. 2, 1986.

———, 'Coins and Trade: A Study of Bihar Economy in the Seventeenth Century', in Amal Kumar Jha (ed.), *Coinage, Trade and Economy*, Anjanery, Nashik, 1991, pp. 210-13.

———, *Commerce and Crafts in Gujarat, Sixteenth-Seventeenth Centuries*, Delhi, 1975.

———, *Patna in the Nineteenth Century: A Socio-Cultural Profile*, Naya Prakash, Calcutta, 1982.

Gordon, Leonard A., *Bengal: The Nationalist Movement 1876-1940*, Delhi, 1974.

Griffiths, Sir Percival, *The History of the Indian Tea Industry*, London, 1967.

Guha, A.C., *A Brief Sketch of the Land Systems of Bengal and Behar*, Thacker Spink & Co., Calcutta and Simla, 1916.

Gupta, Nagendra Nath, *Reflections and Reminiscences*, Bombay, 1947.

Hardy, Friedhalm, *The Religious Culture of India, Power, Love and Wisdom*, Cambridge University Press, Cambridge, 1995.

Heber, Reginald, *Narrative of a Journey through the Upper Provinces of India, from Calcutta to Bombay 1824-1825*, vol. I, London, 1849.

Heidrich, Petra, 'Ochre Robe and Tricolour, Sanyasis and Sadhus in Social Movements in the First half of 20th Century', in Annemarie Hafner (ed.), *Essays on South Asian Society, Culture and Politics*, Berlin, 1995.

Henningham, Stephen, *A Great Estate and its Landlords in Colonial India*, Oxford University Press, Delhi, 1990.

Hodge, William, *Travels in India*, London, 1793.

Hubback, J.A., *Final Report on the Survey and Settlement Operations in the District of Shahabad 1907-1916*, Patna, 1928.

Hunter, W.W., *The Statistical Account of Bengal*, XV, London, 1877.

———, *A Statistical Account of Bengal*, vol. XV, Monghyr, London, 1871.

Jackson, Paul (trans.), *Sharfuddin Maneri: The Hundred Letters*, New York, 1980.

Jackson, Paul S.J., *Sharfuddin Maneri: The Hundred Letters*, Khuda Bakhsh Oriental Public Library, Patna, 2002.

Jackson, V.H. (ed.), *Journal of Francis Buchanan kept during the Survey of the Districts of Gaya and Patna in 1811-12*, Patna, 1925.

Jaffrelot, Christophe, *India's Silent Revolution*, Delhi, 2005.

Jagmohan, 1930, *Bihar and Orissa in 1929-30*, Patna, n.d.

Jayaswal, K.P., *The Rajniti Ratnakar of Chandeshwara*, Patna, 1936.

Jha, Ganganath, *Autobiographical Notes of Dr. Sir Ganganath Jha*, Allahabad, 1976.

Jha, Hetukar, 'Promises and Lapses: Understanding the Experience of the Scheduled Castes in Bihar in Historical Perspective', *Journal of Indian School of Political Economy*, vol. XII, nos. 3 & 4, July-December 2000.

Jha, Hetukar et al., *Social Structures and Alignments*, Delhi, 1985.

Jha, J.C., *The Migration of Maithil Pandits*, Patna, 1991.

Jha, J.S., *Records of the Judge and Magistrate of Patna for the Years 1820-25*, Patna, 1966.

Jha, Jata Shankar, *Biography of an Indian Patriot Maharaja Lakshmeshwar Singh of Darbhanga*, Patna, 1972.

Jha, Radhanandan, 1998, *Origin and Development of Bihar Legislature*, Patna, n.d.

Kalapura, Jose, 'Challenge of Socio-Religious Structures: The Christianisation of the Ravidasis of Bihar', *IHC*, 56th Session, Madras, Calcutta, 1997.

Kamal, Ritu and Gopal Kamal, *Prapanch Kanya: Indian Philosophy in the Second Millenniam*, Viva Books, New Delhi, 2008.

Karim, Abdul, *Murshid Quli Khan and His Times*, Dhaka, 1974.

Khan, A.R., 'Chieftains in Bihar during the Mughal Period', *IHC*, Goa, 1987.

Kotnala, M.C., *Rammohun Roy and Indian Awakening*, New Delhi, 1975.

Kuber, W.N., 'Dalit Movements in India', in V.D. Divekar (ed.), *Social Reform Movements in India*, Bombay, 1991.

Kumar, J., *Indo-Chinese Trade 1793-1833*, New Delhi, 1974.

Lal, Bishwanath, 'Language Journalism in Bihar: Retrospect and Prospect', *Souvenir*, Indian Federation of Working Journalists, Patna.

Lall, Awadh Bihari, *English Poems*, Patna, 1918.

Land Revenue Proceedings, no. 48 (May 1870), no. 49 (May 1870), no. 59 (August 1870), no. 63 (April 1871) and no. 64 (April 1871).

Majumdar, B.B. and B.P. Mazumdar, *Congress and Congressmen in the Pre-Gandhian Era, 1885-1917,* Firma K.L. Mukhopadhyay, Calcutta, 1967.

Martin, Montgomery, *Eastern India,* vol. II, rpt., Delhi, 1976.

Majumdar, Bimanbehari and Devendra Kumar (eds.), *Great Men of Shahabad,* Prasad Publishing House, Patna, 1946.

Mittal, S.K., *Peasant Uprisings and Mahatma Gandhi in North Bihar,* Meerut, 1978.

Mozoomdar, P.C., *Heart Beats,* Calcutta, 1935.

Mundy, Captain, *The Journal of a Tour in India,* vol. 1, London, 1803.

Narain, V.A., 'Munshi Peyare Lall and the Anti-Dowry Agitation', *PIHC,* Muzaffarpur, 1972.

'The Role of Bihar Scientific Association in the Spread of Western Education in Bihar'. *PIHC,* Varanasi, 1969.

Oman, John Campbell, *The Brahmans, Theists and Muslims of India,* Delhi, 1973.

Parekh, M.C., *The Brahma Samaj,* Kathiawad, 1929.

Patna University Calendar, 1925-6; 1934-5; 1935-6; 1936-7; 1939-42; 1952-5.

Patna University Golden Jubilee Souvenir, Patna, 1970.

Patna University Proceedings of the Convocation and Minutes of the Senate, Syndicate and Faculties, Patna, 1935-6.

Patna University Silver Jubilee Souvenir, Patna, 1944.

Pemble, John (ed.), *Miss Fane in India,* London, 1885.

Pinch, William, 'Poppy and the Peasants: A Look at the Structure of Agrarian Society in Twentieth Century Bihar', *Explorations,* no. 2.

Prakash, Om, 'The Dutch East India Company in Bengal', *Indian Economic and Social History Review,* September 1972.

———, *The Dutch East India Company and the Economy of Bengal, 1630-1720,* Princeton, 1985.

Prasad, Satya Narain, 'Origins of Technical Education in Bihar (1854-1915)', *PIHC,* Jabalpur, 1970.

———, '"The *Behar Times* and News" and the Social Awakening in Bihar (1894-1912)', *Proceedings of the Syndicate,* Patna University Syndicate, 1936.

Ram, Rajendra (ed.), *Intellectual Perspective of Rahula Sankrityayana: Essays and Reminiscences,* Janajagaran Prakashana, Patna, n.d.

Report of the Census of Bengal, II, 1881, pp. 22-3.

Rizvi, Syed Najmul Raja, 'The Lifestyle of the Zamindars of Eastern Uttar Pradesh in the Eighteenth Century', *Proceedings, PIHC,* Burdwan, 1983.

Roy, Rammohun and Kissory Chand Mitter, *Rammohun Roy and Tuhfatul Meshwahhiddin,* Calcutta, 1975.

Roerich, Dr. G., *Biography of Dharmasvamin,* Kashi Prasad Jayaswal Research Institute, Patna, 1959.

Salim, Ghulam Hussain, *Riyazu-s-Salatin,* Text and English translation by Abdus Salam, Calcutta, 1902.

Sarkar, J.N. and J.C. Jha, *A History of the Patna College,* Patna, 1963.

Sarkar, Jagdish Narayan, *Glimpses of Medieval Bihar Economy,* Calcutta, 1978.

_____, *Private Traders in Medieval and British India,* Calcutta, 1990.

Sastri, Sivanath, 'Rammohun Roy: The Story of His Life', in *The Father of Modern India: Commemoration Volume of the Rammohun Roy Centenary Celebrations,* Calcutta, 1933.

Science College Old Boys' Association Souvenir, Patna, 2000.

Selected Works of Mahatma Gandhi, vol. 63.

Sen, Guru Prosad, 'The Aristocracy of Bihar', n.d.

Sen, P.K., *Biography of a New Faith,* II, Calcutta, 1954.

Sen, Punyamoy, 'Hundred Years of Hazaribagh Brahmo Samaj', *The Searchlight,* 30 April 1967.

Sen, Sunil, *Agrarian Relations in India,* Calcutta, 1979.

_____, *Peasant Movements in India,* Calcutta, 1982.

Sen, Sushma, *Memoirs of an Octogenarian,* New Delhi, 1971.

Singh, Shayam Narayan, *History of Tirhut from the Earliest Times to the End of the Nineteenth Century,* Darbhanga, Bihar, 2012.

Sinha, P.B., *Development of the Mineral Industries of Bihar,* Muzaffarpur, 1975.

Sinha, Sachchidanand, *Some Eminent Behar Contemporaries,* Himalaya Publications, Patna, 1944.

Sohoni, V.S. and B.B. Keskar, *Spiritual Power-house,* Bombay, 1940.

Srivastava, N.M.P., 'Peasant Movement in Bihar', *The Journal of the Bihar Puravid Parisad,* Patna, 1980-1.

Statistics of the District of Patna, n.d.; published from Calcutta in 1850s.

Stavorinus, John Splinter, *Voyages to the East Indies,* vol. I, London, 1798.

Thakur, Upendra, *History of Mithila,* Darbhanga, n.d.

The Apostles and Missionaries of the Navavidhan, 1967.

The Autobiographical Notes of Mm. Dr. Sir Ganga Natha Jha, ed. Hetukar Jha, Allahabad.

'The Universal Man and the Yellow Dog; The Orientalist Legacy and the Problem of Brahmo Identity', in Rachel van M. Baume (ed.), *Aspects of Bengali History and Society*, Delhi, 1976.

Valentia, *Voyages and Travels to India, Ceylon, The Red Sea*, vol. I, London, 1809.

Wilson, C.R., *The Early Annals of the English in Bengal, III*, Calcutta, 1917.

Wyatt, A. Esq. (Revenue Surveyor), *Geographical and Statistical Report of the District of Tirhoot*, Thos. Jones, 'Calcutta Gazette' Office, Calcutta, 1854.

———, *Statistics of the Districts of Saran and Sircar Saran*, n.d., (probably published in 1850s).

Yang, A., *Limited Raj Agrarian Relations in Colonial India: Saran District, 1793-1920*, Delhi, 1989.

LITERATURE IN HINDI

Abhedanand, Swami and Pandit Mahadev Sharan (eds.), *Bihar Arya Pratinidhi Sabha ka Itihas*, Patna, 1985.

Bihar Bandhu, 7 August 1894.

Devi, Sumitra, *Sri Jagjivan Ram Jeevan Aur Mahanta*, Patna, n.d.

Jha, Jharkhandi, *Bhagalpur Darpan I*, pt. I, Vaijani/Bhagalpur, 1933.

Kane, P.V., *Dharmasastra Ka Itihas*, vol. I, n.d.

Kunal, Kishor, *Dalit-Devo Bhava*, Publication Division, Patna, 2006.

Pandey, Braj Kishor, *Dalit Samasya ki Rajniti*, Delhi, 2003.

Prasad, Rajendra, *Atmakatha*, Sasta Sahitya Mandal, New Delhi, 2002.

Sahni, Dinanath, *Mahan Khagolbid-Ganitigya Aryabhatta*, Prabhat Prakashan, Delhi, 2012.

Saraswati, Swami Sahajanand, *Kisan Sabha Ke Sansmaran*, Allahabad, 1947.

———, *Mera Jeewan Sangharsha*, Bihta, Patna, 1952.

Sarkar, J., *A History of the Patna College*, Patna, 1963.

Sarvadeshik Arya Pratinidhi Sabha Ka 27 Varshiya Itihas (Karya Vivaran Twenty-seven Year), Delhi, 1939.

Shastri, Sarvendra, 'Bihar Rajya Ke Pratham Asthawan Aryasamaji Svargiya Babu Madhav Lalji', *Aryasankala*, vol. X, no. 9, April 1988.

_____, *Bihar Mein Swami Dayanand*, Sastri Sadan, Pahleja Barka, Dist. Saran, 1984.

Singh, Babu Ramdin, *Behar Durpan*, 2nd edn., Patna, 1883.

Sinha, Anugraha Narayan, *Mere Sansmaran*, 2nd edn., Patna 1961.

Sinha, Indradeep, *Bihar Mein Communist Party Ka Vikas*, Patna. n.d.

URDU

Al Panch, 26 April 1897.

Eqbal, Dr. Muzaffar, 'Suba Bihar ki Urdu Sahafat Key Sau Saal (1853-1953)', *Souvenir*, All India Editorial Conference, Patna, 1972.

Gilani, Syed Abdul, *Hayate Reza*, Aligarh, 1935.

Iqbal, Dr. Muzaffar, 'Sube Bihar Ki Urdu Safat ke Sau Saal', *Souvenir*, Patna, 1972.

BANGLA

Basu, Prabhat, *Doctor Bimalchandra Ghoser Jivan Kotha*, n.d.

Basu, Satya Sundar, *Bhakta Hari Sundar Basu Mahasaya Charit-Katha*, Calcutta, 1350 BS.

Basu, Prem Sundar, *Keshav, Brahmananda*, pt. I, Bhagalpur, n.d.

Bose, Suresh Chander, *The Life of Pratap Chunder Mazoomdar*, Nobabdhan Trust, Calcutta, 1929, vol. II.

Chakravarti, Satish Chandra, *Sivanath Sastri*, Calcutta, 1375 BS.

Chakravarty, Sudhakaran (comp.), *Srishchandra Chakravarty Sradharghya*, Calcutta, 1361 BS.

Guha, Rajni Kant, *Atma Charita*, n.d.

Gupt, Manmathnath, *Acharya Sivanath*, Calcutta, n.d.

Kundu, Ranjita, *Shishu Sahitya Bhagirath Yogindra Nath Sarkar*, Calcutta, n.d.

Mukherjee, Nibran Chandra, *Brahmatatva*, Calcutta, 1931.

Mukhopadhyay, Bhudev, *Bhudev Charit*, vol. II.

Nivedan-Svargiya Prakashchandra Roy Mahasayer Updesh O Prarthna, Calcutta, n.d.

Niyogi, Niranjan, *The Apostles and Missionaries of the Navavidhan*, Calcutta, n.d.

_____, *Brajgopal Janmshatvarshiki*, Calcutta, 1957.

_____, *Brajgopal Tamshatvarshiki Shradeya Bhai Brijgopal Niyogi*, Calcutta, 1957.

Smritir-Gawrab-Smritir Saurabh, Calcutta, 1969.

Sastri, Sivanath, *Atma Charita*, Calcutta, 1359 BS.

Sen, Navinchandra, *Navinchandra Rachnavali*, vol. I.

Sen, P.K., *Keshub Chandra Sen*, Calcutta, 1938.

JOURNALS AND NEWSPAPERS

English

Amrita Bazar Patrika, 1 December 1932, 23 December 1932, 3 January 1933, 5 January 1933.

People's War, 22 August 1943, 19 September 1943, 26 September 1943, 7 November 1943 and 26 March 1944.

The Behar Times, 25 February 1897.

People's War, vol. II, no. 2, 11 July 1943.

Times of India, 2 April 2000.

Hindi

Aryavarta, 5 May 1999.

Bihar Bandhu, August 1881.

Hunkar, 6 December 1942, 20 December 1942, 21 December 1942, 27 December 1942, 10 January 1943, 17 January 1943, 31 January 1943, 7 February 1943, 14 February 1943, 23 February 1943, 20 August 1944.

Lok Yuddha, 13 February 1943, 4 July 1943, 17 October 1943, 31 October 1943, 14 November 1943; 26 December 1943, 16 January 1944, etc.

Index